ICONS OF BLACK AMERICA

Recent titles in
Greenwood Icons

Icons of the American West: From Cowgirls to Silicon Valley
Edited by Gordon Morris Bakken

Icons of Latino America: Latino Contributions to American Culture
Roger Bruns

Icons of Crime Fighting: Relentless Pursuers of Justice
Edited by Jeffrey Bumgarner

Icons of Unbelief: Atheists, Agnostics, and Secularists
Edited by S.T. Joshi

Women Icons of Popular Music: The Rebels, Rockers, and Renegades
Carrie Havranek

Icons of Talk: The Media Mouths That Changed America
Donna L. Halper

Icons of African American Protest: Trailblazing Activists of the Civil Rights
Movement
Gladys L. Knight

Icons of American Architecture: From the Alamo to the World Trade Center
Donald Langmead

Icons of Invention: The Makers of the Modern World from Gutenberg to
Gates
John W. Klooster

Icons of Beauty: Art, Culture, and the Image of Women
Debra N. Mancoff and Lindsay J. Bosch

Icons of Mystery and Crime Detection: From Sleuths to Superheroes
Mitzi M. Brunsdale

ICONS OF BLACK AMERICA

Breaking Barriers and Crossing Boundaries

VOLUME 2

Matthew C. Whitaker, Editor

GREENWOOD ICONS

GREENWOOD

AN IMPRINT OF ABC-CLIO, LLC
Santa Barbara, California • Denver, Colorado • Oxford, England

Library of Congress Cataloging-in-Publication Data

Icons of Black America : breaking barriers and crossing boundaries / Matthew C. Whitaker, editor.
    p. cm. — (Greenwood icons)
    Includes bibliographical references and index.
    ISBN 978–0–313–37642–9 (hard copy : acid-free paper) — ISBN 978–0–313–37643–6 (ebook)
1. African Americans—Biography. I. Whitaker, Matthew C.
E185.96.I26   2011
920.009296073—dc22   2010030784

ISBN: 978–0–313–37642–9
EISBN: 978–0–313–37643–6

15 14 13 12 11   1 2 3 4 5

This book is also available on the World Wide Web as an eBook.
Visit www.abc-clio.com for details.

Greenwood
An Imprint of ABC-CLIO, LLC

ABC-CLIO, LLC
130 Cremona Drive, P.O. Box 1911
Santa Barbara, California 93116-1911

This book is printed on acid-free paper ∞

Manufactured in the United States of America

For Jackson Asanté Whitaker and Anastacia Ami Whitaker,
and the future of Black America.

Contents

List of Photos   xiii

Series Foreword   xxiii

Foreword by *William Jelani Cobb*   xxv

Acknowledgments   xxix

Introduction   xxxi

Volume 1

Muhammad Ali   1

Maya Angelou   13

Apollo Theater   23

Louis Armstrong   33

Arthur Ashe   43

Ella Baker   53

Joséphine Baker   63

James Baldwin   73

Charles Barkley   83

Harry Belafonte   93

Halle Berry   103

Barry Bonds   113

Carol Moseley Braun   127

Ralph Bunche   137

Stokely Carmichael (Kwame Ture)   147

George Washington Carver   159

Ray Charles   169

Shirley Chisholm   179

Bill Cosby   189

Dorothy Dandridge   199

Angela Davis   209

Miles Davis   219

Sammy Davis, Jr.   229

Frederick Douglass   239

W. E. B. Du Bois   249

Duke Ellington   259

Ralph Ellison   271

Louis Farrakhan   281

54th Massachusetts Infantry   291

Ella Fitzgerald   301

Aretha Franklin   311

Marcus Garvey   319

Marvin Gaye   329

Nikki Giovanni   337

Volume 2

Alex Haley   345

Fannie Lou Hamer   355

Harlem Globetrotters   365

Jimi Hendrix   377

Billie Holiday	387
Lena Horne	395
Langston Hughes	405
Zora Neale Hurston	415
Michael Jackson	425
Jay-Z	435
Earvin "Magic" Johnson	445
Jack Johnson	455
James Weldon Johnson	471
Robert L. Johnson	481
Quincy Jones	491
Barbara Jordan	499
Michael Jordan	509
Florence Griffith Joyner	519
Martin Luther King, Jr.	531
Spike Lee	541
Joe Louis	551
Malcolm X	561
Thurgood Marshall	571
Hattie McDaniel	583
Morehouse College	593
Toni Morrison	603
Motown Records	613
Elijah Muhammad	623
Negro Baseball Leagues	635
Huey P. Newton and Bobby Seale	645
Barack Obama	657
Michelle Obama	667

Jesse Owens   677

Rosa Parks   687

Sidney Poitier   697

Colin Powell   707

Richard Pryor   717

Volume 3

A. Philip Randolph   727

Ishmael Reed   741

Condoleezza Rice   751

Paul Robeson   761

Jackie Robinson   771

Bayard Rustin   783

Dred Scott   793

Tupac Shakur   803

Russell Simmons   813

Tommie Smith and John Carlos   819

Will Smith   829

Spelman College   837

Mary Church Terrell   847

Sojourner Truth   857

Harriet Tubman   867

Nat Turner   877

Tuskegee Airmen   887

Alice Walker   897

Madam C. J. Walker   905

Booker T. Washington   919

Denzel Washington   931

Ida B. Wells-Barnett   943

Cornel West   957

Venus Williams and Serena Williams   967

Oprah Winfrey   979

Stevie Wonder   989

Tiger Woods   999

Carter G. Woodson   1009

Richard Wright   1019

Selected Bibliography   1027

About the Editor and Contributors   1053

Index   1063

List of Photos

Muhammad Ali (page 1). Muhammad Ali, who was born Cassius Marcellus Clay, Jr., is regarded by millions as "The Greatest" boxer of all time, and one of the most distinguished proponents of peace in the modern era. (Getty Images)

Maya Angelou (page 13). Maya Angelou is one of the premier U.S. poets of the twentieth century. (National Archives)

Apollo Theater (page 23). The Apollo Theater, located in Harlem, a neighborhood in New York City. (Getty Images)

Louis Armstrong (page 33). Louis Armstrong is one of the towering figures in the history of jazz. (Library of Congress)

Arthur Ashe (page 43). Tennis legend Arthur Ashe. (Courtesy ProServ, Arlington, VA)

Ella Baker (page 53). Ella Jo Baker was a founder of the Student Nonviolent Coordinating Committee during the civil rights movement of the 1960s. (Library of Congress)

Joséphine Baker (page 63). Josephine Baker, a young dancer from New York City's Harlem neighborhood, was the star attraction in the 1920s at the Folies Bergères in Paris. (Library of Congress)

James Baldwin (page 73). James Baldwin, author of the novel *Go Tell It on the Mountain* (1953), wrote about the effects of race, religion, and sexuality on personal identity. (Library of Congress)

Charles Barkley (page 83). Phoenix Suns forward Charles Barkley shoots over Houston Rockets forward Robert Horry during the first quarter in their playoff game on Thursday, May 11, 1995 in Phoenix. (AP/Wide World Photos)

Harry Belafonte (page 93). Singer Harry Belafonte appears on the Broadway stage in *Belafonte At The Palace*, January 5, 1960, in New York. (AP/Wide World Photos)

Halle Berry (page 103). Academy Award-winning actress Halle Berry poses during a press conference for the film *X-Men: The Last Stand*, at the 59th International Film Festival in Cannes, France in 2006. (AP/Wide World Photos)

Barry Bonds (page 113). San Francisco Giants" slugger Barry Bonds watches the ball flying over the right field wall after hitting his record-breaking 73rd home run on October 7, 2001 in San Francisco, California. (AFP/Getty Images)

Carol Moseley Braun (page 127). In 1992, Carol Moseley Braun became the first African American woman elected to the U.S. Senate. (U.S. Senate)

Ralph Bunche (page 137). As a high official of the United Nations for 25 years, Ralph Bunche led peacekeeping efforts in troubled areas of the world. (Carl Van Vechten Collection/Library of Congress)

Stokely Carmichael (Kwame Ture) (page 147). Stokely Carmichael, an effective leader of the Student Nonviolent Coordinating Committee (SNCC), brought the concept of black power into the U.S. civil rights struggle. In 1967, Carmichael, an advocate of militancy rather than nonviolent cooperation, broke with SNCC and joined the more radical Black Panthers. (Library of Congress)

George Washington Carver (page 159). Born enslaved in the United States, George Washington Carver nevertheless rose to national prominence as a chemist and inventor of uncommon genius. His special talent was developing industrial applications from farm products, including more than 300 discoveries derived from the peanut, about 100 from the sweet potato, some 75 from pecans, and others from a variety of clay. (Library of Congress)

Ray Charles (page 169). Ray Charles (shown here on March 16, 1979), the Grammy-winning crooner who blended gospel and blues and heartfelt ballads such as "Georgia on My Mind," died on June 10, 2004 in Beverly Hills, California at the age of 73. (AP/Wide World Photos)

Shirley Chisholm (page 179). Congresswoman Shirley Chisholm announces her candidacy for presidential nomination, January 25, 1972. (Library of Congress)

Bill Cosby (page 189). Bill Cosby is one of the best-loved comedians in the world and has perhaps the widest appeal due to the gentle, inoffensive nature of his humor. (AFP/Getty Images)

Dorothy Dandridge (page 199). Portrait of Dorothy Dandridge, ca. 1950. (Photofest)

Angela Davis (page 209). A militant communist and fervent civil rights activist, Angela Davis is most recognized for causing a nationwide uproar in the 1970s when she was charged with several crimes in connection with a gunfight at a California courthouse. She was acquitted and in 1980 she ran unsuccessfully for vice president on the Communist Party ticket. In 1991, Davis became a professor at the University of California at Santa Cruz. (AP/Wide World Photos)

Miles Davis (page 219). Miles Davis was always at the cutting edge of modern jazz. His extraordinary trumpet improvisations and fine ensemble work pushed boundaries of rhythm, harmony, and melody and continuously posed musical challenges that suggested future paths for jazz. (AP/Wide World Photos)

Sammy Davis, Jr. (page 229). Entertainer Sammy Davis, Jr. (Popperfoto/Archive Photos)

Frederick Douglass (page 239). Frederick Douglass, leader in the abolition movement, author, speaker, ambassador to Haiti, and one of the most famous and influential Americans during the nineteenth century. (Library of Congress)

W. E. B. Du Bois (page 249). W. E. B. Du Bois, called the father of pan-Africanism for his work on behalf of the emerging African nations, devoted his life to the struggle for equality for African Americans and all people of color. (Library of Congress)

Duke Ellington (page 259). Jazz musician and band leader Duke Ellington. (Library of Congress)

Ralph Ellison (page 271). Ralph Ellison, whose novel *Invisible Man* has become a classic of modern American fiction, wrote compellingly of the experience of African Americans in a society that has tended to ignore their problems. (National Archives)

Louis Farrakhan (page 281). Nation of Islam leader Louis Farrakhan addresses the National Press Club in Washington, D.C. on May 3, 2004. The charismatic African American leader has been criticized as a racist for his extreme separatist views, but has also been praised for his role in calling for a renewed community commitment to assisting others in need. (Photo by Mark Wilson/Getty Images)

54th Massachusetts Infantry (page 291). The assault on Fort Wagner at Charleston Harbor on July 18, 1863. The Confederacy delivered a crushing defeat to the Union forces lead by Brig. Gen. Quincy A. Gillmore and the mostly African American 54th Massachusetts Volunteer Infantry Regiment. Although the loss was embarrassing to the Northern states, the battle proved the worth of African American soldiers and helped to raise Union Army recruitment. (The Illustrated London News Picture Library)

Ella Fitzgerald (page 301). Jazz vocalist Ella Fitzgerald in 1940. (Library of Congress)

Aretha Franklin (page 311). Aretha Franklin performs at New York's Radio City Music Hall, July 6, 1989. (AP/Wide World Photos)

Marcus Garvey (page 319). Marcus Garvey launched the first mass movement of African Americans in the United States that was based on racial pride, self-help, and separatism. (Library of Congress)

Marvin Gaye (page 329). Soul singer Marvin Gaye was Motown's top-selling solo artist during the 1960s. (AP/Wide World Photos)

Nikki Giovanni (page 337). Poet Nikki Giovanni (left), Kay Mazzo, ballet dancer with the New York City Ballet, and fashion designer Betsey Johnson receive the first Sun Shower Award in New York City in January 1971. The award is given to outstanding women who have achieved new heights in their careers. (AP/Wide World Photos)

Alex Haley (page 345). Alex Haley won the Pulitzer Prize for his best-selling book *Roots: The Saga of an American Family*. His book, which was made into a popular television miniseries, marked the first time an African American descended from enslaved people had traced his family's history back to its origins in Africa. (Hulton Archive/Getty Images)

Fannie Lou Hamer (page 355). Fannie Lou Hamer, a Mississippi field hand for most of her life, became a prominent advocate of civil rights. As Mississippi's Democratic Party refused African American members, Hamer helped form the Mississippi Freedom Democratic Party (MFDP) whose members attempted to unseat the regular party delegation at the Democratic National Convention in 1964. (Library of Congress)

Harlem Globetrotters (page 365). Basketball acrobatics are displayed by Michael Wilson of The Harlem Globetrotters in 2002. (AP/Wide World Photos)

Jimi Hendrix (page 377). Jimi Hendrix discovered an unknown world of expression within the electric guitar. Though his superb, highly amplified guitar playing was often upstaged by galvanizing theatrics, his brief, explosive career was a relentless quest to expand the horizons of music and sound. (Hulton Archive/Getty Images)

Billie Holiday (page 387). Billie Holiday performs in 1947 in New York. (William P. Gottlieb/Library of Congress)

Lena Horne (page 395). One of the United States's best and most enduring performers, Lena Horne worked tirelessly to promote equal rights for African Americans. Unlike most of her fellow entertainers, Horne's career hit its apex in her later years when she starred in the one-woman Broadway show *Lena Horne: The Lady and Her Music* in 1981. (Hulton Archive/Getty Images)

Langston Hughes (page 405). For more than five decades, Langston Hughes wrote poetry, fiction, and plays that were meant to capture the essence of the black experience in the United States. A prolific writer of rare versatility, he wrote for the men and women he saw struggling first for survival and then for equality from the 1920s through the 1960s. (Library of Congress)

Zora Neale Hurston (page 415). Zora Neale Hurston was an American novelist, folklorist, anthropologist, and prominent member of the circle of writers associated with the Harlem Renaissance of the 1920s. (Library of Congress)

Michael Jackson (page 425). Michael Jackson, the number-one selling pop vocal artist in history, performs at opening night of his Victory Tour at Dodger Stadium in Los Angeles, California, December 1, 1984. (AP/Wide World Photos)

Jay-Z (page 435). Rapper and current president and CEO of Def Jam and Roc-A-Fella Records, Jay-Z, 2001. (Photofest)

Earvin "Magic" Johnson (page 445). Earvin "Magic" Johnson, is a five-time National Basketball Association (NBA) Champion, a highly successful businessman, and a distinguished humanitarian. (UPI/Bettmann/Corbis)

Jack Johnson (page 455). Jack Johnson was the first African American heavyweight boxing champion of the world. (Library of Congress)

James Weldon Johnson (page 471). Portrait of author and civil rights activist during the Harlem Renaissance, James Weldon Johnson. (National Archives)

Robert L. Johnson (page 481). Robert L. Johnson, founder of the Black Entertainment Television (BET) cable network, and Lifetime Achievement Award winner, comments at the fourth annual CNBC Executive Leadership Awards at the New York Public Library in New York on March 31, 2008. (AP/Wide World Photos)

Quincy Jones (page 491). Composer and record producer Quincy Jones poses onstage of the Auditorium Stravinski at the 42nd Montreux Jazz Festival in Montreux, Switzerland in 2008. (AP/Wide World Photos)

Barbara Jordan (page 499). Sen. Barbara Jordan sworn in as governor of Texas in 1972. Jordan became the first black woman to serve as governor of any state, became governor for a day when the Texas governor and lieutenant governor were out of the state. (AP/Wide World Photos)

Michael Jordan (page 509). Widely regarded as the best basketball player in history, Michael Jordan is an NCAA basketball champion, six-time NBA champion, two-time Olympic gold medalist, and current majority owner of the NBA's Charlotte Bobcats. (Photofest)

Florence Griffith Joyner (page 519). Sprinter Florence Griffith Joyner wins the women's 100-meters final at the Seoul Olympics on September 25, 1988. Joyner gained worldwide fame for her performance in the 1988 Summer Olympics in Seoul, South Korea and for the style and glamour she brought to the sport.

Martin Luther King, Jr. (page 531). Theologian, civil rights activist, and proponent of peace, Martin Luther King, Jr. answers questions at a press conference in March 1964. King was a strong opponent of the Vietnam War. (Library of Congress)

Spike Lee (page 541). U.S. filmmaker Spike Lee, looks at the camera as he arrives at the Bellas Artes Museum in Caracas in 2009. (AP/Wide World Photos)

Joe Louis (page 551). Heavyweight boxer Joe Louis served as a symbol of the power of the American dream in the 1930s, promoting racial unity, national strength, and opportunity. (Hulton Archive/Getty Images)

Malcolm X (page 561). Portrait of Malcolm X, spokesman for the Nation of Islam who later converted to Sunni Muslim. He was assassinated on February 21, 1965. (Library of Congress)

Thurgood Marshall (page 571). Thurgood Marshall, the first African American appointed to the U.S. Supreme Court, built a remarkable legal career on the premise that all forms of racial segregation were unconstitutional. (Joseph Lavenburg, National Geographic Society, Collection of the Supreme Court of the United States)

Hattie McDaniel (page 583). Hattie McDaniel, the first African American to win an Academy Award, plays a tune as she portrays the title role of "Beulah" in the CBS Radio Network's comedy series in New York City in 1951. (AP/Wide World Photos)

Morehouse College (page 593). Students walk on the campus of historical Morehouse College in Atlanta, Georgia, in 2009. (AP/Wide World Photos)

Toni Morrison (page 603). Toni Morrison is one of the most significant American authors of the twentieth century. She was awarded both the Pulitzer Prize and the Nobel Prize for literature. (Olga Besnard)

Motown Records (page 613). Stevie Wonder and Marvin Gaye around a microphone at the Motown recording studio in Detroit in 1965. (Redferns/Getty Images)

Elijah Muhammad (page 623). Elijah Muhammad, as spiritual leader of the Nation of Islam in the United States, established a religious organization that gave poor urban African Americans a sense of racial pride and economic and political self-sufficiency. (Library of Congress)

Negro Baseball Leagues (page 635). Negro Leagues baseball star Buck O'Neil stands with a statue of himself at the Negro League Baseball Museum in Kansas City in 2005. Since 1990, he's been a tireless fundraiser and goodwill ambassador for the Negro Leagues Baseball Museum in Kansas City's historic jazz district, traveling the country to keep the legacy of black baseball alive. (AP/Wide World Photos)

Huey P. Newton and Bobby Seale (page 645). Huey Newton (right), founder of the Black Panther Party, sits with Bobby Seale at party headquarters in San Francisco, July 1967. (Ted Streshinsky/Corbis)

Barack Obama (page 657). Democrat Barack Obama became president of the United States in 2009. The first African American to hold that position, his election promised to usher the United States into a new era of opportunity, diversity, and multinationalism. (U.S. Department of Defense)

Michelle Obama (page 667). Michelle Obama, first African American first lady of the United States (2009–). (Department of Defense)

Jesse Owens (page 677). American sprinter, Jesse Owens, is pictured with the four gold medals he won at the 1936 Olympic Games in Berlin. (The Illustrated London News Picture Library)

Rosa Parks (page 687). Rosa Parks is fingerprinted in Montgomery, Alabama. Parks's arrest for refusing to give up her seat on a bus to a white man on December 1, 1955, inspired the Montgomery Bus Boycott, a prolonged action against the segregated Montgomery, Alabama, bus system by African American riders and their white supporters. (Library of Congress)

Sidney Poitier (page 697). In 1958, Sidney Poitier became the first African American to be nominated as Best Actor by the Academy of Motion Pictures Arts and Sciences for his costarring role in the Hollywood film *The Defiant Ones*. In 1963, he became only the second African American actor to win an Oscar, and the first to win the Academy Award for Best Actor, for his performance in the film *Lilies of the Field*. He is credited with paving the way for public acceptance of African American men in U.S. films, and such contemporary film figures as Eddie Murphy and Spike Lee have him partially to thank for their huge success. (AP/Wide World Photos)

Colin Powell (page 707). The first African American man to serve as chairman of the Joint Chiefs of Staff of the U.S. military, and as U.S. Secretary of State,

Colin Powell is one of the most highly regarded military authorities and political leaders in U.S. history. (AP/Wide World Photos)

Richard Pryor (page 717). Trailblazing comedian-actor Richard Pryor, performing in 1977. (AP/Wide World Photos)

A. Philip Randolph (page 727). A. Philip Randolph won respect for his quiet dignity and his firmness in a lifelong commitment to racial justice. A union organizer and socialist early in life, he became the country's best-known African American trade unionist and a nationally prominent leader in the struggle for civil rights during the early to mid-twentieth century. (Library of Congress)

Ishmael Reed (page 741). Novelist, essayist, and poet Ishmael Reed. AP/Wide World Photos.

Condoleezza Rice (page 751). Secretary of State Condoleezza Rice speaks at a news conference near President George W. Bush's Crawford, Texas ranch on August 6, 2006. During the news conference, Rice discussed the Iraq War and the conflict between Israel and Lebanon. (AP/Wide World Photos)

Paul Robeson (page 761). Paul Robeson, world famous stage and film performer, leads workers in singing "The Star-Spangled Banner" at the Moore shipyard in Oakland, California in September 1942. Robeson entertained Allied forces during World War II. (National Archives)

Jackie Robinson (page 771). Jackie Robinson was the first African American to play Major League Baseball, playing for the Brooklyn Dodgers from 1947 until 1956. Robinson won the first Rookie of the Year award in 1947 and the Most Valuable Player award in 1949. He was inducted into the Baseball Hall of Fame in 1962. (Bettmann/Corbis)

Bayard Rustin (page 783). Bayard Rustin was one of the most skillful organizers among the leaders of the civil rights movement. He was also influential in a range of other causes: pacifism, refugees, nuclear disarmament, Japanese-American rights, and gay rights. (Library of Congress)

Dred Scott (page 793). Dred Scott, plaintiff in one of the most important cases of constitutional law in U.S. history. (Library of Congress)

Tupac Shakur (page 803). Tupac Shakur as Ezekiel "Spoon" Whitmore in the 1997 movie *Gridlock'd*. (Photofest)

Russell Simmons (page 813). Russell Simmons arrives at the 2008 MTV Video Music Awards held at Paramount Pictures Studio. (AP/Wide World Photos)

Tommie Smith and John Carlos (page 819). At the Summer Olympic games in Mexico City, Mexico in October 1968, runners Tommie Smith and John

Carlos outraged the U.S. Olympic Committee by giving a black power salute during the medal ceremony. (Bettmann/Corbis)

Will Smith (page 829). Actor Will Smith poses at the *Hitch* photocall during the 55th annual Berlinale International Film Festival on February 18, 2005 in Berlin, Germany. (Dreamstime)

Spelman College (page 837). Spelman College in Atlanta, Georgia. (Spelman College)

Mary Church Terrell (page 847). Activist, Philanthropist, first African American Woman to earn a college degree, and co-founder of the National Association of Colored Women. (Library of Congress)

Sojourner Truth (page 857). A poster celebrating Sojourner Truth's fight for suffrage, and commemorating her famous " 'Ain't I a Woman?' " speech from the 1851 Women's Rights Convention. Not until the 1960s did African Americans truly receive the right to vote throughout the United States, with the help of additional federal legislation and sometimes military force. Women of all races received the right to vote through the Nineteenth Amendment, ratified in 1920, but due to poll taxes and confusing ballots many African American women's votes were never counted. (Library of Congress)

Harriet Tubman (page 867). Portrait of Harriet Tubman, leader of the Underground Railroad. (Library of Congress)

Nat Turner (page 877). A newspaper cartoon depicts the violent slave uprising led by Nat Turner that began on August 22, 1831 when Turner killed his master and his master's family. The revolt only lasted about a week but Turner eluded capture until October of that year. He was later tried and hanged for the crime. (Library of Congress)

Tuskegee Airmen (page 887). Tuskegee Airmen, including Benjamin O. Davis, Jr. (third from left), in Alabama, 1942. The Tuskegee Airmen were the first African American pilots in the U.S. Army Air Corps. (Library of Congress)

Alice Walker (page 897). One of the best and most influential writers of her generation, Alice Walker (shown here in 1990) has affected modern American life not only through her brilliant poetry and novels, but through her actions as a black feminist ("womanist") and social activist. Her novel *The Color Purple* is perhaps her most popular work so far. It was made into a movie starring Oprah Winfrey in 1985. (AP/Wide World Photos)

Madam C. J. Walker (page 905). Madam C. J. Walker founded a successful cosmetics business, actively spoke out on African American political issues, and sponsored philanthropic organizations. She was the wealthiest African American woman of the early twentieth century and an influential voice for the economic self-empowerment of African American women. (Madam C. J. Walker Collection, Indiana Historical Society)

Booker T. Washington (page 919). As the head of Tuskegee Institute (a leading center of African American education), Booker T. Washington was a major spokesperson for African Americans during the late nineteenth and early twentieth centuries. (Library of Congress)

Denzel Washington (page 931). Actor Denzel Washington won an academy award for Best Supporting Actor in 1990 and another for Best Actor in 2001. (AP/Wide World Photos)

Ida B. Wells-Barnett (page 943). As an anti-lynching crusader and the founder of the African American women's club movement and other civil rights organizations, Ida Wells-Barnett was one of the most influential African American women of the late nineteenth and early twentieth centuries. (Department of Special Collections, University of Chicago)

Cornel West (page 957). Dr. Cornel West speaks at the Conference on the State of the African-American Professoriate hosted at Ramapo College of New Jersey April 20, 2002. (AP/Wide World Photos)

Venus Williams and Serena Williams (page 967). Williams sisters Venus and Serena pose with trophy following the US Open in 2009. (Dreamstime)

Oprah Winfrey (page 979). Oprah Winfrey on the cover of her O magazine. (PRNewsFoto/Oxmoor House)

Stevie Wonder (page 989). Singer-songwriter Stevie Wonder at the 39th NAACP Image Awards in Los Angeles. (Shutterstock)

Tiger Woods (page 999). Professional golfer Tiger Woods. (Shutterstock)

Carter G. Woodson (page 1009). Carter G. Woodson established a model for African American history through the Association for the Study of Negro Life and History, which helped to correct the prejudice with which historians and the general public viewed African American abilities. (AP/Wide World Photos)

Richard Wright (page 1019). Richard Wright (photographed in 1939) is best known for his first published novel, _Native Son_, which introduced a new realism to literary treatments of the United States's racial problems, rendering sympathetically the always fearful, sometimes violent psychology of the oppressed. (Library of Congress)

Alex Haley (1921–1992)

Alexander Murray Palmer Haley was born on August 11, 1921, in Ithaca, New York. Though he spent a significant portion of his adult life serving in the Coast Guard, he is most known for his groundbreaking contributions to the writing of black history, and U.S. history in general. A simple statement made by an aging Haley characterizes his view toward the past: "a nation's history is only the collective histories of all its people." His ascent into the public eye began with the widespread acclaim given to the publication of his first book, *The Autobiography of Malcolm X: with the assistance of Alex Haley*, which was released shortly after **Malcolm X**'s assassination in 1965. The popular acceptance of this work provided Haley a subsequent contract in which he sought to write a large-scale study of his family's history. He begins the story in a West African village in 1767, and traces them across the Atlantic Ocean to America, where through the generational experiences of his forbearers he describes American life in the antebellum South, through Emancipation, and up to the early years of sharecropping. In September 1976, after over a decade of researching and writing, which had carried him to over 50 archives, across three continents, and included thousands of interviews, *Roots: The Saga of an American Family* hit the bestseller list in less than a month. Over half a million copies sold by the end of the year, which further prompted its immediate translation into 31 languages. The eight million copies purchased worldwide in the first year, while establishing Haley as an important voice for African Americans, was but a glimpse of the iconic stature he would obtain in the coming years. The American Broadcasting Company (ABC) television adaptation of *Roots* into an eight-part miniseries then landed the once-broke writer a million dollar contract, and solidified him as a household name for the over 90 million viewers who tuned in on the final evening. At this point, a Roper poll placed Haley as the third most admired black man in America, rivaled only by boxer **Muhammad Ali** and musician **Stevie Wonder**. This newfound fame and wealth, while providing Haley the means to further pursue his writing, did not shelter him from criticism. Contending with it, however, was not out of the ordinary for Haley, who since his days in the Coast Guard had persisted writing despite countless rejections from publishers and confrontations from members of the black community. Through thick and thin, Haley's perfectly candid demeanor combined with an unrelenting drive to publish and promote his work, kept him at the pinnacle of the African American community for the rest of his life. As a public intellectual, he drew from generations of genealogical history and so placed the African American experience clearly within the borders of U.S. society at large.

Alex Haley spent the first years of his life in Henning, Tennessee, where his grandfather, George Palmer, owned the local lumber company. Alex's father, Simon Alexander Haley, and mother, Bertha George Palmer, were both teachers. Although Simon Haley had taught at several Southern colleges, upon the death of Bertha's father, he took over the lumber business. During this time, Alex Haley lived and learned in close proximity to his mother's extended family. Hot afternoons on his grandmother's screened front porch brought long, winding stories about his African ancestry, told by his grandmother, Cynthia Palmer, and her visiting sisters, Plus and Liz. These dramatic stories about Uncle Mingo, Masa Waller, Miss Kizzy, Tom, and "Chicken George," were further enlivened by a contingent of other female relatives who would spare no time in pulling a rocking chair to the porch where they would exchange their own fragments of the story. These stories all began in Africa with their great-grandfather, Kunta Kinte, who as a child, went looking for wood to build a drum, was captured by slave-traders, and transported to America where he was sold. Though some elements of the story changed, and the ladies would use words that the young Haley could not understand, he did pick up on certain parts, which sparked his lifelong interest in his family's history, and genealogy in general. These parts, that Kinte had played a guitar-like instrument called a *ko*, and that his family had lived near a river called the Kamby Bolongo, stuck with Haley, and would serve as the basis of his research for *Roots*, which he began almost 40 years later.

Simon Haley spent about a year after George Palmer's death putting business affairs in order and then sold the lumber company so as to return to teaching. The Haley family traveled much in the coming years as Simon took teaching jobs at colleges for African Americans in Oklahoma and Alabama. He even earned his master's degree from Cornell in 1931. Less than a year later, Bertha died, leaving Simon Haley with Alex and his younger brother George. Simon's mother Queen then came to live with the family until 1933, when he married another professor on campus, Zeona Hatcher. Even though they were constantly on the move, Haley's father always stressed the importance of a strong education. He tried to impart this on his children by taking them to visit African Americans, such as the famous scientist **George Washington Carver**, who had elevated the circumstances and public perceptions of their fellow people.

In high school, Haley took classes in mathematics, English, history, geography, and typing, but despite his father's best wishes, did not excel in his studies. He graduated from high school in 1936 with only a "C" average. Poor performance in the classroom did not prevent him from continuing his education, and in 1937 he enrolled in the college to which his father had transferred to in North Carolina. After two years, he found that he could no longer handle the classroom and decided to drop out. His father strongly opposed this and would not forgive Alex for years to come. In an effort to curb his son's apparent waywardness, Simon Haley had him enlist in the U.S. Coast Guard. He hoped his son would have a renewed interest in his studies after completing a three-year enlistment with the services.

So in the summer of 1939, Alex Haley entered the Coast Guard at the rank of steward. This time with the Coast Guard would set him in motion toward his eventual career as a writer. Unlike his father had thought, however, he would spend a full 20 years in the service before venturing out on his own as a full-time writer. During the initial three-year stint, his ship would frequently dock at a North Carolina port. Within two years, he developed an interest for a local woman, Nannie Branch, and in 1941 they were married. Now when his ship was on three-month voyages at sea he would write back to her. These letters, while helping Haley avoid the turmoil experienced by his fellow sailors who were unable to communicate clearly with their loved ones while away, did not occupy enough of his spare time to fill the monotonous void, which appeared when sailors failed to create their own amusements once duties were finished each day. Supplementing the letters to Nannie, Haley would write to his father, former teachers, his friends, and anyone else to whom he felt compelled. These apparent fits of writing came at such a pace that it was not unusual for him to mail 30 or 40 letters at once. As Haley increasingly viewed his typewriter as the single most important piece of property he had at sea, his supervisor Scotty saw his typing ability as something he could himself benefit from by catching up on personal letter writing.

Haley typed one letter in particular that in saving the relationship of one of Scotty's shipmates also opened a door for paid writing. As the story goes, under Scotty's guidance, Haley wrote to this shipmate's girlfriend after she broke their engagement. The letter was so powerful that the woman replied, begging forgiveness. As others on board caught wind of this incredible feat, they too asked him to write letters to their girlfriends. These sailors enjoyed the wonderful response they received from their girlfriends so much that they began paying him for his prose. That his writing not only earned him extra money but was also warmly accepted by the readers, provided Haley the impetus to try to have his writing published. His first attempts were love stories for magazines, and though none were published, the experience further drove his ambition. It was at this point that Haley made a discovery that would shape the rest of his life: "The idea that one could roll a blank sheet of paper into a typewriter and write something on it that other people would care to read challenged, intrigued, and exhilarated me" (quoted in Gonzales, 1994, 32).

By 1945 the Coast Guard had taken notice of Haley as a particularly skilled writer, and established an office position for him in New York where he served as an intermediary between the Coast Guard and newspapers. His wife, and newborn daughter Lydia moved with him to Harlem, and in 1946 his son William was born. At Haley's new post, he took charge of the public information telephone, immediately showing a zealous drive to convey accurate information about incidents at sea to newspaper reporters in New York. While diligently working for the Coast Guard, Haley learned to maintain a professional commitment to journalists in general. Those reporters who worked with him held him in the highest esteem, and spoke of him as amiable, industrious, and ever helpful. This dynamic work ethic helped Haley gain the editorship of a Coast Guard magazine, *The Helmsman*, begin another called *The Outpost*, and contribute articles to a third, *The United States Coast Guard Magazine*.

In December 1949, the Coast Guard recognized Haley's unparalleled performance by promoting him to Chief Journalist, a previously nonexistent position. As the first person to hold this specialty rank he wrote speeches for officers and stories for various publications. Ever since moving to New York to take on full-time office duties, Haley had also continued to work on his own articles to sell, waking at 4:30 a.m. every morning to write before heading to the office. This too finally paid off, and during the Christmas holidays, a popular men's magazine, *Coronet*, purchased three of his stories.

Over the following decade Haley balanced his role as Chief Journalist with an increasingly fruitful writing career outside of the Coast Guard. He published a first article with *Reader's Digest* in 1954, "The Harlem Nobody Knows," which marked his entrance to the ranks of established authors. In the following years this publication provided Haley occasional opportunities to write. Although these initial pieces were of only minor significance, they established Alex Haley as a recognized name among the magazine's global audience, with 24 million subscribers receiving issues in 13 different languages.

By 1959, Haley had completed 20 years of service with the Coast Guard and, determined to make it as a writer, took an early retirement. Now, each day of the week, Haley invested himself in writing for 16 to 18 hours. His unabated passion to publish overwhelmed his entire life; he became almost completely disinterested in material possessions and while staying in the austere accommodations of a dark one-room basement apartment in Greenwich Village, was prepared to starve. Understandably discouraged at this point, with little more than 18 cents and a couple cans of sardines, Haley turned to his curious ability to write letters eliciting action from the receiver. He wrote to six black writers who were currently living in the Village and in close proximity to its burgeoning cultural scene. This scene drew energy from the bohemian-inspired Beat movement of the early 1950s, with authors, playwrights, musicians, and artists continuing to gather and develop powerful commentaries on the imposing drive toward social conformity. Though **James Baldwin** was the only one to respond, his advice and encouragement gave Haley the needed support to continue. As Haley would recount later in his life, more than anything, Baldwin had simply treated him as a fellow writer.

Haley made a substantial break in late 1959 when *Reader's Digest* commissioned him to do a series of short biographical sketches of popular celebrities and others with particularly exciting lives. Making the most of his situation, Haley proposed an interview with the fervent young Muslim minister Malcolm X, a volatile figure even within the Nation of Islam (NOI) itself. Haley successfully persuaded the magazine that its mostly white, generally conservative readers would find the fiery young leader of interest and his article, "Mr. Muhammad Speaks," definitely delivered. In providing the general public its first honest profile of Malcolm X, Haley also showcased his exceptional talent as a writer and interviewer. While the popular and critical success of this article was unparalleled by Haley's previous work, equally important was the close friendship which had begun to unfold between he and Malcolm X.

Haley's able handling of the piece on Malcolm X drew the attention of editors from across the country and in the following years a variety of highly regarded publications sought his work. After three years of these scattered, though substantive articles, *Playboy* invited him to do a series of interviews with controversial public figures. This assignment fit Haley's character well. His time in Harlem and Greenwich Village and interviews with Malcolm X had made him quite conscious of a range of popular movements, from bohemianism to radicalism. His calming presence put the most skeptical or paranoid interviewees at ease. For his first piece he even got the acclaimed jazz trumpeter **Miles Davis** to speak freely about his life and music. While other journalists had failed to get past Davis's moody withdrawn mannerisms or his open suspicion of the white establishment, Haley's informal style of recording long casual conversations between himself and the interviewee provided an entirely new glimpse into Davis's life. Haley generally cut parts from the lengthy transcripts so as to provide a condensed, yet coherent product to the magazine. This process could take quite awhile and he had become quite notorious for missing deadlines. With Davis's article, however, he came up against a firm due date and decided to turn in the full transcript. To his surprise, the editors responded with thrill and published the entire interview. Haley's work habits, which had strained his relationship with other editors, paved the way for an entirely new form of journalism that disregarded the polished edited standard of the day, opting instead for stream of consciousness.

About this time, Malcolm X was approached by Doubleday to publish an autobiography for the general public. Some accounts have Haley as the one responsible for persuading Malcolm X that his story could benefit the public perception of the NOI. Others have Doubleday proposing the idea to Malcolm X who turned to Haley because they had worked together on a few projects. Either way, over the following years Malcolm X visited Haley's apartment in the Village weekly, and began telling of his time with the NOI, of the organization's foundation, of their revolutionary claims and demands for what the United States did to blacks. It would take months before Haley, in what was becoming his trademark style, broke the ice; after asking Malcolm X about memories of his mother, the strident Muslim minister went into detailed stories of his past. Haley spared little in transcribing Malcolm X's accounts–having agreed from the start to put nothing in the manuscript not said by Malcolm X himself, and to leave nothing out he wanted in. Though the manuscript was completed only weeks before Malcolm X's death, he felt it accurate enough that the book initially went to press simply as *The Autobiography of Malcolm X*. Subsequent editions, published with the addendum "with the assistance of Alex Haley," would directly recognize his work as ghostwriter. The longstanding value of this contribution was acknowledged when the autobiography made the top 10 list of books published in the 1960s, and again reaffirmed when *Time* magazine placed it among the 10 most important nonfiction books of the twentieth century.

Haley found himself increasingly occupied with his work. While his writing now reached people in all walks of life, helping them better appreciate the impact of controversial public figures, he was unable to bring the same energy and dedication to his own family. This strain brought his marriage with Nannie Branch to an end in 1964. Within a year, he married another woman, Juliette Collins. Together they had a daughter, Cynthia Gertrude, but this relationship, too, was fraught with hardship. The author's romantic life proved similar to that of other prominent African American men he interviewed during this turbulent time, as he himself had commented about Malcolm X and **Martin Luther King, Jr.** who while holding such opposing viewpoints were both "obsessed with their work but felt guilty about being away from their families" (Gonzales, 1994, 45). Fortunately, these troubles at home did not prevent Haley from capitalizing on the success of the autobiography.

Haley's sensitivity and devotion, which helped place *The Autobiography of Malcolm X* among the permanent literature of the African American struggle, enabled him to maneuver his next contract, whereby he agreed to complete the story of his African ancestors. He had begun this book while undertaking Malcolm X's autobiography, with the tentative title *Before this Anger*. By the time he finished in February 1976, he had worked 10 years and $91,000 beyond his initial two year, $5,000 proposal, and in the process changed the title to *Roots: The Saga of an American Family* so as to emphasize both the genealogical and collective dimensions of the historical narrative. His research had carried him far: to linguists, who identified the language of those African words spoken by his grandmother as Mandinkan, a language still spoken in West Africa; to archives, where he found written records verifying the name of the ship Kunta Kinte had traveled to America in while shackled to its hull; to Africa, where griots—Mandingo elders trained orally in their village's genealogical history—corroborated Haley's findings with more extensive knowledge of members who had been captured and shipped to America; and culminating in Annapolis, Maryland, where his great-great-great-great-grandfather landed in 1767, with Haley at the port his ancestors knew of as Naplis.

Recognizing that some of the historical content was hard to verify, the Pulitzer Committee awarded Haley with a special prize commending him for his work, which "did not accommodate itself to the category of history but transcended it." Even after some bitter controversy was sparked by a London newspaper's scathing editorial, which brought both the integrity of Haley's research and the accuracy of his account into question, the Pulitzer Committee maintained its stance, stating, "regardless of error, the historical essence of [Haley's] book was truthful." Haley himself had promoted his work as a "historical novel," referring to his approach as faction: "All the major incidents are true, the details are as accurate as very heavy research can make them, the names and dates are real, but obviously when it comes to dialogue, and people's emotions and thoughts, I had to make things up" (Shirley, 2005, 81). To know what a historical actor such as Kunta Kinte thought, Haley emphasized the need to subject oneself to the same discomforts—to imagine what he saw, heard, felt, smelled, tasted.

Interpretive reservations aside, book buyers across the globe testified to the story's appeal as both interesting family narrative and critical retelling of U.S. history. With his special Pulitzer Prize and a citation from the National Book Awards in hand, Haley secured a million dollars in contract negotiations between Doubleday and ABC for the rights to produce a miniseries based on *Roots*. His hard work had finally paid off, as he literally became a millionaire overnight. While this enabled him to make a few purchases—a stereo, a television, and a VCR to watch reruns of the forthcoming miniseries—it had, more significantly, opened the door to a less-stressful life for the author, who no longer had to live wondering if he had enough money for bills from one month to the next.

When the *Roots* miniseries initially aired in September 1977, it was an event that dominated the national consciousness, with more than half of the people in the United States having watched at least one segment. Many felt that it galvanized a potentially fractious society in the aftermath of civil rights era strife, as it was about more than African Americans, and by telling an American story, about an American family, convincingly portrayed the country's collective history. This unprecedented appeal to television audiences across the nation lead ABC to immediately produce a sequel, *Roots: The Next Generation*, which aired the following year. With this widespread success, Haley found himself swept away, rotating between tight schedules of public speaking and further consulting on the film set. These public appearances included everything from book signings at rural libraries, to speaking engagements in Africa, Latin America, and the former Soviet Union, to guest appearances, such as his visit to *The Tonight Show Starring Johnny Carson*. He maintained his presence on the film set into the early 1980s, helping co-produce two seasons of *Palmerstown, U.S.A.*, which portrayed autobiographical fragments from his time as a youth in Henning, Tennessee.

In his later years, Haley again found time to write. He published a book, *A Different Kind of Christmas*, in 1988 and contributed to *Queen* with David Stevens, who would not complete the work until after Haley's death. Years later, Stevens also wrote another book, *Mama Flora's*, based on Haley's research. Following the trend of Haley's now prolific set of miniseries, *Queen* and *Mama Flora's* were both adapted into successful television productions. Though none of these later works won the acclaim of his earlier projects, they retold stories that continue adding depth to the history of African Americans.

Haley will always be remembered most by his first two iconic works, *The Autobiography of Malcolm X* and *Roots*; two cultural phenomena that maintained universal appeal while showing a dark, tormented, and at times triumphant history. In 1991, Haley's body of work was singled out for special recognition by his colleagues in the National Association of Black Journalists, an honor that Haley felt rivaled only by his Pulitzer Prize. In leading

Americans to better understand and embrace their past, Haley had inspired individuals everywhere to appreciate their lineage and forefathers. His work reinforced this idea by maintaining a historical dimension, as if to say "you have to understand where people have been to understand what they have come into." A proud Haley affirmed this when he reflected, "If I have become a symbol of the shared search for ancestral roots, then indeed I am blessed" (Shirley, 2005, 98).

Always the avid promoter, Haley was on his way to a public engagement in Seattle, Washington when he suffered a fatal heart attack on February 10, 1992—by this point celebrated as an American biographer, scriptwriter, novelist, and historian writ large. Much like Malcolm X, who died only months before the release of his autobiography, Alex Haley died only months before the release of **Spike Lee**'s cinematic adaptation of *Malcolm X*, which is dedicated "In Memory of Alex Haley," and "based upon his *The Autobiography of Malcolm X, as told to Alex Haley*." The Kunta Kinte-Alex Haley Foundation, founded in 1992, carries on Haley's legacy as a cultural icon worldwide; with a mission to "be the world's premier organization for African Americans and all others to come to for a fuller awareness and appreciation of their history, the universality of human experiences, and a deeper understanding of slavery and its impact on race relations in America today" (www.kintehaley.org).

Bradley T. Wiles
Arizona State University

FURTHER READING

Gonzalez, Doreen. *Alex Haley: Author of Roots*. Hillside, NJ: Enslow, 1994.

Haley, Alex. *A Different Kind of Christmas*. New York: Doubleday, 1988.

Haley, Alex. *The Playboy Interviews*. New York: Ballantine, 1993.

Haley, Alex. *Roots: The Saga of an American Family*. New York: Doubleday, 1976.

Haley, Alex, and David Stevens. *Alex Haley's Queen: The Story of an American Family*. New York: Morrow, 1993.

Kunta Kinte–Alex Haley Foundation, Inc. Web site: www.kintehaley.org.

Shirley, David. *Alex Haley*. New York: Chelsea House, 1994.

X, Malcolm, and Alex Haley. *The Autobiography of Malcolm X: with the Assistance of Alex Haley*. New York: Grove Press, 1966.

Library of Congress

Fannie Lou Hamer
(1917–1977)

Fannie Lou Hamer was born Fannie Lou Townsend on October 6, 1917, in Sunflower County, Mississippi (also the home of future ardent segregationist Senator James O. Eastland). Raised in the heart of the Jim Crow South, Hamer rose to prominence as perhaps the most important rural working-class leader of the Civil Rights Movement that included so many other middle-class people. She challenged a U.S. president, faced down hostile white law enforcement officers, and encouraged poor African Americans throughout rural Mississippi to register to vote and work together for social justice. Despite some physical ailments leftover from a childhood bout with polio and a vicious beating at the hands of white law enforcement officers in Winona, Mississippi, Hamer possessed a deep reservoir of physical and emotional strength in advocating for equal voting rights and economic justice. Her heartfelt oratorical skills and deep passion for singing Christian spirituals and freedom songs would become some of her trademarks as she pursued her activism on a national, state, and local level. Hamer is unique among civil rights figures because of her sharecropping background and relative lack of education. Her life represents how factors of race, class, gender, and religion intersected with one another during the black freedom struggle in both complementary and contradictory ways.

Hamer's early life was crucial in shaping the contours of her future political activism. She was the youngest of the 20 Townsend children that included 14 brothers and 5 sisters before she was born. Her parents, James Lee Townsend and Lou Ella Bramlett Townsend, were both sharecroppers on cotton plantations in the Sunflower County countryside. Much like Hamer would do later in her own life, both of her parents took on various odd jobs to supplement their income to survive. Like many other black women of the time, Lou Ella worked as a domestic servant in a white home for extra money. In an unusual pairing of jobs, Hamer's father worked as both a Baptist minister and a bootlegger. Her family also engaged in the practice of "scrapping" cotton, or picking what was left on the cotton stalks after a day of picking, to sell their own bales of cotton on the market. With all the hard work the Townsends put into sharecropping and their other odd jobs, they were able to save enough money to get to the point where they could become more financially independent and rent some land of their own. During this time, the Townsends had enough money to buy livestock, farm equipment, and even a car. However, the Townsends' prosperity did not go unnoticed by their neighbors, black and white. In fact, a white man poisoned the Townsends' livestock trough with an insecticide containing arsenic. The poison killed all the livestock and stifled the Townsends' ability to break away from the cycle of indebtedness that trapped so many sharecroppers.

One of the other formative parts of Hamer's family background was her grandmother's experience with white plantation owners and how it shaped her mother. Hamer's mother was one of three children of Liza Bramlett who was conceived in a consensual relationship, but Lou Ella Bramlett had 20 other siblings who were the product of her mother being raped. After listening to her mother's experience with being raped by white plantation owners, Lou Ella became very protective of herself and her children. She gained a reputation for talking back to the plantation owners and even hit the son of an owner when she was a child. Hamer even noticed that her mother carried a pistol out into the cotton fields with her to protect herself or her children against whites for fear of reliving Liza Bramlett's experience with rape. The story of her grandmother's sexual victimization and her mother's tough attitude conditioned Hamer to be bolder in resisting the status quo in the life of a sharecropper in the Mississippi Delta.

In Hamer's first direct conflict with the white power structure of the Jim Crow South, the Townsends' plantation owner tricked Hamer into picking cotton at the young age of six. While she was playing outside one day, the plantation owner came by and asked her whether she could pick cotton. Hamer sheepishly admitted that she was not sure whether she could pick cotton. The owner then told the young Hamer that he would give her some treats from the plantation commissary if she could pick 30 pounds of cotton by the end of the week. Her parents refused to give her any of their cotton so she could make her 30-pound quota. After successfully picking 30 pounds of cotton, Hamer claimed her treats, but was soon entrapped in working the cotton fields on a regular basis. She proved her mettle in picking cotton and found herself in debt to her family's plantation owner. Hamer later recalled, "What had happened was he was trapping me into beginning the work I was to keep doing and I never did get out of his debt again" (quoted in Asch, 2008, 54).

In 1944, Hamer married Perry "Pap" Hamer, a tractor driver from another plantation. The two worked as sharecroppers on W. D. Marlowe's plantation in Ruleville. After two attempts at having children and two stillbirths, the Hamers adopted two girls, Dorothy Jean and Vergie Lee, who needed help because their biological parents were unable to care for them. In 1961, doctors performed surgery on Hamer to remove a small cyst on her stomach. However, the surgeons also performed a hysterectomy on Hamer without her consent thus preventing her from attempting to have any children of her own in the future. However, Hamer's involuntary sterilization was not an isolated incident because lawmakers in Mississippi and elsewhere had considered forced sterilization programs for mothers on welfare or other indigent women. Like many other black women, Hamer's body was violated by the larger white power structure that felt it could control the bodies of black women either through rape or involuntary sterilization.

On the Marlowe plantation, Hamer held a position of high esteem among black sharecroppers because she was a timekeeper who helped determine wages. Plantation owners would pay sharecroppers according to the amount of cotton they picked, but would often cheat the sharecroppers by using a scale that was altered to produce a lower weight for the picked cotton. Hamer earned a reputation as a fair timekeeper who would try to prevent plantation owners from cheating their sharecroppers. When it came time for sharecroppers to weigh their cotton, she would add a counterweight to the plantation owner's scale to produce the accurate cotton weight. However, she would be on the lookout for the owner and would stealthily remove the counterweight if the plantation owner happened to be nearby to observe the weighing process. Hamer explained her daily acts of resistance in the following way, "I didn't know what to do and all I could do is rebel in the only way I could rebel" (quoted in Asch, 2008, 59). Like her parents, Fannie Lou and Pap Hamer had to take on a variety of odd jobs to support their family with additional income. She worked as an insurance saleswoman for the black community in Sunflower County because of her skill with numbers and her good reputation with the community. The Hamers also engaged in hunting, bootlegging, and even running a juke joint because their work as sharecroppers on the Marlowe plantation was insufficient even though Fannie Lou worked in a higher position as the timekeeper.

Hamer's participation in traditional political activism began in Williams Chapel Church in August 1962. The Student Nonviolent Coordinating Committee (SNCC) began talking to black sharecroppers in the homes about registering to vote. They had organized a large meeting at Williams Chapel Church in which to make their pitch to a much larger audience. Composed primarily of college students and young adults, SNCC hoped to reach out to a broader audience by joining together with the National Association for the Advancement of Colored People (NAACP), the National Urban League (NUL), and the Southern Christian Leadership Conference (SCLC) to form the Council of Federated Organizations (COFO) to reduce competition among civil rights groups. The larger COFO campaign reached out to Mary Tucker, a family friend of the Townsends, to help recruit other people to come to the mass meeting at Williams Chapel Church. Tucker reached out to Hamer and suggested that she come to the meeting. At first, Hamer was reluctant to attend, but after consulting with her husband, she decided to attend the meeting at the church. She had been involved in church for almost her entire life and was most fascinated by Bible stories of the Exodus and the Kingdom of God as described by Jesus. When James Bevel preached on Luke 12:54 and interpreting the signs of the time in the context of a SNCC voter registration drive, Hamer was deeply moved and made a commitment to become a registered voter. In her own words, she described the experience, "Until then I'd never heard of no mass meeting and I didn't know that a Negro could register and vote" (quoted in Lee, 2000, 25).

On August 31, Hamer was 1 of 18 people who responded to SNCC's call to register to vote at the county seat of Indianola. Hamer explained her decision to go to Indianola in bold terms, "I guess if I'd had any sense I'd a-been a little scared, but what was the point of being scared. The only thing [the whites] could do was kill me and it seemed like they'd been trying to do that a little bit at a time since I could remember" (quoted in Marsh, 1997, 12). Once the bus arrived at the Sunflower County courthouse in Indianola, the 18 aspiring voters were hesitant to disembark at first until Fannie Lou Hamer led the way into the courthouse. The circuit court clerk asked the group why they had come to the courthouse and Hamer explained for the group that they had come to register to vote. Once he had dismissed 16 of the 18 prospective registrants, the clerk begrudgingly initiated the voter registration application for Hamer and one of the others. The application for voter registration included a literacy test that asked questions about a registrant's name, their employment, and interpreting the Mississippi state constitution. To make local whites aware of African Americans attempting to register so that they might launch reprisals against prospective black registrants, Mississippi local newspapers frequently published the names of everyone who registered to vote for several weeks. While filling out the application and taking the literacy test, Hamer realized the consequences of her attempt to register to vote. She and her family would probably be fired and displaced by plantation owner W. D. Marlowe for her attempt to assert her fundamental right to vote. When she came to the section of the literacy test on interpreting the state constitution, Hamer knew her chances of succeeding were slim. The question asked her to analyze a section of the constitution dealing with de facto laws. She later noted that, "I knowed as much about a facto law as a horse knows about Christmas Day" (quoted in Marsh, 1997, 14). After working on the literacy test until the end of the day, Hamer boarded the bus to return to Ruleville.

On the way back to Ruleville, a local law enforcement officer pulled the bus over and arrested the driver for driving a bus that resembled a school bus. The group of aspiring registrants was petrified because they no longer had a way home. Drawing on her deep emotional strength, Hamer began singing hymns like "Just a Little Talk with Jesus" and "This Little Light of Mine" to encourage the others who soon joined Hamer in song. After their bus driver was released from jail, the group finally returned to Ruleville. However, the drama for Hamer was not yet over because plantation owner W. D. Marlowe had already been notified about her attempt to register. Marlowe drove down to the Hamer home to issue an ultimatum to Mrs. Hamer, demanding that she withdraw her registration application or leave the plantation. Hamer decided on the latter option, responding to Marlowe, "Mr. Dee, I didn't go down there to register for you. I went there to register for myself" (quoted in Lee, 2000, 33). She left the Marlowe plantation to stay with Mary and Robert Tucker while her husband and daughters stayed behind to finish the harvest season. At the end of the harvest, Marlowe fired Pap Hamer and confiscated their family's furniture and car to pay off a debt that the Hamers still supposedly owed.

Even after moving off the Marlowe plantation, Hamer was not through being a victim of retribution for her attempt to register. A group of whites riddled the Tucker home with bullets in an attempt to kill Hamer. After the attempt on her life, she moved to Tallahatchie County where she resided for two months with her daughters. During her time in Tallahatchie County, Hamer reflected on her experiences with the Jim Crow power structure and how it had affected her parents and grandparents. Drawing on her Christian faith, she resolved that she would run no more from those who threatened her fundamental American right to vote. Then she made the bold decision to return to Ruleville to attempt to register to vote for a second time. She defiantly told the registrar, "Now you cain't have me fired because I'm not livin' in no white man's house. I'll be here every thirty days until I become a registered voter" (quoted in Lee, 2000, 37). Assuming she had failed the literacy test for the second time, she returned to Indianola in January 1963 to take the test for a third time, but the registrar informed her that she had passed. However, Hamer was not yet able to vote because Mississippi had a law that required registered voters to have two poll tax receipts from consecutive years before they could actually vote. The Hamer family suffered a considerable amount of retaliation after Fannie Lou Hamer's successful registration was published in the local newspaper per Mississippi law. Other than violence and physical intimidation, the Hamers received a water bill one month for thousands of dollars because the water company claimed they had used several thousand gallons of water.

While continuing her attempts to register to vote, Hamer attended a variety of civil rights training workshops and conferences. Bob Moses, a SNCC activist, invited Hamer to attend a SNCC-sponsored workshop at Fisk University in Nashville because Hamer exemplified the type of grassroots community leadership that SNCC sought to develop. At the Fisk University conference, Hamer learned about tactics of nonviolence, problems of economic injustice, and strategies of organizing civil rights activists. Hamer began working as a field secretary for COFO, launching a long career of paid civil rights work. She conducted citizenship classes for the SCLC and canvassed for potential voters, but her heart was most dedicated to SNCC and its young activists because they were committed to the people of the local community. Hamer sometimes showed contempt for other civil rights organizations, calling the NAACP the "National Association for the Advancement of Certain People" and questioning the commitment of black ministers to civil rights that often put her at odds with the SCLC. In June 1963, Hamer and several other local Mississippi activists traveled to Charleston, South Carolina for a joint SCLC-SNCC workshop on training people for voter registration drives. The return journey from Charleston would change Hamer's life and provide her with the most compelling story of Jim Crow violence and intimidation that she would tell in her later political work.

At a bus stop in Winona, Mississippi, the group of activists returning from Charleston was arrested after they took down the license plate numbers of police who harassed them at a lunch counter. Hamer had remained on the bus because she was tired, but she came off the bus to inquire what the people on the bus should do. After getting off the bus, she too was arrested and taken with the others to the county jail. At the county jail, the group was beaten and tortured by local law enforcement officers. When it came time for Hamer to be "interrogated," the prison guards brought in two black inmates who were coerced into beating Hamer with blackjacks. She was forced to lay on the jail bed on her stomach while she received blow after blow. At one point, her dress was riding up, but when she tried to adjust it, the white police officers pushed the dress back up. The white law enforcement officers asked a few questions during the beating, but were not concerned with getting any sort of answer. Instead, they took perverse pleasure in watching male black inmates torture Hamer in a recreation of racial and sexual stereotypes held by many whites. The Winona experience was seared in Hamer's memory as she recalled the incident in her speeches to civil rights groups.

One of Hamer's fundamental beliefs was that broader voting rights for disenfranchised African Americans and more progressive officeholders would change the American status quo and lead to a more just society. Despite SNCC's voter registration campaign, many Mississippi African Americans were still intimidated by whites who threatened them both physically and economically. In November 1963, COFO launched the Freedom Vote, a mock election to demonstrate the level of potential black turnout when barriers to voter registration were removed. Approximately 83,000 African Americans turned out to participate in the Freedom Vote, selecting COFO-endorsed candidates by wide margins over Mississippi's regular Democrats. After the success of the Freedom Vote, SNCC activists organized the Freedom Summer in 1964. Hamer participated in the Freedom Summer by training young white college students in the realities of Jim Crow Mississippi and by speaking at black churches to encourage voter registration. Even while some SNCC activists were trying to keep whites out of their organization, Hamer advocated for racially integrated civil rights activism and offered the opinion of an older, more traditional person to a group dominated by younger and more radical people.

The year 1964 not only marked the Freedom Summer in Mississippi, but also a presidential election that pitted Democratic President Lyndon B. Johnson against Republican Senator Barry Goldwater. Part of SNCC's summer activities included organizing the Mississippi Freedom Democratic Party (MFDP) that was created to challenge the delegates of the regular Democratic Party slated to attend the Democratic National Convention in Atlantic City. Hamer was one of the MFDP delegates chosen to attend the convention in Atlantic City and to bring the story of the racism of Jim Crow Mississippi to a larger national audience. She made an immediate impact on the convention by leading groups in song or addressing audiences attending MFDP events on the Atlantic City boardwalk. Her story riveted audiences and reporters from almost every medium that provoked the ire of President Johnson who was afraid of losing the electoral votes of the "solid South" to Goldwater over civil rights issues. To get seated in the place of the regular Democrats as Mississippi's delegation to the convention, the MFDP had to receive 11 votes from the Credentials Committee to get a chance for a vote on the convention floor and eight states would have to support a roll call vote on the floor of the convention.

In the Credentials Committee meeting, Hamer got an opportunity to address the committee and told her story about trying to register to vote and the beatings at the Winona jail. She challenged the committee with a provocative statement, "All of this [intimidation and retaliation by whites] is on account we want to register, to become first-class citizens, and if the Freedom Democratic Party is not seated now, I question America" (quoted in Marsh, 1997, 38). Hamer's testimony before the Credentials Committee was being televised, but was cut short when President Johnson called an urgent press conference to stop television coverage of Hamer's story. Much to Johnson's chagrin, the television networks televised her testimony in prime time later that evening when they realized that they had been tricked. Johnson was determined to keep "that illiterate woman" (as he called her) away from major press coverage that might disrupt his nominating convention.

Johnson enlisted vice-presidential candidate Hubert Humphrey and his protégé Walter Mondale to find a solution to the MFDP crisis that would silence the civil rights activists and not upset the Mississippi regular Democrats. Their solution was a compromise that would give the MFDP two at-large delegates without replacing the regular delegates. While a few of the MFDP delegates accepted the compromise, Hamer and other poorer delegates were livid about the two-seat solution. After one last vigil, Hamer and other MFDP delegates left Atlantic City, disheartened by what had transpired. Despite having their hopes dashed at the convention, the activism of the MFDP and SNCC had increased the number of black voters in Mississippi.

After being rebuffed in Atlantic City, Hamer and several other SNCC activists traveled to Guinea at the expense of singer **Harry Belafonte**. In the three weeks they were in Guinea, Hamer and the others met Guinea's president Sekou Touré and marveled at how blacks in Guinea ran the recently decolonized country in stark contrast to the Jim Crow South where blacks' political participation was proscribed. After Toure's visit, Hamer remarked, "Imagine the president coming to see us, when in the United States we couldn't even go to see the president" (quoted in Lee, 2000, 104). Hamer's trip to Guinea left a significant impact on her future activism because she now felt connected to a larger global struggle for black liberation.

In the 1964 elections, she and other MFDP leaders ran against the regular Democrats in the Democratic primaries. Losing in the primaries, the group tried to run in the general election as independents, but Mississippi state law prohibited the primary losers from running in the general election. The MFDP contested the seating of the Mississippi congressional delegation and held a second Freedom Vote to show voter support for the MFDP candidates who were prevented from running in the general election. However, the challenge was eventually dismissed by the House of Representatives.

The fallout of the Atlantic City convention led to a radical transition in the larger Civil Rights Movement as well as Hamer's personal philosophy. Both Hamer and the movement began to move away from electoral politics and more toward economic justice issues because they realized that gaining the vote would not dislodge the white power structure. Despite her frustration with the political process, Hamer persisted in her political activism, ran for elective office on several more occasions, and even attended the 1968 Democratic National Convention as an official part of the Mississippi state delegation.

As SNCC became more radical with the influence of Black Power ideology, Hamer became less involved with SNCC and electoral politics and focused more on local economic issues and self-help activities. She became a strong advocate for the Mississippi Freedom Labor Union (MFLU), formed in 1965 to support the efforts to day laborers, truck drivers, and domestic workers. Although not involved in MFLU's creation, Hamer participated in the organization through fund-raising and recruitment drives and through becoming a well-recognized symbolic leader of the union. Hamer also participated in fund-raising for a local community-supported Head Start program funded by Johnson's War on Poverty. However, middle-class whites and blacks collaborated to ensure that the funding would be directed away from the program run by the poor to establish a separate program run by middle-class citizens. She helped create the Freedom Farm Corporation, a cooperative farm in Sunflower County that would help support poor families in making a living. However, the Freedom Farm eventually failed because of mismanagement and people taking advantage of the free food and lodging without giving any work back to the cooperative.

In her later life, Hamer continued to fund-raise for different civil rights and social justice causes, but the constant traveling led to deterioration in her health. She eventually died of breast cancer at the age of 59 on March 14, 1977. Activists, scholars, and others remember her as a strong advocate for African Americans, women, and the poor. Even though she lived to see many advances in social justice causes, injustice and inequality still frustrated Hamer until her death. It is only fitting that her tombstone's epitaph is "I am sick and tired of being sick and tired."

Blake Jones
Arizona State University

FURTHER READING

Asch, Christopher Myers. *The Senator and the Sharecropper: The Freedom Struggles of James O. Eastland and Fannie Lou Hamer*. New York: New Press, 2008.

Hamer, Fannie Lou. *To Praise Our Bridges*. Jackson: KIPCO, 1967.

Lee, Chana Kai. *For Freedom's Sake: The Life of Fannie Lou Hamer*. Athens: University of Georgia Press, 1999.

Marsh, Charles. *God's Long Summer: Stories of Faith and Civil Rights*. Princeton, NJ: Princeton University Press, 1999.

Mills, Kay. *This Little Light of Mine: The Life of Fannie Lou Hamer*. New York: Dutton, 1993.

AP/Wide World Photos

Harlem Globetrotters

As a collective, the Harlem Globetrotters are the soul and wit of world basketball. The organization is more than a team; it is a spirit that permeates sport, entertainment, and even race to be a humanitarian force serving as goodwill ambassadors to the world. At a modern Globetrotters game audiences are awed by the showmanship, basketball talent, and hilarious on-court antics and jokes the team uses as part of their routine.

Sports in the early part of the twentieth century served as a vehicle for assimilation to Americanism and American ideals. To this end, neighborhood club sports took on an extremely local flavor with team names that carried some sort of local identifier. Team names like the Hebrews, Terrible Swedes, and Celtics were common in the 1920s for club athletic teams.

In the early part of the twentieth century, local, ethnic club basketball teams played low-scoring matches in nearly every imaginable indoor venue throughout the United States. Some local teams played in dance halls as a means to get crowds in the doors as an exhibition before the evening's dancing began. According to team lore and three-quarters of a century of propaganda, it is at the Savoy, a dance hall, where the first game by the players who became the professional Harlem Globetrotters played under the name of the Savoy Big Five.

The members of the Savoy Big Five originally hailed from Chicago. The team's three core members were former Wendell Phillips High School basketball standouts from that school's heavyweight basketball division. The core players from Wendell Phillips were Tommy Brookins, Randolph Ramsey, and Toots Wright.

The Savoy Big Five eventually disbanded. Incongruities involving the team's pay led some of the original team members to create another team and they invited high school teammates Willis "Kid" Oliver, Inman Jackson, Bill Watson, and their former coach Bobby Anderson to form a team called the Globe Trotters. At least for a short time, the team was named the Tommy Brookins Globe Trotters.

It was not easy for a team made up of African American basketball players to get paying games against local white teams around the Midwest in the 1920s. The Globe Trotters consequently sought out a "white face" who could help them schedule games. They found Abe Saperstein, a man who had gotten games for some Negro Baseball League teams in white towns in the region. Saperstein is one of the most controversial and important figures in the history of the Harlem Globetrotters and basketball. His motives and business practices, beginning with his first contact with the Globe Trotters, were unorthodox at best and immoral and racist at worst.

Since the team Saperstein led came to represent America throughout the world, it is only fitting that he was born on July 4, 1902. However, Saperstein was not an American, but rather a Polish Jew born in London as his parents fled czarist Russia's imperial reach. The Saperstein family eventually made its way to Chicago where Saperstein's father obtained a tailoring job after posing as a non-Jew in the Ravenswood area of the Windy City. Abe, like other immigrants, sought out sports as a way to both assimilate and prove himself to his Irish and German neighbors.

A good memory, a love for sports, an outsider in his own neighborhood, and a tireless knack for salesmanship made Saperstein very good at scheduling and promoting games. This was just the skill set that Tommy Brookins and his Globe Trotters needed when they decided to go from town to town or barnstorming to play basketball.

Brookins's Globe Trotters agreed to pay Abe Saperstein 10 percent of their take as their Booking Agent. Saperstein told the team he would need $100 in expenses to travel to the countryside of Wisconsin and Michigan so that he could arrange their first games. The team voted to give him the $100, though according to Brookins he double-booked and double-crossed the team. While the Globe Trotters were playing in rural Michigan, Saperstein fielded another five players simultaneously in Wisconsin. Once Brookins found out about this malfeasance, he confronted the booking agent, but Brookins soon left the Globe Trotters. He had an offer to sing professionally in Chicago and made the career change as a financial means to quit the tiring barnstorming circuit of basketball.

With Brookins' departure, Saperstein had better access to the Globe Trotter name as well as access to many of the former Wendell Phillips high school stars and Chicago South Side African American athletes. Saperstein used the team's name, connections, and a Model T Ford to re-shape the Globe Trotters and take them barnstorming throughout the Midwest.

As a marketing scheme, Saperstein took the team's uniforms to his father's tailor shop where he had the name New York sewn on the uniforms to add a level of exoticism to the team as it traveled the Midwest. Saperstein also added the New York moniker to the team's name to make small towns feel like they were playing a game against a far-off powerhouse on the basketball court. He added Harlem soon thereafter, making the team's new official name the New York Harlem Globe Trotters.

Saperstein's ignobility seemed boundless. By adding New York and Harlem to the team's name, he was not only fictionalizing the team's background but was also trying to capitalize on the fame of the New York Renaissance, an actual New York also regularly known as the Rens and the Harlem Renaissance. Saperstein knew that by adding New York to the team's name he would add value to his club's own name by trading on the fame of the popular New York team. In reality, however, he stripped his team of their Chicago background. He also simultaneously belittled and helped erase the Rens, one of the foremost and most formidable basketball teams in American history, from popular memory.

The Harlem Renaissance basketball team name came from the Harlem Renaissance Casino, where the team played home games. These basketball games were used as a way to get people into the ballroom and, in the Harlem team's case, the casino. The Rens did not play many of their games in the ballroom though, as white teams would not come to Harlem to play them. They consequently took to the barnstorming circuit as early as 1922 and played in predominantly white towns throughout the East Coast and near the Midwest.

The Harlem name was not all the Globe Trotters borrowed from the Harlem Renaissance. The Rens were renowned for masterful play. Members of the team could pass the ball effortlessly and without looking, often confusing and dizzying their opponents. This style of play was not something the Rens had trademarked, but they played in this manner when the original Globe Trotters were still students at Wendell Phillips High School. The Rens also amassed an amazing winning record 2,588–539.

The Rens and the Globe Trotters faced many of the same problems during their early barnstorming years, including racism, discrimination, and poverty. It is this last problem, that Abe Saperstein was particularly adept at overcoming. Unlike the Rens, the Globe Trotters only carried a five-man team plus Saperstein when traveling. Having no substitute meant one fewer persons to pay, transport, feed, and house as the team barnstormed the American Midwest. In the early years, Saperstein even kept a uniform on under his suit so that if a player fouled out or became ill he could come in as the team's substitute. Remaining box scores and sporting accounts report that the five foot three inch tall Saperstein was no dynamo on the court.

When the banks were all out of money Saperstein took the team to towns without banks. Oftentimes this meant five large men and Saperstein crammed into a Model-T traveling at 30 miles per hour for 120 or 200 miles to play one game, only to return to the car to travel and play again. Players from the Depression era likely were happy to be employed at a time when it was very hard for anyone, and particularly for African American men, to find work.

Watching sports provided respite to many during the Great Depression. At this time, banks closed, and millions of Americans were homeless. Yet the Depression era was some of the best eras for the Globe Trotters. The team's success is not surprising given the historical significance placed on sporting events in the Depression era. As the Great Depression swept the United States, Americans needed a way to escape their misery. Athletics was a way for Americans to forget their own pain for just a few minutes. For city dwellers this meant listening to a fight, or perhaps hearing or maybe even seeing a ball game. Yet for rural Americans, there were not similar opportunities; that is, until the Globe Trotters arrived in their town.

The Globe Trotters offered escapist sports entertainment for only a few cents to small-town Americans. Unlike Yankees games or Max Schmelling fights, those in attendance knew half of the competitors when the Globe Trotters came to town, because the basketball team played locals. These games were opportunities for hometown teams to prove themselves to the world by playing the renowned Globe Trotters of Harlem, New York. When the games did not go the way of the home team, the Globe Trotters had something else to offer:

extreme athletic prowess and showmanship. The Globe Trotters featured talent that was virtually unknown and rarely seen in small towns. The Globe Trotters wins were capped off with extremely good sportsmanship and bits of athletic showmanship during the early years.

While the team was successful, their financial earnings remained limited due to the Depression. The team worked hard, playing 150 games in just one season. Sixty-one of these games were played on consecutive nights and some were played outdoors and in the rain. While the Globe Trotters made some money during the Depression, Saperstein still managed the team's affairs shrewdly, for instance he changed the team's name from the New York Harlem Globe Trotters to just the Harlem Globe Trotters to save money on the extra two words when telegram costs increased. Saperstein also assumed more than a booking agent role during the Depression years. In 1934 Saperstein announced that the players would no longer share the profits from the team, but rather that they would be paid a flat rate of $7.50 a game. This shifted the team from a collaborative effort between Saperstein and the players to a team owned by Saperstein.

The change did not go unchallenged. Team star Runt Pullins along with George Easter and Fat Long had serious problems when Saperstein changed his role to team owner instead of coach, manager, and driver. These problems manifested themselves most notably with the exodus of one of the Depression Era team's biggest stars, Runt Pullins and along with him went Long and Easter. Not only did Pullins leave the team over Saperstein's Globe Trotter ownership grab, he also decided to form his own Globe Trotter squad using the same name. The country suddenly had at least two Harlem Globe Trotter teams. Saperstein, who considered Pullins a former employee, did not enjoy the competition Pullins created with a second Harlem Globe Trotters team. Most of the white towns did not know that there were two different teams and often did not know which Globe Trotter team they had contracted to play. On at least one occasion, Runt Pullins showed up with his squad of five Globe Trotters and stole the evening's game and pay away from Saperstein's Globe Trotters. The feud between Saperstein and Pullins came to an end because Saperstein was able to convince the all-white controlled Amateur Athletic Association (AAU) that his team was the only one on the barnstorming circuit that was purely amateur. The AAU's pseudo sanctioning of Saperstein's team meant that teams that played against the "Original Harlem Globetrotters" as Saperstein began calling them were under no threat of losing their amateur credentials. Those teams who played other barnstorming units that might be construed as professionals, such as Pullins's team could lose their amateur status.

Sports during the Depression era were largely about promotion, and especially self-promotion, an area in which Saperstein excelled. As the self-titled team owner, he began talking more often with sports writers as a promotional measure, but he added outright fabrications about the team and his own accomplishments. Lies were a major part of sports in this era in the

United States, as was racism. The white owner's hyperbole indeed embodied both as he spoke about men with whom he once shared beds, rooms, and car space. He now considered these men to be his employees. This change in his relationship to the team brought out the worst in his own attitudes and speech about the African American players on his team. For example, he claimed that his team's African roots made them "natural entertainers." He also forbade players from interracial dating, but he himself had a number of African American girlfriends.

Beyond Saperstein's racist claims, the Globe Trotters were often described as a continuation of minstrelsy. In minstrel shows, blacks are degraded for the amusement of whites. This criticism remains the hardest legacy for the Globe Trotters to shake. It indeed has elements of truth in it, as at various times the team does use humor, and particularly humor aimed at black stereotypes such as speaking with a southern dialect or worse, to garner laughs.

> I wanted to be the best comedic basketball player of all time.
> —George "Meadowlark" Lemon

Like the Globe Trotters themselves their performance was complicated. Comedian and sometimes Globetrotter **Bill Cosby** made two important points about this criticism. He claimed that Globetrotter humor is only funny because the team is backed up by tremendous sportsmanship and athleticism. In essence, the team uses humor to defuse situations in which an all-black team comes into a white town and soundly defeats its local heroes. Cosby also argued that the team does not fit the pattern of minstrelsy. If the Globetrotters of the present day are minstrels, then who are the Washington Generals, the all-white team who travels and plays against the modern Globetrotter team, in the minstrel show? The Washington Generals serve as the straight men for most of the Globetrotters' jokes. No minstrel show continually perpetuated gags against whites.

While the Globe Trotters' name was associated with showmanship throughout the Depression era, the Harlem Rens became increasingly known for their on-court basketball prowess. Saperstein knew that his team needed to play and beat the Rens to prove his claims about the Globe Trotters' abilities. Building a team capable of beating the Rens and promoting a game of that magnitude were just the kind of challenges that Saperstein enjoyed. The first meeting between the Globe Trotters and Rens took place as part of the *Chicago Herald*'s World Pro Championship series in Chicago in 1939. Few sports fans realize it, but basketball permitted on-court integration at the professional level, or what might be considered the semi-professional level in modern times, whenever the Globe Trotters played. Until the Globe Trotters faced the Rens, the mainstream media paid little attention to black teams. Once the two teams faced each other in the semi-finals of the World Championship game, however, everyone took notice. While Saperstein's promotions stole away the Rens' place in history as one of the greatest teams, in 1939 the Rens secured a place in the record books by defeating the Globe Trotters and silencing Saperstein, albeit only temporarily.

The loss in Chicago indeed was hard for the Globe Trotters, but it set Saperstein on a mission to rebuild the Globe Trotters. His rebuilding involved Toledo's Sonny Boswell, one of the best pure shooters in basketball. Boswell's shooting and height made the 1940 Globe Trotter team even better than their third-place predecessors. In Chicago's 1940 World Professional Championship game, no team, including the Rens, were a match for the Globe Trotters. The Globe Trotters and Rens played in front of the largest audience ever amassed for basketball up to that time.

The World Championship victory opened promotional doors to Saperstein and the Globe Trotters. The victory gave the team a chance to play against the 1940 College All-Stars. This game was an epic battle that went into overtime before the All-Stars won what was described by many in attendance as the greatest sporting spectacle there would ever be. What was more impressive was the world record-setting attendance of 20,583 fans. The number of fans in attendance was impressive but so was the fact that the crowd was racially mixed. Saperstein felt that despite the loss, this game was "the night we came into our own."

The Globe Trotters continued to find new players. While Saperstein worked with the Globe Trotters, he never stopped working as a booking agent for the Negro Leagues. His work as a booking agent for baseball gave him a network for scouting athletic talent. His connections are exactly why Reece "Goose" Tatum, a very good baseball player from Alabama, came to play basketball. Tatum took the performance and humor of the Globe Trotters to a new level and expanded the team's repertoire. He was an imposing spectacle at six feet three, with a wingspan of more than seven foot three inches. His comedic timing and on-court gags also made him one of the most loveable Globe Trotters of all time. While he clowned around on the court, he also learned the game of basketball to become a fantastic player.

The war brought out Saperstein's best improvisational skills. While World War II stopped many sports teams from meeting their regular demands, Saperstein saw the war as an opportunity to expand the reach of the Globe Trotters by booking games at military bases around the country. The games also gave him a means to circumvent rationing rules on gasoline, oil, and rubber, which were supplies a traveling team needed. Despite these concessions many of the Globe Trotters were still drafted and sent to bases where they ended up playing on segregated military base leagues. When players were drafted, Saperstein simply found more players, brought old players out of retirement, and found a way to field teams. When Goose Tatum was drafted his absence left a real hole in the show portion of the team's routine. Saperstein filled this hole with Bob Karstens, a professional white player from Iowa. The Globe Trotters integrated professional basketball by first playing Saperstein and then more prominently featuring Karstens.

The Globe Trotters regrouped at the end of World War II. Saperstein capitalized on his sports connections by hiring Satchel Paige to run and coach one of the Globe Trotter farm teams and four-time Olympic Gold Medalist **Jesse Owens** to manage the business affairs of Saperstein's Kansas City Stars. At halftime of many of the games, Owens performed track and field demonstrations as part of his contract with Saperstein. The runner's relationship with Saperstein also led him to exploitative exposition events, in which he ran against a horse and at other times a dog. Saperstein also expected Owens to give speeches about the 1936 Olympics, Hitler, and Owens's experiences in Berlin. Owens delivered these speeches with patriotic overtones at a time when in his own country, even as a national hero, he was treated with disrespect because of his race.

Racial issues also plagued the Globetrotters as the team began actually trotting the globe. They traveled to Hawai'i, Cuba, Puerto Rico, Canada, and Mexico to play basketball. It was not uncommon for the players to be treated better abroad than they were at home. In many areas of the United States, they were still expected to drink from separate water fountains, eat from the back doors of diners, and sleep any place but a town's only hotel. The team, whose name evolved to the Globetrotters after World War II, found their social status limited by every ugly image of segregated Jim Crow America when they were not performing on the basketball court.

Globetrotter players were disallowed in the newly formed, segregated professional basketball leagues. Although Marques Haynes, Nat Clifton, and Ermer Robinson were widely heralded as the greatest basketball players on earth, they were not welcome to play in these leagues. Segregation in basketball was of course a great absurdity in the United States post–World War II because the Globetrotters had already played white teams for nearly 20 years by this time. Yet the professional leagues simply could not imagine white audiences paying to see black players play basketball. This racial assumption gave Saperstein the kind of promotional opening he loved. He immediately hounded the Basketball Association of America (which later joined with the National Basketball League to become the National Basketball Association) to allow the Globetrotters to play against the Minnesota Lakers, the league champion team.

The Globetrotters not only got a game with the Lakers but defeated the team. The win against the Lakers in 1948 was celebrated throughout the Chicago Southside as a victory for African Americans everywhere. Many in white America argued that the win was simply a fluke or that the Lakers had not taken the clown princes of basketball seriously enough to win. White fans clamored for a rematch immediately. Saperstein wanted to capitalize on the excitement from the first game and managed to schedule a rematch for the following year. Again the Globetrotters were victorious. In the second game with the Lakers, the Globetrotters not only won, but they were able to get a lead commanding enough that they began doing "the show." Fans loved their performance. Even more importantly, movie newsreels filmed both the 1949 game and the team's showmanship. As a result Americans watched a few seconds of the Globetrotters before their featured presentation at movie houses around the country. This game gave the Globetrotters free built-in, nationwide marketing.

As the various all-white professional basketball organizations floundered, they turned to the Globetrotters for help. Organizations asked Saperstein to have the Globetrotters play on the front half of a bill, hoping the crowds would stay to see a second game. At one such event, the Globetrotters played college all-stars from Loyola, DePaul, Marquette, and Notre Dame. This event created the College All-Star tour. The Globetrotters and All-Stars played 18 games in 3 weeks on this tour and covered over 9,000 miles. The tour exposed fans across the country to both college players and the Globetrotters, thus building modern professional basketball. The tour also became the foundation, in Saperstein's mind, for other tours across Europe, Asia, and the world. Saperstein hired a secretary, Marie Linehan, to help him organize tours around the world and because of her outstanding organizational skills the team was able to truly travel the globe.

In many countries, Globetrotter visits were treated like official Head of State visitations. The team entertained and played for Eva Peron, Pope Pius XII, and royalty throughout the world. The U.S. State Department did not hesitate throughout the cold war era to use the team's fame and goodwill as a way to ease tensions. Simply put, national problems waited if the Globetrotters were in town. In 1951 the team traveled to Berlin, Germany. On this trip Jesse Owens returned to Berlin's Olympic Stadium, where he had earned four gold medals in 1936. As Owens sat on the sidelines and more than 75,000 people watched from the stands, the players brought their combination of athleticism and humor to Germany and their presence along with Owens helped heal their national wounds from World War II.

National Basketball Association (NBA) team owners finally broke the color barrier of modern basketball by recruiting and drafting three black players. Globetrotters Nat "Sweetwater" Clifton and Chuck Cooper were two of the first players to integrate the NBA. The owners initially feared Saperstein's reaction to this draft, worrying that he would not play the Globetrotters in the front bill of their games. Eventually the owners decided if they had the best players in their organization fans might come just to see NBA games, Globetrotters or no. In typical Saperstein style, the Globetrotters owner did not deal with Clifton's departure for the NBA with grace, style, or fairness.

Yet the Globetrotters' allure wore thin by the late 1970s and early 1980s. The NBA now provided much of the spectacular play that used to be unique to the Globetrotters. Many NBA players openly admitted that they got their ideas from former Globetrotter greats. The NBA provided Globetrotteresque play, which the technology of televisions streamed into living rooms around the United States. Changes in media and the NBA draft were hard on the Globetrotter organization. To remain innovators, the team hired Olympic star and Kansas University player Lynette Woodard in 1985 as the first female "professional basketball player." Even Woodard's charisma and appeal could not save the organization. By the early 1990s, many people thought the Globetrotters would be sent out to pasture as a relic of the past.

The Globetrotters' fortunes changed when the most important Globetrotter of all time returned to resurrect the team. Mannie Jackson played for the Globetrotters in the early 1960s before becoming a multi-millionaire through his hard work in the business world. In June 1993, the world learned that Jackson owned the team, which made him the first African American to own a major sporting franchise. He was also the first Globetrotter since Tommy Brookins to have control over the team's destiny.

The team continues to perform, play, and reach audiences to the present day. Jackson recently explained that he is proud of the Globetrotters' legacy and ability to build cultural bridges. Through laughter and sports, the Globetrotters communicate beyond language, beyond conflict. When asked if the Globetrotters would persevere in this new modern age, Jackson responded as follows:

> The Globetrotters are like fine art, every year they play and every mile they travel they change. They mean something different at different times in your life, they represent different things to different people in different eras—art is something you may see everyday and then suddenly you see something new and beautiful and meaningful in it that you've never seen before and you rediscover your love of that art.

As the mesmerizing Globetrotter soundtrack "Sweet Georgia Brown," played by Brother Bones, pulses in the background, the Globetrotters remain one of the original American art forms.

Brian S. Collier
University of Notre Dame

FURTHER READING

Abdul-Jabbar, Kareem. *On the Shoulders of Giants: My Journey through the Harlem Renaissance*. Boston: Simon and Shuster, 2007.

Biography. *The Harlem Globetrotters: America's Court Jesters*. A&E Television Networks, 2005.

Boskin, Joseph. *Sambo: The Rise & Demise of an American Jester*. Oxford: Oxford University Press, 1988.

Christgau, John. *Tricksters in the Madhouse: Lakers vs Globetrotters, 1948*. Lincoln: University of Nebraska Press, 2004.

Green, Ben. *Spinning the Globe: The Rise, Fall, and Return to Greatness of the Harlem Globetrotters*. New York: Amistad, 2005.

Kline, Johnny. *Never Lose: From Globetrotter to Addict to Ph.D.: An Autobiography*. New York: Papa Joe's Book Company, 1996.

Kuska, Bob. *Hot Potato: How Washington and New York Gave Birth to Black Basketball and Changed America's Game Forever*. Charlottesville: University of Virginia Press, 2004.

Rhoden, William C. *Forty Million Dollar Slaves: The Rise, Fall and Redemption of the Black Athlete*. New York: Random House, 2006.

Sharman, Jay, Mike Sear, David Houle, and Mannie Jackson, executive producers. *Harlem Globetrotters: The Team that Changed the World*. Burbank, CA: Warner Brothers, 2005.

Thomas, Ron. *They Cleared the Lane: The NBA's Black Pioneers*. Lincoln: University of Nebraska Press, 2002.

Hulton Archive/Getty Images

Jimi Hendrix
(1942–1970)

James "Jimi" Marshall Hendrix was born Johnny Allen Hendrix in Seattle, Washington, on November 27, 1942, and was re-named James Marshall Hendrix by his father Al Hendrix on September 11, 1946. Hendrix is widely regarded as one of the greatest guitarists of all time and his music has influenced musicians in several musical genres including rock, blues, heavy metal, funk, and hip-hop. Hendrix made groundbreaking studio innovations using feedback, distortion, and stereophonic sound, changing how music was recorded and played, while his live performances, characterized by his colorful, flamboyant clothing and his many guitar "tricks," have influenced countless artists ever since. As a man of both Cherokee and African ancestry playing music to mostly white audiences, Hendrix found himself caught between three worlds in which he was an outsider to all. He was loved by young fans and other musicians and became a symbol of the hippie counterculture, but allegations of drug use and his opposition to the Vietnam War tarnished his reputation with many people who saw him as a bad influence on young people. Nevertheless, the music of Jimi Hendrix remains popular and relevant as countless re-issues and re-releases of his albums continue to sell extremely well and he is introduced to new generations of listeners. Hendrix's talent and influence on modern music and popular culture have been recognized by music magazines including *Rolling Stone* and *Guitar World*, both of which have ranked him as the greatest guitarist of all time.

Throughout his childhood, Hendrix was surrounded by music. His grandmother Nora Hendrix used to tell him stories of her time in a chorus line as well as tales of Native American music, dances, and rituals that were a part of her childhood. His mother and father were also serious dancers who would often practice their routines at night to Al Hendrix's record collection during the short time they were together. In black Pentecostal services that he attended, Hendrix saw that music could convey messages as it elicited powerful emotional responses. It was not long before Hendrix became very interested in playing music and because his father could not afford to buy him a proper instrument, Hendrix took to fashioning makeshift guitars out of whatever he could find, destroying several old brooms in the process. Hendrix became so obsessed with playing the guitar that while he was in elementary school, a social worker tried to get him a guitar by using school funds for needy children, arguing that not having a guitar was damaging Hendrix psychologically (Shapiro and Glebeek, 1995, 35).

Eventually his father bought Hendrix a harmonica on which his son began learning some old blues standards. Even though Al found an old ukulele with one string that Hendrix was able to begin playing the songs he grew up with including those of Buddy Holly and Henry Mancini's "Peter Gunn," Hendrix needed a "real guitar" if he was to progress any further in music. So when a friend of his father offered to sell him his acoustic guitar for five dollars, Hendrix jumped at the chance and talked his father into buying it for him. Because it was a right-handed guitar and Hendrix was left-handed, Hendrix learned to re-string and tune the guitar on his own. Despite a lack of any formal training, he quickly became proficient on the instrument. After two years of learning and experimenting with his acoustic guitar, Al took 17-year-old Hendrix to the music store to buy him his first electric guitar, a white Supro Ozark guitar, and a saxophone for himself so that he could play along with his son. He soon realized that Hendrix was far too advanced on the guitar than he ever would be on the saxophone, and it was not long before Hendrix began performing for audiences in Seattle.

His first band, The Rocking Kings mainly played covers of '50s bands such as The Coasters and became very successful in the Seattle area, playing parties, dance halls, and small clubs. These shows gave Hendrix experience playing in front of crowds, while on off days he gained an education in stage performance as he hung around clubs waiting for a chance to play and watched how other musicians whipped crowds into a frenzy, clapping, cheering, and stomping their feet, much like the Pentecostal preachers he had seen as a boy at church. In addition to bandmates and local musicians, Hendrix also learned much from the blues guitarists of the day such as Muddy Waters, B. B. King, Elmore James, and John Lee Hooker, as well as earlier artists including Charlie Patton and Tommy Johnson. This confluence of jazz, blues, and rock influences in Hendrix's early career would have a huge influence on the direction his musical style would take as elements of all three styles can be easily heard in much of his later work.

In 1960, Hendrix and a few members of The Rocking Kings formed The Tom Cats who, like The Rocking Kings, were very successful playing local gigs, but his music career would be put on hold temporarily as Hendrix's attention was drawn to life outside of music. During the fall of 1961, Hendrix dropped out of high school without graduating and after working with his father and running into some minor trouble with the law, he decided to find adventure and himself by joining the Army. Hendrix's short stint in the Army allowed him to travel outside of Seattle, and as a member of the 101st Airborne, he met bassist Billy Cox and formed the band the King Kasuals in which Hendrix played lead guitar. After Hendrix received a medical discharge from the Army in July 1962, he and Cox continued playing together in Indianapolis, Clarksville, Tennessee, and later in Nashville where he made his first recording with Cox and hooked up with The Marvelettes and Curtis Mayfield and The Impressions for a one-month tour.

By 1963 Hendrix became so popular and sought after that he was backing up big name artists such as Jackie Wilson, The Supremes, and Sam Cooke. In 1964, he moved to New York and throughout the year, recorded and toured extensively with The Isley Brothers, which included playing the southern "chitlin circuit," where Hendrix witnessed and experienced discrimination unlike any he had seen in New York or his native Seattle. In January 1965, Hendrix met Little Richard and was given the guitar slot in Little Richard's band, which dramatically increased his visibility and hastened his rise to stardom.

As lead guitarist for Little Richard, Hendrix honed his flashy stage act and his guitar playing, learning much from the veteran bandleader. After Hendrix left Little
Richard in the summer of 1965, he recorded once more with The Isley Brothers
and then Hendrix joined Curtis Knight & The Squires. While with Curtis Knight,
Hendrix was noticed by producer Ed Chalpin of PPX Inc., who offered him a
three-year contract in which Chalpin would own the rights to all Hendrix's work
produced during that period (Hendrix got $1 and a guarantee of 1% royalties
while with The Squires). Though Chalpin would maintain his claims on Hendrix's assets long after Hendrix's death, Hendrix soon forgot about the deal as
he continued to tour and record with Curtis Knight and other artists such as Ike
and Tina Turner, King Curtis, and Joey Dee and the Starlighters through the
end of 1965 until the summer of 1966.

By the summer of 1966, Hendrix had become frustrated with his role as a
backup musician and decided it was time to form Jimmy James and the Blue
Flames, which he led as guitarist and singer. In July, Hendrix and the Blue
Flames were seen live by Animals' bassist Chas Chandler, who was looking to
leave his band for a career in record production. During the Animals' 1966
U.S. tour, Chandler stopped by Greenwich Village to check out the music scene,
which is where he saw Hendrix in concert. Chandler instantly realized that
Hendrix's skills were something special and introduced himself to Hendrix as
he raved about Hendrix's version of the folk song "Hey Joe." Hendrix was not
sure what to make of this English musician turned manager/producer who
promised to return as soon as he finished with his band, but he liked the new
Animals single and thought Chandler might be a good connection.

Chandler did return after six weeks to manage Hendrix's burgeoning music
career along with former Animals manager and business partner Michael
Jeffrey, as the pair took care of all of Hendrix's financial issues (except for
the contract with Chalpin which Hendrix had forgotten about), took him to a
doctor for a physical, and got him a passport. Chandler's plan was to take
Hendrix to London where he thought Hendrix would be more appreciated
and hoped to find him a recording contract. Before they left, Chandler and
Hendrix decided that Jimmy Hendrix and Jimmy James belonged to the past
and that from then on, he would be known as Jimi Hendrix. Hendrix arrived
in England on September 23, 1966, and was immediately recognized as something special. In London, Hendrix quickly acquired a fan base made up of the
era's most popular artists including John Lennon, Paul McCartney, Mick
Jagger, and Pete Townsend. During a guest spot with Cream on October 1,
Hendrix found yet another admirer in Eric Clapton, who was so in awe of
Hendrix that he stopped playing with his band so that he could watch Hendrix
from off stage.

Once settled in London and with a reputation already established, Hendrix
and Chandler set out to form a band. On the same day Hendrix was issued a
work permit, an out-of-work guitarist named Noel Redding came up to London
looking for a job with Eric Burdon's New Animals. Redding was told by Chas

Chandler that he might be better off auditioning for Hendrix, who was looking for a bassist at the time. Despite never having played bass before, Hendrix immediately took a liking to Redding's freestyle playing as well as his afro-style hair, which Hendrix took as a sign of the Englishman's individuality. Hendrix hired Redding on the spot and then began looking for a drummer. Several drummers were auditioned, but none played in the style that Hendrix was looking for. At the same time, a British R&B band, also called the Blue Flames, had just broken up and their drummer, John "Mitch" Mitchell was looking for work. Hendrix liked that Mitchell was highly proficient, had a busy, exciting style, and was a versatile drummer who had experience playing jazz, blues, rock, and R&B, so eventually gave him the job after a few days of tryouts.

As these auditions were taking place, Hendrix continued to play with bands in London clubs where he was seen by singer Johnny Hallyday, who was hugely popular in France and was known as "the French Elvis." Hallyday invited Hendrix to support him on his upcoming tour of France once Hendrix got his band together, and Hendrix eagerly accepted. Hendrix toured France for one month as Hallyday's opening act, so despite his short set, Hendrix and his new band, The Experience, received great exposure at the sold-out shows. Anchored by blues standards such as Howlin' Wolf's "Killing Floor," The Troggs' "Wild Thing" and his soon–to-be-released single "Hey Joe," Hendrix's performances were marked by a momentum that grew with each show. French fans were at first shocked by Hendrix's appearance as he took stage in a blue mohair jacket while playing a solo and making his guitar roar with just one hand (McDermott and Kramer, 22). Thanks to a repertoire of guitar "tricks," his colorful appearance, a dynamic stage presence, emotionally powerful and skilled playing, Hendrix's became a huge draw in France and throughout Europe.

After his triumphant tour of France, Hendrix returned to England to complete the recording of his first single, "Hey Joe," and the record's b-side, "Stone Free," which greatly increased Hendrix's popularity and was soon followed by his signature hit "Purple Haze" as well as "The Wind Cries Mary," written about his mother, who had died when Hendrix was 15. English and European audiences were intrigued by and enthusiastic about the innovative African American guitarist who played blues and rock in such a unique and sometimes disturbing way (Lawrence, 60). Guest spots on British programs such as *Top of the Pops* and *Ready, Steady, Go* as well as another successful tour of Great Britain and Western Europe allowed millions of people to finally see him, which brought him more fans as well as the attention of those who felt threatened by what Hendrix represented. Not until the release of *Are You Experienced?*, which included hits such as "Purple Haze," "Hey Joe," and "Foxey Lady," and a tour of the United States in the summer of 1967 were American audiences finally able to see what European fans were so excited about.

Hendrix's live introduction to American audiences came at the Monterey Pop Festival where he headlined a concert that included major, established acts such as Otis Redding, The Who, The Grateful Dead, Simon & Garfunkel, and Jefferson Airplane. Originally slated to headline the show, The Who was hesitant about going on after Hendrix, and the matter was resolved with a flip of a coin which resulted in Hendrix getting top billing. Hendrix knew that the performance was to be filmed and that The Who would be destroying their instruments at the end of their performance, so he employed many of the guitar "tricks" that he became known for like playing with one hand, with his teeth, and with the guitar held behind his back. At the end of his set, Hendrix rolled on the floor, turned up the amplifiers as loud as they would go, and then attacked them with his guitar. He then threw the instrument to the ground, poured lighter fluid over it, and set his guitar alight before proceeding to smash it against the floor. Hendrix's burning of his guitar became an iconic image in rock history and brought him national attention.

As Hendrix's popularity soared after performance at Monterey and the release of *Are You Experienced?* in the United States, Jimi Hendrix and the Experience went to Los Angeles to play the famed Fillmore West where Hendrix was introduced to members of the Black Panther Party backstage after the show. After calling Hendrix a "white nigger" for his refusal to make political statements, the two men were thrown out by club owner Bill Graham. Nevertheless, the episode greatly affected Hendrix, as he had never disowned his heritage musically or emotionally. Songs such as "House Burning Down" addressed the issues of discrimination and segregation in the United States, while "I Don't Live Today" tied his own sense of being an outsider with the plight of Native Americans. One of Hendrix's most famous and controversial pieces was his live performance of the National Anthem at the Woodstock Festival in 1969, as he punctuated the distorted melody with what sounded like falling bombs and explosions in protest against the war in Vietnam. To the dismay of groups such as the Black Panthers, Hendrix preferred to use his music to express his political sentiments, and as an advocate of peace, was more a believer in the methods of King rather than the Panthers. Ultimately, Hendrix's songs of war, peace, and social conflict, whether it was interpersonal or interplanetary, reflected his own inner turmoil and could only be addressed on his terms (Shapiro and Glebeek, 180).

Though his return to the United States had been marked by some of his best and most inspired performances, the run-in at the Fillmore and an ill-advised tour with the made-for-television pop band The Monkees put a damper on an otherwise triumphant return to North America. As they toured the Midwest and South, Experience members Mitchell and Redding were also shocked when they realized that Hendrix could not eat in the same restaurants as them, although none of it surprised Hendrix, who had seen it all before. In addition, Ed Chalpin got in touch with Hendrix and his management while they toured the United States, demanding his share of the royalties from *Are You Experienced?*. Chalpin's claims would continue to dog Hendrix for the rest of his life, adding to the pressure he was already feeling from fans, management, and political activists. Not surprisingly, Hendrix was happy to go back to England in August of 1967 to start another European tour and begin work on his next album, *Axis: Bold as Love*.

Following another successful tour of the United Kingdom and Western Europe, Jimi Hendrix and the Experience released *Axis: Bold as Love* in the United Kingdom on December 1, 1967. *Axis* was a creative step forward for Hendrix as it also showed great progress in recording and songwriting. Though it was more psychedelic and experimental than *Are You Experienced?*, the album contained commercial hits such as "Crosstown Traffic," the instrumental ballad "Little Wing," and his version of Bob Dylan's "All Along the Watchtower." The success of his first two albums and the overwhelming support from fans gave Hendrix the confidence he needed to move forward with the innovations and creative direction he was taking his music. The release of the album was followed by a sponsorship from Fender Guitars and yet another tour of Europe and North America.

During the tour for *Axis: Bold as Love*, Hendrix was once again forced to deal with issues involving race both in the United States and Europe. After the assassination of **Martin Luther King, Jr.**, Hendrix did a show in a predominantly black area of Newark where he came on stage to great applause and said, "This number is for a friend of mine," and then played a haunting lament for King. After bringing the crowd to tears, Hendrix finished the piece, gently laid his guitar down, and walked off the stage. A month later, Hendrix traveled to Italy to for a few dates in Milan, Rome, and Bologna. The Italian media, taking their cue from a writer in the British press who referred to Hendrix as "the wild man of Borneo," portrayed Hendrix as an "unwashed child molester" whose image was shown by mothers to children who would not eat their meat. Once they met Hendrix however, the Italian press conceded that he was very polite and bathed regularly, although headlines would still read, "The Youngsters Go Wild for the Ugly Man with a Perm" (Shapiro and Glebeek, 272).

After the shows in Italy and a few shows in Switzerland, Hendrix returned to the United States in June to continue touring and to record his next album with the Experience, which was released at the end of 1968 with the title *Electric Ladyland*. *Electric Ladyland* was a double album with the most diverse material of all his albums to date and featured advances in the use of studio technology and guitar technique. Jimi Hendrix and the Experience covered a range of musical styles on the album from the more experimental and psychedelic "1983 ... A Merman I Should Turn to Be" to more traditional rock with "Crosstown Traffic," and also included blues tracks such as "Voodoo Chile." Hendrix also chose to address sociopolitical issues to a greater extent on *Electric Ladyland* with "House Burning Down" and his cover of Bob Dylan's "All Along the Watchtower," which became the album's biggest hit.

Despite legendary performances such as his show at the Woodstock Festival and well-received appearances on television programs including The Dick Cavett Show in 1969, the year would also see Hendrix face problems with the law and within his band. On May 3, Hendrix was arrested at the Toronto International Airport by Canadian customs officials for carrying heroin in his luggage, although he was released on bail to play a show in Toronto that night. Hendrix later argued at his trial that the drugs had been planted and was acquitted of all charges, but the court's decision did little to dispel rumors of Hendrix's drug abuse at the time, and since his death. Despite Hendrix's arrest, the tour continued through the United States, supported by the Buddy Miles Express and Noel Redding's band, Fat Mattress. During the last months of the tour, Redding had grown restless within the Experience and wanted to devote time to his solo project. At the same time, Hendrix had been jamming with friend Buddy Miles and had gotten into contact with old army buddy Billy Cox, who was eager to play bass for him again. Jimi Hendrix and the Experience would play their last concert on June 29, 1969, in Denver as Redding announced to the crowd that he would be leaving the band.

Though the rest of 1969 was spent recording with his new bandmates and several guest musicians, little would come of the Band of Gypsys and no new recordings would be released during his lifetime with the exception of a poorly recorded Band of Gypsys live album. Hendrix's desire for perfection in the studio and his frustration with the limited ability of the equipment he had to work with led to days of wasted studio time and hundreds of hours of unused material, although some of these recordings would be released posthumously on albums of varying quality and legal standing. Thanks to Hendrix's success however, he was able to invest in the creation of Electric Ladyland in New York's Greenwich Village, which he would run and help design for himself and other musicians. Opened in August 1970, Hendrix would only have two months to record at Electric Ladyland, but it has served its purpose as a musician's studio in the decades since. In the meantime, after just two nights of concerts in New York on New Year's Eve and New Year's Day, the Band of Gypsys broke up as Buddy Miles returned to the Express and Mitch Mitchell resumed his role as drummer.

This new version of the Jimi Hendrix Experience began the grueling "Cry of Love" tour in April 1970, which would take a heavy toll on Billy Cox and especially Jimi Hendrix. The band once again played North America and Hawaii through the summer and after the opening of Electric Ladyland at the end of August, the band flew to England for another tour of Europe. The European tour began with what would end up being his last great performance, filmed live at the Isle of Wight Festival in England, as a relentless schedule would soon take its toll on Hendrix. At a show in Arhus, Denmark on September 2, Hendrix had to leave the stage due to exhaustion after playing just two songs, commenting to the audience, "I've been dead a long time." Despite his condition, the tour continued as Hendrix played the following night in Denmark and then flew to Germany for the final shows, after which he returned to England with Mitchell while Billy Cox flew back to the United States to recuperate from mental and physical fatigue.

Jimi Hendrix spent the next two weeks doing interviews and jamming with friends in London, but constant touring and the demands on his time had weakened Hendrix both mentally and physically. Prone to bouts of insomnia, on the night of September 17 Hendrix took nine Vesperax sleeping pills that had been prescribed to girlfriend Monika Danneman. He was found choking and semi-conscious the next morning by Danneman who called an ambulance to her apartment in the Hotel Samarkand. Despite the efforts of paramedics, by the time they arrived at the hospital Hendrix had already passed away. Even though the ensuing investigation ruled Hendrix's death an accidental overdose, rumors have circulated ever since over whether his death was actually suicide or a murder conspiracy but none have been proven. Regardless of the controversy over his death and drug use, Jimi Hendrix's status as a talented guitarist, musical innovator, and major influence on modern music and musicians has never been disputed as he continues to be cited by artists, music fans, and writers as one of the greatest musicians of all time.

Jason Bell
Arizona State University

FURTHER READING

Burrell, Ian. "Hendrix Hits Top Note Again as Best Guitarist in History." *The Independent*, August 28, 2003.

Cross, Charles R. *Room Full of Mirrors: A Biography of Jimi Hendrix*. New York: Hyperion Books, 2006.

Kramer, Edward, and John McDermott. *Hendrix: Setting the Record Straight*. New York: Grand Central Publishing, 1992.

Lawrence, Sharon. *Jimi Hendrix: The Intimate Story of a Betrayed Musical Legend*. New York: Harper Paperbacks, 2006.

Murray, Charles Shaar. *Crosstown Traffic: Jimi Hendrix and the Post-War Rock & Roll Revolution*. New York: St. Martin's Griffin, 1991.

Roby, Steven. *Black Gold: The Lost Archives of Jimi Hendrix*. New York: Billboard Books, 2002.

Shadwick, Keith. *Jimi Hendrix, Musician*. Milwaukee: Backbeat Books, 2003.

Shapiro, Harry, and Caesar Glebeek. *Jimi Hendrix: Electric Gypsy*. New York: St. Martin's Griffin, 1991.

William P. Gottlieb/Library of Congress

Billie Holiday
(1915–1959)

Billie Holiday was born Eleanora Fagan in Center City, Philadelphia, on April 7, 1915. Many music historians consider her the most influential female vocalist of the twentieth century. She is certainly one of the premier jazz and blues vocalists of all time. Prior to Holiday, most pop singers aimed for anonymity in their vocals. Music producers wanted songs to sound the same no matter who sang them. Holiday changed all this. She sang with intensity and pathos. Her idiosyncratic, emotional delivery inspired generations of singers to make the songs they sang their own. Holiday sang with pain for a reason. Her childhood was about as tumultuous an upbringing as one could imagine. Her adult life proved just as turbulent. Her ghostwritten-memoir (1959) and the subsequent film *Lady Sings the Blues* (1972) made her abusive relationships, incarceration, and drug problems legendary. Over the course of her 44 years, Holiday made use of her pain to craft some of the finest vocal performances ever laid to wax. Her performances of "Lover Man," "I've Got My Love to Keep Me Warm," and "God Bless the Child," a song she co-wrote, are all considered canonical in the history of American music. Holiday's haunting version of "Strange Fruit," a 1939 song detailing the lynching of two men, stirred up an immense amount of controversy at the time of its release. In 1999, *Time* magazine, which profiled Holiday at the time of its release, ranked "Strange Fruit" the greatest song of the twentieth century.

Billie Holiday, born Eleanora Fagan (referred to henceforth as Billie Holiday), grew up in circumstances that remain a subject of mystery and conjecture. Her mother, Sadie Fagan, was 13 years old at the time of her birth. Fagan had grown up in Baltimore, but was kicked out of her home when her parents discovered her pregnancy. Clarence Holiday, a 16-year-old jazz guitarist, was the father of the child. Fagan and Holiday broke up soon after Eleanora's birth. He was never a part of her life. In later years, Billie Holiday and Clarence Holiday were both prominent players in the New York jazz community. Billie refused to hire the man who abandoned her as a child, even though he was a superb rhythm guitarist. Clarence Holiday died in 1937 at the age of 39.

Billie Holiday moved frequently as a child. Her mother left her with several different relatives who took the child in for varying lengths of time. Sadie Fagan married a stevedore named Philip Gough in October 1920. The new family settled in West Baltimore, but three years later Gough abandoned his wife and stepdaughter. Holiday and her mother moved around frequently over the next two years before settling in a Durham Street row house in impoverished East Baltimore. The already densely populated neighborhood became even more crammed as the Great Migration brought many southern blacks to the city. Sadie Fagan, like many of her neighbors, supplemented her income by taking in boarders. The city's segregated housing market made living space of any quality extremely valuable to black newcomers. Around Christmas 1926, Fagan caught one of the boarders sexually assaulting her 11-year-old daughter. The man was arrested, but, following the tragic legal logic of the day, a judge sent Holiday to the Good Shepherd Home for Colored Girls, a

Catholic reform school, to restore the child's moral grounding. Holiday had been in trouble before, so the judge took the sexual assault as a sign of her continued poor behavior. It took Holiday's family nearly two years of legal wrangling to get her out of the reform school. Following her release, Holiday joined her mother in Harlem. Sadie rented a room in a home owned by a local madam. Holiday and her mother worked during the day as domestics and earned extra income in the evening as prostitutes. She was arrested for prostitution during a police raid shortly after her 14th birthday. Holiday spent 100 days in at a workhouse on Welfare Island. Upon her release, Holiday moved with her mother to the predominately black Bedford-Stuyvesant neighborhood in central Brooklyn.

Soon after moving to Brooklyn, Holiday began pursuing a career as a professional singer. Saxophonist Kenneth Holton, a friend of Holiday's, helped her get her first professional singing gigs at cabarets and clubs in Brooklyn and Queens. In 1930 or 1931, Eleanora Fagan started using the stage name "Billie Holiday." She chose the name "Billie" as a tribute to the silent film star Billie Dove. "Holiday" came from her biological father. The legend propagated by *Lady Sings the Blues* suggests that Holiday got her big break in 1933 during an impromptu audition at a speakeasy. In fact, Holiday spent the early 1930s honing her skills and developing a reputation as one of New York's premier nightclub singers. By the time famed producer and talent scout John Hammond discovered Holiday in 1933, she was an experienced live performer. Hammond set up a recording session for Holiday with Benny Goodman and several members of his Orchestra. The session produced Holiday's first single, "Your Mother's Son-in-Law," an upbeat number driven primarily by Goodman's brass section.

Holiday's first big hit, the sultry "Riffin' the Scotch," was also recorded during these sessions. Over the next two years, Holiday recorded little but built up further name recognition in the New York jazz scene. In April 1935, Holiday made her debut at Harlem's **Apollo Theater** with Ralph Cooper and his 18 Kings of Melody. The band performed primarily upbeat tunes, which was ill-suited to Holiday's style. The Apollo audience did not hesitate to show its disapproval. The sting of the Apollo shows proved short-lived. In June 1935, John Hammond arranged for Holiday to record with pianist Teddy Wilson for Brunswick Records. The sessions relied primarily on the lesser Tin Pan Alley songs which they were assigned by the record label. Holiday made exquisite use of such marginal Swing-era material as "Yankee Doodle Never Went to Town," "Twenty-Four-Hours-A-Day," and "Eeny Meeny Miny Mo." In true jazz style, she used the bland tunes as a framework for improvisation. Holiday's vocals added a bittersweet tone to songs which sounded dramatically different when performed by other singers. Her delivery oozed with sensuality and heartache simultaneously. Fluff such as "If You Were Mine" became jazz classics when rendered by Holiday. The singles "Miss Brown to You" and "What a Little Moonlight Can Do" became jukebox mainstays in the late 1930s. Holiday's unique vocals made both singles instantly recognizable to audiences who were used to carbon-copy pop vocal performances.

Holiday followed up her sessions with Teddy Wilson in 1937 by recording and touring extensively with the Count Basie Orchestra. John Hammond set up the initial meeting of Basie and Holiday. Count Basie's saxophonist Lester Young became a close friend and confidant of Holiday. Young was one of the few constants in Holiday's life. He nicknamed her "Lady Day" in 1937, a moniker which followed her for the rest of her career. Holiday nicknamed Young "Prez." The two died only a few months apart in 1959.

Following the tour with Count Basie, Holiday began singing with Artie Shaw's band. This gig was short-lived as promoters and sponsors proved uncomfortable with a black female singer working with an all-white orchestra. Holiday soon quit Shaw's band and took a gig at Café Society, a new interracial nightclub at Sheridan Square in Greenwich Village. Café Society catered to a progressive clientele and treated all customers equally. During her tenure at Café Society, Holiday incorporated two songs into her repertoire that became a pair of her signatures. "God Bless the Child," a song Holiday co-wrote with Arthur Herzog Jr., sounds like Old Testament prophecy cloaked in Holiday's matter-of-fact moan. Holiday's own life taught her that the world favors the child "that's got his own." "God Bless the Child" became a major hit for Holiday upon its release by her new label, Columbia Records, in 1941. Holiday recorded an alternate version of the song in 1950 for Decca Records which also proved highly successful on the charts.

The other tune that Holiday debuted at the Café Society was written by one of the club's regular patrons, Abel Meeropol, a writer and schoolteacher from the Bronx. Meeropol, who wrote under the pseudonym Lewis Allen, wrote "Strange Fruit" in response to the epidemic of lynching. Meeropol wrote "Strange Fruit" after seeing the notorious photograph of the March 1930 lynching of two black males in Marion, Indiana. When Barney Josefson, owner of the Café Society, became aware of the song's popularity in left-wing circles, he asked Holiday, his most prominent vocalist, to include it in her repertoire. Holiday's haunting rendition of the song became the centerpiece of her live shows. John Hammond, who had brought Holiday along with him to Columbia Records, refused to produce the song, fearing the dour tune would have little commercial appeal. Holiday brought the song to Commodore Records' Milt Gabler, who produced the song and ensured its wide release in summer 1939. The song proved one of Fitzgerald's most popular. News of radio station and record store boycotts only added to the song's mystique. Seats at Holiday's Café Society performances became some of the most sought-after tickets in New York.

Holiday enjoyed relative peace in her private life during the late 1930s. This changed in the 1940s as Lady Day's personal affairs started impacting her recording career. On August 25, 1941, she married a trombonist named

Jimmy Monroe. Infidelity and spousal abuse led to the dissolution of the marriage in 1947. "Don't Explain," a single Holiday recorded for Decca Records in 1944, told the story of an evening on which Monroe came home covered in lipstick and smelling of perfume. Holiday herself had an affair with Joe Guy, a trombone player who apparently introduced her to heroin. She had long dealt with a serious drinking problem. The combination of drug use and heavy drinking contributed to Holiday's serious health problems, which plagued her for the rest of her life. Guy and Holiday broke up soon after Holiday's divorce from Monroe. Holiday's love life remains a topic of great speculation. Rumored affairs with Orson Welles, Marlene Dietrich, and Tallulah Bankhead are frequently credited to the singer.

During the Second World War, Holiday left Columbia Records. Following the advice of Milt Gabler, she signed on with Decca Records, a label for which Gabler worked as an artists and repertoire (A&R) man. She recorded her first single for Decca in 1944, the emotive smash hit "Lover Man." "Lover Man" features a wistful Holiday, wondering where her lover is and when he will come for her. The gin-soaked grittiness which characterized her later vocals is already evident on "Lover Man," a tune which sounds more like a torch song than a jazz standard. Smooth, subtle strings back Holiday's vocals. The brass section responds in a heartbreaking cacophony to Holiday's every cry for her "Lover Man." Few songs in the history of popular music create as affecting an atmosphere as "Lover Man."

Holiday recorded infrequently during the mid-1940s. Problems in her personal life distracted her from following up on the momentum of "Lover Man." Decca Records gave Holiday the opportunity to record with excellent musicians and to choose from the high-quality material Gabler put at her disposal. Holiday recorded several excellent songs, including "There is No Greater Love," "No Good Man," and "Good Morning Heartache," during this period, all of them big hits, but her total output amid favorable circumstances proved decidedly small. During this time period, she appeared in her only major film role. Holiday starred alongside **Louis Armstrong** in the musical *New Orleans*. Holiday sang several tunes with Armstrong in the 1947 film. As a black woman, she was upset with her typecasting as a maid in a film that very well could have featured her as a nightclub singer.

Soon after the film's release, a series of legal issues derailed Holiday's career. She was arrested on May 16, 1947, for drug possession in New York. Holiday pled guilty to a narcotics charge. Her extensive criminal record led the judge to sentence her to one year of incarceration at the Alderson Federal Prison Camp for Women in Monroe County, West Virginia. Holiday spent 10 months at the minimum-security prison. She refused to perform at the facility. Released early for good behavior, Holiday faced intense media scrutiny upon her return to New York. The drug conviction cost Holiday her cabaret license in New York, limiting the number of venues she could perform at in the city. Public interest in Holiday's music proved as intense as their interest in her legal troubles.

A March 27, 1948, comeback concert drew a sold-out crowd at Carnegie Hall. Nine months later, in January 1949, San Francisco detectives arrested Holiday for possession at the Hotel Mark Twain. Holiday claimed the opium and drug paraphernalia found in the room belonged to her former manager, then-boyfriend John Levy. In late 1949, Holiday was cleared of the charge.

Holiday maintained a busy recording schedule in the years following her release from prison. She recorded several singles in 1948. Backed by the Stardusters vocal group, she cut "Weep No More" and "Girls Were Made to Take Care of Boys." Holiday sounds superb on both songs, but the Mitch Miller-like backing vocals detract from the intimacy of the recordings. Holiday recorded "My Man" and a version of Gershwin's "I Loves You Porgy" around the same time. Mercifully, no one invited the Stardusters to accompany Lady Day on either song. Holiday sings of the simultaneous pain and pleasure of love in her 1948 recordings of "My Man" and "I Loves You Porgy." The minimal accompaniment on both tunes gave Holiday space to fully intonate her blues.

The late 1940s marked Holiday's commercial peak. Her 1948 singles proved highly successful. In 1949, she scored a major hit with a version of her idol Bessie Smith's "T'Ain't Nobody's Business if I Do." Holiday recorded several other hits in 1949 including "Somebody's on My Mind," a song she wrote, and "Crazy He Calls Me." In spite of her success, Holiday was considered a troublesome artist by Decca Records. She recorded infrequently, showed up late for recording sessions, and lived a self-destructive lifestyle that was taking a toll on her voice. When Milt Gabler, Holiday's number-one advocate at the label, left Decca Records, the company decided to drop Lady Day from its roster.

Idle time proved disastrous for Holiday. Her often-changing management (often her current manager and current boyfriend were one in the same) failed to secure her a long-term deal in the early 1950s. Financial troubles plagued the singer. Record companies clearly stiffed Holiday on royalties over the course of her career and big band recording sessions proved costly for the singer, but Holiday's drug habit and extravagant lifestyle played an important role in bringing about her money woes.

In October 1951, Holiday's freefall appeared to end when she hired jazz impresario Norman Granz as her new manager. He featured her in his "Jazz at the Philharmonic" concerts along with Louis Armstrong, **Ella Fitzgerald**, Buddy Rich, and Count Basie. Granz signed Holiday up with Verve Records and got Holiday back in the studio. Backed by the likes of Ray Brown and Oscar Peterson, a gravely voiced Holiday recorded excellent versions of "Stormy Weather" and "He's Funny That Way" in July 1952. Earlier in 1952, 36-year-old Billie Holiday began a long-term relationship with 43-year-old Louis McKay, a long-time friend who was heavily involved in organized crime. Initially, McKay offered stability in Holiday's life. Quickly, Holiday's relationship with McKay devolved into a tumultuous on-again, off-again drama. He tried unsuccessfully to get Holiday to quit drugs. At the same time, McKay abused his wife and stole money from her to invest in real estate. They split up briefly in 1956 following their arrests on drug charges in Philadelphia. The couple got back together after Holiday did a two-month stint in a detoxification center. They married on a whim in Chihuahua, Mexico on March 28, 1957, but separated shortly before Holiday's death in 1959.

Despite her troubled personal life, Holiday, with the help of Norman Granz, revived her career in the mid-1950s. Granz booked Holiday her first European tour in 1954. The highly successful tour garnered her widespread acclaim from fans and critics who had been waiting for years to see her perform. Holiday performed a superb set that summer at the first annual Newport Jazz Festival. Joined on stage by Oscar Peterson, Ray Brown, and Lester Young, Holiday gave an impassioned performance to the crowd of over 13,000.

Holiday's mid-1950s recordings were equally impressive. One of Holiday's most passionate vocals is "Willow, Weep for Me," the product of a 1954 studio session. Holiday throaty delivery on the swinging "I've Got My Love to Keep Me Warm" sounds something like Louis Armstrong. Lady Day's best-known mid-1950s performance is 1956's "Lady Sings the Blues," a title used later that year for the singer's ghostwritten autobiography. Holiday's raspy, whisper of a voice exudes as much feeling as any song in her catalog. Many posthumous interpretations of "Lady Sings the Blues" focus on its cryptic, epitaph-like quality. At the same time, the song can be read optimistically, as the testimony of a woman who has experienced all the pain the world has to offer and is slowly working her way through the worst of the blues.

The 1956 release of Holiday's autobiography, *Lady Sings the Blues*, introduced the public to her remarkable life story. Ghostwritten by the *New York Post*'s William Dufty, *Lady Sings the Blues* is widely acknowledged to have taken a great deal of artistic license in rendering the details of Holiday's life. Holiday herself claimed to have never read the book. None of this appears to have detracted from the enthusiastic public reception to the book. Public demand for Billie Holiday increased exponentially following the fall 1956 release of her memoir. She performed for two sold-out nights at Carnegie Hall in November 1956. In December 1957, she gave a stellar performance of "Fine and Mellow" on CBS's *The Sound of Jazz*.

Holiday recorded her final studio album in February 1958 with the Ray Ellis Orchestra. *Lady in Satin* features Holiday's voice at its weakest physically. The album includes some excellent performances, including "You've Changed" and "I'm a Fool to Want You." It is evident from the vocals that Holiday was straining to get even the minimal sound she mustered out of her throat. Her health was already in serious decline during the recording of the album. Heart and liver problems limited her stamina considerably. The cash-strapped Holiday performed occasionally over the next year, picking up extra money whenever possible. She continued drinking and using heroin in spite of her health problems.

Holiday collapsed in her Manhattan apartment on May 31, 1959 and was rushed to the emergency room at New York's Knickerbocker Hospital. Later that day, she was transferred to Metropolitan Hospital, a facility better equipped to deal with liver ailments, which had caused Holiday a great deal of pain for several years. Doctors at Metropolitan Hospital soon realized that she was suffering from both acute liver and heart disease. Police arrested Holiday in her hospital bed on June 12 for heroin possession. They maintained a guard outside her room as she lay dying of cirrhosis and heart failure. Holiday passed away early in the morning of July 17, 1959. At the time of her death, Holiday had 750 dollars in bills in her purse, but less than a dollar in the bank.

Tributes to the deceased singer commenced immediately after her death and have continued for the last 50 years. About 10,000 people paid tribute to the singer at a memorial service held on July 20, 1959, at the Universal Friends Chapel in Midtown Manhattan. Holiday's actual funeral took place on July 21 at St Paul's Catholic Church. A who's who of the jazz world turned out to pay tribute to Lady Day.

Holiday's reputation as one of the greatest vocalist in the history of American popular music has remained constant in the more than 50 years since her death. The critically acclaimed 1972 biopic *Lady Sings the Blues* starring Diana Ross as Billie Holiday introduced the singer's work to a new generation of films. The film received five Oscar nominations and the accompanying soundtrack reached number one on Billboard's album charts. Countless compilations and live recordings have been consumed by several generations of music lovers on several different media formats. Any serious list of the great singers and songs of the twentieth century has included Billie Holiday and her music. Lady Day's status as an iconic performer will be secure for as long as there are people interested in American music.

Clayton Trutor
Boston College

FURTHER READING

Blackburn, Julia. *With Billie*. New York: Pantheon, 2005.
Gourse, Leslie, ed. *The Billie Holiday Companion*. New York: Schirmer, 1997.
Nicholson, Stuart. *Billie Holiday*. Boston: Northeastern University Press, 1995.
White, John. *Billie Holiday, Her Life & Times*. New York: Universe Books, 1987.

Lena Horne (1917–2010)

Before there was **Halle Berry**, or her predecessor **Dorothy Dandridge**, representing the beauty of African American womanhood in the cinema, there was the groundbreaking legend, Lena Horne. Lena Mary Calhoun Horne was born in Bedford-Stuyvesant, Brooklyn, New York, on June 30, 1917. Her birth made her a part of what **W. E. B. Du Bois** called the "The Talented Tenth." This was a description given to the social class to which she was born. Its scholars, education, activities, social organizations, fairness of skin, and exclusivity distinguished the black bourgeoisie, or upper-middle class. This peculiarity of her birth set Lena Horne apart from 90 percent of her peers.

Lena Horne's background was rooted deeply in the black upper-middle class. Her maternal grandfather, Samuel Scottron, was an engineer, and inventor, who spent his leisure time as an organizer and public speaker who promoted racial harmony. The Horne family was also composed of activists who were organizers in the NAACP and other community organizations that promoted racial equality. The Horne family included many notable figures. Frank Horne, an uncle of Lena Mary Calhoun Horne, was an adviser to Franklin Delano Roosevelt, as well as the dean of students at Fort Valley Junior Industrial Institute (Fort Valley State University), a historically black university, located in Fort Valley, Georgia. Horne is also said to be a direct descendant of John C. Calhoun, the seventh vice president of the United States, and a leading proponent of slavery.

Edwin "Teddy" Horne and Edna Scottron were married in 1916, and Lena was born the next year. Upon leaving the hospital, Lena was taken home to the residence of her paternal grandparents, where her parents were living. Her parents were young, and generally focused on their own pursuits. Teddy, who was a gambler, and considered by many to be extraordinarily handsome, moved out of the house when Lena was still a toddler. Edna, a beauty in her own right, soon set her sights on an acting career. Lena was to become an only child, abandoned by both of her parents. She spent her formative years being raised by her grandmother, Cora Calhoun Horne, and her grandfather, Edwin Horne. Cora Calhoun Horne, who was devoted to her activities in the NAACP, made Lena a member of the organization at the age of two.

Cora Calhoun Horne was said to be a tough taskmaster. She ruled her home with an iron will. She was not an emotional person, and would not tolerate emotion from Lena. Lena was raised in the very proper ways of her grandmother, and the ladies in her grandmother's social and political circles. She was schooled in the proper way to talk, how to act in public, and how to carry herself as a lady in general. She was also schooled in Cora Calhoun Horne's racial attitudes. Cora Calhoun Horne, a suffragette, had an intense dislike for white people. Horne was not allowed to associate with white people, as a result of her grandmother's distrust of them. This had to cause some confusion for the young Lena, as many of the people in her immediate family appeared white. Her own grandfather Edwin, while living the life of a black man, was of English and Native American descent. Cora Calhoun Horne also carried a disdain for lower-class or dark-skinned black people.

Starting at the age of four, to the dismay of Cora Calhoun Horne, Lena began to spend more time with her mother Edna, who had become a member of the Lafayette Players, a Harlem Renaissance theater troupe, founded by Anita Bush in the early twentieth century. Edna took Lena to Philadelphia with her in 1921, while she was with the Lafayette Players. This is where Lena as a small girl played her first role, as a sleeping child, in the play *Madame X*. Eventually, Edna reclaimed her daughter, and Lena spent the next six years on the road with her mother, looking for acting work. Lena lived in Miami and Jacksonville, Florida; Ohio; and Macon, Fort Valley, and Atlanta, Georgia. These were difficult years for the young Lena. Though Horne met many people who were kind to her, and undoubtedly made a lasting impression on her, she was often left in foster homes where her treatment was sometimes harsh. She was often in the position of living off of whatever others were willing to give her including eating the leftovers from the tables of whites who employed those with whom she lived. She was often called "yaller," by other blacks, or "cute little nigger," by whites. Lena was emotionally and physically abused by some of her caretakers. Edna would come back, pick up Lena, and they would move on to the next town.

While Horne was living in Macon, Georgia, her uncle Frank picked her up and took her with him to his home in Fort Valley, Georgia, where he was dean of students at Fort Valley Normal and Industrial School. She stayed in the dorm there with college-aged women until her uncle married. Upon the marriage of her uncle, Horne moved in with him and his new wife, Frankye. At Uncle Frank's, Horne had her own room. During her stay with Frank and Frankye Horne, Horne got a visit from her father Teddy, whom she adored. Her joy was short-lived. Edna reappeared, and Lena was once again on the move. In Atlanta, Edna enrolled Lena in a dancing school.

In 1929, Horne was returned to Brooklyn to her grandmother. It was difficult returning to the discipline of Cora Calhoun Horne after the upheaval of the previous few years. Horne attended junior high school at P.S. 35. When her grandmother went on a trip given to her by Lena's father, Horne was left with Laura Jean Rollock. She joined the Junior Debs, a social club for the black bourgeoisie, attended the theater, and participated in a show at her high school. When Cora Calhoun Horne returned from her trip, she was in poor health. Horne moved in with her mother and her mother's new husband, Miguel Rodriguez, a Cuban immigrant. The pillar of the Horne family, Cora Calhoun Horne, died in September of 1933. A few months later, Edwin Horne followed his wife in death. The people who represented stability in the life of young Lena Mary Calhoun Horne were both gone.

After the death of her grandfather, Horne quit high school. Her stepfather was having a difficult time finding suitable work, and this was exacerbated by his marriage to a black woman, albeit one who appeared white and Edna's opportunities were few. Horne began pursuing jobs on the stage to help support herself, her mother, and her stepfather. Under the mentorship of Laura Rollock she enrolled in the Anna Jones Dancing School. The Jones girls performed at the Lafayette Theatre where Edna Scottron Horne had gotten her start in show business. Horne had grown into a beautiful girl, and was a stand-out wherever she went. In 1933, the obvious next stop for a beautiful, fair-skinned, black girl who liked to perform was the Cotton Club.

The Cotton Club located at Lenox Avenue and 142nd Street in New York City began as Club De Luxe in 1920. It was opened by heavyweight boxing champion Jack Johnson as a supper club. In 1923 the struggling club was purchased by Owen "Owney" Madden, a bootlegger who at the time of the purchase was imprisoned for manslaughter. He changed the name to the Cotton Club. Under the ownership of Owney the décor of the Cotton Club displayed the racial stereotypes of the day. Performers were portrayed as savages and plantation workers. The girls of the chorus line however had to be "tall, tan, and terrific," and under the age of 21. Duke Ellington and his band provided the music. The Cotton Club, although in the heart of Harlem, had a whites-only policy for its customers. The clientele was made of the notorious of the day, including gangsters, bootleggers, and those who socialized with them. The club also boasted some of the best entertainers of its day. **Duke Ellington**, Ethel Waters, Fletcher Henderson, Count Basie, Cab Calloway, Bessie Smith, The Nicholas Brothers, **Ella Fitzgerald**, Bill "Bojangles" Robinson, Fats Waller, **Louis Armstrong**, Dizzy Gillespie, Nat King Cole, and **Billie Holiday** appeared at the Cotton Club. The Cotton Club was the pinnacle for young African American entertainers in 1933. By 1933 the club had slightly relaxed its color code. Entertainer's families could attend as long as they sat near the kitchen, and as long as they were light-skinned. This is the world that Horne entered shortly before her 16th birthday.

Although the age minimum for working at the Cotton Club was eighteen, Horne became a member of the Cotton Club chorus line at the age of 16. The air of quiet sophistication that had been instilled in Lena by Cora Calhoun Horne paid off. Lena had an innate sense of pride and sophistication. The Cotton Club prided itself on the air of professionalism and sophistication. By the time Horne became a member of the Cotton Club chorus line, Cab Calloway and his orchestra provided the music. Under the constant guidance of her mother, Edna, Horne quickly went from the chorus line, to singing. She studied the blues singers who were the headliners at the Cotton Club, and worked with Cab Calloway on the songs that she was given to sing. She was such a standout at the Cotton Club that she also made her first film and Broadway appearances during this time period after being picked out of the chorus line. She appeared with Cab Calloway in a short film called *Jitterbug Party*, and she appeared on Broadway as a quadroon girl in the play *Dance with Your Gods*.

Horne left the Cotton Club in 1935. Some accounts surround this departure with a great deal of controversy as Edna had signed Lena to a lifetime contract, at 25 dollars a week. Some versions have her stepfather, Miguel Rodriguez, being violently assaulted by gangsters or thugs at the club. Whatever the circumstances, Horne joined the Noble Sissle Society Orchestra in 1936 as a singer and dancer. The Sissle Orchestra was a perfect match for Horne at the time. Noble Sissle was known for the decorum and sophistication that had been instilled in her by her grandmother. There were no color distinctions placed on the people employed by Sissle. Black people of all shades worked for him; however Horne continued to face discrimination and prejudice. While traveling with the Noble Sissle Society Orchestra, Horne and other band members still had to enter the back doors of the venues where they entertained. They had difficulty finding lodging wherever they went. They had to stay with local black families in the cities where they performed as they were not permitted to stay in the local hotels. There were often no bathroom facilities that they were allowed to use. Many black entertainers learned to sleep on the buses that they traveled on.

Although Horne sang, danced, and had begun to do some modeling during this time with the Noble Sissle Society Orchestra, she was mostly recognized for her great beauty. However, this changed for a brief period when Sissle was involved in a near-fatal car crash. He instructed Horne to take over his job of conducting the orchestra at the Moonlite Gardens in Ohio. In Sissle' absence, Lena sang, conducted, and bantered with the audiences, and received rave reviews. Eventually Sissle returned, and reclaimed his baton.

At the end of 1936, Lena went to Pittsburgh to visit her father. During this visit, Teddy Horne introduced his daughter to Louis Jones. Louis Jones was the 28-year-old son of a Baptist minister. Apparently this was not important to the 19-year-old Catholic, Horne. Weeks after they met, they were married. Louis Jones had very strict ideas about marriage, and did not hold show business in high regard. Lena tried to become a housewife. In December 1937 Lena gave birth to a daughter, Gail. During this time in their marriage, Louis was having a hard time with finances and Ralph Cooper, of the Apollo Theater, was looking for someone to star opposite him in the movie *The Duke Is Tops*. His original choice for this role was Nina Mae McKinney, also known as the "Black Garbo." Because McKinney was not available, Cooper went in pursuit of Horne. Louis Jones agreed to have her play the role because of their financial circumstances.

In 1938, Lew Leslie, a Broadway writer and producer, sought out Horne for his revue, *Blackbirds*. The show lasted only a week, but Horne received rave reviews. She ended up returning home to her husband and daughter, where her husband quit his job to pursue a political career. In 1939, Lena Horne found that she was expecting their second child. On February 7, 1940, the family grew by one when Lena gave birth to a son, Edwin Fletcher Jones. Teddy, as the new baby was called, was born into an unstable family environment. His father, had returned to a regular job that did not make him happy and his mother, had the possibility of making more money if she performed, and that meant traveling without her family. Shortly after Teddy's birth, she found someone to care for them, and went to New York.

Once Lena was back in New York, she found it difficult to find work. Although she was thought of as an up-and-coming star in the black community, she was told by some that she didn't sing, "colored enough," and should, "pass for Latin," to find work. Lena became aware that Charlie Barnet, conductor of a swing orchestra, needed a vocalist. Although she was hesitant about singing with a white orchestra, as this was a rare occurrence in 1940, she went to meet with Barnet. After hearing Horne sing, Barnet offered her a six-month contract, which she signed. The contract was for more money than Horne had ever made. She took criticism from many in the black community and the white community when it was made public that she would be singing with a white orchestra. When they performed, primarily for white audiences, she could hear malicious remarks about her as she left the bandstand. In some locations she could only be on the bandstand while she was singing. She could not eat at the same restaurants as the orchestra, and she missed her children, whom she needed to help support.

Lena returned to Pittsburgh after about six months of traveling with Charlie Barnet and his orchestra to find her unhappy marriage irreparably broken. Louis Jones informed Horne that she could take their daughter, Gail, but that he intended to retain custody of their son, Teddy. Newspapers carried the story that Lena had been charged with desertion. Lena's cousin, Edwina, moved to the house in Brooklyn, New York where Lena had spent her early childhood, to help Lena care for Gail. The divorce was to become a bitter one, with accusations from both sides. Lena blamed the break up of their marriage on her husband's overbearing personality, inflexibility, and her need to make a living. Louis Jones blamed the discord in their marriage on his wife's show business career. He had no desire to share her with the rest of the world.

The next stop in Horne's growing career was a 10-month engagement at Café Society Downtown, in New York City. Café Society was a nightclub opened in 1938 by Barney Josephson to break down racial barriers. Café Society was the first integrated nightclub in a white neighborhood. Barney Josephson modeled it after the cabarets he had seen in Prague and Berlin. He was outraged by the treatment that blacks had to endure in existing clubs of the time such as the Cotton Club. Café Society employed many notable performers of the day such as Billie Holiday, who became a friend of Horne, Sarah Vaughan, Hazel Scott, Big Joe Turner, **Paul Robeson**, as well as many other notable African American entertainers. Horne is said to have found the working environment at Café Society very enjoyable. The prejudice, bigotry, and color consciousness that existed in the other places where she had worked did not exist at Café Society. The progressive politics of those who worked at Café Society as well as the clientele was a good fit for her. Many of the people she met, such as Robeson, had known her grandmother Cora Calhoun Horne, and were intrigued by that lineage. During her time at Café Society Horne made the short film, *Boogie*

Woogie Dream, which though not widely viewed, resulted in the suggestion by nightclub owner Felix Young that she come to Hollywood and become one of the stars in his new cabaret.

In late 1941, Lena Horne moved to Hollywood, California, with Gail and her cousin, Edwina, and waited for Felix Young to open his new cabaret. During this time she was dating heavyweight champion Joe Louis, but later had a relationships with Orson Welles, the famous director, producer, writer and actor, and Artie Shaw, the jazz musician and composer. She also established one of the most important relationships in her life during this time. While attending *Jump for Joy: A Sun-Tanned Revu-sical*, starring her friend Duke Ellington, she met arranger, composer, and musician, Billy Strayhorn, who remained her mentor, close friend, and confidant until his death in 1967. While waiting for Young's club, which would be called the Little Trocadero, to open, Lena recorded her first full album, *Moan' Low*.

Metro-Goldwyn-Mayer, or MGM, the movie giant founded in 1924, under the direction of then president Louis B. Mayer, decided in the early 1940s that they could try to move away from the stereotypes that had always been the presentation of African Americans in the cinema. This was a result of pressure from the NAACP, and the realization that African Americans spent some of their disposable income on movies, and would perhaps like to see themselves portrayed as something other than mammies, and servants. Walter White, the executive secretary of the NAACP, having seen Horne perform, considered the beautiful, talented, sophisticated young woman anything but a stereotype. Shortly after having brought Lena to the attention of the people at MGM, she found herself in the office of Louis B. Mayer. Early in 1942, Lena Horne became the first African American to sign a long-term contract with a major studio. The contract was for seven years and made her the highest paid African American actor of her time. MGM presented in *Panama Hattie* later that year. Lena performed two songs in the movie.

There were a couple unanticipated problems involved with the signing of Horne. Max Factor was enlisted to create a special makeup for her that was called "Light Egyptian." This makeup was used to make her skin appear darker because it was thought that she photographed and filmed too fair-skinned. The second problem was the studio wanted to be progressive without offending audiences in the South. Her scenes were filmed so that they could be easily cut out in theaters where her appearance could be considered racially offensive. This was to set a tone for her movie career.

Cabin in the Sky, Stormy Weather, Thousands Cheer, I Dood It, and *Swing Fever*, with Lena Horne, were all made during 1943. *Cabin in the Sky* was the first all-black musical released by MGM since 1929. The film, considered a cinema classic, was the first Hollywood movie directed by Vincente Minnelli. It was groundbreaking in its treatment of African Americans in a nonstereotypical manner. It is infamous for the censorship of a scene in which Horne appears in a bubble bath, although she was completely covered. *Stormy Weather*, which included the song of the same title, became a signature song for Horne. In 1943, Horne appeared in *Newsweek, Life,* and *Time* magazines. Between films, she went back to appearing in cabarets, and became a favorite pinup of black servicemen with whom she enjoyed visiting at every opportunity.

From 1944 until 1950, Horne continued her busy acting and singing career. She filmed *Boogie-Woogie Dream, Broadway Rhythm, Two Girls and a Sailor, Till the Clouds Roll By, Ziegfeld Follies, Words and Music, Some of the Best,* and *Duchess of Idaho,* usually singing, and looking glamorous, in parts that could be excised from the films for racial reasons. Because of her continuing interest in politics, and her support of Harry S. Truman, in 1948 Lena was invited to sing at his inaugural ball. Also because of her progressive political beliefs, she was later accused of being a communist sympathizer, and blacklisted.

Another important event that occurred in 1950 was the official announcement of the marriage of Horne to Lennie Hayton. Leonard George Hayton, or Lennie, a Jewish composer, conductor and arranger, was an Academy Award-winning musician. He was musical director for MGM from 1940 until 1953. Although they married in 1947, the couple kept their nuptials a secret until they were in Paris in 1950 for a performance. They had feared the repercussions of revealing their interracial marriage in the United States. Lennie and Horne remained married until his death in 1971.

Possibly one of the biggest disappointments in Horne's life occurred during the casting of MGM's 1951 movie, *Show Boat.* Because Horne had played the role of Julie LaVerne previously in *Till the Clouds Roll By,* it was assumed that she would reprise the roll in the movie *Show Boat,* especially considering the character of Julie LaVerne was a mulatto. However, because of the code forbidding interracial relationships in films, the role was given to Horne's very good friend Ava Gardner, and to add insult to injury, Light Egyptian makeup, that had been originally developed to make Horne appear darker, was used on her friend Gardner for the role. Gardner also used recordings of Horne to practice the songs for the film. Although Horne and Gardner remained friends until Gardner's death in 1990, this may have been a defining moment in Horne's career.

During the 1950s, Horne became more focused on her performances in nightclubs both in the United States and Europe, where she was much sought after. She made the movies *Duchess of Idaho in 1950, Meet Me in Las Vegas* in 1956, and *The Heart of Show Business* in 1957. She re-signed her recording contract with RCA Victor and released one of her biggest selling albums, "At the Waldorf Astoria." Also in 1957, Horne was finally able to have her name cleared from the Hollywood Blacklist, but seldom appeared in films. She often appeared on television, and performed at The Sands in Las Vegas. In 1957, Horne also appeared in the play *Jamaica* on Broadway. *Jamaica* also starred Ricardo Montalbán.

Horne had spent most of her life being involved in civil rights starting with her registration in the NAACP by her grandmother as a toddler and continuing with her concern for black troops during World War II. She refused to perform for segregated audiences, or for groups in which German POWs were seated in front of African American servicemen. She worked with Eleanor Roosevelt to pass anti-lynching laws. In the 1960s, she stepped up her activism. The week before Medgar Evers was assassinated, Horne had attended an NAACP rally with him in Jackson, Mississippi. She participated in the March on Washington, and spoke at rallies around the country for the National Council for Negro Women. She also met with Attorney General Robert Kennedy to discuss race relations. In addition she did civil rights work with Delta Sigma Theta, Incorporated, of which she is a member.

In the span of one year, Horne lost the three most important men in her life. Her father, Edwin "Teddy" Horne died on April 18, 1970. Her son, Teddy, had been living with health difficulties for a long period of time. He needed dialysis and was in need of a kidney transplant. He passed away on September 12, 1970. Her husband, Lennie Hayton suffered a ruptured aorta on April 23, 1971, and died the next day.

Since starring in her first U.S. television special, *Monsanto Night Presents Lena Horne*, in 1969, Horne has appeared in many television specials and been a featured guest on many television programs. In 1978 she returned to film as Glinda the Good Witch in *The Wiz*, which was directed by her son-in-law Sidney Lumet. She appeared on Broadway again in 1981 in the one-woman show *Lena Horne: The Lady and Her Music*, which received much acclaim, and for which she received a Tony Award and a Grammy Award. In 1984 Horne was honored at the Kennedy Center for her contribution to the world of entertainment. At age 93 and retired, Horne has received almost every award available to an entertainer. She has received Grammies, Emmys, and Tonys. She has been inducted into the **Martin Luther King, Jr**. National Historic Site, and she has received an NAACP Image Award. However the one award that she never had the opportunity to win was an Oscar, for she was never given the opportunity. She came along too soon. Most of her films relegated her beauty and grace to sections that could be clipped out. She came along when African American women played mammies, and Lena Horne was never anyone's mammy.

Covey L. Whitaker
Independent Writer

FURTHER READING

Buckley, Gail Lumet. *The Hornes: An American Family*. New York: Applause Books, 1986.

Gavin, James. *Stormy Weather: The Life of Lena Horne*. New York: Atria Books, 2009.

Haskins, James. *Lena Horne*. New York: Putnam Juvenile, 1983.

Horne, Lena. *Lena*. New York: Doubleday & Co., 1965.

Jet Magazine. November, 1988.

Lena Horne on *The Rosie O'Donnell Show*, 1998, Parts 1 and 2.

Langston Hughes
(1902–1967)

Langston Hughes was born James Langston Hughes in Joplin, Missouri, on February 1, 1902. One of the most prolific writers of the twentieth century, Hughes was also an outspoken critic of racism and segregation and a leading figure in the Harlem Renaissance. Although he is most widely recognized for his poetry, Hughes excelled in virtually every literary genre and was the author of two novels, two autobiographies, several operas, three collections of short stories, and more than 30 stage plays. Hughes also produced five collections of stories and newspaper articles based on the popular fictional character Jesse B. Semple from Hughes's column in the *Chicago Defender*.

While Hughes was widely acclaimed during his lifetime, receiving the prestigious Spingarn Medal in 1960, he often struggled to make a living as a writer. Despite his financial troubles, Hughes traveled throughout the world in both his youth and his later years, visiting countries in Africa, Europe, Latin America, and Asia, even living in Moscow for a brief period in the 1930s. Intent on forging connections between American blacks and Africans and conveying the culture and customs of African Americans to the rest of the world, Hughes quickly became an international icon. His time in the Soviet Union and the socialist message of many of his works, however, was also detrimental to his career, as his reputation as an alleged communist prohibited Hughes from participating in certain engagements and subjected him to investigation by both the FBI and the U.S. Senate.

Hughes's personal life was no less complicated. Somewhat of an enigma, the author was known as much for his striking good looks as his solitary demeanor. Throughout his life, Hughes avoided prolonged entanglement in intimate relationships. While he was pursued by (and said to have relationships with) both women and men, Hughes never married or had a long-term intimate partner. Many of Hughes's biographers suggest that the author's lonely and unstable childhood was responsible for Hughes's isolation; however, it was also this upbringing that fostered a fierce sense of independence and self-reliance in Hughes that would contribute to his immense success as a writer. The first black American whose work was characterized by racial consciousness to make a living as a writer, Hughes is perhaps most significant for his incorporation of African American vernacular and the rhythms of black music, such as the blues, into his poetry. Coupled with this innovation, Hughes's role in the Harlem Renaissance, his political activism, and his mentorship of younger writers such as **Alice Walker** define Hughes as the most prominent African American writer of the twentieth century.

Although Hughes's early life was marked by rejection, abandonment, and instability, it was also during his first 13 years that he developed his racial consciousness, which would permeate his writing and his activism for years to come. Hughes's parents, James Hughes and Carolyn Mercer Langston, had a tumultuous and short-lived marriage. By the time of Langston's birth, his father was already largely absent, living abroad in countries such as Cuba and Mexico. Meanwhile, Langston's mother, Carrie, often left her young son in the care of his maternal grandmother, Mary Sampson Patterson Langston, while she traveled and looked for work. Carrie Hughes sent for Langston from time to time, however, her presence in his life was fairly minimal for the first 13 years. Hughes's grandmother, Mary, had a deep impact on the burgeoning young writer. A free woman of African, Indian, and French heritage, Mary Hughes Patterson moved northward from her home in North Carolina to Oberlin, Ohio at the age of 21, where she attended the university, became active in the abolitionist's movement, and served as a conductor on the Underground Railroad. While Mary Hughes was well advanced in years by the time Langston came to live with her, and thus unable to care for him in many ways, she did enrich his life with stories of the past and the greatness of his ancestors, including a great-uncle who served in the U.S. Congress as a representative from Virginia. Inspired by these tales of heroism and struggle, the values of racial uplift were instilled in Hughes from an early age.

At age 13, Hughes's world changed drastically with the death of his grandmother. Because his mother had remarried, Hughes remained in Lawrence for several months to finish out his seventh grade year in the care of family friends. Then, in the summer of 1915, Hughes relocated to Lincoln, Illinois to live with his mother, stepfather, and stepbrother. There, he enrolled in the eighth grade at Central School, where he and one other classmate were the only black students. Hughes adjusted well to the new environment, excelling academically and being elected class poet by his fellow classmates. While Hughes attributed this honor to his white classmates' racist view that black people possessed some innate rhythm, Hughes did indeed have a talent for writing. Thus, the task of writing a graduation poem for his class marked the beginning of Hughes's poetic career. Four years later, when Hughes graduated from high school in Cleveland (after relocating with his family yet again) he would receive the title of class poet once more.

The summer following his junior year of high school, Hughes traveled to Mexico to visit his estranged father. Although the young Hughes looked forward to the visit, it soon became apparent that he and his father were quite incompatible in both temperament and attitude. Hughes would later write in his autobiography, *The Big Sea*, that this was one of the worst summers of his life. According to Hughes, his father hated his own blackness and often made disparaging comments about his own race. Furthermore, for much of the summer that Hughes spent in Mexico, his father was largely absent, leaving young Langston alone and isolated in a country where he did not know the language. At the end of the summer Langston grew ill, and spent three weeks recovering in an American hospital in Mexico City. According to Hughes, his experience was largely psychosomatic, brought on by his hatred of his father and his inability to express it. Throughout his life, Hughes would experience such bouts of illness during times of intense stress.

Hughes soon recovered and returned to Cleveland to complete his senior year. After graduating in 1920, Hughes again returned to his father in Mexico, despite the unpleasantness of the previous summer. This decision was likely motivated by the fact that Hughes's mother, Carrie, expected her son to begin working to support her following graduation. Hughes's desire to continue his education, however, prompted him to go back to Mexico to try to convince his father to finance his education at Columbia. On his journey to Mexico, Hughes composed one of his most famous and widely anthologized poems, "The Negro Speaks of Rivers," which was soon published in **W. E. B. Du Bois**'s literary magazine, the *Crisis*. While Hughes's father ridiculed his son's aspirations to make a living as a writer, after a year he grudgingly agreed to finance Hughes's first year at Columbia. Hughes enjoyed his proximity to Harlem, which was quickly becoming the cultural center of black America, however financial troubles, quarrels with his father, and the racism he encountered from his white classmates caused Hughes to drop out of college after his first year.

Hughes worked various odd jobs in New York following his brief stint at Columbia. He also spent as much time in Harlem as he could and established important relationships with other writers such as Countee Cullen and Alian Leroy Locke. In June 1923, Hughes eagerly accepted a position as a messman on a ship bound for Africa, looking forward to the opportunity to travel and to make analogies between the situation of blacks in Africa and black Americans. Hughes soon realized, however, that the Africans did not recognize him as a black man, possibly in part because of his light complexion. Horrified by the racism and the suffering that he witnessed, Hughes would later write a great deal about his experiences in Africa.

After his six-month journey, Hughes briefly returned to Harlem, where he found that his literary reputation had increased in his absence. Although the literary scene in Harlem was thriving, Hughes struggled to support himself. He accepted yet another position as a messman, this time on a ship bound for Rotterdam. After a brief return to Harlem, during which Hughes celebrated his 22nd birthday, in February 1924, Hughes again sailed for Europe and settled in Paris. There, he had a brief romance with a black British woman named Anne Marie Cousey. Meanwhile, back in the United States, Hughes's reputation continued to grow, as his friend Countee Cullen helped to place some of the poems Hughes wrote while in Africa. After his relationship with Cousey ended, Hughes traveled to Venice. He returned to New York in November just as the Harlem Renaissance was beginning, a period of great artistic and literary achievements by black Americans based in Harlem from roughly 1925 to 1930.

Hughes made several important connections during this period, including ties to Carl Van Vechten, a white author and an important link to the publishing world, and Arna Bontemps, a teacher who became a dear friend and a collaborator. Hughes also abruptly ended his friendship with Countee Cullen for undisclosed reasons. Hughes's primary biographer, Arnold Rampersad, suggests that Cullen possibly made unwelcome sexual advances toward Hughes and invaded his privacy.

After receiving an invitation to join his mother and stepbrother in Washington, DC, Hughes came to stay with them at the home of some wealthy cousins. During this period, Hughes worked various jobs, attempting to save money to go back to college. While in Washington, the author found that he was unhappy not only with the level of segregation in the city but with the snobby attitude of its prosperous, middle-class blacks. Hughes consequently distanced himself from high society, spending time in slum areas and working on poems that captured the mood of the blues music that floated throughout the city. During the year and two months that Hughes spent in Washington, DC, he published more poems than ever before, many of which conveyed a socialist message. During this time, he also became acquainted with **Zora Neale Hurston** at an awards ceremony in New York and, with the help of Van Vechten, secured a contract with Knopf to publish his first volume of poetry, *The Weary Blues*. Hughes was accepted in 1925 to Howard University, but he was not offered a scholarship in spite of his literary success and thus, could not afford to attend. Hughes did, however, manage to enroll in Pennsylvania's prestigious Lincoln University for the spring semester, with the assistance of patron Amy Spingarn. In his second year at Lincoln, Hughes published his second book, *Fine Clothes to the Jew*, a collection of blues poems in which Hughes attempted to capture the common experiences of African Americans. Hughes also spent his time at Lincoln writing short stories and completing a draft of his first novel, *Not Without Laughter*.

Hughes was further aided in his success in 1927 when his friend Alain Locke introduced him to Charlotte Mason, an elderly, wealthy white woman who wished to invest in black artists and writers. Mason soon became Hughes's patron and asked the writer to call her "Godmother." Hughes cultivated his relationship with Godmother through letters and visits in which he discussed his work. In exchange, Mason provided Hughes with a monthly salary to support his writing. However, their relationship soon became strained, as Hughes and Mason quarreled over artistic differences. In addition, Hughes resented Mason's request that he track and record his spending. Dissatisfied with Hughes's progress despite his graduation from Lincoln in 1929 and the publication of *Not Without Laughter* in 1930, Mason gradually severed all ties with Hughes, first refusing to see him and later discontinuing her financial support of the author. Hughes, greatly distressed by Godmother's rejection of him, became ill with stomach pains, tonsillitis, and toothache. Eventually, however, he recovered and accepted that the relationship was over.

Hughes also quarreled with fellow Harlem Renaissance writer Zora Neale Hurston over the authorship of the play *Mule Bone*, which the two collaborated on in early 1930. While the original inspiration for the project came from a short story by Hurston, entitled "The Bone of Contention," Hughes was largely responsible for the dramatic structure of the play and made some significant changes to the plot. Hurston, on the other hand, contributed her knowledge of Southern dialect and folklore to make the dialogue more authentic. After the play was complete, however, Hurston claimed sole authorship of the work, insisting that Hughes had contributed little and that she had not really incorporated any of his suggestions into the finished product. Hughes contested this claim and argued for his recognition as a co-author. Sadly, Hughes and Hurston could not come to an agreement, and the play was not published or performed in its entirety until its Broadway debut in 1991.

In a more positive turn of events, Hughes was awarded the Harmon medal for literature in 1930, an honor that enabled him to travel to Cuba and then Haiti with his friend, the young, black artist Zell Ingram. After four months abroad, Hughes returned to the United States and made preparations to embark on a reading tour of the South in 1931. During this time, Hughes wrote some of his most radical works, including several pieces about the Scottsboro boys, a group of nine black teenagers wrongfully accused of raping two white women on a train in Alabama. Hughes also generated several publications in the early 1930s, including *Dear Lovely Death* (1931), *The Negro Mother and Other Dramatic Recitations* (1931), and several children's books.

In the summer of 1932, Hughes, along with 21 others, embarked on a trip to Moscow to work on a Soviet film about the experiences of American blacks. Ultimately the project fell through and the film was never made, however Hughes's journey to Russia was extremely significant in his life and his work. Although he was never formally a member of the Communist Party, Hughes clearly expressed his admiration for the freedom that the Soviet Union provided to racial minorities in contrast to the racism and segregation that characterized race relations in the United States. These sentiments inspired some of Hughes most dramatic socialist verses, including the controversial poem, "Goodbye Christ," a work that would haunt Hughes's reputation for many years to come.

From 1932 to 1933, Hughes continued to travel widely, visiting Soviet Asia, Japan, Korea, Shanghai, and Hawaii. He returned to the United States in late 1933, settling in California to work on a collection of short stories, *The Ways of White Folks*, which was published in 1934. Hughes also continued to write radical poetry. In October, Hughes's father died, and the author soon traveled to Mexico to settle his father's affairs. After several months, Hughes returned to the United States, where his writing began to flounder. Although Hughes received a Guggenheim Fellowship to support his work on a proposed new novel to be set in Chicago, by December of 1936 Hughes's nine-month grant had run out without the author making any progress. Hughes also produced several plays that were received poorly. Moreover, while in the past Hughes had often relied on lectures and public speaking engagements as a reliable source of income, his reputation as a radical and a communist sympathizer caused many organizations to shy away from hosting the successful writer. Hughes also had a difficult time publishing his revolutionary poems. Hughes began to distance himself from the Communist Party and avoiding speaking arrangements that would link him to the radical group, although he refused to publicly denounce communism altogether.

In 1937, Hughes sailed to Europe to cover the Spanish Civil War for several black newspapers. The author returned to New York in early 1938 and established the Harlem Suitcase Theater. His first production was a one-act "poetry play" entitled *Don't You Want to Be Free?* A huge success in Harlem, the play contained recitations of many of Hughes's poems. The author's happiness was marred, however, in June 1938 by the death of his mother, who passed away following a three-year struggle with cancer.

Following his mother's death, Hughes attended a conference in Paris and embarked on a reading tour of the Southwest. Hughes then spent several months in California working on a Hollywood script with Clarence Muse entitled *Way Down South*, a film that would later be accused of depicting black Americans as Uncle Tom-like, loyal slaves. Hughes also founded the New Negro Theater in Los Angeles, which staged a production of *Don't You Want to Be Free?* in March 1939. Eventually Hughes resigned as the director of the Harlem Suitcase Theater in New York, because his affairs in California prohibited him from being more actively involved with the playhouse. After attending the premiere of the commercially successful (among white audiences), but widely criticized film, *Way Down South*, Hughes vowed to devote himself to more serious work, namely, his autobiography, *The Big Sea*. Hughes completed the book in the fall of 1939, and it was published the following August. Given the tumultuous state of international affairs with the Second World War looming on the horizon, in his autobiography Hughes attempted to distance himself from radical politics, ending his story in 1931, and thus leaving out his radical poetry and his time spent in the Soviet Union. Furthermore, in 1939 Hughes stopped writing radical verse and drama altogether, returning instead to blues poetry.

Struggling financially, Hughes spent the latter part of 1939 and early 1940 vigorously promoting *The Big Sea*. While the book was reviewed favorably, Hughes found himself under attack for his radical views, and in particular, what audiences perceived as the anti-Christian tone of his 1932 poem, "Goodbye Christ." After several of the author's speaking engagements were cancelled due to protests and picketers, Hughes publicly denounced the poem; however, sales of his autobiography remained low. Moreover, several of Hughes's friends and acquaintances disapproved of him for caving into public pressure and repudiating his work. Hughes soon grew ill at the close of 1940, suffering from various symptoms likely associated with a venereal disease the author had contracted a few weeks earlier. In February of 1941, the author was forced to sell the rights to his books to his publisher, Knopf, for $400 to pay off his medical expenses, thus giving up his claim to any future royalty payments.

Hughes's financial situation began to improve in June 1941 when he was awarded a Rosenwald Fellowship to write a series of one-act plays featuring black heroes. However, as with his previous Guggenheim Fellowship, Hughes procrastinated on the project and only completed one play, *The Sun Do Move*, by the time his grant ran out. In the aftermath of the attack on Pearl Harbor in

December, Hughes concentrated on several war-related projects, including various poems and radio broadcasts. As these efforts proved financially unviable for Hughes, he turned to songwriting in the hopes of producing a popular hit. This ambition, too, yielded lackluster results. Indeed, Hughes's earnings from all lyrics written between 1926 and 1942 totaled a mere $400.

However, a promising opportunity presented itself to Hughes in late 1942 when the author accepted an offer to write a 1,000-word weekly column for the *Chicago Defender*. Through this column, Hughes developed the popular fictional character Jesse B. Semple (also known as Simple), a folk character the author used to address racial issues and life in Harlem. Hughes's Simple character became wildly popular, so much so that the author was able to publish five collections of stories and articles based on the column between 1950 and 1965. The author's success began to mount in the early 1940s. Hughes toured the country vigorously, addressing the war effort and racial issues, including the increase of racial violence that occurred in several U.S. cities as a result of the draft creating more opportunities for blacks to move into previously white-dominated jobs. In 1943, Hughes received an honorary doctorate from his alma mater, Lincoln University. In 1944, the author's financial success enabled him to repurchase the rights to his first five books from Knopf.

Allegations that Hughes was a communist began to resurface in 1944, when the House of Representatives Special Committee on Un-American Activities again turned their attention to the writer. Once again, Hughes lost several speaking engagements as a result of these allegations. By 1948, the poet had practically been forced off of the lecture circuit due to persistent rumors regarding his political and religious beliefs.

Meanwhile, Hughes's time away from his public appearances allowed the author to settle in New York, moving into a house with friends Toy and Emerson Harper in Harlem in 1948, where the author would live for the rest of his life. Hughes also devoted more time to his writing, producing several works, including the poetry volumes *Montage of a Dream Deferred* (written in 1948 and published by Holt in 1949) and *One-Way Ticket* (1948), as well as *The Poetry of the Negro*, an edited anthology released at the end of 1948. In the spring of 1949, Hughes accepted a position as a visiting lecturer at the University of Chicago's Laboratory School, marking his second teaching position. (The author also taught creative writing at Atlanta University in the spring of 1947.)

In the 1940s and 1950s, Hughes devoted much of his time to musical theater projects, including the opera *Troubled Island*, the Broadway show *Street Scene*, and the opera *The Barrier*. Of these three, *Street Scene* would prove to be Hughes's most successful endeavor, providing the bulk of his income after 1948 when the writer was banished from the lecture circuit due to political oppression. Hughes also served as the lyricist for the musical *Just Around the Corner*, which debuted in 1950 in Maine. As anti-communist sentiment continued to mount against Hughes, the author was finally called to appear before the Senate Permanent Sub-Committee on Investigations, which was chaired by Senator Joseph McCarthy. While Hughes denied that he was or ever had been a member of the Communist Party, he refused to denounce Communism altogether. In addition, he defended some of his more controversial works and expressed his faith in the democratic process. Hughes's testimony helped to alleviate many of the attacks against him, although the author would be faced with strong antiradical sentiment for the remainder of his life.

Hughes spent the later years of his life continuing to advocate for racial justice and the end of segregation through his writing. He declined, however, to become a more visible figure in the Civil Rights Movement, refusing an invitation from **Martin Luther King, Jr.**, to join him on the march from Selma to Montgomery and expressing his disapproval of radical leaders such as **Malcolm X** and **Stokely Carmichael**. In 1956, Hughes also published the second installment of his autobiography, entitled *I Wonder as I Wander*.

One of Hughes's greatest achievements came in 1960, when he was awarded the prestigious Spingarn Medal, an annual award given by the NAACP to a black American on the basis of high achievement in any field. In his acceptance speech, Hughes dedicated the award to his fellow black Americans, who provided much of the material for his life's work.

In his final years, Hughes continued to write and publish in nearly every literary genre. He also continued to travel widely, most notably embarking on a State Department-sponsored tour of Europe in 1965. The beloved author was accepted into the National Institute of Arts and Letters in 1961, and received an honorary doctorate from Howard University in 1963. Hughes died in New York on May 22, 1967 from septic shock as a result of a bacterial infection the author contracted following prostate surgery. His final collection of poems, *The Panther and the Lash*, was published posthumously later that year.

Corie Hardy
Arizona State University

FURTHER READING

Bernard, Emily, ed. *Remember Me to Harlem: The Letters of Langston Hughes and Carl Van Vechten*. New York: Vintage, 2002.

Gates, Henry L., Jr. *Langston Hughes: Critical Perspectives Past and Present*. New York: Amistad Press, 1993.

Hughes, Langston. *The Big Sea*. New York and London: Alfred A. Knopf, 1940.

Hughes, Langston. *The Collected Poems of Langston Hughes*. New York: Knopf, 1994.

Hughes, Langston. *The Collected Works of Langston Hughes*. Columbia: University of Missouri Press, 2001.

Hughes, Langston. *I Wonder as I Wander*. New York: Rinehart, 1956.

Leach, Laurie F. *Langston Hughes: A Biography*. Westport, CT: Greenwood Press, 2004.

Rampersad, Arnold. *The Life of Langston Hughes. Volume I: 1902–1941, I, Too, Sing America*. New York and Oxford: Oxford University Press, 1986.

Rampersad, Arnold. *The Life of Langston Hughes. Volume II: 1914–1967, I Dream a World*. New York: Oxford University Press, 1988.

Zora Neale Hurston (1891–1960)

Zora Neale Hurston was born Zora Neal Lee Hurston on January 7, 1891, in Notasulga, Alabama. An American folklorist, author, and anthropologist, Hurston is best known for her 1937 novel, *Their Eyes Were Watching God*. The fifth of eight children born to John Hurston and Lucy Potts Hurston, Zora Neale Hurston grew up in the all-black town of Eatonville, Florida, a setting that would greatly influence Hurston's passion for storytelling and her development as a writer. Despite Hurston's successful and productive career, producing four novels and more than 50 short stories, essays, and plays, the author died in poverty. Moreover, despite Hurston's preeminence during the Harlem Renaissance and her success in the 1930s and 1940s, by the time of her death in 1960 Hurston's work had already begun to fade into obscurity. Indeed, Hurston's work was not rediscovered until 1975, when author **Alice Walker** published the article "In Search of Zora Neale Hurston" in *Ms.* Magazine. Today, Hurston is widely recognized for her contribution to black American literature. In particular, she is known for her immense knowledge of Southern folklore, her use of dialect, and her realistic depictions of Southern black life.

Although she was born in Alabama, Zora Neale Hurston always considered Eatonville, Florida home. Throughout her life, she claimed Eatonville as her birthplace and even referred to it as her "native village." Still a toddler when her family relocated, Hurston may not have even known of her true birthplace. If she was told, perhaps the author considered this detail insignificant. Whatever the case, it is certain that everything Hurston would grow up to write and to believe had its roots in the all-black Southern town. Full of examples of black achievement, Hurston grew up never knowing racial prejudice. A spirited and adventurous girl, she took to exploring, roughhousing with the local boys, and storytelling, all activities that her stern father disapproved of. A Baptist minister, John Hurston discouraged his children from pursuing what he considered to be fanciful dreams. Conversely, Hurston's mother, Lucy, nurtured her daughter's imaginative spirit, encouraging her to "jump at de sun." For the first 13 years of her life, Hurston relished in the company of her mother, who would often protect Zora from her father's wrath. While Lucy admitted that Zora could be impudent at times, she refused to "squinch" her daughter's spirit for fear that she would grow up meek and mealy-mouthed.

Curious from a young age about people and their stories, Zora was prone to flagging down Eatonville's white visitors and accepting rides from them up the road, an activity she was harshly punished for whenever her parents found out. The young Hurston also often lingered in Joe Clarke's convenient store, which served as the social center of Eatonville. Here, adults often gathered on the front porch to share stories and gossip. While as a child Zora was not permitted to listen to "grown up" conversation, she would often drag her feet whenever her mother sent her to the store to purchase something to listen in on the day's chatter. Of greatest interest to Hurston, however, were the folktales or "lying sessions" the people of Eatonville so often engaged in. Stories of talking animals, allegories regarding the differences between men and women, struggles of good versus evil, and tales of how black folks got their color provided the backdrop to Zora's childhood. Huston was also a voracious reader. She particularly admired literary heroes such as Hercules, who were strong and thirsty for knowledge.

Hurston's fiercely independent spirit caused her to be a loner among the children of Eatonville. Too rough and adventurous to play with other girls, and prohibited by her parents from playing with boys, Zora often spent time alone exploring and making up elaborate fantasies. While her mother encouraged such inventiveness, the disapproval Hurston encountered from her grandmother and her father caused her to keep many of her stories to herself. This fostered a rich inner life for the burgeoning young writer, but it also led to loneliness. The young Hurston began to feel particularly alone when, at an unspecified point in her childhood, she began to have ominous visions of things to come. While Hurston correctly predicted that everything she saw in her dreams would come true, she never confided in anyone, not even her mother, for fear of being dismissed as a liar. Hurston would later claim that these pronouncements marked the end of her childhood.

The first of Hurston's prophetic visions was fulfilled in September of 1904 with the death of her mother. At just 13, Hurston was quickly sent away by her father to Florida Baptist Academy in Jacksonville. For the first time in her life, Hurston encountered racism and segregation. Whereas in all-black Eatonville she enjoyed the privilege of expressing her individuality while still belonging to the larger community, in Jacksonville Hurston felt she belong to no one. Feeling displaced and alone, Hurston had a difficult time adjusting at the new school. Soon after her arrival in Jacksonville, Hurston received word that her father had remarried. Hurston and her siblings were hurt that their father had taken a new bride less than five months after their mother's death. The trauma was further exacerbated by the fact that John Hurston's second wife was just 20 years old, only 6 years older than Zora, and 24 years John's junior. Hurston barely had time to react to this news when she learned that her father had failed to pay her room and board. Lacking financial resources, she finished out the school year by cleaning and cooking on the weekends and after her classes. At the close of the school year, Hurston watched her classmates hurriedly leave for the summer, while she was instructed to stay behind until her father came for her. However, after several weeks, the school received a letter from Hurston's father asking the academy to adopt his youngest daughter. The administrator, however, claimed that there was no place for Zora, and provided the funds for Hurston to travel home to Eatonville.

Hurston did not receive a warm welcome when she returned to her father's house. After several conflicts with her father and his new wife, Hurston, like her other siblings, soon fled. Few details are available regarding the next phase in Hurston's life, which historians have referred to as "the lost years." Indeed, since Hurston wished to erase these years from her history, little is known about her whereabouts during this time. According to her limited account, Hurston moved from place to place, staying with various friends and family. Often, her unpleasant attitude was such that she was not welcome in any one place for very long. Hurston also worked a variety of odd jobs during this period, mainly cleaning or looking after children, though like the families that took her in, Hurston's employers quickly grew dissatisfied with her services. At age 20, Hurston's father located his daughter and insisted that she come home. However, Hurston's return was short-lived. Within a month after moving back into her father's house, Zora disappeared once again after a quarrel with her stepmother in which she bludgeoned and almost killed her father's wife.

Hurston vanished from the public record once more, until she was invited to live in Nashville with her older brother, Bob, and his family in 1912. While Bob promised he would send Zora to school if she helped his wife with their young children, soon after her arrival Bob informed Hurston that he could not enroll her in school right away, as his wife had just given birth to their third child and needed Zora's help around the house. In 1913, he moved the family, including Hurston, to Memphis, where he set up a medical practice. While Hurston was materially more comfortable than she had been in years, she soon grew inpatient with cleaning and caring for her brother's family. With no school in sight, Hurston soon fled.

The years 1914–1915 mark yet another gap in Hurston's history. Eventually, she landed a job as a maid working for a singer in a traveling theater group. Hurston soon fell in love with the stage, and enjoyed the company of her employer, Miss M, and the other members of the company. After roughly a year and a half, Hurston's employer announced that she was retiring, and encouraged Zora to return to school. At a tour stop in Baltimore, Miss M warmly bid Zora farewell, sending her on her way with a hug and a small sum of money.

When Hurston arrived in Baltimore in 1917, she was 26 years old. Since Maryland law provided free admission to public schools to all black youths between 6 and 20, Hurston shaved 10 years off of her life, posing as a 16-year-old. Blessed with a youthful appearance, for the remainder of her life Hurston would continue to present herself as at least 10 years younger than she actually was. Hurston quickly began to excel at Baltimore's night high school, and soon switched to Morgan Academy where she could take college prep classes. She later switched to Howard Academy after the daughter of a Howard dean encouraged her to pursue a spot at America's largest black university. In May 1919, she finally received her diploma, and began classes at Howard University the following fall.

Hurston's literary career began to blossom when she joined the staff of *The Stylus*, the annual journal published by Howard's literary club. In addition to facilitating Hurston's acquaintance to important figures such as Professor Alian Locke, *The Stylus* provided the forum for Hurston's first publications in 1921—a poem entitled "O Night," and more importantly, her first short story, "John

Redding Goes to Sea." Meanwhile, Hurston's love life also flourished, as she began a relationship with fellow Howard student Herbert Sheen. Hurston also began to develop a vibrant social life as a member of the Zeta Phi Beta sorority.

The author's success continued in 1924, when Locke recommended Hurston's work to Charles S. Johnson, the editor of *Opportunity: A Journal of Negro Life*. After reading "John Redding Goes to Sea," Johnson invited Hurston to submit material to the prestigious journal. Hurston sent the short story "Drenched in Light," and it was published in the December 1924 issue of *Opportunity*. Hurston's first nationally published short story, "Drenched in Light" explored a day in the life of Isis Watts, a playful and adventurous child modeled after the spirited young girl Hurston had once been.

At Johnson's urging, Hurston moved to New York to join the New Negro movement, planning to continue her college education once she settled into her new environment. Hurston instantly felt at home in Harlem, where she enjoyed the freedom to express herself as well as a sense of community for the first time since her youth in Eatonville. She regularly attended parties and social gatherings, and met fellow writers and artists such as **Langston Hughes**, Countee Cullen, and Ethel Waters. In May 1925, Hurston's achievements as a writer continued to mount, as she claimed four prizes at an awards banquet for *Opportunity* magazine's literary contest. A newcomer to Harlem, Hurston turned heads as she accepted a second-place fiction award for her short story "Spunk," a second-place prize in drama for her play *Color Struck*, and two honorable mentions for other works.

At the party following the awards dinner, Hurston made a memorable entrance, flinging a colorful scarf around her neck as she bellowed out the title of her prize-winning play: "Coloooooooor Struuckkk!" Hurston's flamboyant nature quickly charmed her colleagues and peers, in addition to paving the way for important connections to influential whites who supported the New Negro movement (whom Hurston referred to as "Negrotarians") such as Annie Nathan Meyer, Fannie Hurst, and Carl Van Vechten. As Hurst once aptly noted, Hurston had "the gift" of "walking into hearts."

Hurston's relationship to this particular trio of Negrotarians soon began to pay off. First, Annie Nathan Meyer, the founder of Barnard College, offered Hurston admission to the independent women's college. Meanwhile, Hurston continued to publish short stories and essays. While Hurston was doing well both academically and professionally, financially she struggled to pay her school fees and other expenses. Soon, however, Hurston's monetary problems were alleviated when she began to work as a secretary for the famous novelist Fannie Hurst. This arrangement not only helped Hurston financially, but also aided the author in gaining the admiration and respect of her fellow Barnard classmates, who were initially unwelcoming to Hurston, the only black student at the all-white school. While Hurston's employment with Hurst was short-lived, the affection that the two women felt for each other lasted well beyond their formal financial arrangement. Hurst continued to bolster

Hurston's career by acquainting editors with Hurston's work and introducing her to her celebrity friends.

In her second term at Barnard, Hurston branched out from her English and History-heavy curriculum, undertaking the study of anthropology with renowned German anthropologist Franz Boas. Hurston found her new interest deeply fulfilling, as this academic discipline yielded a fresh lens through which to view the black folk culture that was at the center of her work.

The summer of 1926, Hurston moved into a downtown apartment to be closer to her summer job. Her new flat quickly became a popular haven for what Hurston termed "the Niggerati," a playful and evocative name for the group of black writers and artists who were Hurston's contemporaries, such as Langston Hughes, Wallace Thurman, Gwendolyn Bennett, and Richard Bruce Nugent. Hurston, congenial as always, frequently housed visitors and hosted get-togethers, and always had something cooking on the stove. While Hurston enjoyed her popularity during the Harlem Renaissance and was often considered the life of the party, in actuality she published little during this time. In fact, for the latter part of the Renaissance, Hurston was rarely even in Harlem, as she spent most of her time on the road conducting anthropological research.

Hurston said farewell to Harlem in February 1927 after being awarded a scholarship to collect Negro folklore in the South. Naturally, Hurston chose Florida as the site of her research, rationalizing that the state drew people from all over the country and thus would yield a good cross-section of the black South. While her assignment was to collect stories, superstitions, songs, dances, and jokes, Hurston found it difficult to separate her interests as a writer and a researcher, and thus struggled to collect the kind of material Franz Boas, her supervisor for the project, instructed her to obtain. While Hurston was enamored with the content of the stories and songs she heard, as an anthropologist she was expected to focus on the form, method, and other technical aspects of Southern folklore. Rather than befriending and entertaining the people that she met, as Hurston was accustomed to doing, her task as a social scientist was to study them, not get to know them. For the outgoing Hurston, this work was certainly difficult, and rather lonely.

Hurston did manage to take two brief detours during her travels. The first was to Memphis, to visit her older brother, Bob. The second, and far more significant break from her fieldwork came in May 1927, when Hurston met her long-term boyfriend, Herbert Sheen, in St. Augustine, Florida and married him. After a brief honeymoon, Hurston was already back at work, fearful of the constraints matrimony might place on her life. Predictably, given Hurston's strong sense of independence and the distance between she and her husband, who lived in Chicago, the marriage did not last. Indeed, relations soured between the couple within a year, and the two were formally divorced in 1931.

After completing her fieldwork in the South, Hurston returned to New York, where she was introduced to Charlotte Mason, an elderly, wealthy white woman who wished to become a patron to young black writers and artists. In December 1927, Hurston signed a contract to work for Mason collecting Negro folklore in the South for the entire year of 1928. While Mason paid Hurston a handsome salary and furnished her with an automobile and a video camera for her travels, Hurston soon found the arrangement oppressive, as her contract stipulated that she could not use any of the material she collected for her own work. In 1932, Hurston's stifling arrangement with Mason finally came to an end, and the author was free to publish the material she collected during her travels.

Despite finally receiving her degree from Barnard College in 1928 and for once having a steady income from Mason, the early 1930s were a difficult time for Hurston. In addition to the stress brought on by her relationship with Mason, Hurston quarreled with friend and colleague Langston Hughes over the authorship of a play that the two worked on together entitled *Mule Bone*. Unable to come to an agreement, the play was neither published nor performed during Hurston's lifetime. Moreover, her close friendship with Hughes abruptly came to an end. To make matters worse, the harsh economic conditions of the Great Depression further blackened Hurston's mood. Hurston's despair deepened in mid-1933 when she learned of the death of her only sister, Sarah. Around the same time, Mason, whom Hurston affectionately referred to as Godmother, had a nasty fall and broke her hip, leaving her hospitalized indefinitely. To cope with these tragedies, Hurston threw herself into her writing, publishing her first piece of fiction since 1926, a short story called "The Gilded Six-Bits" in *Story* magazine in August 1933.

While Hurston received only a modest payment for the story, "The Gilded Six-Bits" would pave the way for publication of the author's first novel. After receiving an offer from publisher Bertram Lippincott of the J. P. Lippincott Company to submit a book-length work of fiction, Hurston wrote and submitted *Jonah's Gourd Vine* in just nine weeks. Largely autobiographical, the book told the story of Hurston's parents, and in particular, her father. Hurston's next book, a critically acclaimed collection of Southern folktales entitled *Mules and Men*, soon followed in 1935. However, the author's greatest success would come in 1937 when she wrote and published her most famous novel, *Their Eyes Were Watching God*. Remarkably, Hurston wrote the novel in just seven weeks while in Haiti on a Guggenheim Fellowship.

While Hurston's success continued into the 1940s with the publication of works such as *Tell My Horse* (1938), *Moses, Man of the Mountain* (1939), and her autobiography, *Dust Tracks on a Road* (1942), the author was never able to support herself solely as a writer. For example, while successful white authors such as Fannie Hurst routinely received $5,000 book advances, Hurston's received only $200 for her first novel. Thus, racism in the publishing world forced Hurston to pursue other sources of income throughout her career, up until the time of her death.

Hurston's other achievements included being featured in the 1942 editions of *Who's Who in America*, *Current Biography*, and *Twentieth Century*

Authors. The following year, Hurston was presented with Howard University's Distinguished Alumni Award. The most well-known black woman author during her time, Hurston's ambitions appeared to be endless despite her lack of financial success. In January 1935, the author was awarded a fellowship from the Rosenwald Foundation to pursue a PhD in Anthropology at Columbia University, although she never completed the degree program. Hurston did, however, receive an honorary doctorate in 1939 from Morgan State College.

In 1939, Hurston married for the second time; at 23, Albert Price III, was 25 years Hurston's junior. The marriage, however, only lasted several months, though the two attempted to reconcile briefly in 1940 before their divorce was finalized in 1943. Nonplussed, Hurston continued to write and publish throughout the 1940s. In 1947, she traveled to Honduras to research black communities in Central America. Hurston remained in Honduras until 1948. While she was there, she wrote her last published novel, entitled *Seraph on the Suwanee*.

Shortly after her return to the United States, in September 1948 Hurston was accused of molesting three 10-year-old boys. While the case was dismissed in 1949 after the accusers admitted that they had fabricated the allegations, the ordeal took a mental and physical toll on the author. In 1950, Hurston finally settled in Florida where she had lived on and off throughout her life. However, given that all the royalties she might have earned from the sale of her last book went toward paying off the legal fees that she accumulated during the molestation trial, Hurston was in need of a steady income. Therefore, at age 59 she decided to take a job as a maid for a couple in a wealthy Miami suburb. Ironically, during this same period of time one of Hurston's last short stories, "Conscience of the Court," was published in the *Saturday Evening Post*. A string of other undesirable jobs followed, including librarian, substitute teacher, and newspaper columnist. Hurston also wrote several political essays, covered the trial of Ruby McCollum (a black woman accused of killing her white lover), and began her biography of Herod the Great in her final years. Despite the fact that Hurston's work had already been largely forgotten by the last decade of her life, the author never stopped writing.

In early 1959, Hurston suffered a stroke. Later that year, she reluctantly entered the Saint Lucie County welfare home in Fort Pierce, Florida, where she would live out the remainder of her life. On January 28, 1960, the 69-year-old author died of hypertension heart disease. Due to Hurston's poverty, her Florida neighbors took up a collection to pay for Hurston's funeral services. Without enough money for a headstone, Hurston was buried in an unmarked grave in the Garden of Heavenly Rest cemetery in Fort Pierce, Florida.

Some 13 years later, a young author named **Alice Walker** traveled to Fort Pierce to place a marker on Hurston's grave. Two years later, Walker's article, "In Search of Zora Neale Hurston," was published in *Ms.* magazine, inspiring a revival of the long-forgotten author's works. Today, Hurston is recognized as one of the most significant African American authors of the twentieth century. Moreover, she was the first black female author to attempt to make a living solely as a writer. Remembered not only for her vivacious personality but her realistic depictions of Southern black life and use of dialect, Zora Neale Hurston paved the way for several younger generations of black female writers, including Alice Walker, **Maya Angelou**, and **Toni Morrison**. For these women, Hurston's literary children and grandchildren, Hurston is not remembered as an individual who died largely forgotten and unrecognized, but as a fiercely independent and brave literary pioneer who would set the stage for many women writers to come.

Corie Hardy
Arizona State University

FURTHER READING

Boyd, Valerie. *Wrapped in Rainbows: The Life of Zora Neale Hurston.* New York: Scribner, 2003.

Hemenway, Robert E. *Zora Neale Hurston: A Literary Biography.* Urbana: University of Illinois Press, 1977.

Hurston, Zora Neale. *Dust Tracks on a Road.* New York: HarperCollins, 1996.

Kaplan, Carla, ed. *Zora Neale Hurston: A Life in Letters.* New York: Doubleday, 2002.

Plant, Deborah G. *Zora Neale Hurston: A Biography of the Spirit.* Westport, CT: Praeger, 2007.

Walker, Alice. "In Search of Zora Neale Hurston." *Ms. Magazine*, March 1975, 74–79, 84–89.

AP/Wide World Photos

Michael Jackson
(1958–2009)

Michael Joseph Jackson was born August 29, 1958, in Gary, Indiana, to father, Joseph "Jo" Jackson, and mother, Katherine Jackson. The Jacksons, a large, African American working-class family, was closely knit and extremely talented. Jo Jackson played the guitar semi-professionally until he dispensed with his musical goals to support his family as a crane operator. Jo Jackson, recognizing his sons' musical and dancing prowess, worked them into a musical group during the early 1960s. In the beginning, the performers in the Jackson family included Michael's older brothers Jackie, Jermaine, and Tito. Michael joined his brothers when he was five, and after he shocked his father and almost everyone else with his stunning singing and dancing talents, he quickly emerged as the group's lead vocalist and principal attraction. He demonstrated exemplary range and power for his age, astonishing crowds and industry professionals, including Smokey Robinson, with his ability to communicate adult, multifaceted emotions. When Marlon Jackson, Michael's older brother, eventually joined the band, they named themselves the Jackson 5.

Joseph Jackson was a taskmaster in driving his sons to excel as artists and entertainers. He was also rumored to erupt into fits of anger and violence when his children did not meet his soaring standards or conform to his rule without question or comment. Despite the harsh ways in which Jo Jackson lorded over his children, Michael Jackson would late credit his father's unyielding authority and meticulousness as both the curse of his youth and the foundation of his own unsurpassed determination and commitment to excellence. Michael and his brothers studied music, dancing, and singing relentless, and their rehearsal schedule and related efforts to perfect their act was grueling. Initially, the Jackson 5 performed in venues near their home in Gary, where they garnered a robust fan base. They produced their first self-recorded single, "Big Boy," during the period. "Big Boy" boasts a b-side tune titled "You've Changed." Both songs, however, were unsuccessful at generating significant attention.

Despite their early struggles as recording artists, the group soon attracted enough attention to transition into performing as an opening act for famous R&B artists such as James Brown, Sam and Dave, and Gladys Knight and the Pips. Many of these celebrities were contractually bound to the renowned **Motown Records**. In fact, Gladys Knight is considered by many to have discovered the Jackson 5, and delivered the group to Motown founder, Berry Gordy. Gordy was thoroughly impressed with the group, especially Michael Jackson, who Gordy considered to be a prodigy. Gordy signed the group to the Motown label in 1968. Jo Jackson then moved their family to Los Angeles to polish their act and position stars-in-the-making in the center of the music industry. The Jackson 5 began working on the music and dancing even harder, while Jo Jackson assumed the role of their manager. When the Jacksons first arrived in Los Angeles they moved in with Gordy. They also lived, at intervals, with Diana Ross, the superstar lead of the celebrated group, The Supremes.

In August 1969, the Jackson 5 was presented to the music world at an exclusive event in Los Angeles, and they would soon secure the position of opening act for the Supremes. Their first album, *Diana Ross Presents the Jackson 5*, debuted on the charts in December of 1969. The group's first single on that album was "I Want You Back." It was a smash hit that topped the charts at number one on the *Billboard Hot 100* in January of 1970.

The Jackson 5 rocketed to the top of the charts again one year later with a string of hits, including as "ABC," "The Love You Save," and "I'll Be There." Michael Jackson, who had established himself as the most talented, visible, and adored of the group by age 13, embarked on a solo career while continuing to work as the front man for the Jackson 5. He released the album *Got to Be There*, which scored the hit, title-track single, "Got to Be There." His 1972 album, *Ben*, introduced the emotional and distinctive ballad about a young boy and his beloved pet rat. The song was lauded for its depth of feeling and for Michael's rousing vocals. It also became Jackson's first number-one single as a solo artist. Despite Michael Jackson's taxing schedule, he continued to pursue his own professional interests while leading the Jackson 5, all under the guidance of Berry Gordy and his Motown personnel. Gordy, in fact, wrote a number of the songs that were recorded by the Jackson 5 and by Michael Jackson as a solo artist. The Jackson 5's popularity became so ubiquitous that they were given their own self-titled cartoon show, which aired from 1971 to 1973.

In the face of tremendous artistic and financial success as a member of the Jackson 5 and as a solo artist, however, tension emerged between the Jackson camp and Motown Records. Hostilities intensified between Gordy and Jo Jackson over the supervision of his children's professional lives, and the extent to which they shared in production of their music. The Jacksons demanded greater command of their recordings. This unyielding position facilitated the acrimonious departure of the most of the Jacksons from Motown in 1975. Jermaine Jackson, who launched his own career as a solo artist, continued to work as a member of the Motown recording family. Jermaine Jackson went on to release a number of albums with some success. None of his albums, however, came close to equaling the success of his younger brother Michael.

After leaving Motown Records, the group signed a new recording deal with Epic Records and renamed themselves the "Jacksons." They released their album *Destiny in 1978*, and Michael, Marlon, Tito, Jackie, and the newest addition, Randy Jackson, proved themselves to be gifted songwriters, in addition to musicians, singers, and dancers, as they wrote every song on the album. Reaching even greater heights, Michael Jackson paired up with renown producer, Quincy Jones, to deliver his solo album, *Off the Wall*, in 1979. *Off the Wall* astonished the record industry and the artistic world with its contagious and transcendent mix of R&B, funk, and pop. This remarkable album produced a string of hit singles, including the Grammy Award-winning "Don't Stop 'til You Get Enough," "Rock with You," and the title track, "Off the Wall." His pained and remorseful song "She's Out of My Life," was also a success, though it did not receive the same critical acclaim of the other, more popularly songs on the album.

The tremendously affirming response to *Off the Wall* helped sustain the Jacksons' career as well. *Triumph* (1980) sold in excess of one million copies, and the brothers went on a large-scale concert tour to buttress the album's success. Michael Jackson, however, began to place a higher premium on his solo career. He teamed up with rock legend, Paul McCartney, on their 1982 duet, "The Girl Is Mine," which almost reached number one on the pop charts.

The song also appeared on Michael Jackson's next solo album, *Thriller* (1982), which spawned a staggering seven top 10 hits. On a television special honoring Motown's 25th anniversary, Jackson performed "Billie Jean"—eventually a number one hit—and unveiled his now-celebrated dance move, the moonwalk. Jackson, a learned and skilled entertainer at this point, refined the fairly obscure, sliding, reverse-walking movements that had been exhibited by crack tap, free style, and B-Boy dancers for decades, and added his own grace and unmatched style to it. He also co-choreographed the dance sequences for the video of his other number-one hit, "Beat It." Millions of Americans tuned into the "Motown 25" show to see a seasoned, dynamic, and astounding Michael Jackson. The next day, millions of Americans, enthralled with the moonwalk, attempted to imitate the move—in school yards, family rooms, and dance studios.

Jackson's most elaborate video, however, was for *Thriller*, the album's title track. Directed by John Landis, the video was a horror-themed production. Complex dance scenes, special effects, and a voice-over done by actor Vincent Price added to the video's allure. The already-successful album got an additional boost in sales after the release of the video, keeping the album on the charts for 80 weeks, 37 of which were spent in the number one spot. The charts were not the only place where the song and album's success were recognized. *Thriller* earned 12 Grammy Award nominations, and won in 8 of the 12 categories, showcasing the diverse nature of Jackson's work. He won the Grammy Award for Best Rhythm and Blues Song for "Billie Jean," which highlighted his songwriting skills. He won Best Pop Vocal Performance, Male for "Thriller" and added a win under Best Rock Vocal Performance, Male for "Beat It." With co-producer **Quincy Jones**, he shared the highly coveted Grammy Award for Album of the Year.

Thriller was an unparalleled and unstoppable musical movement. Epic Records was reveling in success. At its 1984 presentation of upcoming releases, executives boasted the company's success, inserting stock footage of semitrucks with a voice-over announcing, "There goes another load of Michael Jackson's *Thriller* albums!" Surpassing the industry's wildest expectations, *Thriller* was still breaking records and bringing in high sales more than a year after its late 1982 release, averaging more than one million copies per month in U.S. sales alone. Now, 27 years after its release, *Thriller* still stands as the best-selling studio album in the United States, certified 28-times platinum, and has sold over 50 million copies internationally.

Sales statistics alone cannot set the benchmark for the album's success, however. As Jackson moonwalked his way into music history, *Thriller* set a new standard for blockbusters that changed how the music business promoted and marketed superstar releases. The album, and its video, also changed MTV, breaking down the cable network's racial barriers, with Jackson becoming the first black artist to break into the burgeoning music video scene. It significantly raised the bar for video quality and ingenuity. The album also redefined expectations for blockbuster releases, as demonstrated through its synchronized worldwide release, its increased production time, and its amount of radio-released tracks. In fact, Columbia released seven singles, the same number of singles that Thriller spawned, from Bruce Springsteen's *Born in the U.S.A.* (1984). All of these singles made their way into the *Billboard Hot 100*'s top 10. Warner Bros. copied this model, sending five of Prince's *Purple Rain* singles to radio. Mercury released seven pop-chart placed hits from Def Leppard's *Hysteria*. All of these albums, though not reaching nearly the level of success of *Thriller*, sold over 10 million copies each.

Thriller also made a contribution to the music sales industry, giving the business a much-needed boost during its second slump in just the previous three years. The sales were so low, in fact, that CBS staffers deemed August 13, 1982 as "Black Friday." From 1980 to 1982, *Billboard* reported a decline in record shipments of 50 million units. On "Black Friday," Epic fired many of its employees, including half the marketing department. Jackson revolutionized and revitalized the business. *Thriller* was the driving force behind what became the hottest span in Epic's history. After *Thriller*, Epic went on to have major hits with Cyndi Lauper, Culture Club, and REO Speedwagon. The *Flashdance* soundtrack and The Police's *Synchronicity* also helped draw fans and increase sales.

During the peak of *Thriller*'s success, Jackson was at the top of his game, both creatively and commercially. He signed an endorsement deal with Pepsi-Cola, to the tune of five million dollars. During a commercial shoot for Pepsi-Cola in 1984, Jackson was severely injured by burns to both his face and scalp. To repair the damage from these unfortunate accidents, Jackson had reconstructive surgery. This event, many believe, triggered Jackson's experimentation with plastic surgery. Eventually, his face, most notably his nose, would become altered significantly.

In the same year as his tragic accident, Jackson toured, for what was then the final tour, with the Jacksons, promoting the album *Victory*. Jackson's duet with Mick Jagger, "State of Shock," was the major hit from the album, garnering much attention and fanfare. Recovered from his burns, Jackson showed his altruistic side in 1985 with "We Are the World," a charity single for USA For Africa that he co-wrote and sang. A number of other notable stars also participated in this project, including Lionel Ritchie, **Ray Charles**, Bob Dylan, Willie Nelson, Bruce Springsteen, and Tina Turner.

Now a handful of years after the release of *Thriller*, Jackson released his follow-up, *Bad* (1987). While the record placed him, again, at the top of the charts, and included five number-one hits, it was unable to replicate the phenomenal sales of *Thriller*. "Man in the Mirror," "The Way You Make Me Feel," and the title track, which was supported by a video directed by Martin Scorsese, were major players on the album. Jackson spent more than a year on the road, promoting the album with numerous high-energy concerts and appearances.

While his onstage persona was anything but calm, Jackson was actually quite shy and a quiet person off-stage. His religious upbringing as a Jehovah's Witness may have contributed to this demeanor. Although he received a lot of media attention, that was never Jackson's preference, as he rarely gave interviews. To escape many of the stresses brought on by his career, and events in his childhood, Jackson created his own personal fantasy retreat in the late 1980s, Neverland Ranch in California. At Neverland he had exotic pets, including the now-well-known chimpanzee, Bubbles. Jackson also had a number of his own amusement rides at the ranch, perhaps, as some maintain, to aid in an exploration of a second childhood. He did not keep Neverland to himself alone, however, as he would occasionally open up the ranch for children's events. Because of his reclusive nature, odd behaviors, and preference to avoid the media, rumors began to circulate. Three of the initial rumors involved his skin color, sleeping habits, and sexuality. Many say that he intentionally lightened his skin to appear white, although this was later dispelled by Jackson in a rare televised interview. His sleeping routine came under speculation when a rumor spread that he slept in a special chamber in order to increase his life span. In reality, Jackson suffered from a severe version of the skin disease, vitiligo, and his chamber sleeping was likely staged and overblown. Some also posited that Jackson was a homosexual, but Jackson dismissed these claims.

In 1991, his first album of the early 1990s, Jackson released *Dangerous*, which featured the hit song "Black or White." The video for this song, directed by John Landis, included an appearance by child star Macaulay Culkin, of *Home Alone* fame. The video's final minutes sparked some controversy based on Jackson's sexual gestures and violent actions. The gestures, in particular, were a departure from Jackson's typical asexuality and became the catalyst for much speculation. Despite the controversy over the "Black or White" video, Jackson continued to enjoy widespread popularity. In 1993, he performed several important events, including the halftime show at Superbowl XXVII, and making a rare televised interview appearance. Sitting down with **Oprah Winfrey** in February of that same year, he attempted to dispel rumors, explaining that the change in his skin tone was, in fact, the result of vitiligo, a skin condition in which there is a loss of pigment that results in irregular white patches of skin. During the same interview, Jackson also opened up about the abuse he suffered from his father.

Later in 1993, the first allegations of child molestation against Jackson emerged when a 13-year-old boy claimed that the music star had fondled him. While Jackson was known to have sleepovers with boys at his Neverland Ranch, prior to this accusation there were never any known charges of wrongdoing. Jackson maintained his innocence at the onset and throughout all of the allegations. Police officers searched Neverland Ranch, but never found any evidence to support the molestation claim. In 1994, Jackson settled with the accuser's family out-of-court. However, the allegations of molestation were not behind him, as others emerged claiming the same type of events occurred.

In August 1994, Jackson announced that he had married Lisa Marie Presley, daughter of rock icon Elvis Presley, in what would be a short-lived union that ended in divorce in 1996. Because of the timing, many believed that the marriage was merely a publicity stunt to restore Jackson's image after the molestation allegations. Presley, though, denied these claims, and argued that their love was genuine and that their marriage was legitimate, a claim she still maintains today.

In the same year as his divorce from Presley, Jackson shared marital vows with Debbie Rowe, a nurse. Jackson and Rowe had two children, both through artificial insemination. Their first, a son, Prince Michael Jackson, was born in 1997, and their daughter, Paris Michael Jackson, was born in 1998. Shortly after the birth of their second child, Rowe and Jackson divorced in 1999. Jackson received full custody of their two children. Jackson had a third child, Prince Michael Jackson II, nicknamed "Blanket," whose mother is unknown.

Around the mid-to-late 1990s, Jackson's musical career began to lose steam in many populations, particularly America's younger, white community. His 1995 album, *HIStory: Past, Present, and Future, Book I*, was anticipated to do incredibly well on the sales charts, but fell short of the expectations. The album featured both well-known, earlier hits and new material. And although the record as a whole did not sell as expected, two individual tracks achieved the status that the album as a whole did not. "You Are Not Alone," which reached number one on the Pop and R&B charts, and his duet with sister Janet Jackson, "Scream," which reached the top 10 on the same charts became wildly popular. "Scream," in fact, earned Michael and Janet a Grammy Award for Best Music Video Short Form, that year. Another track from the album, "They Don't Care About Us," however, brought Jackson intense criticism for using an anti-Semitic term. *HIStory*, and *Bad* for that matter, were evaluated against the backdrop of *Thriller*'s record-breaking success. So, by *Thriller*'s standards *HIStory* and *Bad* were disappointments. By any other measure, however, *HIStory* and *Bad* were undisputed successes.

By the release of 2001's *Invincible*, Jackson was better known in many circles, primarily white, and young, as an eccentric whose quirks were reported in the tabloids, than as a performer. The album sold well, but stories of his odd behavior started to overshadow his talent. He often appeared in public wearing a surgical mask, and he hid his children's faces under veils. In 2002, Jackson seemed confused and disoriented on stage at an MTV awards show. Soon after, he received enormous criticism for dangling his son, Prince

Michael II, over a balcony while greeting fans in Germany. In a later interview, Jackson explained that "We were waiting for thousands of fans down below, and they were chanting they wanted to see my child, so I was kind enough to let them see. I was doing something out of innocence."

Jackson's reputation was served another blow in 2003 with the television documentary, *Living with Michael Jackson*. British journalist Martin Bashir spent several months with Jackson, and he got Jackson to discuss his relationships with children. He admitted that he continued to have children sleepover at his ranch, even after the 1993 allegations. Jackson said that sometimes he slept with the children in his bed. "Why can't you share your bed? That's the most loving thing to do, to share your bed with someone," Jackson told Bashir.

Jackson faced more legal woes in 2004 when he was arrested on charges related to incidents with a 13-year-old boy the previous year. Facing 10 counts in all, he was charged with lewd conduct with a minor, attempted lewd conduct, administering alcohol to facilitate molestation, and conspiracy to commit child abduction, false imprisonment, and extortion. The resulting 2005 trial was a media circus with fans, detractors, and camera crews surrounding the courthouse. More than 130 people testified, including Macaulay Culkin who appeared on Jackson's behalf. He said that he had been friends with Jackson as a young teen. While he had stayed over at the Neverland Ranch, he told the court that Jackson never tried to molest him. Jackson's accuser also appeared via videotape and described how Jackson had given him wine and molested him.

On June 14, 2005, Jackson was acquitted of all charges, and many speculated that the star was merely the victim of false accusations and carefully executed extortion attempts. He stayed at Neverland for only a short time after the trial and then moved to Bahrain. A friend of the king of Bahrain's son, Jackson was able to avoid the intense media scrutiny he had been subjected to during the trial. Plans were made for Jackson to record a comeback album with the king's son's record company, but the album never materialized. Reportedly in dire financial straits, Jackson sold his Neverland Ranch in 2008. He, however, sued to block the auction of some of his personal items from the home the following year. Around this same time, the largely reclusive Jackson announced that he would be performing a series of concerts in London as his "final curtain call." There had been some speculation regarding whether the often fragile-appearing singer would be able to handle the rigors of 50 concerts. However, despite all of the allegations and stories of odd behavior, Jackson remained a figure of great interest, as demonstrated by the strong response to his concert plans. Set to appear at the O2 Arena beginning July 8, 2009, Jackson saw the tickets to these shows sell out in only four hours.

Michael Jackson, one of the most popular artists of all time, died suddenly of cardiac arrest on June 25, 2009, in Los Angeles just before the concert series. He was 50 years old. His death stunned millions and prompted many to reflect upon his impact upon the entertainment industry and popular culture. His vast charitable work was also the target of a great deal of attention. In addition to being the record-breaking "King of Pop," Michael Jackson was one of the most generous entertainers of all time. Many argue that he paved the way for the current surge in celebrity philanthropy. Jackson supported dozens of charities during his life, including USA For Africa, the Make-a-Wish Foundation, and the Elizabeth Taylor AIDS Foundation.

Jackson reportedly was listed in the 2000 edition of the *Guinness Book of World Records* for "Most Charities Supported by a Pop Star." The number was 39. As a humanitarian, he is perhaps best known for "We Are the World," the 1985 song he wrote with Lionel Richie that raised millions of dollars for famine relief in Africa. To honor Jackson's philanthropy, some fans and small companies have pledged to make donations to his favorite charities.

Millions of people were shocked by Michael's Jackson's death. Throughout the cosmos, the brightest stars often have the shortest life spans, so many suspected that humanity would only have Jackson for a relatively short period of time. Still, millions of people feel a tremendous void now. His music was the soundtrack of millions of lives, and many identified with the loneliness of his crowded and overbooked existence, as well as the optimism he embodied in a world rife with pessimism and bitterness. His music comforted his fans. His success buoyed them, and his altruism, activism, and philanthropy uplifted them. No matter how confusing and dismal things got for many of his admirers, his artistry, energy, work ethnic, artistic genius, and unsurpassed accomplishments were always there for them.

Even in the midst of scandal and his often eccentric and inexplicable behavior, much of the music he produced and the performances he rendered bordered on perfection. He was one of a kind, an original who will never grace the earth again, and even though few of his fans met him, millions miss him. He gave the world 45 years of his brilliance. His impact on the music industry is mind-boggling, and he single-handedly changed the music video industry. It was he who made MTV a household name. He was one of, if not the, greatest entertainer of all time, and his brilliance will echo through the ages.

Matthew C. Whitaker
Arizona State University

FURTHER READING

Ebony Magazine Editors. *Ebony Special Tribute, Michael Jackson: In His Own Words and Notes from Those Who Loved Him*. Chicago: Johnson Publishers, 2009.
Gray, Todd. *Michael Jackson: Before He Was King*. New York: Chronicle Books, 2009.
Jackson, Michael. *Moonwalk*. New York: Harmony, 2009.
Jefferson, Margo. *On Michael Jackson*. New York: Vintage, 2007.
Taraborrelli, J. Randy. *Michael Jackson: The Magic, the Madness, the Whole Story, 1958–2009*. New York: Hachette Book Group, 2009.

Jay-Z (1969–)

Shawn Corey Carter, most popularly known to the world as Jay-Z, was born on December 4, 1969, in New York City. In the realm of hip-hop he has no peer. His successes as a recording artist, business executive, brand developer, and philanthropist distance him from others by virtue of his uncanny ability to rise to challenges, and exceed expectations in a very discreet, matter-of-fact way. He is a self-described "hustler" who transformed himself from Brooklyn drug dealer into a global music and business icon. As a recording artist he is responsible for over 33 million records sold, charting 11 number-one albums, and turning Roc-A-Fella Records into a household name. Outside the realm of music, his business interests include Roc-A-Wear clothing, 40/40 Club (sports bar), Translation Advertising, and minority ownership in the National Basketball Association's New Jersey Nets. His aliases range from Jigga, and variations of the Hebrew name for God, Jehovah. These variations include Jay-Hova, Hova, and Young Hov. As if to cement his god-like status, he is married to one of the biggest music stars of all time, Beyoncé Knowles. Jay-Z is a living embodiment of the "rags-to-riches" narrative and uses this to inspire underdogs and outwit those who underestimate his hustle.

Jay-Z is the youngest of four children born to Adnes (AJ) Reeves and Gloria Carter. According to his grandmother, Hattie White, he was a happy-go-lucky child growing up in the Bedford-Stuyvesant section of Brooklyn, New York. His parents were working-class and finances were a consistent issue during childhood. At the age of six his family moved into the Marcy Housing Projects. His life took a dramatic turn when his father left the family when Jay was 11. Gloria Carter attributes Adnes's departure to his inability to constructively cope with the murder of his brother, Jay-Z's uncle, which consumed him with rage and the need for revenge. As a result, Gloria became a single mother of four and Jay-Z became more guarded in fear of becoming close to anything and having it taken away so abruptly. This character trait would later be interpreted as a trademark coolness he exuded while hustling in the streets or brokering deals in high rises.

Two things about Jay-Z were evident at an early age, he loved music and he was intelligent. His relatives remember there being crates of music in the house filled with the soulful sounds of Earth, Wind and Fire, Ohio Players, The Whispers, and The Temptations. His sister Michelle vividly remembers young Shawn's enthusiasm whenever he heard the Jackson 5's "Enjoy Yourself." As a student Jay-Z claims that he tested at a 12th grade level while in sixth grade. He showed promise in the areas of math and writing. He would seek refuge in writing to cope with the absence created by his father's departure.

Rapping was a way he could combine both his passion for music and composition. Jay-Z would keep his siblings awake at night by pounding out beats on the wall and kitchen table while writing his songs. He was so committed to lyricism that he studied rhyming dictionaries. In an effort to not have his rhymes stolen by "biters," he wrote in an illegible fashion only understood by him. His early rap style was very rapid-fire with tongue-twisting cadence.

He began to build a reputation as one of the neighborhood's best emcees and took on the nickname "Jazzy" which would eventually become "Jay-Z." As rap music cemented itself as the music of inner-city youth of the 1980s, Jay-Z and many of his peers became enamored with the idea of becoming rappers. Two of his high school classmates at George Westinghouse Vocational and Technical High School were Trevor Smith and Christopher Wallace, who would go on to respectively become hip-hop legends Busta Rhymes and Notorious B. I. G. Rap music was not the only phenomena infiltrating inner-city neighborhoods in the 1980s, it was also the era of crack cocaine.

Marcy Projects was engulfed by the crack epidemic and became a war zone. Like many of his peers, Jay-Z became a soldier but was determined not to become one of its casualties. He dropped out of school and began to sell drugs on the streets while simultaneously pursuing opportunities to break into the music industry. The two lifestyles proved to be inseparable for Jay-Z the artist and Shawn Carter the man. Ironically, the majority of the content of his music is filled with tales of his life as a street hustler and his business acumen is a direct result from dealings in the crime world. In his music he often compared his life in the streets to the realities of the recording industry by using the association of "the rap game vs. crack game."

His first experience with the music industry came in 1989 as a featured artist on neighborhood friend Jaz-O's *Word to the Jaz*. Analogous to Dr. Dre's less-than-flattering introduction to the world in a sequenced one-piece jumpsuit as a member of the World Class Wrecking Crew, Jay-Z's appearance in Jaz-O's video for the single "Hawaiian Sophie" would prove not to be indicative of his future status as a hip-hop mogul. Jaz-O was signed to Capitol Records and this opportunity was seen as the break Jay-Z needed to secure himself a record deal. However, the experience proved to be a disaster as the record label attempted to market Jaz-O, progeny of the Marcy Projects, as an act comparable to the suburban Fresh Prince.

Jay-Z was disappointed by this turn of events and returned to the streets, selling drugs, and writing raps. These two pastimes would again combine to catapult Jay-Z into mythological status as the drug dealing kept him away from his access to paper and pen. Therefore, on the streets between transactions he would be creating songs in his head and then rush into a corner store to write them onto paper bags. Eventually this method became a bit cumbersome so he began to commit entire compositions to memory without having to write them down. This talent would later earn him the moniker, "One-Take Hov" because of his ability to nail a song in a recording session in one take.

His next attempt at entering the music industry came after he formed a relationship with Brooklyn emcee Big Daddy Kane. Big Daddy Kane was one of the seminal artists of hip-hop's Golden Era (1986–1993) and unlike the start-up Jaz-O, was an established artist. Kane was the total package at the time. He was a world-class lyricist, a gold-certified recording artist, and a sex symbol. After hearing Jay-Z rap Big Daddy Kane took Jay-Z under his wing. The two recorded a demo tape together and Big Daddy Kane invited Jay-Z to join him on tour. Jay-Z and his closest friends saw this as his real chance at securing a record deal. Big Daddy Kane would allow Jay-Z to perform during breaks in his set. Initially the crowd would give him a cold welcome but once he started rapping he would have them in the palm of his hands. This still didn't impress music industry executives and was unable to leverage the Big Daddy Kane relationship into a record deal. Jay-Z returned to his street hustling roots.

It is the early 1990s, he had been in pursuit of his passion for several years and had been exposed to every level of the business and yet had no record deal. DJ Clark Kent, former deejay for rapper Dana Dane, believed in Jay-Z's potential and did not want to see him succumb to the twin traps of street life; death or incarceration. With the encouragement of a cousin and DJ Clark Kent, Jay-Z recorded a demo tape. DJ Clark Kent began to use his relationship as an industry insider, as an A&R at East/West Atlantic, to secure Jay-Z a record deal. Kent, rejected at every turn, decided Jay-Z would benefit from having professional management and introduced Jay-Z to a young ambitious music executive name Damon Dash. Dash, who would take on the name "Dame" had successfully secured record deals for two groups, Original Flavor and Future Sound, while still in his teens. Although Dame was from Harlem and Jay-Z was from Brooklyn the two bonded on their passion for success and began to work toward securing Jay-Z a record deal.

Jay-Z was featured on Original Flavor's first single, "Can I Get Open?" As in the case with the Jaz-O record, he was featured in the video and mirroring the scenario with Kane, Jay-Z shined during performance. The result—no offers for a recording contract. They decided to take matters into their own hands and recorded a single and a video for "I Can Get With That." The video was shot on location in the Marcy Projects and directed by Abdul Malik Abbott. The video cost $5,000 and according to Abbott the funding budget came from a paper bag filled with small denomination bills. This led them to a single deal with Pay Day Records who financed a larger-budget video for a song titled, "In My Lifetime." This video featured Jay-Z and Dash on yachts in the Virgin Islands. They still failed to garner sales so they went back into the studio and began recording what would become Jay-Z's debut album, *Reasonable Doubt*.

Dame and Jay-Z took on a business partner, Kareem "Biggs" Burke and formed the independent record label, Roc-A-Fella Records. Tone Hooker, a member of Original Flavor, is credited with naming the label as a play off of the tycoon family the Rockefellers. The name had a twofold meaning, one of association with the prestige of the Rockefeller family, and the other addressing the aggressive way someone would get "rocked" if they posed a threat to the crew. The Roc-A-Fella team rented a low rent office space in downtown New York and began the work of building a record label from the ground up.

For Jay-Z, *Reasonable Doubt* served as a testimonial for a repenting drug dealer seeking meaning for his life as a sufferer and a contributor to human suffering. Roc-A-Fella secured a distribution deal for *Reasonable Doubt* through Priority Records based on the strength of its features. "Can't Knock the Hustle" featured the Queen of Hip-hop Soul Mary J. Blige, Bad Boy Records' new star. Notorious B. I. G. collaborated on "Brooklyn's Finest" and Def Jam's newest artist Foxy Brown shined on the Jaz-O (now big Jaz) produced "Ain't No Nigga." Producers on the album included the legendary DJ Premier, DJ Clark Kent, and Ski of Original Flavor. The lead single "Dead Presidents" featured a voice sample from Queensbridge rapper Nas on the chorus.

Reasonable Doubt was released on June 25, 1996. The album was a critical success as evident in the "4 mics" rating it received in the then, "Hip-hop Bible" the *Source* magazine. However sales didn't take off until "Ain't No Nigga" was included on the soundtrack to Eddie Murphy's *Nutty Professor*. Jay-Z and Foxy trade rhymes about a relationship between a man and his materialistic, ride-or-die chick over a sample of The Whole Darn Family's "Seven Minutes of Funk," and an interpolated chorus of the Four Tops, "Ain't No Woman (Like the One I've Got)." The video, directed by Malik Abdul Abbott, generated moderate rotation on BET and MTV and landed Roc-A-Fella a distribution deal with Def Jam recordings. The deal, brokered by Def Jam president Lyor Cohen, allowed Carter, Dash, and Burke to retain 50 percent ownership in Roc-A-Fella Records.

In the midst of his burgeoning rap career Jay-Z is dealt a blow by the tragic death of his friend and colleague Christopher Wallace popularly known as the Notorious B. I. G. Wallace was a rap star based off the success of his debut album *Ready to Die* and was gunned down in Los Angeles, California while promoting his sophomore effort *Life After Death* on March 9, 1996. This news shook the rap world and served as the final chess move in the bubbling East Coast/West Coast beef which cost the lives of many young men, the most popular being Wallace and **Tupac Shakur**. Jay-Z pushed through the tragedy and controversy and began to focus on his second album, *In My Lifetime, Vol. 1*. He appreciated the congratulatory remarks and critical accolades he received from his first effort but he wanted to sell more records. Jay-Z enlisted Bad Boy Entertainment founder and Wallace's mentor, Sean "Puff Daddy" Combs as executive producer for *In My Lifetime*. Jay-Z's Def Jam debut simultaneously earned him the record sales he desired while losing him much of his street credibility.

The album featured more pop-oriented production and features by R&B artists including Blackstreet and Babyface. In fact, the video for the lead single "Always Be My Sunshine" featured Jay-Z, Foxy Brown, and Babyface in a Hype Williams directed, Fisheye-lensed video. The video and song were not a fit and immediately caused many to question if the promise Jay-Z had shown on *Reasonable Doubt* was a fluke. Without the assistance of Def Jam, Roc-A-Fella went into damage control mode and shot a street film with an accompanying soundtrack titled, *The Streets is Watching*. The video and songs repositioned Jay-Z back as a streetwise hustler and won back the hearts of many who had criticisms of *In My Lifetime, Vol. 1*. The Roc-A-Fella relationship continued with Bad Boy Records as they were invited to tour with Puff Daddy and his Bad Boy affiliates. Due to a variety of unsatisfactory conditions, Roc-A-Fella's participation in the tour was short-lived but they left the tour with one of the most valuable pieces of music the young label would secure.

DJ Kid Capri serving as the host deejay for the Bad Boy tour played an instrumental produced by The 45 King every night of the tour. The song was a laid-back sample of piano chords and thick baseline with a vocal sample from the Broadway musical *Annie*. Dash and Jay-Z fell in love with the song, purchased it from The 45 King, and recorded "Hard Knock Life (Ghetto Anthem)." It served as the lead single to Jay-Z's third album *Vol. 2 ... Hard Knock Life* earning Jay-Z his first number-one Billboard chart position and the 1998 Grammy for Best Rap Album. The song went gold and the album was certified five times platinum having sold over five million copies in the United States. Jay-Z had solidified his position as a bona fide contender to fill the void left by the deaths of Tupac and the Notorious B. I. G. Jay-Z showed a sign of activism by not attending the Grammy Award ceremonies as a protest for the failure to nominate his friend and label mate DMX for an award.

In many ways, 1999 proved to be a pivotal year for Jay-Z and the Roc-A-Fella organization. Jay-Z followed up his success from *Vol. 2* by releasing *Vol. 3 ... Life and Times of S. Carter*, which sold well off the strength of singles, "Jigga My Nigga," "Do It Again," and "Big Pimpin" featuring Port Arthur, Texas natives UGK. The launch of Roc-A-Wear clothing also occurred in 1999. By paying attention to their concert artists, Dash, Burke, and Jay-Z recognized the impact they had on popular fashion trends. They wanted a piece of the action and began to approach fashion companies they believed benefited from Jay-Z's inadvertent promotion of their brand. As with their previous efforts at attempting to secure a record deal, the door was shut on them in fashion as well. In an unorthodox attempt to kick-off their own clothing line, they purchased three sewing machines and enlisted a team of people to begin to manufacture apparel they would wear and promote. Eventually they became aware of the limits of this approach and sought counsel from Def Jam and Phat Farm founder Russell Simmons who assisted them in making the right connections within the fashion industry. The apparel company took off and as of 2009 did $700 million in sales globally.

The street ethos caught up to Jay-Z in 1999. He was accused of stabbing music executive Lance "Un" Rivera at an album release party in New York. The incident centered around Rivera's apparent bootlegging of Jay-Z's music. Initially, Jay-Z plead not guilty and claimed to have eyewitnesses and videotape surveillance as proof. After the grand jury came back with an indictment, he plead down to a misdemeanor charge and received three years probation. The incident was apparently sobering for Jay-Z as he saw how quickly he could "lose it all."

Roc-A-Fella Records next project was slated to be a compilation showcasing the label's roster of talent titled *The Dynasty: Roc La Familia*. Although it contained a host of features from Roc-A-Fella artist Beanie Sigel, Memphis Bleek and Freeway, it became Jay-Z's fifth studio album. The album's lead single, "I Just Want to Love You (Give it 2 Me)," was an up-tempo club track produced by the Neptunes and featured Pharell Williams singing the hook. Commercially and critically the album was a success. In a bit of foreshadowing, *The Dynasty* was the first time Jay-Z would work with up and coming producers Justin "Just Blaze" Smith and Kanye West. Their demonstration on the *Dynasty* project earned them in-house producer status for the Roc-A-Fella label. The combination of Carter, Smith, and West would be responsible for a plethora of hit records for years to come.

Before the September 11, 2001 release of his sixth studio album, *The Blueprint*, Jay-Z found himself in an old-fashion rap music battle through a variety of verses on multiple songs aimed at Queensbridge rap duo Mobb Deep. The Mobb Deep "battle" manifested itself into a Kanye West-produced song called "The Takeover." The song not only targeted Mobb Deep, it included a verse aimed at Nasir "Nas" Jones, another heir to the throne, left by the deaths of Tupac and B. I. G., who had yet to have the commercial success of Jay-Z. Jones initially reported that he would not respond to the record. On his 2001 release *Stillmatic*, Jones responded with one of the most famous "diss" tracks in rap history, "Ether." The song was the undisputed knockout blow in the feud and helped to reestablish Jones as a viable recording artist. Most importantly, the situation set up one of rap music's finest moments as the two reconciled in 2005 at Jay-Z's *I Declare War* concert in New York City where the two united on stage and performed Jay-Z's first single "Dead Presidents" with Jones on the chorus.

Jay-Z released the highly successful The Blueprint 2: The Gift and the Curse in 2002. He began working on what was marketed as his last solo album, *The Black Album*, in 2003. He visually documented the entire process of beat selection, song composition, and recording to be used for the production of a film, *Fade to Black*. The entire process was to crescendo into his final concert at Madison Square Garden November 25, 2003, a week after the album's release. The album included hits such as "Change Clothes," "Dirt Off My Shoulder," and the Rick Rubin produced "99 Problems." One of the most revealing moments on the album is the song "Moment of Clarity" where he addresses issues ranging from his father's absence to "dumbing down" his lyrics in an effort to garner record sales. After his "retirement" Jay-Z never stopped recording and went into the studio and produced a mash up album *Collision Course* with California rock band Linkin Park. The album won a Grammy and added to Jay-Z's growing list of platinum albums.

Apparently while Jay-Z, the artist, rode off into the sunset, Shawn Carter, the executive, arrived ready to shake up the industry. His career as an executive began as he dissolved his long-standing partnership with Dash and Burke. Neither side has offered a clear concise explanation for the split and it caused turmoil within the Roc-A-Fella family as artists felt they had to choose between Jay-Z and Dash. Kanye West had begun a breakout career outside of producing with his debut release *College Dropout* (2004) and was determined to show loyalty to both Jay-Z and Dash before ultimately opting to stay with Jay-Z. Dash and Biggs's interest in their joint ventures including Roc-A-Fella Records, Roc-A-Wear Apparel, and Roc-A-Fella Films were bought out officially ending both the personal and business relationships among the parties.

L. A. Reid, president of the Island Def Jam Music Group (IDJMG), offered Jay-Z the position of president and CEO of Def Jam/Roc-A-Fella once all parties sold their interest to Def Jam, which he accepted. Jay-Z's tenure as president of Def Jam, which he dubbed "The Carter Administration" lasted three years and was filled with praise and criticism. Under Jay-Z's leadership Def Jam launched the careers of future stars Rihanna, Ne-Yo, and Young Jeezy. Kanye West continued to exceed everyone's expectations as he released *Late Registration* (2005) and *Graduation* (2007). Jay-Z admitted in an interview that he had initially only agreed to offer West a recording contract to keep the production within the Roc-A-Fella family, he had no idea West would grow into an international superstar.

As Jay-Z began to consider a return to the recording booth, veteran emcee and the first artist signed to Def Jam, LL Cool J, began to publicly criticize Jay-Z. LL Cool J saw Jay-Z's role as both an artist and executive as an inherit conflict of interest and cited this as one of the reasons his *Todd Smith* (2006) album undersold his previous efforts. Nevertheless, Jay-Z continued working on his new project *Kingdom Come* (2006). The project used cross marketing most notably with Budweiser as segments from the lead single "Show Me What You Got" were used in a Budweiser advertisement. Jay-Z recorded *American Gangster* his last album for Def Jam after having a preview screening of the Ridley Scott film of the same name starring **Denzel Washington**. The album was not a soundtrack but was inspired by the film and was released on November 6, 2007.

Live Nation, a live events company, began to offer contracts to recording artists with controlling interests in their merchandising and Web sites. In April 2008, Jay-Z inked a $152 million deal as he formed his new label, Roc Nation. Roc Nation serves as both a record label and an artist management firm. Coming full circle, Jay-Z released his *Blueprint 3* album on Roc Nation and had it distributed by Atlantic, now headed by Lyor Cohen who brought Roc-A-Fella to Def Jam. *Blueprint 3* was released on September 8, 2009 and debuted at number one on the billboard charts. This milestone placed Jay-Z ahead of Elvis Presley as the record holder for the most number-one albums by a solo artist on the Billboard 200.

His influence on popular culture continues to expand. Jay-Z invested $4.5 million for a minority ownership in the New Jersey Nets and has planned to move the team to his home borough of Brooklyn. In 2007 he sold the rights of the Roc-A-Wear brand to Iconix Brand Group for $204 million while maintaining his ownership stake and overseeing marketing and brand development.

He has partnered with former record executive Steve Stoute to form Translation Advertising, specializing in helping marketers reach multicultural consumers. His upscale sports bars, 40/40 Club, have locations in New York and Atlantic City with plans to expand to Tokyo and Singapore. Venturing into real estate, he has formed a company J Hotels and has purchased a $66 million dollar parcel of land in Chelsea, New York with plans to develop a high rise on the property.

His status as a pop icon has not gone unrecognized by world leaders. In 2006, he met with UN Secretary General Kofi Annan to raise awareness about the global water shortage crisis. He partnered with MTV to film a documentary *Diary of Jay-Z: Water for Life* about the crisis while he toured Africa that aired in November of 2006. In 2005, he teamed with Sean "P-Diddy" Combs to contributed $1 million to the American Red Cross to assist with Hurricane Katrina relief effort. In 2008 Mayor Michael Bloomberg enlisted Jay-Z to kick off Summer Streets, an initiative aimed at providing positive recreational opportunities for New York youth. He also provides scholarships to students through his Shawn Carter Scholarship Fund. He and his wife, Beyoncé publicly supported the presidential campaign of Barack Obama and were guests of the Obama family for the inauguration.

Jay-Z has navigated the gritty streets of "do or die" Bed-Stuy and the quarterly earnings-focused corporate boardrooms to stand as an example of success in both areas. He has participated in some of the petty fights inherit with the rap world and emerged as a shining example of how to resolve conflict constructively, as demonstrated by his truce with Jones. His lyrics have evolved from detailing the triumphs and pitfalls of street hustlers to challenging young people to live their dreams.

He is unassuming in his presence so his power sneaks up on even the most guarded of critics. While promoting his *Blueprint 3* album in 2009, he did an interview with **Oprah Winfrey** for her *O* magazine and her television show. Jay-Z took Oprah to the Marcy housing projects he grew up in. She challenged him on his use of derogatory language and miscegenation in his music. They engaged in a friendly debate for a few minutes and agreed to disagree. By the end of the television show he was teaching Oprah how to freestyle rap. Jay-Z's ability to enter into a situation an underdog and not only survive but prevail and win over his harshest critics places him into the stratosphere of icon.

Adam P. Boyd
University of California, Los Angeles

FURTHER READING

Chang, Jeff. *Can't Stop, Won't Stop: A History of the Hip-Hop Generation*. New York: St. Martin's Press, 2005.

Dee, Kool Mo. *There's God on the Mic: The True 50 Greatest MC's*. New York: Thunder's Mouth Press, 2003.

Def Jam.com: http://www.islanddefjam.com/artist/bio.aspx?artistID=7304.

Driven: Jay-Z. The Rise and Rise of Jay-Z, VH-1, 2003.

Fade to Black. Dir. Patrick Paulson and Michael John Warren. Perf. Jay-Z, Sean "P. Diddy" Combs, Damon Dash, Rick Rubin, Kanye West, Common, Afeni Shakur, Voletta Wallace, and Pharrell Williams. DVD. Paramount, 2005.

Kitwana, Bakari. *Why White Kids Love Hip Hop: Wangstas, Wiggers, Wannabes, and the New Reality of Race in America*. New York: BasicCivitas Books, 2005.

Earvin "Magic" Johnson (1959–)

Earvin "Magic" Johnson remains in the minds of many the epitome of basketball athleticism with his style, flair, and smile. Over the years, he built upon his impressive resume as a player by reaching out into other endeavors, sometimes by choice, sometimes by fate. As a basketball player he was perhaps best known for his ability to raise the level of his teammates' play; in his business and charitable activities he has sought to improve opportunities for people. Many people attribute the growth of the National Basketball Association (NBA) to the renewed interest that he, along with Larry Bird and **Michael Jordan**, brought to the game. He remains an iconic figure in the world of professional sports, and now he thoughtfully employs the opportunities offered by his celebrity.

Born August 14, 1959, in Lansing, Michigan, Earvin Effay Johnson, Jr. was the fourth of seven children (his parents had three children prior to their marriage). Earvin Sr., his father, worked in the local General Motors plant, and augmented the family income with second jobs, including pumping gas and collecting trash. His mother, Christine, supplemented the family income as a school custodian and working in a cafeteria. They had migrated to Michigan from the South, and occasionally the family took trips to Mississippi, where the elder Johnson described the world of Jim Crow segregation. His parents reminded Johnson that race relations, while far from ideal, had evolved since their childhoods. As a fifth-grader, Johnson became the favorite of his teacher, Greta Dart, who with her husband Jim, looked after Johnson: as a result, Johnson began feeling comfortable around white people.

The Johnson household was managed by parents who believed in hard work and discipline as essential to raising a family with love. Johnson absorbed the lessons. He did chores to earn money, including cleaning out the offices of two of Lansing's more successful black businessmen: he dreamed of one day having an office and a lifestyle just like theirs. Although he adored his mother, he found her embrace of the Seventh-Day Adventist Church entailed too stifling a lifestyle, and remained a Baptist with his father. Father worked with son on playing one-on-one basketball, with the father playing hard, fouling his son, never letting up, as he urged him to develop a complete game.

From an early age, Johnson loved basketball. He adored his hometown Detroit Pistons, and could not get enough opportunities to play. By the time he entered high school, his skill was evident. Observers noted that he played the game with a certain flair and charismatic style. At Everett High School, his stellar play earned him the nickname of "Magic," when sportswriter Fred Stabley, Jr. recounted a performance where the teen scored 36 points, grabbed 16 rebounds, and dished out 16 assists. In his junior year, Johnson scored 54 points against Sexton High School, a then-record for Lansing schools. He led Everett to the Class A state championship in his senior year with a record of 27–1, averaging just under 29 points and 17 rebounds per game.

Entering Michigan State University in 1978, Johnson impressed observers. Coach Jud Heathcote noted that the new team member's playmaking skills helped his fellow players improve their games. Michigan State claimed the

Big Ten conference title and finished the year with a 25–5 record. Johnson won All-American honors in his sophomore year as he spearheaded the Spartans' drive to a National Collegiate Athletic Association (NCAA) championship. In the Finals Michigan State faced upstart Indiana State, led by top scorer and playmaker Larry Bird. The highly anticipated match drew a record number of television viewers. Michigan State claimed a 75–64 victory, with Johnson winning Final Four MVP honors. It was a foregone conclusion that he would turn pro at the season's end.

The Los Angeles Lakers chose Johnson first overall in the 1979 NBA draft. It was Lakers' owner Jack Kent Cooke's last major decision before selling the team to Dr. Jerry Buss. Johnson's acquisition proved essential in restoring the Lakers to the ranks of the NBA's elite franchises. The restoration had already involved several years of rebuilding, commencing with the acquisition of center Kareem Abdul-Jabbar in 1975. The rookie brought his trademark enthusiasm to professional basketball, beginning with his first game, where he was so excited driving to the hoop that he tripped over himself. Although Abdul-Jabbar tried to get him to curb his enthusiasm, Johnson's ebullience persisted throughout his rookie season.

Playing power forward with the additional skill set of a guard, Johnson quickly became a contributor. The Lakers won the Pacific Division and blew through the Western Conference playoffs to the Finals, where they confronted Julius Erving and the Philadelphia 76ers. After splitting the first four games, the Lakers took Game 5 due to a heroic performance from Abdul-Jabbar, who scored 40 points despite spraining an ankle. Up 3–2, the Lakers readied to travel to Philadelphia without their dominant center. Johnson boarded the plane, settled in the seat traditionally reserved for the absent Abdul-Jabbar, and announced, "Never fear, EJ is here" (Lazerby, 2005, 198). As game time approached, the rookie proposed that he start at center. What followed was astonishing. Johnson moved all over the court, playing like a man possessed. Scoring 42 points, gathering 15 rebounds, dishing out 7 assists, with 3 steals and a blocked shot, he led the Lakers to a 123–107 victory. The performance became the stuff of legend, including claims that he won the game "single-handedly," which neglected the contributions of his teammates. The decision to name Johnson the MVP of the Finals also seemed to overlook his teammates. Several people, including Abdul-Jabbar and even Johnson, thought this honor should have gone instead to the sidelined center. Still, it was a wonderful beginning for the rookie.

Johnson's second year proved far more trying. He missed much of the regular season due to a knee injury, and the Lakers were ousted in the first round of the playoffs. During the summer of 1981, however, Johnson again made news when the Lakers signed him to a 25-year personal services contract for 25 million dollars, a contract far more astonishing for its length than for the dollars involved. Fully recovered from his injury, Johnson stormed back in the 1981–1982 season, as did the Lakers. Coach Paul Westhead attempted to install a half-court offense featuring Abdul-Jabbar, replacing the fast-breaking attack under which Johnson had flourished. Dissatisfied, Johnson finally demanded to be traded: instead, Buss replaced Westhead with assistant coach Pat Riley. Johnson celebrated Riley's hiring by assuring reporters that it was "show time" again. Although Johnson was unpopular with fans for forcing the issue with Westhead, their resentment soon faded as the Lakers rolled through the season and the playoffs, beating Philadelphia once more in the Finals with Johnson securing his second playoff MVP award.

Turnabout proved foul play for the Lakers in 1982–1983. Once more they tore through the regular season and the Western Conference playoffs: this time, however, it was Philadelphia who prevailed in a stunning four-game sweep. Johnson's magic took a temporary tumble. The following season, the Lakers reached the Finals again: it was a rematch of the 1979 NCAA tournament game pitting Johnson against Larry Bird, but this time it pitted Johnson's Lakers against Bird's Celtics. Given the fine players on both teams, too much was made of the Bird-Johnson rivalry, but it proved to be marketing magic for the NBA. Once more the Lakers marched through the schedule and made their way through the playoffs: this time the Celtics, led by season MVP Bird, responded in kind, and at last the dream was a reality. In a hard-fought seven-game series, the Celtics prevailed and Bird was named Finals MVP. For Johnson, the series was a disaster, as his poor play contributed to several Boston victories. Sensitive to the criticism, he vowed to recommit himself to the game. The results became evident the following year. Once more the Lakers met the Celtics in the Finals, and this time, at long last, it was the Lakers' turn to beat Boston, with the clinching game taking place at Boston Garden. It marked the fourth straight year Johnson played in the Finals.

In retrospect, these two Lakers-Celtics Finals were key to the development of the NBA. The league struggled in the later 1970s. The absorption of several teams from the competing American Basketball Association did nothing to spark fan interest. Television ratings were so bad that games were regularly aired on a tape-delayed basis, and tinkering with the schedule did not improve matters. It was not until Bird and Johnson faced each other for the first time in the 1984 Finals that ratings really improved. Moreover, CBS, which televised the NBA nationally, began to promote telecasts as clashes between stars as well as teams. In such an arena Johnson was sure to draw his share of attention.

Johnson had been linked with Larry Bird ever since they played each other in the 1979 NCAA championship game. During that season, it had been Bird and his upstart Indiana State team, not Johnson's Michigan State squad, that had attracted public interest and contributed to the large viewership for the 1979 Final Four tournament. The 1979 championship game offered Johnson a chance to perform in front of a large audience. Over the next four years, while Johnson's teams won more games, Bird received more attention, despite winning only one championship. Perhaps this was due to an East Coast bias in media coverage, including television's preference to broadcast games played in the eastern and central time zones. Johnson's popularity also suffered due to the reputation he gained as a selfish and spoiled superstar in the aftermath of the Westhead firing. Finally, two other issues worked in Bird's favor: he played for the legendary Boston Celtics and he was white. Some observers even called him "the great white hope," making explicit the racial reason for his popularity.

The media's comparisons of Bird and Johnson emphasized contrasting styles of play. Reporters portrayed Bird as a hard-working, team-oriented rural boy while they described Johnson as a flashy Hollywood star with his razzle-dazzle play and effervescent smile. In truth, their playing styles were more alike than different, as passing was key to their games. Yet Bird's passes, sometimes delivered with a great deal of flair, were never described with the "Showtime" imagery associated with Johnson's no-look deliveries. The Celtics were presented in the press as East Coast, workmanlike, and unselfish team players. Many of the Celtics players were white, although the team had their share of African-American players, including center Robert Parish and guard Dennis Johnson. In contrast, the Lakers were portrayed in the media as West Coast celebrities whose "Showtime" label bespoke basketball as entertainment and individual performances from a number of African American players. The play of Kurt Rambis, a white player on the Lakers team, only cemented this racialized conception. Rambis took the court complete with black-rimmed glasses, emphasizing his gawkiness and the contrast in styles supposedly delineated by race. Along with the all-too-real rivalry between Bird and Johnson, these artificial contrasts helped propel the NBA toward widespread popularity. The stereotypes both concealed and revealed realities that no one really wanted to discuss. The Bird/Johnson contrast could only add to the rivalry between the two men by forcing it to carry a certain amount of societal baggage.

> That first game, I was so excited and so nervous that I ran out of the court leading
> my team out.   —Magic Johnson

The NBA was not the only institution to emphasize the rivalry between the players. Basketball sneaker manufacturer Converse played upon the Bird/Johnson contrast in a 1984 commercial. It opened with Bird practicing alone on a court near his rural hometown of French Lick, Indiana. Suddenly a limousine pulls up. Johnson emerges in uniform and challenges Bird to play one-on-one. The irony of the commercial became richer than the portrayal of two styles that exploited their differences, for during production Bird and Johnson began developing a real friendship. Yet the commercial reaffirmed the rivalry and the stereotypes upon which it was based. The comparison was distorting. Johnson implied as much in a 1984 interview in reflecting on how he had adjusted to life in Los Angeles, reminding a reporter that he was at heart a Midwestern kid who liked the outdoors, picnics, and fishing, the very rural activities associated with Bird. He explained that to some extent "Magic" was an on-court persona that did not reflect what Earvin Johnson was all about off the court. While "Magic" was an intense ballplayer who visibly enjoyed playing the game with a certain flamboyant style, Earvin was an easygoing, laid-back fellow who was something of a homebody, taking the occasional walk or going to the movies.

Friendship with Bird in no sense dampened the rivalry: it may have enriched it. Johnson admitted that he kept an eye out for Bird's statistics and pushed himself to surpass his rival's standards. The rivalry had even larger implications for professional basketball. It proved essential to marketing the NBA on television, ending the days of delayed telecasts and buried contests. Just as both men needed each other to excel, the league needed them to compete to prosper.

The Lakers failed to defend their title in 1984–1985, with Boston reclaiming the crown against the Houston Rockets, who had defeated the Lakers in the Western Conference finals. This served as a prelude for the 1986–1987 season, which may well have been Johnson's finest performance at the height of his prowess. Averaging a career-high 23.9 points per game with a league-leading 12.2 assists per game, he took over from Abdul-Jabbar as the Lakers' dominant player. Johnson finally won his first regular season MVP, and was the first guard to do so since Oscar Robertson in 1964 (the always-competitive Johnson observed that Bird had already won the award three times). For the third time in four years, the Lakers battled in the Finals against Bird's Celtics, the defending champions. Up 2–1 in the fourth game of the series, played in Boston Garden, Johnson astonished fans, television viewers, and players. In the closing seconds of the game, with the Celtics up 106–105, he took the inbounds pass, moved toward the foul line, and released a sky hook— Abdul-Jabbar's trademark shot—and found nothing but net as he capped a furious fourth quarter comeback to allow the Lakers to take a commanding 3–1 lead in a series they eventually won in six games. Johnson secured his third playoff MVP with his performance: even Bird said that his rival was the best player he'd ever seen.

In many ways, the 1986–1987 season marked the beginning of a major shift in Johnson's career. He was now the brightest star in the Lakers' constellation. At long last his regular season play gained the recognition it deserved. It would also be the last time that the Lakers and Celtics met in the NBA Finals during the Johnson-Bird era. Johnson's fourth NBA championship bettered Bird's three rings. Before long it was evident that the Celtics were in decline, with the Detroit Pistons and the Chicago Bulls emerging as the dominant powers in the Eastern Conference. In 1987–1988, Johnson added his fifth ring as the Lakers, spurred on by Riley, became the first team to repeat as NBA champions since the Celtics had accomplished the task in 1968–1969. This time, however, the Pistons, Johnson's boyhood team, were the Lakers' opposition in the Finals. They put up quite a fight, extending the match to seven games. Given the Pistons' reputation as "Bad Boys," this time there was no doubt as to who the good guys were, at least in the eyes of many fans. Johnson fought through a bout with the flu that lasted over several games to claim another championship ring. It proved to be his last.

Riley spoke of a "three-peat" for the Lakers in 1988–1989, but it was not to be. Although Johnson garnered his second regular season MVP award, the Lakers were a year older and the Pistons a year better when the two teams clashed again in the Finals. Whatever doubt remained that it was the Pistons' year vanished when Johnson went down with a hamstring injury. The Lakers lost in four straight. The season proved to be Abdul-Jabbar's farewell to the league. If Abdul-Jabbar had never won a championship without world-class guards Oscar Robertson or Johnson, neither Robertson nor Johnson could win a championship without the big guy with the sky hook. This interdependence became evident the following season, when, despite yet another regular season MVP, Johnson found only frustration once more when the Phoenix Suns upset the Lakers. Matters did not improve the following season. Johnson led a players' rebellion that resulted in the ouster of Pat Riley as coach. That spring the Lakers, now directed by Mike Dunleavy, managed to reach the Finals once more, although they played the role of spectators as Michael Jordan and the Chicago Bulls clinched their first NBA championship. The torch had been passed to a new generation.

Johnson realized that things were changing, both on and off the court. For years there had been stories of his relationships with women, which usually were no more than one-night stands. In August 1991, however, he finally proposed to longtime girlfriend Earlitha "Cookie" Kelly. Within weeks Kelly learned she was pregnant. As he prepared for fatherhood and the opening of the 1991–1992 season, Johnson took a physical. The results of his exam came back on October 25, 1991. For weeks afterwards, no one could explain why he was not participating in preseason contests. Eventually the season began, and still Johnson was not playing. Why?

On November 7, 1991, the eve of what was to have been his thirteenth season in the NBA, Earvin Johnson announced that he had tested positive for HIV. As a result, he was retiring from basketball. The news stunned basketball fans. In a tribute to Johnson, fans voted him to the 1991–1992 All-Star team. This was the 12th time he had been named to the mid-season contest; only in 1981, when he was injured, was he not selected. Johnson chose to suit up, and in a startling performance, scored 25 points and was named the game's MVP, the second time he had been so honored. Ironically, 1991–1992 also proved to be Larry Bird's last year in the NBA.

Johnson was determined not to be sidelined by his condition. In the summer of 1992 he joined a spectacular lineup of players, all but one an NBA star, to form the U.S. men's basketball team. It was the first time professionals were allowed to participate in Olympic competition, and the results were predict-able. The United States won the gold medal in convincing fashion and the team became known as the Dream Team. Encouraged by his performance, Johnson considered making a comeback, but chose to stay retired after the conclusion of the preseason.

At first, Johnson tried to remain active in basketball with the Lakers. He replaced Randy Pfund as coach in April 1994, but he was unable to prevent the team from missing the playoffs and declined to continue as coach. However, he chose to make a comeback as a player for the 1995–1996 season. Playing power forward for the Lakers, Johnson demonstrated flashes of his former skill, although he averaged less than 30 minutes playing time per game. After the Lakers lost in the first round of the playoffs, he retired from the NBA again, this time for good. In years to come he would take to the court for short spurts, including two stints with two European teams that he also owned.

Johnson thus called it quits on a marvelous career. He had five champion-ship rings, three regular season MVP awards, and three playoff series MVP awards. Although his regular season totals were curtailed by his premature retirement, he still left his mark on the record book, with 11.2 assists per game during the regular season and a playoff career total of 2,346 assists. He was selected to appear in 12 All-Star games, and only his injury in 1980–1981 may have prevented a thirteenth selection. Both the Lakers and Michigan State honored him with statues outside their arenas in 2001. The Professional Basketball Writers Association established the Magic Johnson Award, given to the player who best combines on-court excellence with cooperation with the media. And yet it was Johnson's commitment to winning and his enjoy-ment of the contest that proved most memorable. He keeps in touch with the game, playing the occasional exhibition or appearing as a commentator on national television broadcasts.

> Everyone looks at me and still sees basketball, but I run my companies. People who don't know me may not believe that. But if they come in here and want to do some business, they'll find that out fast enough.   —Magic Johnson

Even as he slowly let go of basketball, Johnson moved on to other endeav-ors. For all the attention paid to his 1981 contract and subsequent negotiated basketball contracts, he made far more money in business since retirement from basketball. He was not always successful, however. Especially embar-rassing was "The Magic Hour," an ill-fated talk show that lasted two months. His efforts to educate other people about HIV and AIDS proved far more last-ing and important. During his retirement announcement, he declared that he intended to be a spokesman addressing and educating people on the issue. He made good on the pledge. He worked with Arsenio Hall to produce an AIDS awareness video called "Time Out." He also appeared with Linda Ellerbee on a television special for kids. At the same time, his very activity as a basketball player became something of an education experience. At first some NBA players were reluctant to come into contact with him, and questioned the wisdom of his comebacks. Other players met the challenge and the whispers head-on, hugging Johnson and showing their support, both in NBA contests and during the 1992 Olympics. Johnson established the Magic Johnson Foundation, a nonprofit charitable group that supports community organizations to help children and young people, as well as to educate children and adolescents about HIV/AIDS.

The Magic Johnson Foundation proved but a first step in Johnson's efforts to revitalize and assist challenged communities. Bearing the slogan "We are the communities we serve," Magic Johnson Enterprises became a way for Johnson to engage in numerous activities. The organization focused on education, development, opportunity, and uplift through entertainment. For example, Johnson Development Corporation sought to revitalize urban areas by constructing entertainment complexes, frequently anchored by a movie theater bearing Johnson's name, restaurants, and retail centers. Johnson also partnered with Canyon Capital Realty Advisors to establish the Canyon-Johnson Urban Fund to assist in funding revitalization efforts. He has also worked with AMC to build movie theaters, with Starbucks to open more than 100 coffee shops in a joint venture, with Burger King and T.G.I. Fridays to establish franchises in various urban areas, and with 24 Hour Fitness to construct fitness centers. He branched out into producing shows for television and has also invested in the music industry. He bought into a Los Angeles-based bank to help finance these varied ventures. Johnson is not simply a name or an absentee investor, however. He takes pride in his business acumen and is quick to point out that he personally runs his companies.

In all these activities, Earvin Johnson maintained what may be the signature theme of his basketball career; he makes those around him better. He sets up some to score on the court and prepares others to succeed in life. What may seem to some to be simply magic is in fact the result of hard work and deep thought. Johnson may have come to America's attention as a basketball player, but the imprint he made on American society transcends its foundation.

Brooks D. Simpson
Arizona State University

FURTHER READING

American Express Magic Johnson 2004 All Star Game Tribute: http://www.nba.com/allstar2004/magic_tribute/.

Bird, Larry, Earvin Johnson, and Jackie MacMullan. *When the Game Was Ours.* Boston: Houghton Mifflin Harcourt, 2009.

Johnson, Earvin, with William Novak. *My Life.* New York: Random House, 1992.

Lazenby, Roland. *The Show: The Inside Story of the Spectacular Los Angeles Lakers in the Words of Those Who Lived It.* New York: McGraw-Hill, 2005.

Magic Johnson Enterprises: http://magicjohnsonenterprises.com/.

National Basketball Association: http://www.nba.com.

NBA @ 50 interview: http://www.nba.com/history/players/magic_johnson_nba50_pt1.html; http://www.nba.com/history/players/magic_johnson_nba50_pt2.html.

Library of Congress

Jack Johnson
(1878–1946)

Jack Arthur Johnson, also nicknamed the "Galveston Giant," was the best heavyweight boxer of his generation and arguably in the history of boxing. He was the first African American heavyweight champion of the world, holding the title between 1908 and 1915. His boxing record was exceptional including 113 official fights with 79 wins (44 by knockout), 12 draws, and 8 losses.

Johnson was not only an African American sports icon but, perhaps more importantly, an American social icon who used boxing and fervent individualism to challenge white supremacy in the United States and beyond. He challenged the philosophy and practice of racial superiority of whites over non-whites as expressed through state sanctioned violence and the repressive control of America's sociopolitical, legal and economic system. He was one of the country's most well-traveled, wealthy, and successful citizens. Johnson's life and legacy unveiled the myth of white superiority and consequently threatened the foundational premise upon which white supremacy rested in the United States and beyond. He single-handedly forced whites throughout the world to confront their racist misconceptions of blacks and defied the character of race relations in the United States; Johnson is consequently one of the most famous, infamous, and influential figures of the twentieth century.

Jack Johnson was born in Galveston, Texas, to Henry and Tina (Tiny) Johnson on March 31, 1878, one year after the remaining Union troops withdrew from the former Confederacy. Johnson's parents were born into slavery: Henry was born on a plantation in Maryland or Virginia in 1838 and was known for amusing his masters as a feared bare-knuckle exhibition boxer, and Tiny was born in North or South Carolina. Although the exact year of her birth is not known, she was younger than Henry.

Henry Johnson served in the U.S. Army's 38th Colored Infantry as a civilian teamster servant and likely as a carpenter during the American Civil War. He later worked as a bar porter, school janitor, and a supervising school janitor in Galveston's East School District. Tiny Johnson was a housewife who washed clothes to supplement the family's income. Despite the fact that they were illiterate, Henry and Tiny worked together to ensure that all of their children had at least five years of schooling and lived as law-abiding Christians. Henry settled in Galveston in 1867, but it is unclear when Tiny did.

Johnson had eight siblings, but only five lived to adulthood. He had four sisters, including older sisters Lucy and Jennie, younger brother Henry, and adopted brother Charles. As the eldest brother, Johnson assisted his father with his janitorial duties and earned 10 cents and a new pair of red socks each week for riding along with and watching the milkman's horse-drawn wagon on Saturday mornings.

Galveston was the largest city in Texas and among the most prosperous in the country. It was a progressive city for blacks because there was gainful employment and longshoremen were paid the same as whites, $2 a day, which was significant in 1877, particularly for African Americans who were lawfully considered property only 10 years prior. The city was said to have a northern optimism that did not manifest in acute racial tension, although racial segregation and inequality were a fact of life. There were no laws prohibiting black and white children from playing together, though the city's school system was segregated. It was on the streets, alleys, and docks of Galveston where Johnson befriended white children, joined racially mixed gangs, and ate, fought, and slept at the homes of whites. Johnson's experiences led him to respect but not fear whites. From his childhood, Johnson had a naturally high opinion of himself that could not be destroyed by racism.

As a youth Johnson was often beaten up by neighborhood bullies and teased because he was physically frail and a bit cowardly. Johnson's older sisters often protected him from them until one day his mother threatened to beat him if he did not learn to defend himself, which led him to dismantle one of the older and tougher neighborhood bullies. Johnson's newfound fighting prowess gave him enormous confidence and quickly earned him a reputation as a hard-hitting tough guy.

Johnson dropped out of school after the sixth grade to work on Galveston's docks and later held various menial jobs as sweeper, porter, and baker's assistant. He then went to Dallas in search of employment, working at a racetrack caring for horses and then as an apprentice to a man named Walter Lewis, who owned a business that painted carriages. It was Lewis who sparked Johnson's interest in boxing by encouraging him to spar with friends for fun, which the young man took to with great ease. While Johnson appeared to be on course with his training in the profitable carriage painting trade, he sought more.

Johnson traveled to New York at the age of 16 and with less than a nickel in his pocket as a stowaway on a cotton steamer, in search of Steve Brodie, an Irish immigrant saloonkeeper who became famous in 1886 for claiming to have jumped off the newly constructed Brooklyn Bridge. Johnson was however discovered aboard by the ship's captain and forced to earn his fare by shoveling coal and peeling potatoes. When the steamer landed in New York, Johnson concocted a phony suicide plot to jump overboard referring to himself as a "worthless colored boy" with no family or friends, thereby appealing to the sentiments of white passengers, who filled his cap full of money. It was Johnson's natural inclination to adapt to adverse circumstances and manipulate black/white power relations that separated him from most blacks.

Johnson does not appear to have ever found Steve Brodie but his independence, drive, and confidence took him to Boston to track down Joe Walcott, a famous West Indian welterweight boxer also known as the "Barbados Demon." Johnson worked in a horse stable to support himself and eventually met Walcott. His interaction with Walcott and idolization of other black greats such as Isaac Murphy, a famous jockey, and Marshall "Major" Taylor, a nationally recognized bicycle racer, taught him that blacks could excel in sports irrespective of America's Jim Crow system.

Upon returning to Galveston in 1894, Johnson worked in a custodial capacity for a boxing gym. Here Johnson seemed to develop and refine his boxing skills.

By the age of 16 he was extremely well-built, standing six feet tall with a powerful frame, muscular arms and legs, and immense hand and foot speed. Johnson tested his prowess by challenging members of his gang and others. The critical incident that appears to have given Johnson the confidence to become a boxer is when he beat an older, bigger, and rugged man named Davie Pierson, who accused Johnson of snitching on him after the two were arrested for playing craps.

Johnson earned his living fighting on the docks and in the alleys, clubhouses, and private boxing clubs in the area from 1895 to 1898, ultimately entering the world of the Battle Royal. The Battle Royal was a blood sport where around four to eight or more blacks, sometimes blindfolded or tied together, would pulverize each another in a ring for the amusement of an all-white audience until the last man stood. The winner collected the change thrown into the ring by white onlookers. Johnson became the king of the Royal. His experiences as a black fighter in a racist and segregated society provided him with the "ring" experience that prepared him for national prominence. In March 1899, Johnson turned 21 and was keen to leave Galveston. After a brief marriage to Mary Austin, an African American childhood friend, Johnson's thirst to become a national prizefighter led him to Springfield, Illinois.

To many, Jack Johnson was the best boxer who has ever lived. Although, as previously noted, his boxing record comprises 113 official fights with 79 wins (44 by knockout), 12 draws, and 8 losses, it was the era in which he boxed, his flamboyant style, and raw power that allowed him to become a giant among men in the annals of history. Unlike the boxers of today who fight no more than 10 rounds, Johnson routinely fought 20.

Johnson's professional career began in 1899 and by 1915 he had conquered the boxing world. His stellar career, however, was almost derailed by early losses and personal tragedy. While traveling to Chicago, Johnson's train stopped in Springfield, where he disembarked in search of a meal. He was immediately spotted by Johnny Conner, a former fighter–turned-saloon owner and promoter, and offered room and board and an opportunity to win 50 dollars if he participated in a Battle Royal. Desperate for money, Johnson accepted and pummeled his opponents before a crowd including journalists and boxing promoters. His performance created a buzz and landed him a fight with John "Klondike" Haynes in Chicago.

> The search for the "white hope" not having been successful, prejudices ... piled up against me, and certain unfair persons, piqued because I was champion, decided if they could not get me one way they would another.
>
> —Jack Johnson

Although Johnson had fought for money since 1895, it was not until May 5, 1899, that he made his debut at the Howard Theatre in Chicago against Haynes that his professional career began. The Haynes bout was a far cry from fighting strongmen on the docks of Galveston. Johnson was defeated by a body blow in the fifth round and had his 10 dollar purse withheld for allegedly quitting the fight, forcing him to beg its promoters for money to buy food. Johnson had no job, income, or home in Chicago, making him homeless and desperate; he moved between the residences of friends and homeless shelters. After fighting in Indiana and skipping out on his landlord in Chicago, Johnson traveled to Pittsburgh, New York, and New Haven, sometimes fighting and other times working as a trainer. Johnson eventually returned to Galveston and reconnected with white childhood friend Leo Posner, who was matchmaker for the Galveston Athletic Club. Johnson solicited Posner to organize fights for him while he sought out a manager and spent his spare time moonlighting as president of the Twelfth Ward Republican Club in Galveston.

Posner organized a fight between Johnson and Bob White, an experienced heavyweight and top fighter in Texas, which ended in a 15-round decision for Johnson and earned him $100 and wide respect. Johnson quickly became regarded as one of the top black fighters in the region, at times fighting as many as two times per week. On May 1, 1900, he fought his first white opponent, an Australian fighter named Jim Scanlon. Johnson knocked him out in the seventh round and seemed to relish the opportunity to defy the baseless theory of white supremacy by knocking whites out in the ring.

Soon after the Scanlon fight, Johnson took on and defeated Jim McCormick and Horace Miles and battled Haynes to a 20-round draw. Johnson became stronger with each fight and developed into a gifted fighter; however, his career was put on hold when, in September 1900, Galveston was devastated by up until that point the United States' worst hurricane and natural disaster. The hurricane killed more than 8,000 people, displaced tens of thousands, and obliterated about 70 percent of Galveston, including the home of Henry and Tiny Johnson. Johnson was deeply affected by the hurricane and its impact on Galveston—he served as a part of a black crew who assisted in both the relief and clean-up efforts. The hurricane also created a heightened incentive for Johnson to generate money for his family.

He took on a promoter from Dallas by the name of "A. Busch," who organized a few fights for him in Tennessee. Johnson fought his old foe Klondike and eventually found his way into the ring with Joseph Bartlett Choynski, a boxing icon and the first Jewish American athlete to rise to international repute. Although by 1901 Choynski was past his prime, white promoters were keen to keep Johnson from rising in the ranks too quickly and believed Choynski was the right antidote to their problem. On February 25, 1901, Choynski and Johnson fought in Galveston, where Johnson was knocked out in the third round. Both men were arrested in the ring and taken to jail by five Texas Rangers for prizefighting or fighting for financial gain, which was a felony in Texas punishable by two years in state prison. Oddly enough, Choynski and Johnson were placed in the same jail cell for 24 days, during which time Choynski taught Johnson invaluable boxing lessons. On March 8, 1901, a Galveston grand jury chose not to indict the fighters and the County Sheriff immediately released and advised them to leave town before the State Attorney levied additional charges against them. Johnson went to Denver, Colorado and joined a boxing club named Ryan's Sand Creek House. He sparred with a string of fighters while in Denver.

Mary Austin visited and temporarily lived with Johnson in Denver and even accompanied him to California, then boxing capital of the country. He linked up with several fight managers and promoters and eventually settled with Frank Carillo, a hard-nosed Mexican American who dabbled in several professions including the saloon, racehorse, and dogfight businesses. Johnson temporarily settled in Bakersfield and chose to live in the white part of town against the community norm of segregated living. Johnson viewed himself above the color line. Johnson fought and lost a decision to Hank Griffen, son of a former slave, on November 4, 1901. Following this loss, Johnson took several menial jobs until he had a rematch with Griffen in Oakland that December resulting in a draw.

Johnson next fought Frank Childs to a draw in Chicago and proceeded to knockout several no-name fighters in New England, Texas, and California. It was not until he fought Jack Jeffries, that Johnson became recognized and even vilified by the United States. Jeffries was the younger brother of heavyweight champion Jim Jeffries, who was renowned for refusing to fight black boxers. Johnson's fight with Jack took place on May 16, 1902 in Los Angeles, and the prefight media blitz was replete with racial stereotypes and slurs. Johnson, who predicted he would knock Jeffries out 50 seconds after the fifth round began, was not fazed by the racial frenzy and appeared in the ring in pink ring wear. The packed building cheered for Jack Jeffries and hissed at Johnson. From the onset, Johnson toyed with Jeffries and just as he predicted knocked him out in the fifth only to roll him over and fan him in front of the white boxer's champion brother, who Johnson said that he could "lick" too. This victory over Jack Jeffries and several subsequent fights made Johnson a household name.

Johnson then fought George Gardner, another well-known white fighter, for 20 rounds in October 1902, barely squeezing out the decision. Carillo, Johnson's corner man, who allegedly placed a significant bet on the fight, brandished a gun and threatened to shoot his boxer if he lost. If this were not enough pressure, the media and white spectators castigated Johnson whenever he faced a white opponent. He nevertheless had a great deal of pride, a strong mind, and little fear of people, particularly white men. On December 5, 1902, he fought Fred Russell, a boxer trained by Jim Jeffries (who wanted revenge on Johnson for dismantling his brother), and known to be a dirty fighter. Russell ended the bout with Johnson by punching him in the genitals, causing Johnson to collapse in the ring. While whites wanted to see Johnson fall, many were offended by Russell's dirty tactics and rushed the ring only to be repulsed by police. Johnson was awarded the victory on a foul.

After firing Carillo for stealing funds, Johnson signed on with Tom McCarey, a bookmaker and poolroom owner from Los Angeles who immediately arranged for Johnson to fight Denver Ed Martin. Martin was called the black heavyweight champion because no white champion was willing to fight him. Johnson defeated Martin by decision in front of 4,000 spectators to become the black heavyweight champion of the world; however, Johnson would not be fulfilled until he defeated Jim Jeffries for the "white heavyweight championship." Jeffries used race as a justification to avoid Johnson. Although Johnson won a $1,260 purse in the Martin fight, which is equivalent to $25,000 today, he was eager for a big money fight that could yield $10,000 as he needed to fuel his flamboyant lifestyle, which included numerous cars, clothes, and women. For example, Johnson was one of the first Americans to own a Winton automobile manufactured by the Winton Motor Carriage Company. He was an avid driver.

After the Martin fight, Johnson became increasing frustrated that the top white boxers refused to fight him. Nevertheless, he continued to box hoping that one day his mastery in the ring would generate public outcry for a championship match with one of the "white greats." Between 1903 and October 1904, Johnson traveled and won half of his fights by knockout and the rest by decision. His October 27, 1903, fight with Sam McVey in Los Angeles earned him $2,796, which was his largest payday to date. The fight improved his image with the media and was the most profitable boxing event Los Angeles had ever hosted. The Johnson/McVey fights were so popular and profitable that their handlers scheduled another bout on April 24, 1904 in San Francisco, where Johnson jeeringly toyed with McVey and angered the crowd. Some fans were so incensed with Johnson's cat and mouse game with McVey that they flipped lit matches on his back, threatened his life with racial slurs, and attempted to assault him in the ring. Johnson responded by throwing the contents of his spit bucket at them and bolting out of the building. His masterful defeat of McVey caused the media to discuss his readiness for Jim Jeffries.

Johnson met and entered into relationships with two black prostitutes from Philadelphia, named Clara Kerr and Etta Reynolds, in the summer of 1903. While his relationship with Reynolds was of limited duration, he developed a long-term relationship with Kerr and lived happily with her for about two years. Johnson moved to Chicago with Kerr, whom he loved, and made Chicago his base of operations. However, when Kerr allegedly had an affair with William Bryant, one of Johnson's childhood friends, the boxer lost all faith in black women. Following his fallout with Kerr, Johnson suffered a loss in the ring, where race played a significant role in a decision against him.

Johnson fought Marvin Hart, a top white Kentuckian contender for the heavyweight title, in San Francisco on March 28, 1905. Hart was an avowed white supremacist; prior to the bout he openly hurled racial insults at Johnson, who responded by calling Hart a coward to his face. Although both men fought valiantly, Hart won the bout in a controversial decision by the fight's promoter and self-appointed judge, Alex Greggains. Jim Jeffries attended the bout and relished the outcome. After the Hart fight Johnson went on a rampage, fighting 12 more times in 1905, winning the majority of bouts by knockout and losing one match in November in the second round for a foul.

The racist commentary of sports writers, bloodthirsty spectators who reveled in the notion of a white boxer defeating Johnson, and the dirty tricks of opponents in these fights revealed that Johnson was at the epicenter of a sick society and sport. In his 1905 fight against Sandy Ferguson, Johnson punished and embarrassed the white hope so badly that the boxer kneed Johnson in the genitals three times to the roaring approval of his fans, causing him to collapse. When the referee declared Johnson the winner on a foul, Ferguson and his spectators started a riot, though Johnson managed to slip away. The Ferguson incident was reminiscent of Johnson's bout with Fred Russell; white men unable to defeat him in the ring sought to castrate him as slave owners did on plantations to keep their "black bucks" in check.

After his July 24, 1905, bout with Joe Grim, Johnson moved back to Los Angeles with Kerr, with whom he had reconciled. Johnson's life took yet another turn for the worse, however, when Kerr unexpectedly departed with what little money he possessed, she left Johnson broke in the heart and pocket book. Taken together, these events deeply affected Johnson, who swore never to settle with other black women and in the year that followed cleansed the heavyweight division while waiting feverishly for a bout with a white heavyweight champion. Johnson hired Sam Fitzpatrick as his new manager and even traveled to Australia with Alec McLean to show films of their fights and take on any contenders.

Johnson arrived in Australia on January 24, 1907, with great fanfare. He was an enigma to the Australians, who respected him as one of the United States' leading boxers but unsurprisingly shared the same racist attitudes toward blacks as white Americans. After Johnson defeated Peter Felix, Australia's "colored champion," for the colored heavyweight title of the world on February 19, he dismantled Australian Bill Lang, another white hopeful, before 20,000 spectators on March 4, 1907. Johnson made plans to leave Australia, but not before having an affair with a white Australian woman from a prominent family. He was also arrested for physically assaulting McLean, who had filed a breach of contract claim against Johnson for failing to pay him a debt. Johnson was forbidden from leaving Australia until the claim, which was decided in McLean's favor, was adjudicated that April.

Johnson returned to San Francisco in May, but had enormous difficulty finding anyone credible to fight, as the white heavyweight contenders stayed clear of him. Johnson managed to muster two fights in the first months of 1907 before getting what ultimately was one of his most strategic fights with ex-champion Bob Fitzsimmons, one of the hardest hitting heavyweights in history. Fitzsimmons fought Johnson on July 17, 1907 in Philadelphia, only to suffer an embarrassing knockout in the second round. Johnson's victory and public persona as a fearless and independent black man were celebrated by blacks all over the country and elevated the boxer to the status of an icon.

While Johnson fought nearly 30 more challengers over 12 years, his bouts with Tommy Burns in December 1908 and Jim Jeffries in July 1910 were the most important of his career and collectively the single greatest blow to white supremacy in the first half of the twentieth century. While Johnson's standing in the boxing world was at an all-time high, his fights with Burns and Jeffries would not occur for six more fights and another year and a half.

After defeating six other boxers in 1907 and 1908, Johnson and Fitzpatrick lobbied for a match with Burns, the Canadian world champion. Though they followed him to France to argue their case, Burns would not fight Johnson. Burns refused to fight a black boxer for less than $30,000 and berated Johnson with racial slurs in the press. An Australian promoter raised the capital for a fight between Burns and Johnson, however, offering $30,000 to the former and $5,000 to the latter. Johnson was not happy about receiving one-sixth of the amount of Burns but nonetheless agreed to fight in Sydney on December 26, 1908.

As Johnson entered the ring, 20,000 white Australians jeered at him in a seamless epithet of racial slurs; they did not come to see Johnson win but rather Burns thrash the black aspirant. Johnson was used to such abuse and walked down the aisle to the ring undaunted, cheery and shaking his head with confidence. When Burns entered the stadium he received a standing ovation from the crowd. He also earned roaring cheers when he refused to shake Johnson's hand before the fight. Johnson pulverized Burns once the fight began, sending him to the canvas in the first and second rounds. With a smile on his face, Johnson methodically talked to and beat Burns bloody round after round. He could have knocked out the champion in the first round but wanted to demonstrate his fighting skills to the world. Johnson made a mockery of Burns by speaking to the press while pummeling him, only to knock him down a third time in the seventh round. His clinical handling of Burns was a silent retort to the widely held view among whites that blacks were weak in the stomach, yellow under pressure, and unintelligent in the ring. Johnson was holding Burns up and beating him by the thirteenth round to the utter dismay of the crowd, who called for the police to stop the fight. Burns wanted to continue, though in the fourteenth round he was so badly beaten that the police stopped the fight and the referee declared Johnson the victor. Johnson's victory created a numbing quiet as the stunned audience left the stadium. After defeating Burns, Johnson visited the grave of Peter Jackson, the black Australian heavyweight champion who former white American world champion John L. Sullivan refused to fight, on racial grounds, for the world heavyweight championship that Johnson now held.

Johnson's victory sent shock waves of hope and pride into blacks in the United States and beyond and acute fear into white Australians and their Anglo-Saxon brethren in the United States. Many commentators responded with praise for the legal constraints on non-white immigration to Australia and *de jure* segregation in the United States. Johnson's triumph over Burns caused some sportswriters to wish that there had never been a Slave Trade and that Johnson had remained in the trees of Africa. Even though Johnson was an American, white Americans were indifferent to his world championship victory and had preferred that the white Canadian defeat him. They feared the new champion's victory would empower and embolden blacks with racial pride: an unacceptable proposition given the United States' racial caste system. In contrast, black America reveled in Johnson's victory, making him the most famous and respected athlete in that community.

After his fight with Burns, Johnson and his girlfriend Hattie McClay traveled to Vancouver, British Columbia, where the boxer was prohibited from staying in white-only hotels, to fight Victor McLaglen. He defeated this boxer in the sixth round on March 10, 1909. Johnson's flamboyant lifestyle, combined with his alleged "marriage" to McClay, engendered significant attention. Interracial marriage was an aberration in Canada and the United States; in fact, thousands of black men were lynched or murdered for even the insinuation of relations with white women. Notwithstanding, he didn't care about the social status quo and continued to publicly enjoy the company of other white women, such as Belle Schreiber, after parting ways with McClay. When Johnson defeated a string of boxers in 1909, the media pressure on Jeffries was too great and purse too big to allow race to continue to serve as a cloak of avoidance.

Shortly thereafter Johnson fired Fitzpatrick and hired George Little, a Chicagoan businessman who ran a brothel among other enterprises, to be his new manager. Johnson lived lavishly, spending money on his women companions such as McClay, who reappeared, Schreiber, and another prostitute named Etta Terry Duryea. Even Kerr reappeared, claiming to be his wife, and sued Johnson for $406 she was allegedly owed. Finally, after years of ducking Johnson, Jeffries agreed to fight him. The fighters met on October 29, 1909 at New York's Albany Hotel, negotiated terms, and gave promoters until November 30 to submit their bids. George Lewis "Tex" Rickard, a successful businessman and casino owner, approached Johnson offering a $101,000 purse, which was the biggest offer in boxing history and worth nearly two million dollars today, as well as two-thirds of the film rights to be split between the boxers. Rickard partnered with another promoter named Jack Gleason to avoid controversy after learning that Jeffries had secretly signed on with that promoter. Johnson agreed without consulting Little, as did Jeffries through his manager Samuel Berger. Both men received a $10,000 advance and the fight was set for July 4, 1910.

In the months preceding the bout, Johnson and Jeffries traveled on the road touring with various vaudeville shows and other carnival tours, while Rickard dealt with the politics of finding a venue for the fight. It was supposed to take place in San Francisco, but California Governor J. N. Gillette barred it for alleged moral and political reasons. Rickard moved the fight to Reno with the blessings of Nevada Governor Denver S. Dickerson. The run-up to the fight was filled with excitement, rumors, racial tension, heartbreak, scandal, and violence, particularly for Johnson. Johnson created a love quadrangle with McClay, Schreiber, and Terry, resulting in feuds among the women. He also engaged in a violent skirmish with a taxi driver who refused him service, pulled a gun on Sam Langford for threatening him, beat Schreiber after a domestic dispute, and was arrested for beating a man in a bar who insulted him. For his part, Jeffries made a considerable sum on the road but grew weary from all of the hype surrounding the fight. The pressure of being the "Great White Hope" wore him down to the point where he wanted to quit touring; however, Jeffries readily accepted the role of the great white redeemer.

The contest between the so-called "colored heavyweight champion of the world," an interesting title given that Johnson had already defeated white champion Burns in Australia, and the "champion of champions" who had retired several years earlier, was the biggest news in the nation and people from around the world tuned in to hear the fight via radio broadcast. The country's racial division was reflected in blacks' support for Johnson and whites' support for Jeffries. Americans did not consider this an ordinary fight but rather a clash of the races: a test to determine whether white subjugation of blacks was a natural right or an arrangement of limited duration.

As Johnson walked into the ring for his fight with Jeffries, the majority of the nearly 30,000 spectators hissed and hurled racial slurs at him reminiscent of the Burns fight. Jeffries' entry into the stadium was met with the thunderous roar of nearly all those in attendance, who firmly expected him to dismantle Johnson. When the fight began, the boxers spent the first few minutes feeling one another out, and by the second round Johnson seems to have had his opponent's number. Johnson did a lot of talking and smiling while seeming to dominate Jeffries with uppercuts. The white boxer retaliated with insults, powerful body blows, and head shots, which by the fourth round had cut open Johnson's mouth. Nevertheless, Johnson incrementally wore Jeffries down in rounds 5 through 15 while the crowd became more incensed with the cavalier and masterful way Johnson dismantled the former white champion. By the middle of the 15th round, Jeffries was bloodied with a broken nose, swollen shut eyes, and other cuts. After Johnson knocked Jeffries down several times, white spectators began shouting racial epithets and demanding that Jeffries' corner not allow Johnson to knock out the white boxer. Soon after, Jeffries' camp threw in the towel, ending the fight. Rickard declared Johnson the winner.

> Always, a woman has swayed me—sometimes many have demanded my attention at the same moment.
>
> —Jack Johnson

Black Americans celebrated throughout the country and whites responded with ugly and pernicious violence. White citizens and police throughout the country openly spat on, beat, burned, lynched, and shot black Americans in an orgy of violence that resulted in the murder of at least 30 blacks with hundreds more severely wounded. The most detestable acts of violence occurred in Manhattan's San Juan Hill neighborhood—a warren of densely packed tenements in the West 60s—a mob set fire to a building occupied by blacks, then tried to block the doors and windows so no one could get out. A white passenger on a Houston streetcar slit a black man's throat because he dared to cheer for Johnson. When whites in Wheeling, West Virginia, came upon a Negro driving a handsome automobile, as Jack Johnson was now famous for doing, they dragged him out from behind the steering wheel and hanged him. Near Uvalada, Georgia, white riflemen opened fire on a black construction camp, killing three and wounding five.

Johnson's victory meant more to blacks than any since Emancipation; however, Johnson was aware that too much chest pumping would only exacerbate the violence and dissuaded blacks from doing so while at the same time cautioning whites not to be uncivilized. He attended celebration parties all over the country, but Chicago was where he had the biggest following. He deposited his $101,000 purse in the First Trust and Savings Bank in Chicago and bought new cars, clothes, and even shared some of his purse with his old friends in Galveston. Johnson was on top of the world, but soon the world would be on top of him.

The media characterized Johnson as a black villain throughout his career due to his "ethnic cleansing" of great "white hopes," his ability to shatter white America's machinations about black inferiority, and his fearless and cavalier attitude toward life, including his fancy for white women. After defeating Jeffries, Johnson became the most famous sportsman in the world. He achieved what he had always wanted: iconic status. However, it was also his win over Jeffries that spurred the wagons of white supremacy rolling. Johnson became the target of public and private discrimination. Nowhere was this more apparent than through the law. Fifteen states and the District of Columbia banned the distribution of the Johnson vs. Jeffries fight for fear that the imagery of a black man legally pummeling a white man would threaten America's segregated status quo. In response to the fight, Congress also banned the interstate transportation of fight films in 1912. Johnson's victory over Jeffries and fiercely independent and boastful character infuriated white American society. He was the world champion in the manliest of sports, bold and defiant of white authority and custom, and a role model for other blacks. Johnson's example scared whites in the United States and beyond.

While Johnson became a soft target of local police for speeding, even going to jail for 25 days in San Francisco as perhaps the first black man to be racially profiled while driving, his real troubles began after he badly beat Terry Duryea, his lover. For most Americans, black and white, it was bad enough that he publicly courted white women, but to beat one bloody, 55 years before Emmett Till was lynched for allegedly making an overture at a white woman, and then publicly marry her was too much for most white Americans to stomach. This was also the case in Britain, where Johnson traveled to fight British heavyweight Billy Mills in 1912. British Home Secretary Winston Churchill barred the bout, however, fearing that any interracial fight resulting in a loss by Mills could destabilize white rule in the colonies in the same way that racial violence ensued after the Jeffries bout.

Upon returning to the United States, Johnson fought Jim Flynn on July 4, 1912 in New Mexico and defeated the "white hope" in the ninth round after police stopped the bout. Soon after, he opened a saloon name Café de Champion on the South Side of Chicago, which was a major hit in the city. Johnson was the champion of the world and a prominent businessman. However, Johnson's life took a serious turn for the worse when Duryea, who was abused by Johnson and shunned by blacks and whites, committed suicide in September. Scrutiny of him heightened when, within a month of Duryea's death, he had an affair with 18-year-old white woman Lucille Cameron against the wishes of her mother. On October 18, 1912, Johnson was arrested and charged with the abduction of Cameron, but was thereafter released on bail to the displeasure of the crowds of whites who jeered for him to be lynched outside of the jail.

Johnson was charged for violating the 1910 Mann Act (also known as the White Slave Traffic Act), a federal act adopted to combat the sexual exploitation of white women, which made it a felony to "knowingly transport or cause to be transported, or aid or assist in obtaining transportation for, or in transporting, in interstate or foreign commerce, any woman or girl for the purpose of prostitution or debauchery or any other immoral purpose." Cameron refused to testify against Johnson, so the government was forced to drop its case. The two married soon after, to the utter dismay of Americans, particularly whites. Their marriage was condemned by local, state, and federal politicians and engendered venomous reactions from the Governors of New York, Pennsylvania, Ohio, and Georgia, among many others. Immediately, antimiscegenation laws were introduced in 10 of the 20 states that permitted interracial marriages, and not less than 21 such bills were introduced in Congress.

Humiliated by its inability to prosecute Johnson, the government aggressively investigated him and co-opted Belle Schreiber, who was scorned by Johnson years earlier, to testify against him. Her testimony enabled the government to obtain an indictment again Johnson for violating the Mann Act. He was charged with transporting Schreiber across state lines for sexual use, engaging her in prostitution and for sexual perversions or physical abuse, the latter of which was later dropped by the government. On May 7, 1913, the case went to trial in the U.S. District Court of Illinois and an all-white male jury found him guilty of the sexual use and prostitution charges. The judge sentenced Johnson to a $1,000 fine and one year and a day in prison. The U.S. Court of Appeals for the Seventh Circuit, however, took issue with the District Court's ruling, reversed the prostitution conviction, and remanded for re-sentencing the sexual use charge, though not before Johnson fled the country. Johnson and Cameron escaped to Paris through Canada, arriving there in June 1913.

Johnson spent seven years living as a fugitive and fighting in England, Paris, Spain, Mexico, and Cuba, among other places. During this period he fought 13 opponents, losing only one bout to Jess Willard in Havana on April 5, 1915. In February 1916, while in England, he was ordered to pay a $1,100 fine for slugging his manager and banned from England under the Alien Restriction Act. With exception to the United Kingdom, Johnson was generally treated well in Europe and traveled with vaudeville shows to make a living. World War I made the continent an inhospitable place for him, however, forcing him to move to Latin America. After his friend and business partner Mexican President Venustiano Carranza was assassinated in May 1920, Johnson was forced to leave the country. He returned to the United States on July 20, 1920, surrendering to federal marshals in California. He later reappeared in District Court in Chicago and was re-sentenced to one year in prison and sent to Leavenworth penitentiary in Kansas.

Johnson was released from prison in July 1921 and greeted as a hero by scores of blacks. Lucille divorced him in 1924 and he married a third white woman. He took on nine professional fights out of financial desperation over the next seven years, losing only two in 1928. Johnson lived out his life as a reluctant national and international hero to blacks all over the world, only to be killed on July 10, 1946, on U.S. Highway 1 near Raleigh, North Carolina, after crashing his Lincoln Zephyr on his way to New York to see **Joe Louis** and Billy Conn fight on July 19, 1946. He was 68 years old.

The boxer's relentless pursuit of excellence shattered and changed the world of sports and America's racist sociopolitical order. Johnson was a maverick revolutionary. He not only transformed the world of sports, particularly boxing, but also American society. He is not simply an African American sports icon; he was one of America's leading sports and social icons in the early twentieth century. No other athlete or social activist during his era or since has provoked the minds and stirred the social consciousness of people while simultaneously exemplifying mastery of a craft. He defied all odds to become the indisputable heavyweight champion of the world and publicly defy social casting. Johnson wore the clothes, drove the cars, dated and married the women, and knocked out the people inside and outside of the ring as he wanted.

Johnson's fearless brand of individualism, courage, and defiance of the United States' racist sports and sociopolitical orders were inimitable. He was an individual rights activist, which wittingly made him a civil rights pragmatist. He achieved what few in world history who faced systematic tyranny and violence could; he employed an a-political philosophy of nonviolence using the weapons of hard work, excellence, and individualism to combat, invalidate, enfeeble, and dismantle a vicious sociopolitical and legal order, in this case American white supremacy. Johnson did not allow America's social status quo to define him, rather, he redefined it.

Jeremy I. Levitt
Florida A&M University

FURTHER READING

Ardell, Jean Hastings. "Baseball Annies, Jack Johnson, and Kenesaw Mountain Landis: How Groupies Influenced the Lengthy Ban on Blacks in Organized Baseball." *Nine*, Spring 2005: 103.

Deardorff, Donald, II. "World Boxing Champion Jack Johnson, Contemptuous and Irritating, Taunted Whites." *St. Louis Journalism Review* 8, no. 3 (October 1995).

Evans, Art. "Joe Louis as a Key Functionary: White Reactions towards a Black Champion." *Journal of Black Studies* 16, no. 1 (September 1985): 95–111.

Gilmore, Al-Tony. "Jack Johnson and White Women: The National Impact." *Journal of Negro History* 58, no. 1 (January 1973): 18–38.

Johnson, Jack. *In the Ring and Out*. Chicago: National Sports Publishing Company, 1927.

Ward, Geoffrey. *Unforgivable Blackness: The Rise and Fall of Jack Johnson*. New York: W. W. Norton, 2004.

James Weldon Johnson (1871–1938)

James Weldon Johnson was a lyricist, a novelist, a lawyer, a principal, a diplomat, and the first black executive secretary of the National Association for the Advancement of Colored People (NAACP). Raised in Florida, Johnson graduated from Atlanta University in 1894. After becoming the first black to be admitted to the bar in Florida in 1897 and developing the first black high school in Jacksonville, Johnson and his brother Rosamond moved to New York City to pursue a musical career. They lived in the center of black bohemia at the turn of the twentieth century. After seven successful years, which saw several of their songs performed on Broadway and the adoption of their 1899 song "Lift Every Voice and Sing" as the Negro National Anthem, the brothers parted to pursue different careers. Johnson entered the diplomatic corps and was posted first to Venezuela in 1906 and then Nicaragua in 1909. During this period, he protected U.S. interests in Nicaragua, married Grace Nail, and wrote his first novel, *The Autobiography of an Ex-Colored Man*. Upon his return to the United States, he joined the NAACP, rising eventually to be the first black executive secretary in 1920. He died in 1938, five years after completing his autobiography, *Along This Way*.

Johnson's parents pursued a different migration course than many African Americans. They had never been slaves. His father, James Johnson, was born in Richmond, Virginia in 1830 and moved to New York as a young man, where he found a job as a head-waiter in luxury hotels. His mother, Helen Dillet, was born on the island of Nassau, in the Bahamas, to parents of mixed French and African heritage. Her family moved to New York City when she was just a child. Johnson and Dillet courted in New York, but when the Civil War started, Dillet's mother returned with her to the Bahamas. Johnson followed her to Nassau and they married in 1864. Johnson built a significant economic nest egg by buying land and continuing his position as head-waiter in hotels. When his finances were severely threatened by a hurricane and a post-war economic slump, he moved his family to Jacksonville, Florida, which was rumored to be the next big tourist destination.

In Florida, the Johnson couple built a secure middle-class home and welcomed two sons, James and Rosamond. That home's interior was filled with books and musical instruments. It was in a neighborhood of many different cultures. The boys learned Spanish and cigar smoking from Ricardo Rodriguez Ponce, a Cuban teenager who came to live with them to learn English. They visited Nassau and New York City as children, which gave them a wider experience of things than their Jacksonville peers. On one trip to New York, James Jr. realized that he was a born New Yorker, who loved cosmopolitanism.

The Johnson family encouraged the education of their children. James Jr. loved the different worlds that he dived into every time he opened a book, a love that never left him as he grew. The Johnsons also shielded their children from most racial realities and they lived in an integrated neighborhood. Jacksonville in the late reconstruction era was a pretty good town for blacks, because few Jim Crow barriers had been established. James Jr. believed that this sheltered upbringing, which protected him from either extreme fear or esteem for whites, was a large part of his later successes. He did not let racist ideas of himself become central to his psyche, as he saw others do.

Johnson went to Atlanta University first for high school and then for his undergraduate education. There he developed lifelong friendships. Among his friends, he started thinking and talking about the complexities of race in the United States in a rigorous way. He realized that for him, education was not meant to prepare him to be a governor (one of his childhood ambitions), but was rather preparation to become a responsible member of the race, who would work to make the world better by extending American democracy to black citizens. This realization came not from the curriculum of the school, which followed closely Yale's academic course, but rather from the atmosphere of the college. Students talked, wrote, debated, and orated about race. Every topic they approached—moral or intellectual—had race at the center.

One summer during his education, Johnson had to remain in Jacksonville during a quarantine and missed the beginning of the semester. Rather than returning in the middle of the term, he hired himself to Dr. Summers, a white physician in Jacksonville, who cemented Johnson's love of learning and travel. Johnson always remembered their relationship as a testimony to the possibility of interracial friendship. Almost immediately upon meeting him, Johnson was impressed with Summers for his culture. He was a literary man and wrote poems that were published locally. Johnson claimed that the relationship between the two of them was not employer to employee or white to black, but rather that of intellectual equals. His light duties gave Johnson ample time to explore the doctor's extensive library, which they would then discuss at length.

After graduating from Atlanta University in 1894, Johnson turned down a medical scholarship to Harvard University because he had had enough of being a student and returned to his elementary school as principal. He had last been there as a student seven years before. He soon decided to convert this school, Stanton elementary, into the first high school in the area for black students. He did this without the permission of the school board or superintendent, but simply convinced the eighth graders and their parents to return to school the next year and taught the class himself. The following year he informed the superintendent about what he had done and asked for an assistant to continue. The superintendent complied and Jacksonville had its first black high school.

After seven years in Georgia, Johnson had found Jacksonville very changed. Public segregation had increased and so African American society retreated into private spaces. One day the intensity of racism in the city came deathly close. A recent fire brought a light-skinned black woman into town to report on the story. She wanted to confirm some details with Johnson. After a long day, he wanted to get out of town and so suggested meeting at a public park that had recently been renovated. He had wanted to see the changes for quite some time and took the streetcar to the end of the line to get to the park. The other passengers slowly left the streetcar until Johnson was the only one. When the driver let him out, he saw Johnson confer with what appeared to be a white woman, but was in actually was the light-skinned reporter.

After seeing what he thought was an interracial liaison, the driver quickly rallied white members of the local militia, who returned to the park in a mob. They surrounded Johnson and began to beat him. He knew if he turned or tried to flee, they would have lynched him so he succumbed to the blows stoically, flinching as little as possible. A lieutenant pushed through the crowd and arrested Johnson. He carefully separated Johnson and the reporter from the mob, putting the two in a private car and sending the others home on the streetcar. Johnson appeared before a Major he knew well and liked, and explained that while the woman in front of him was white, she was not white in the cultural or legal laws of Florida. The man let him go with embarrassment. The journalist then spewed out all her anxiety, blaming him and all his forbearers for what had almost happened.

Johnson told only his brother, not his parents, about how closely he had come to being lynched. For months and years afterward he was tormented by thoughts of "those few frightful seconds, bloodthirsty men in khaki, with loaded rifles and fixed bayonets" (Johnson, *Along This Way*, 170). Throughout his suffering, he realized how strongly sexual desire and racism were bound together. Though racism manifested itself in many different ways, scratching down to the heart of the matter usually revealed an obsession with sex: whites jealousy or fear of black people's supposedly stronger sex drive, the need for white men to protect white women, and the lust white men held for black women.

That summer, Johnson left Florida with his brother, Rosamond, who had already begun to develop a successful music career in New York City. For a year, they had been working on a lyric opera. They entered the city during an exciting time for black bohemia, when many young artists filled the Tenderloin district of New York. At the Hotel Marshall, where they lived, they associated with vaudeville stars, musicians, gamblers, and theatrical stars. Together with Bob Cole, they formed the writing partnership of Cole and Johnson and began to write scores for Broadway shows. Soon, their songs were being performed in three or four different Broadway musicals, and published as sheet music (the most popular way to transmit music before the invention of the phonograph).

In February 1900, even before the brothers had left for New York, the Johnsons contributed a song to an elementary school celebration of Lincoln's birthday. A chorus of 500 school children sang "Lift Every Voice and Sing" before their community. The Johnson brothers enjoyed the performance, but gave little more thought to the song. The children and their parents did not forget, however. They continued to sing the song, and when the children grew up to be teachers, taught their students. Within 15 years, the song was sung throughout the nation and affectionately called the "Negro National Anthem." As such, it is still performed today.

The Negro National Anthem

Lift every voice and sing
Till earth and heaven ring,
Ring with the harmonies of Liberty;
Let our rejoicing rise
High as the listening skies,
Let it resound loud as the rolling sea.
Sing a song full of the faith that the dark past has taught us,
Sing a song full of the hope that the present has brought us,
Facing the rising sun of our new day begun
Let us march on till victory is won.

God of our weary years,
God of our silent tears,
Thou who has brought us thus far on the way;
Thou who has by Thy might
Led us into the light,
Keep us forever in the path, we pray.
Lest our feet stray from the places, our God, where we met Thee;
Shadowed beneath Thy hand,
May we forever stand.
True to our GOD,
True to our native land

Source: James Weldon Johnson, *The Autobiography of an Ex-Colored Man* (Boston: Sherman, French & Company, 1912), 97.

During Johnson and Cole's heights of success, the three traveled the country and the globe, seeing places such as San Francisco and Paris, France. In the French capital, Johnson experienced the freedom that many black people felt there over the next century. He was free from all the fear of imminent harm, scorn, and condescension. He was free to be merely a man. In Paris, Bob and Rosamond began performing a vaudeville act that they continued through a tour of the continent and London. When they returned home, they decided to take the act on the road and asked Johnson if he wanted to be their business manager. He did not want to travel throughout the country on Jim Crow railways and arrive every night unsure of their welcome or what accommodations would be available to blacks. So they all parted ways.

While in New York, Johnson had socialized with Republican Party members. One of these associates, Charles W. Anderson, was New York's leading black politician and a colleague of **Booker T. Washington**, the most powerful black man in the country at the time. Anderson directed Johnson into a

Foreign Service position established through Washington's patronage. Though reluctant to leave a city that had been so good to him, Johnson assumed that with his Spanish he would be posted to an exotic South American locale and would finally have time to write. He had long yearned to put pen to paper in a serious way. He was sent first to Venezuela in 1906, a place he loved. Living in a large, well-appointed house with several servants, he represented France in the area as well as the United States. In addition to his consular duties, he found time to write his first novel, *The Autobiography of an Ex-Colored Man*. He published this anonymously at first, which meant that many people thought that it was indeed an autobiography, rather than a novel. When the Harlem Renaissance began to focus greater attention on novels by and about black people in the 1920s, Johnson's book was republished under his own name and became an important success.

In the novel, Johnson explores an alternative life. The protagonist chooses the opposite answer to the question Johnson often got from white men—the snide what wouldn't you give to be a white man. When asked this in a barbershop in Florida, Johnson had replied that he would lose too much to change into a white man like the questioner. But in the novel, the protagonist is light skinned enough to choose which race to affiliate with. Though his skin color and birthplace are different from Johnson himself, the protagonist ends up in many situations Johnson knew about from personal experience—a cigar factory in Jacksonville Florida (though he had never worked in one, his friends had), black gambling clubs in New York City, and the musical scene in Europe.

Ultimately, the narrator leaves his mentor in Europe, a white man patterned after Dr. Summers, to travel through the American South gathering inspiration from black folk for his own compositions. After witnessing a black man burned at the stake firsthand, the protagonist is filled with shame for being part of a race that was treated like that. He chooses to return to New York and remake his life as a white man. Unlike many African Americans who chose to pass into the white world, the protagonist had no family to leave behind, thus easing his way into that new life. Despite achieving business success and marriage to a beautiful white woman, the novel ends with the protagonist wondering whether he didn't sell his soul for a mess of porridge.

Though he could easily have stayed in beautiful Venezuela, Johnson feared becoming trapped in that one position for the rest of his life, so he applied for a promotion. He was transferred to Nicaragua and entered a wholly different setting. His job had been smooth and easy in Venezuela, but was tempestuous throughout his years in Nicaragua. He witnessed a coup of the Nicaraguan powers, backed by the U.S. government. Part of his job was to aid the U.S. side in this coup, something that earned him criticism in the future. At the same time, he married his New York beau, Grace Nail, a scion of a black Brooklyn family and brought her to Nicaragua. She suffered the deprivations and frequent bouts of violence with admirable calm, but Johnson began to look for a different position in South America, where she would be more comfortable and where he might continue to move up the professional ladder.

The political winds changed in 1912, however, and the Johnsons had to return to the United States. With the election of Democrat Woodrow Wilson, Johnson no longer had his Republican friends in power to reappoint him. Furthermore, Wilson, a Southerner indebted to the South for his election, dramatically reduced the number of African Americans in federal service and brought Jim Crow to the capital. Johnson then had to consider which of his many professions—writing, law, teaching, songwriting—to resume. He and Nail Johnson returned to New York. His wife's parents had followed the tide of African Americans to Harlem. Johnson tried to resume some of his songwriting, but missed the vibrancy of his partners; Bob Cole had committed suicide and his brother was then in London. He had lost the touch of Broadway and did not know what the popular forms were.

The editor of the *New York Age* was looking for a new person to take over the editorial page. Through the influence of his old friend Charles Anderson, the paper offered Johnson the position and he began a 10-year stint as an editorialist for that newspaper. Again, Johnson benefited from the strings Booker T. Washington could pull, without having to publicly ally himself with Washington. He also continued to devote time to literary writing. But he still felt adrift when in 1916, he received a letter from J. E. Spingarn, chairman of the NAACP, inviting him to the First Amenia Conference. **W. E. B. Du Bois**, editor of the NAACP's magazine *The Crisis*, had scribbled at the bottom a note, urging him to come.

The First World War in Europe and its domestic conversations in the United States had broken apart many of the fixed understandings of race. Blacks pointed out that the rhetoric about winning the war for democracy did not apply to them at home. In light of this, and Booker T. Washington's death a year previously, the NAACP leadership believed it was time to reassess the state of race relations. The NAACP had been founded in 1909 by a coalition of liberal whites and blacks determined to confront racial discrimination directly. A significant part of this organization was that white inheritors of the abolitionist spirit were working with African Americans, rather than paternalistically dictating their ideas to them.

Spingarn, a Jewish man and the chairman of the NAACP's board, invited more than 50 black and white leaders to his estate in upstate New York, just outside the village of Amenia. Du Bois's supporters and Washington's followers, as well as those who did not claim a formal affiliation, stayed in tents under the tall buttonwood trees. The calm fields of Amenia witnessed many hard feelings that had to be put to rest between these factions. By the end of the weekend, Washington's followers agreed that the best route forward was bluntly confronting racial realities through political activism. Du Bois' side recognized the special nature of the Southern situation and promised to heed Southerners' advice. As a group, those at Amenia recognized Du Bois as the preeminent African American intellectual. Over the weekend, the tall, cosmopolitan Johnson came to the attention of the NAACP leadership.

After he returned to the city, Johnson received an invitation from Spingarn to join the Association as the national organizer. Johnson was required to travel extensively, write, and organize, as well as tactfully walk a line between white and black supporters. Seventeen years later, he remembered the light of destiny that accompanied that letter. He realized that everything that he had ever done in his life, from being a principal to being a diplomat had prepared him for the NAACP. The organization at this point was still considered a radical one. Yet it was only radical in that it proclaimed rights, guaranteed in the constitution, for those individuals routinely denied them in practice and in law in the United States. The NAACP advocated a direct attack on every legal barrier, a daring method which left many blacks afraid of reprisal.

Johnson decided his first duty as field secretary would be to organize the South. By 1916, the NAACP was still a relatively small organization, with 68 branches in Northern and Western cities, but only 3 branches in Southern ones. Some of the Board members resisted a Southern campaign because they feared that gaining too many Southern members would temper the activist spirit of the organization. Johnson overcame their opposition and with the support of the majority of the board began a tour of the South, stopping in small and large towns holding gatherings in town halls and churches. He believed that the organization not only had fight discrimination, but it also had to awaken African Americans to their constitutional rights and motivate them to fight. No matter what whites did for African Americans, Johnson argued in each place he visited, the greatest work had to be accomplished by African Americans themselves. Two years later, every state in the South had NAACP branches; by 1919, there were 131 branches in the South out of 310 branches in the national association.

At the beginning of the 1920s, the NAACP board promoted Johnson to executive secretary of the organization. He, with his assistant Walter White, decided to devote a major part of his energy to fighting lynching. Johnson spent two years traveling back and forth to Washington DC to lobby for the Dyer Anti-Lynching Bill. Sponsored by Representative L. C. Dyer, the bill sought to create a federal punishment for participants of lynch mobs. Previously, when a lynch mob engaged in their own form of perverted justice, there had been no federal oversight to prosecute the murder. Local police rarely arrested the mob members. Johnson and the NAACP hoped by making lynching a federal crime that they could drastically curb the reality and fear of mob violence. When a representative from the South stood up in Congress and confidently explained that lynchings only ever occurred because a black man had raped a white woman, Johnson made sure that every representative had copies of NAACP literature on their desk the next morning. This literature proved that most lynchings had nothing to do with rape, but rather attempted to prevent prosperous blacks from attaining any more success. The bill passed the House in January 1922, but failed in the Senate because of Democratic filibustering.

Johnson's two years of intense publication did not go to waste. The publicity had been so widespread that Americans, and the rest of the world, began to understand the real causes behind lynchings and to condemn them. Deaths by lynchings began to decrease: in 1916 there had been 96 deaths at the hands of lynch mobs, but by 1926 there had been only 34. These numbers do not express, however, all the close calls that blacks experienced, including Johnson himself who had only barely escaped as a young professional. Following the mixed failure of the Dyer-Anti-Lynching bill, Johnson directed the NAACP through several other causes. He visited Haiti while it was dominated by U.S. troops. He led the continued expansion of the NAACP's local organizations. But perhaps most importantly, he led the NAACP in prosecuting instances of legal discrimination in the courts. By 1954, this became the NAACP's most famous area of interest, when its lawyers won the *Brown v. Board of Education* decision.

Throughout his time leading the NAACP, Johnson encouraged his own and others' artistic talents. Literature finally called Johnson away from his role as executive secretary of the NAACP. He had several projects in mind including a history of African Americans in New York (which became *Black Manhattan*), another book of poetry, and a novel. In 1931, he retired from the NAACP, and spent his days writing, traveling, and participating in organizations, albeit at a slower pace. In 1938, he was killed in a car accident.

Johnson's life was characterized by a tremendous level of diplomacy. He was able to walk between, and bring together, competing groups throughout his life. Perhaps he was able to do this so successfully because his own body contained so many different professions, interests, and pursuits and because he had met so many different people and cultures during his lifetime. Johnson was intent on creating equal opportunity. When others thought about the problems faced by African Americans in the United States, some thought about restitution for all the wrongs done, overthrowing the current political and economic system, or about segregating themselves in a separate state or returning to Africa. But Johnson focused on achieving equal opportunity for the millions of hungry and ambitious African Americans. This meant that whites' mental resistance to black success had to be changed, rather than the structural conditions of poverty and injustice. This was largely the philosophy embraced by Americans during the Civil Rights Movement. But the continued impoverishment and incarceration of large swaths of black Americans has proven that structural injustice must be confronted alongside racist attitudes. Despite this, establishing equal opportunity continues to be one of the strongest currents in U.S. political life.

James Weldon Johnson lived when most African Americans had no access to education or jobs. He succeeded in almost every profession he attempted, including that of principal, lyricist, poet, novelist, diplomat, lawyer, and executive secretary of the NAACP. In each situation, he used his quick facility with language and culture to turn strangers into friends and colleagues. He did not veil his strong opinions about the equality that African Americans were due, but rather successfully fought for those rights through disarming diplomacy and peacemaking.

Lauren L. Kientz
Michigan State University

FURTHER READING

Johnson, James Weldon. *Along This Way: The Autobiography of James Weldon Johnson*. New York: Da Capo Press, 2000.

Johnson, James Weldon. *The Autobiography of an Ex-Colored Man*. New York: Hill and Wang, 1960.

Levy, Eugene D. *God's Trombones: Seven Negro Sermons in Verse*. Viking Compass Edition. New York: The Viking Press, 1969.

Levy, Eugene D. *James Weldon Johnson, Black Leader, Black Voice*. Negro American Biographies and Autobiographies. Chicago: University of Chicago Press, 1973.

AP/Wide World Photos

Robert L. Johnson
(1946–)

Robert L. Johnson is co-founder of the Black Entertainment Television (BET) cable network and the first African American billionaire. Johnson rose to financial success by becoming an astute student of capitalism in the United States and marketing toward an often-ignored group of consumers, African Americans. He is an icon of ingenuity to black Americans who derive a sense of empowerment from BET. Moreover, Johnson is the epitome of success in the business world, as he exceeds corporate America's expectations of African American entrepreneurs. Ultimately, his career serves as a blueprint for other African Americans who strive to excel in business.

Robert Louis Johnson was born April 8, 1946, in Hickory, Mississippi. He was the ninth of Edna and Archie "Peck" Johnson's 10 children. During Johnson's youth, his mother taught African American students at a one-room school in nearby Good Hope, Mississippi, while his father cut and sold wood to local pulp mills. Although racial segregation forced African Americans of Mississippi into second-class citizenship, Johnson's parents taught him to strive for success through education and hard work. Subsequently, the family moved north to the East side of Freeport, Illinois. There, Johnson's parents both found employment at various factories and often picked up additional jobs to provide for their large family. Given these circumstances, Johnson and his siblings also contributed to the household income.

Although Johnson attended a racially integrated school, African Americans only comprised 10 percent of the student body. Therefore, Johnson often felt isolated, particularly in cases when he was the only African American in a classroom of white students. However, Johnson proved to be an outgoing teenager as he was a member of Freeport High School's track, basketball, and football teams. Given Johnson's economic circumstances, he assumed he could not afford to attend college and thus looked forward to joining the U.S. Air Force for fighter pilot training after high school. Yet despite his intended career path and love of sports, Johnson remained committed to his education.

Ultimately, Johnson realized that college was a viable option. During his senior year of high school, Johnson applied to the University of Illinois at Urbana-Champaign (UIUC). Upon his acceptance, he secured a loan to cover the state resident tuition $224 per semester and landed a job cleaning biology labs to pay for his room and board. Thus, in 1964, Johnson became the first person in his family to attend college.

At UIUC, Johnson majored in political science and attempted to balance his academic interests with his social life. He joined the Beta chapter of the Kappa Alpha Psi fraternity, and ultimately moved into the Kappa house on campus. He went on to serve as the Beta chapter president and social chairperson. Ultimately, Johnson devoted much of his free time to his girlfriend Sheila Crump. Sheila grew up in a middle-class suburb of Chicago, Illinois as the daughter of a neurosurgeon. At UIUC she became the university's first African American female cheerleader. After earning his bachelor's degree in 1968, Johnson entered the Woodrow Wilson School of Public and International

Affairs at Princeton University. However, he withdrew from the program after one year and returned to Illinois to marry Sheila.

Johnson and Sheila exchanged vows in 1969 at a chapel on the UIUC campus where they had met. Their wedding cost approximately $50, as Sheila secured the chapel and hors d'oeuvres free of charge, and made her wedding dress from a popular McCall's pattern. While Sheila worked toward her bachelor's degree in music, Johnson secured a high school teaching position on the South Side of Chicago. When Sheila graduated in 1970, the couple moved to Princeton, New Jersey, where Johnson finished his master's program in public administration in 1972.

Upon earning his degree from Princeton, Johnson and his wife moved to Washington, DC. While Sheila worked as a research analyst for New York Senator Jacob K. Javits, Johnson secured a position as director of media affairs for the Corporation for Public Broadcasting (CPB). In addition to his work at the CPB, Johnson coordinated public relations for the National Urban League office in Washington, DC as its director of communications. Yet it was not long before Johnson secured a position as press secretary for the first elected congressperson of Washington, DC, Walter E. Fauntroy. Johnson worked closely with Fauntroy's chief of staff to establish the social connections necessary in their effort to increase the number of elected officials for Washington. While Johnson had already realized the political and economic benefits of knowing influential and wealthy individuals, his time with Fauntroy helped him hone his networking skills and establish long-lasting business partnerships.

After three years with Fauntroy's office, Johnson used his political connections and knowledge of media relations to secure a position as a lobbyist for the National Cable Television Association (NCTA), which represented the interests of cable television companies on a national level. Given Johnson's familiarity with Washington politics, the NCTA asked him to convince lawmakers to lift or modify limitations on cable programming. In doing so, Johnson learned about cable television technology and marketing, in addition to programming. During this time of his career, Johnson began to envision the need for a cable television station directed at African Americans.

While working for Fauntroy, Johnson had considered using television to promote the efforts of the National Black Caucus. However, Johnson did not have the information or social connections necessary to follow through on this idea. Yet as a lobbyist for the NCTA, Johnson came to understand the television industry as a business and began to focus intently on the potential financial rewards of an African American television channel. Johnson recognized that black Americans held power as a consumer group in the United States and viewed more hours of television than non-African Americans. Therefore, he concluded that a cable television network aimed at an African American audience was a potentially profitable business venture.

Eventually, Johnson presented his idea for a black cable network to NCTA board member John C. Malone, who was also head of TeleCommunications Inc. (TCI), then one of the fastest growing cable operators. Malone supported Johnson's vision and encouraged him to develop a business plan. Therefore, Johnson was very receptive when an acquaintance Ken Silverman, a former Columbia Pictures executive, approached him with a plan for a cable network devoted to viewers over 50 years of age. With Silverman's permission, Johnson revised the business proposal by changing references to the over-50 market to focus instead on the African American market.

In 1979, Johnson began putting his business plan into action. To broadcast his network to cable subscribers, he needed to buy time on a satellite transponder. Johnson met with the chief of UA/Columbia Cablevision, Bob Rosencrans, who had recently launched the Madison Square Garden (MSG) Sports Network, later renamed the USA Network. The two negotiated a mutually beneficial agreement, as Rosencrans needed to fill time on his network. Thus, Johnson secured two hours on the MSG Sports Network every Friday night and use of MSG's production facilities, all free of charge.

In August 1979, Johnson announced that his network, BET, would premiere on the MSG channel on January 25, 1980 from 11:00 p.m. to 1:00 a.m. (EST). Johnson resigned from his position at NCTA and convinced the association to grant him a consulting contract for $15,000. He and Sheila secured another $15,000 through a bank loan, and incorporated BET on September 13, 1979. Sheila had secured a job at the elite Sidwell Friends School, and she continued working and giving private violin lessons while helping Johnson establish the network. The company's initial board of directors consisted of Robert and Sheila Johnson as well as Washington attorney Joseph H. Sharlitt.

Johnson also needed additional investments to help his company grow, and assurances from cable system operators to carry his fledgling network. Subsequently, John C. Malone's TCI purchased 20 percent of the company for $180,000, and loaned the company another $320,000 in total over several months, thus contributing $500,000 to the company. Although TCI was part owner of BET, Johnson agreed that Malone would only advise the company in financial matters, as he was not accountable for BET's programming. With this level of support, BET secured agreements from American Telecommunications Corporation, TelePrompTer, and Warner Cable to carry BET programming. Finally, Johnson hired his NCTA coworkers Vivian "Chickie" Goodier and Carol E. Coody, as well as his sister Paulette, and gave them beneficial interest shares in the company to reward them for their loyalty and compensate them for low wages. Johnson later hired one of his fraternity brothers, Virgil Hemphill, as BET's one-man production department.

Johnson rented an office in the Georgetown district of Washington and prepared for BET's initial broadcast. The first program to air on BET was the 1974 film *Visit to a Chief's Son* starring Richard Mulligan, featuring Johnny Sekka. Labeled "Black Classic Night," BET's earliest broadcasts consisted of old films that featured black actors in both minor and major roles, such as *The Emperor Jones* and *Paradise in Harlem*.

In the area of marketing, Johnson initially focused his attention on African American-owned advertising agencies, yet their clients were generally unwilling to market specifically to a black audience. BET's first sponsors were Anheuser-Busch, Cham-pale, Kellogg, Pepsi-Cola, Sears, and Time. Johnson ultimately spent $1,000,000 toward broadcasting football and basketball games from historically black colleges and universities (HBCUs), though the schools themselves received $500 for broadcasting rights to each game. Within the next year, Johnson reluctantly agreed to fill small slots of time with promotional music videos, which the network received free from record labels. The network's series *Video Soul* launched in 1981 with Virgil Hemphill, introducing videos while portraying the fictional persona, Reverend Eldorado.

When Johnson secured more financial investments and broadcasting hours, he immediately increased his staff and expanded the network's programming. In 1982, Johnson sold 16 percent of the company to Taft Broadcasting, later renamed Great American Broadcasting, for $360,000. The network also secured sponsorship from Amtrak, General Electric, Mobil Oil, and Xerox. This allowed BET to begin broadcasting 7 days each week from 8:00 p.m. to 2:00 a.m. on a new satellite transponder.

He then hired recent graduates from HBCUs who viewed BET as a learning experience that prepared them for careers in broadcasting. As an added incentive, Johnson established a lending program, through which he provided small loans to his staff free of interest. He simply deducted small payments from borrowers' paychecks to repay their debt. Meanwhile, Johnson purchased rights to broadcast *The Bobby Jones Gospel Show* and narrowed his selection of athletic events to include only the most popular teams with the best marching bands.

Finally, in 1984, Johnson entered into a profitable arrangement with the Home Box Office (HBO), a premium cable network owned by Time Inc. HBO contributed its Galaxy I satellite to BET in exchange for 16 percent ownership of the company. Furthermore, Time Inc. executive Don Anderson, a former NCTA employee, assisted Johnson in negotiating favorable contracts with cable providers and helped him secure use of HBO's marketing and sales department. HBO's investment in BET encouraged Malone to reduce TCI's share of the network from 20 percent to 16 percent, so that the Johnsons could hold a majority of the company. This arrangement ensured that BET was still a majority African America-owned company.

While BET grew exponentially with the assistance of HBO, Johnson experienced professional setbacks owing to his personal relationships. His small staff experienced a significant amount of tension in the workplace stemming from Johnson extramarital affair with BET's vice president of affiliate relations, Vivian Goodier. Johnson and Goodier ended their three-year relationship in 1982 when Goodier resigned and moved to New York. The same year, Johnson fired his fraternity brother Virgil Hemphill, who served as BET's initial production department. Subsequently, in 1985 Malone at TCI and

Don Anderson with Time Inc. learned that Johnson's sister Paulette had embezzled $28,000 in her role as BET's comptroller. Paulette resigned, as did Johnson's administrative assistant Carole Coody. Thus, BET's founding staff had each left the company within five years.

Johnson also developed a contentious relationship with John H. Johnson, founder and chairperson of Johnson Publishing Company. Robert Johnson had attempted to establish a favorable relationship with John H. Johnson during BET's initial stages, as Johnson Publishing was responsible for the highly successful *Ebony* and *Jet* magazines. However, the two African American entrepreneurs did not meet until the mid-1980s, at which time Robert Johnson audaciously offered to buy Johnson Publishing Company. Robert Johnson's lack of modesty in this instance ignited resentment. Thereafter, John H. Johnson was highly critical of the BET network, as he questioned the company's claim to African American ownership, given the influence of TCI and HBO over the network's affairs. Robert Johnson repeatedly stressed that he owned 52 percent of the company and held control of the network's programming. However, as chief executive at BET, Johnson continued to defend his company against criticism from black America.

As personal scandal and professional criticism temporarily abated, BET began to flourish with new programs and a loyal base of viewers. Although pop music icon Michael Jackson broke the race barrier on MTV in 1983 with his videos for "Billie Jean," "Beat It," and "Thriller," the Music Television network refused to broadcast other videos by black musicians. In broadcasting African American music videos, the network provided a rare outlet for black entertainers. BET hired a local deejay, Donnie Simpson, and Sheila Banks to replace Virgil Hemphill as hosts of *Video Soul*. By 1991, music videos comprised 42 percent of BET's programming.

Johnson also built upon his partnership with Sheila. In 1985, the Johnsons welcomed their daughter Paige into their home, and their son Brett joined them four years later. In 1989, Sheila Johnson developed and managed the network's new series *Teen Summit*, a current affairs program for young people. The following year she held more responsibility at the company as vice president of corporate affairs.

By the early 1990s, Johnson and BET's other owners realized that African Americans had developed a level of pride in the network. Moreover, the company finally generated enough profit for its owners to begin selling shares of the corporation to the public. On November 1, 1991, the recently renamed BET Holdings Incorporated became the first majority black owned company listed on the New York Stock Exchange. BET Holdings Inc. traded under the symbol BTV and offered 21 percent or 4,200,000 shares to the public. Johnson ensured that a little more than 250,000 shares went to individual African American holders. Underwriters Bear, Stearns & Company targeted black celebrities and entertainers to purchase stock, while Johnson solicited support from smaller, African American-owned firms to underwrite shares as well.

Meanwhile Johnson cautiously devoted his time and money to expanding BET Holdings Inc. In 1989, Johnson purchased 27 percent of Wilmer Ames, Jr.'s magazine *Emerge*. Johnson later owned the magazine after buying both Time Inc. and Ames' shares in the publication. In 1991, Johnson developed *YSB* magazine, an acronym for Young Sisters and Brothers. Johnson created the publication under his new venture Paige Publications, named in honor of his daughter. The magazine appealed to African American teenagers but, despite its initial success, the publication only lasted five years. In 1993, Johnson purchased 80 percent of Action Pay-Per-View, and later entered into a project with the Encore Media Corporation to launch BET Movies/Starz!, a 24-hour premium movie channel.

In 1992, Johnson experienced a series of setbacks stemming from his conflicts with BET's founding staff. Vivian "Chickie" Goodier Roberts, Carol E. Coody Jaafar, and Paulette Johnson sued the BET co-founder for their beneficial interest shares of the company, which Johnson had given them when they joined the company. It was under these circumstances that Sheila learned of Johnson's three-year affair with Goodier. Johnson claimed that the plaintiffs surrendered their claims to the shares when they resigned, yet he ultimately settled the lawsuit for $4,000,000. However, the public soon learned that Paulette Johnson's replacement, Antonia Duncan, had embezzled $1,800,000 from the company.

As the 1990s wore on, Johnson came under harsh criticism from African Americans for BET's content and his approach to the television industry. While many BET viewers urged the network to generate original sitcoms, Johnson refused because he did not feel it would be economically viable. By 1996, music videos accounted for over 60 percent of BET's programming, at a time when "gangsta rap" was the most popular form of hip-hop. Although BET was profitable, black political and religious leaders condemned BET for broadcasting music videos that promoted violence, misogyny, and substance abuse. In 2001 national leaders of African American fraternities and sororities met with Johnson to discuss content, yet his primary defense was profit.

Even when BET's content affected Johnson's business deals, he maintained consistency in BET programming. In 1995, the new entity Time Warner sold its $58,000,000 worth of BET shares back to Johnson, as the network had not shown any indication of diversifying its content. Johnson asked that viewers "judge BET for what it is instead of what they'd like it to be" (quoted in Pulley, 115). Therefore, Johnson understood that the public had different expectations of BET, in terms of social responsibility. Yet he refused to conform to a different standard of conducting business simply because he was operating a black network.

Despite ongoing criticism, Johnson ensured that BET provided its African American audience with programming that other networks were unwilling or unable to offer. In 1991, BET presented its viewers with special coverage and analysis of the court case involving four Los Angeles police officers charged with beating Rodney King. Subsequently, in October 1995, Johnson guaranteed extensive coverage of the Million Man March and closed BET's offices to encourage employee participation. Additionally, journalist Ed Gordon, once BET's top news anchor, received widespread praise for his exclusive live interview with O. J. Simpson following the football star's exoneration in the murder of his ex-wife, Nicole, and Ron Goldman. Ultimately, BET met its audience's programming needs, if sporadically, by covering events most important to African Americans.

While BET expanded during the 1990s, so did Johnson's business interests. Major conglomerates valued Johnson's unique insight as a successful African American executive. Therefore, he joined the boards of corporations such as General Mills, Hilton Hotels, and US Airways. He and Sheila also invested in a 168-acre estate in Middleburg, Virginia, which served as their daughter Paige's primary equestrian training facility. The Johnsons acquired prized horses for their daughter and donated as much as $400,000 to sponsor equestrian events. Additionally Johnson provided generous support for Bill Clinton's presidential campaigns, and donated $1,000,000 to the Democratic National Committee in the 1990s.

Yet, in comparison to other corporate executives, Johnson took a different approach to building the BET brand. Instead of remaining focused strictly on the media industry, Johnson branched out into BET restaurants, nightclubs, cosmetics, and jewelry. As the company grew, shareholders became wary of Johnson's business decisions. Johnson wanted to continue to build BET, yet without being accountable to fickle shareholders. Therefore, in 1997 he and Malone bought back the company. Although the two executives ignited controversy by lowballing shareholders with an offer of $48 per share, an investigation by the Securities and Exchange Commission persuaded them to increase their proposal to $63 a share. Johnson held 63 percent ownership of the new company, BET Holdings II, while Malone held 35 percent. The remaining 2 percent of the company went to Debra Lee, who had begun as Johnson's legal advisor in 1986 but had become the president and chief operating officer (COO) of BET by 1996.

However, within three years, Johnson realized that the cable television industry had changed significantly since he first began in 1980. By the late 1990s, large media corporations had begun to dominate the television industry. Therefore, Johnson was receptive when Sumner Redstone of Viacom Inc. asked to purchase BET in 2000. After a relatively brief round of negotiations, the owners of BET Holdings II sold the company for $2,300,000,000 in Viacom stock, $1,400,000,000 of which went directly to Johnson. This deal made Robert L. Johnson the first African American billionaire, as **Oprah Winfrey** was worth an estimated $800,000,000 at the time.

Furthermore, Viacom also assumed $600,000,000 of BET's long-term debt, and Johnson continued as the chief executive officer (CEO) of BET under a five-year contract. He also arranged for COO Debra Lee to secure a five-year contract as well, which stipulated that she would assume the chief executive position upon Johnson's resignation. Although Johnson's deal made him the second largest shareholder of Viacom Inc. stock, he failed to receive a spot on the corporation's board of directors.

Johnson's career after BET has been as controversial and fruitful as his rise to corporate success. In 2002, Johnson divorced his wife and BET co-founder Sheila before going public with his relationship with BET COO Debra Lee. During the 2008 Democratic presidential primaries, Johnson supported his long-time acquaintance Hillary Rodham Clinton and stunned the public by suggesting that her opponent, **Barack Obama**, was unqualified for office because he experimented with illegal drugs as a teenager. Johnson later apologized to Obama for the comment and argued that the media had misinterpreted his statement.

Yet Johnson has continued to broaden his business interests. In 2002, Johnson purchased a new National Basketball Association (NBA) franchise based in North Carolina, the Charlotte Bobcats, as well as Sting, the city's existing women's team. This deal made Johnson the first African American to hold a controlling ownership in a professional athletic team. He established RLJ Development to operate a series of hotels he purchased. Upon the request of Liberia's president Ellen Johnson Sirleaf, Johnson constructed Kendeja Resort and Villas just outside the nation's capital of Monrovia.

Johnson has fought most tirelessly against the estate tax, as smaller estates have born the brunt of taxation. Johnson and his supporters have indicated that newly rich individuals want to give their children the same head start in society as wealthy families who have benefitted from generational wealth. When Johnson began his campaign in earnest, individuals with assets under $5,000,000 contributed to half of all estate taxes, while taxes on estates over $20,000,000 accounted for 17 percent. Thus, Johnson has used his social networks and business acumen to initiate a public conversation about the fairness of taxation.

Johnson has begun to devote some his fortune to nonprofit causes. When his mother Edna died in 2001, Johnson donated $100,000 in her honor to establish an endowed scholarship for African American women at Highland Community College in Freeport, Illinois. In 2002, he received the Humanitarian of the Year Award from the T. J. Martell Foundation for Leukemia, Cancer, and AIDS Research. Subsequently, Johnson provided $3,000,000 to aid the construction of the National Underground Railroad Freedom Center based in Cincinnati.

Ultimately, Johnson's career symbolizes the desire that many African Americans have to secure financial success. Before other iconic black entrepreneurs such as Oprah Winfrey, **Russell Simmons**, and **Jay-Z** entered the business world, Johnson plotted his own course. As he often advised his employees, "We don't need to reinvent the wheel. . . . We just need to paint it black" (quoted in Pulley, 112). He has expanded the boundaries of what is possible for

African Americans in corporate America. Ultimately, African Americans have learned from his successes in business as well as his mistakes, and take pride is willingness to "paint it black."

Monica L. Butler
Seminole State College

FURTHER READING

Buckley, Annie. *Robert L. Johnson*. Ann Arbor, MI: Cherry Lake Publishing, 2008.
Heath, Thomas. "Johnson Readies His Next Gamble." *Washington Post*, February 16, 2009.
"Johnson, Robert L." *Current Biography* 55 (April 1994): 28.
Jones, Felecia Gilmore. "The Black Audience and Black Entertainment Television." PhD dissertation, University of Georgia, 1989.
Pulley, Brett. *The Billion Dollar BET: Robert Johnson and the Inside Story of Black Entertainment Television*. Hoboken, NJ: John Wiley and Sons, 2004.
RLJ Companies. RLJ Companies Management Team: Robert L. Johnson, Founder & Chairman. Accessed July 2009. RLJ Companies Web Site: www.rljcompanies.com/rljTeamRLJ.htm.
Smith-Shomade, Beretta E. *Pimpin' Ain't Easy: Selling Black Entertainment Television*. New York: Routledge, 2008.

AP/Wide World Photos

Quincy Jones (1933–)

Quincy Delight Jones, Jr., was born on March 14, 1933, in Chicago, Illinois. He is one of America's foremost record producers. "Mr. Q," as Jones is nicknamed, is also highly regarded for his work as a music conductor, arranger, and trumpeter. Jones is one of the most highly decorated producers in the history of popular music. By virtue of his musical talent and his personal charisma, Jones became the consummate industry insider. Jones has won 27 Grammys, the second most of any individual in history. Jones's arrangement of "Fly Me to the Moon," as sung by Frank Sinatra was the first music played by humans during the first lunar landing. He has received numerous lifetime achievement awards and honorary degrees. Jones is best known for his work with the late **Michael Jackson**. He is the producer of Jackson's masterpiece, *Thriller*, the best-selling album of all time. Jones has long put his musical talent to work on behalf of social justice. He produced and conducted the "We are the World" single recorded by the star-studded USA For Africa group in 1985. In recent years, Jones has ventured into the film business, television production, and magazine publishing. Jones is a master of the recording studio and a true citizen of the world.

Quincy Jones spent his early childhood on the South Side of Chicago. His father, Quincy Delight Jones Sr., worked as a carpenter. He had played semi-professional baseball before his son's birth. Jones' mother, Sarah Wells Jones, suffered from mental illness. She was eventually institutionalized for schizophrenia. Jones and his younger brother Lloyd were occasionally sent to stay with their paternal grandmother who lived outside of Louisville, Kentucky in a decrepit dwelling without running water. In his memoir, Jones describes how his grandmother would catch rats in traps and then fry them up for Jones and his brother to eat. Quincy Jones Sr. relocated his family to Bremerton, Washington, near Seattle, in 1943 to pick up some of the plentiful government work on the West Coast during the Second World War. In 1947, the Jones family moved into the city of Seattle. They settled in a small home in the city's Central District. Fourteen-year-old Quincy Jones Jr. began attending high school that fall at Garfield High School, a few blocks from their home. Jones pursued his interest in music at the school. He began playing trumpet at age 10. By the time he got to high school, Jones played the instrument proficiently. Jones's music teacher, Parker Cook encouraged Jones to continue training as a musician. Cook introduced Jones to a wide range of jazz and classical music. Around this time, Jones began playing in local jazz combos.

Following his 1951 graduation from high school, Jones attended a new music conservatory named Schillinger House (now known as the Berklee School of Music) in Boston. Schillinger offered Jones a full scholarship based on his audition on the trumpet. Jones's tenure at Schillinger proved short-lived. He came to the attention of legendary band leader Lionel Hampton, who hired Jones as his new trumpeter. Jones quit school and relocated to New York City. He toured the country with the Lionel Hampton Orchestra, making connections with a who's who of musicians. These connections provided Jones with his first opportunities to arrange songs. Lionel Hampton noticed Jones' innate ability for arranging soon after he joined the Orchestra. Hampton took Jones on in an apprenticing role, showing him how the process worked within an ego-filled orchestra. By 1953, Jones was making large sums of money on the side arranging for the likes of Tommy Dorsey and Count Basie.

Jones remained in the fold of the Lionel Hampton Orchestra until 1956. He joined up with trumpeter Dizzy Gillespie's band. *This Is How I Feel About Jazz*, is an album played on by Gillespie's band but arranged by Jones. The swinging album of sunny tunes, such as the 10.5-minute "Walkin," was the first album recorded under Jones' name.

At age 24, Jones moved to Paris. He left behind his young wife Jeri Caldwell Jones and their daughter Jolie. Jones had a job waiting for him at Barclay Records. Over the next two years, Jones expanded his résumé as a producer and arranger. He worked with French pop stars Charles Aznavour and Jacques Brel as well as American stars including Sarah Vaughan. He indulged in the jet-set lifestyle of his new cosmopolitan, globetrotting friends who included Pablo Picasso, Aristotle Onassis, Grace Kelly, Frank Sinatra, Marlene Dietrich, and Maria Callas. While in Lionel Hampton's orchestra, Jones had toured Europe, but he had never partaken in the decadent world of Parisian dinner party culture. Jones proved a superb schmooze. He made further connections with industry insiders including Mercury Records' Irving Green and jazz impresario Norman Granz, which proved particularly advantageous for his career.

The jet-set style of life did not suit Jones's relationship with his wife. She became aware of Jones's numerous affairs with women in Europe. Jeri Caldwell Jones separated from Jones in 1962. They reconciled shortly thereafter, but his philandering ways continued. The couple finally divorced in 1966. Jones soon remarried. In 1967, he tied the knot with 1960s cover girl Ulla Andersson, one of his mistresses throughout the later part of his union with Jeri Caldwell. Andersson was only 20 years old at the time of their marriage. Jones was 34. Andersson and Jones had two children, Quincy III and Martina.

Irving Green, a friend and admirer of Jones, had named the 28-year-old Jones a vice president for Mercury Records in 1961. This made Jones the first African American to hold an executive position at a major U.S. record label. In his previous experience in the United States, Jones worked primarily with jazz musicians. Now, he was called on by Mercury to arrange and produce primarily popular artists, as he had for Barclay Records in France. Jones collaborated with Leslie Gore soon after joining Mercury Records. Jones helped transform the effervescent young pop singer into a major star. Gore scored Jones-produced hits in the early-to-mid 1960s including "It's My Party" and "Judy's Turn to Cry."

In 1964, Jones produced and arranged Frank Sinatra's *It Might as Well Be Swing* album, a collection of jazz standards backed by Count Basie's Orchestra. Jones collaborated with both Basie and Sinatra intermittently for the duration of their respective careers. *It Might as Well Be Swing* included a magnificent version of Bart Howard's "Fly Me to the Moon."

In 1963, Jones scored his first film, Sidney Lumet's *The Pawnbroker*. Jones's haunting score drew wide critical acclaim. Film scoring became one of Jones's fortes. To date, Jones has scored 33 films. The lion's share of Grammy nominations and wins came from his work on films. Jones' earned his first Grammy for his soundtrack to *In Cold Blood* (1967), a film based on Truman Capote's chilling account of the brutal murder of a prominent Kansas farm family. Jones earned another for his steamy score to *In The Heat of the Night* in 1968.

In 1969, Jones recorded his first solo album in many years, an innovative jazz fusion album entitled *Walking in Space*. The album sold well and garnered Jones further critical acclaim. Jones, like his longtime friend and future collaborator **Miles Davis**, was pushing the bounds of jazz and rock and roll by bringing together seemingly disparate elements of both genres. The instrumentation on *Walking in Space* had gone inextricably electric, a move seen as blasphemous by many jazz purists. Shrugging off the criticisms, Jones continued to push the bounds of jazz in his subsequent releases. Jones won the Grammy for Best Instrumental Arrangement for *Walking in Space*. His 1971 follow-up, *Smackwater Jack*, also won the Grammy for Best Instrumental Arrangement. *Smackwater Jack* pushed the bounds of jazz even further. Several of the albums tracks are more or less jazzy television show themes he produced during the early 1970s. *Walking in Space* and *Smackwater Jack* turned Jones into a household name. He was no longer just an icon of the jazz community or a well-conducted industry insider. Mr. Q was a popular performer, producer, and arranger.

The success of *Walking in Space* and *Smackwater Jack* introduced Jones's work to a new generation of performers. In the late 1960s and early 1970s, Jones produced albums with the likes of **Aretha Franklin** and Paul Simon. Franklin became an admirer of Jones's work with Dinah Washington and asked Atlantic Records to procure his services. Their collaboration produced the 1973 album *Hey Now Hey (The Other Side of the Sky)*. *Hey Now Hey* was received poorly at the time of its released. It failed to produce any big hits and Jones's lush, string-laden production actually dominated the Queen of Soul's singing. Jones had more success with Paul Simon, helping to arrange the strings on Paul Simon's classic 1973 album, *There Goes Rhymin' Simon*. Jones's work on the chart-topping album comes through most prominently on the hit "Loves Me Like a Rock," "Something So Right," and "American Tune." The arrangements on *There Goes Rhymin' Simon* exemplify Jones's dexterity as an arranger. Jones bounces from the gospel tinged "Loves Me Like a Rock" to the smooth 1970s adult contemporary pop of "Something So Right" to the Dixieland flavored "Take Me to the Mardi Gras" to the minuet-like "American Tune." Working with Simon, a kindred spirit in his approach to music making, encouraged Jones to experiment with a number of different sounds on the album.

Jones released one of his most popular solo albums in 1974, *Body Heat*. The album included guest appearances by jazz icons Hubert Laws, Frank Rosolino, and Herbie Hancock. It combined the contemporary sounds of soul music with smooth jazz arrangements. *Body Heat* had great crossover appeal on the pop album charts, yet the album drew the ire of many jazz enthusiasts who felt that the always pop-oriented Jones had moved beyond the pale and was no longer a jazz man.

Health problems put Jones' career on hiatus during the mid-1970s. Jones suffered a pair of brain aneurysms in 1974. It was discovered that Jones had a malignant brain tumor. When the tumor was removed, Jones had a metal plate installed and was instructed to never play the trumpet again. During his illness, Jones divorced his wife Ulla Andersson. The couple had been estranged since the early 1970s. Mr. Q married for the third time later in September 1974. Jones and his new wife, the actress Peggy Lipton, best known for her role as Julie Barnes on *The Mod Squad*, had lived together for several years at the time of their marriage. Lipton gave up her acting career to raise the couple's children, Kidada and Rashida. Lipton and Jones divorced in 1990.

Jones's forays into the studio became more sporadic following his illness. No longer a horn player, Jones's health problems relegated him to the roles of arranger and producer. He continued in the vein of *Body Heat* with his solo releases in the latter half of the 1970s. On *Sounds . . . And Stuff Like That* (1978), jazz pianist extraordinaire Herbie Hancock led an all-star cast through Jones' latest compositions in the vein of contemporary sounds. The album combined a disco vibe with a touch of the ribald soulfulness that characterized Jones's albums in the early 1970s. On *The Dude* (1980), Jones experiments heavily with keyboards and synthesizers. Three of the album's James Ingram-sung tracks became Top 40 pop hits, "Ai No Corrida," "Just Once," and "One Hundred Ways." *The Dude* garnered four Grammys in 1981 for Jones and Ingram.

Jones's work on films slowed in the late 1970s as well, though he did help score the soundtracks for the *Roots* miniseries. The music Jones created for *Roots* was compiled on a 1978 LP consisting primarily of snippets of music used during the eight episodes. Some of the tracks on Jones's *Roots* LP were not used in the series, but were written for the film. These include Jones's takes on traditional African music, sea shanties, and American folk tunes. The sheer eclecticism of Jones's work on his *Roots* album reflects his familiarity with mucsical genres throughout the Atlantic world.

In 1980, Jones started his own record company. He formed the now-defunct Qwest Records as a joint venture with his new label, Warner Brothers. Initially, the label featured primarily contemporary rhythm and blues artists such as George Benson, who, like Jones, began his career in the jazz world before moving toward more pop-leaning music. Qwest branched out to artists as diverse as the superstar gospel singing family, The Winans; British post-punk poster boys, New Order; and for a time, Quincy Jones's longtime collaborator,

Frank Sinatra. After many successful years, the label proved unable to develop a stable of new stars in the late 1990s. Qwest ceased operations in 2000.

To many music fans, Jones is best known for his collaborations with Michael Jackson. Their aesthetically groundbreaking and astronomically lucrative relationship collaborations in the studio began with 1979's *Off the Wall*, Jackson's breakthrough as an adult artist. The 21-year-old Jackson entered the studio for his sessions with Jones in an unprecedented position for himself as an artist. No longer was either Jackson's father or Berry Gordy demanding certain sounds out of the young star. Jones, by contrast, treated Jackson as a collaborator.

Arguably the funkiest record to emerge from the disco era, *Off the Wall* shows the producer Jones in top form. He combines the pulsating beat of disco with lushly orchestrated soul music. The album's lushness does not detract from its swagger. *Off The Wall* is an album of emphatic strings, sly keyboards, and exuberant vocals. Jones's jazz background provided the conceptual framework for the album's arrangements. He used Jackson's voice as an instrument, like a vocal soloist in a jazz ensemble. The album produced four top-10 singles, including the roller rink classic "Don't Stop 'til You Get Enough," the vibrant ballad "Rock with You," and the tear-jerking "She's Out of My Life."

The Jones–Jackson collaboration continued on *Thriller* (1982). Widely recognized as the best-selling album of all time, *Thriller* made Jackson the biggest pop star in the world and Jones the world's best-known producer. *Thriller* reflects Jones's background in scoring films. The album's arrangements have a profoundly cinematic quality, from the film noir of "Billie Jean" to the horror flick aesthetics of the title track. The combination of Jones's cinematic production style and Jackson's theatrical singing style makes it no wonder that Michael Jackson was the first superstar of the music video age.

Thriller's success as a coherent artistic statement has always been overshadowed by the stand-alone success of the album's singles. Seven of the album's nine cuts ended up in Billboard's top 10 singles chart. Jones's characteristic eclecticism helped make this possible. None of the album's seven singles come off as a sound-alike. Thriller's 36-week run at the top of the album charts is the result of the album's accessibility. Different singles appealed to listeners of different ages, races, genders, and musical tastes. "Beat It" could pass for 1980s hard rock with its electrifying guest performance by guitar hero Eddie Van Halen. "The Girl Is Mine," a duet with Paul McCartney, has a vaudevillian feel to it. "Wanna Be Startin' Somethin' " was funky enough that P-Funk himself, George Clinton, called Jackson to congratulate him on the song.

Jones's next major project was part of a worldwide move to provide aid to African famine victims, particularly those in Ethiopia, who suffered from a horrific famine in 1984 and 1985. Jackson, Bob Geldof, Lionel Richie, and Jones worked together in 1984 and 1985 to build a coalition of artists who were interested in recording a charity single for the relief effort. Their efforts were inspired by Band Aid, the British charity supergroup formed by

Boomtown Rats front man Geldof. In November 1984, they recorded the single "Do They Know It's Christmas" in time for the holiday season. The single topped the British pop charts and raised tens of millions of pounds for the relief effort. The success of "Do They Know It's Christmas" propelled the efforts of Jones and company. The group they formed called itself USA For Africa. Jones orchestrated a January 28, 1985, recording session in Los Angeles, the day after the previous night's American Music Awards. Jones produced and arranged "We Are the World," the song Jackson and Richie wrote for the group. Mr. Q did a remarkable job balancing the egos of nearly four dozen stars, tailoring solos to singer's particular talents and crafting interesting duets (most interestingly, a striking interplay between Willie Nelson and Dionne Warwick). The stirring seven minutes of "We Are the World" include solos from artists as diverse as Michael Jackson, Billy Joel, Diana Ross, **Stevie Wonder**, Bruce Springsteen, Cyndi Lauper, and Paul Simon. The single skyrocketed to the top of the charts in March 1985, spending five weeks at number one in the United States and four weeks at number one in the United Kingdom. It raised more than $100 million for African famine relief efforts and provided the famine relief movement with a great deal of momentum going into the now-legendary Live Aid concerts in July 1985. USA For Africa won the Grammys for Record and Song of the Year for "We Are the World." The group continues to serve as a model for celebrity-led charity efforts.

Jones's next venture was his first foray into the production side of the film business. He produced the film version of **Alice Walker**'s Pulitzer Prize winning *The Color Purple*. The critically acclaimed film was directed by Steven Spielberg. It starred Whoopi Goldberg, Danny Glover, and Oprah Winfrey. The film deals with the struggles of African American women in early twentieth-century United States and their efforts to persevere in spite of discrimination in both the public and private spheres. The film received 11 Oscar nominations, though shockingly it did not capture any awards.

In 1987, Jones returned to the studio with Michael Jackson to record the much-anticipated follow-up to *Thriller*. *Bad* was seen as a commercial disappointment at the time, even though it sold more than 10 million copies in the United States alone and spawned several smash hits. Sonically, Jones and Jackson created as eclectic an album as its predecessor. The title track "Bad" bears the influence of hip-hop whereas "Smooth Criminal" delves further into the synth-pop sound which was hinted at on *Thriller* and *Off the Wall*. The ballad "Man in the Mirror" continues in the spirit of USA For Africa with its heartfelt call for human brotherhood and sisterhood. *Bad* was the last Jackson album produced by Jones. Jackson, in an effort to update his sound, hired the New Jack Swing production team of Jimmy Jam and Teddy Long to produce his next album, *Dangerous* (1991).

Jones found plenty of ways to keep himself busy in the 1990s. On July 8, 1991, Jones served as guest conductor for jazz legend Miles Davis's epic final concert at the Montreux Jazz Festival in Switzerland. Jones conducted twin orchestras, The Gil Evans Orchestra and the George Gruntz Concert Jazz Band, as Davis worked through material he recorded with longtime collaborator Gil Evans in the late 1950s and early 1960s. Davis rarely played older material in concert, so the evening's spectacular performance was a once-in-a-lifetime treat for jazz enthusiasts. Davis passed away in September 1991 following a stroke. A live album featuring the concert at the Montreux Jazz Festival was released posthumously for Davis in 1993. It was the year's top-selling jazz album.

By the early 1990s, television was one of the few forms of media which Jones had not produced. Jones made the jump into television with *The Fresh Prince of Bel-Air* for the fall 1990 season. The sitcom turned into a smash hit for NBC and transformed former hip-hop MC **Will Smith** into a major star. Like Jones's music, *The Fresh Prince of Bel-Air* had remarkable crossover appeal. It was a light-hearted, though consistently amusing sitcom that charmed a demographically diverse audience. The show ran for six seasons.

Jones made a foray into the publishing world with the formation of *Vibe* magazine in 1994. *Vibe* focused on hip-hop and urban culture. *Vibe* was seen within the publishing world as a challenge to *The Source*, the most prominent hip-hop publication to date. In fact, *Vibe* differed from the music-centric *Source* in its areas of emphasis. *Vibe* focused more broadly on urban lifestyles and culture. It covered the emergence of hip-hop culture in the fashion world, as well as entertainment news and articles on cultural trends. The publication thrived throughout the 1990s, but fell victim to the shrinking of the publishing industry in the 2000s. *Vibe* published its final issue in 2009.

In recent years, Jones has moved into a semi-retirement, still serving in an executive capacity for a number of nonprofit organizations. He resides in Los Angeles, living in close proximity to his pair of famous daughters, Rashida and Kidada. Rashida Jones is a television actress best known for her roles on *Boston Public* and *The Office*. Kidada Jones is an actress, model, and fashion designer. Quincy Jones has proven himself a master of many trades over the course of his six-decade career. He has made use of his seemingly endless talent to benefit the lives of countless strangers around the world. His wide ranging experience makes him an ideal elder statesman of the entertainment world.

Clayton Trutor
Boston College

FURTHER READING

Jones, Quincy. *Q: The Autobiography of Quincy Jones*. New York: Harlem Moon, 2001.

Jones, Quincy, Maya Angelou, and Clint Eastwood. *The Complete Quincy Jones: My Journey & Passions*. New York: Insight Books, 2008.

Kavanaugh, Lee Hill. *Quincy Jones: Musician, Composer, Producer*. Berkeley Heights, NJ: Enslow, 1998.

AP/Wide World Photos

Barbara Jordan
(1936–1996)

Known across the United States as the first black woman to serve in the Senate in Texas and the first black woman in the House of Representatives in Washington, DC, Barbara Jordan made an impact on many Americans for her speech about Watergate in 1974 and her keynote address at the 1976 Democratic Convention. Jordan served only seven years in the Texas legislature and six years in the U.S. Congress, dying at the age of 59, but throughout her life she strove to make a difference in the world around her. The consummate politician, she quickly learned how to work with her white male colleagues and soon became recognized for her eloquent speaking skills and strong ideas. Throughout her tenure, Jordan often was not just one of the few blacks but also one of the few women on the state and national political scenes, and because of this, she often stood as a representative of both groups.

Like most people, Jordan was affected by her family and upbringing. While she certainly faced many struggles in her desire to excel in school, in her dream of becoming a lawyer, and in her push to be recognized as a politician not just as a black woman, Jordan benefitted from a strong family who supported her many endeavors. Her family encouraged both a scholarly and religious education, and these remained interests for Jordan as can be seen through her pursuit of higher education and through her continued devotion to church.

While her education gave her the tools and the background to succeed in politics and move to the national level, religion provided her with fortitude and guided her actions. This focus on religion and prayer influenced Jordan's character and how she acted in politics because she believed that justice and selflessness were the two core values for people of faith. Her belief in justice and selflessness drove her through much of her political career and pushed her to encourage others to act in the same way. Never shy of sharing her beliefs, she gave the opening prayer at the National Prayer Breakfast in Washington, DC, in 1978, and later in 1984 she and President Ronald Reagan were the main speakers for the event, which demonstrated not only her personal convictions about religion but also her presence as an important figure on the national stage.

Born on February 21, 1936, in one of the primarily African American sections of Houston, Barbara Charline Jordan was the youngest of three daughters. Growing up in a district known as the 5th Ward, Jordan, her two older sisters, and her parents Arlyne and Ben Jordan lived with her paternal grandfather until they were able to afford their own home. The family attended church together every Sunday, and Jordan's father eventually became a pastor. The girls were raised in a strict environment where dancing and playing cards were banned. Even though she knew that she wanted to live differently at some point in her life, Jordan also understood that she needed her family's support and care at that age and never rebelled.

More than just valuing religion and offering Jordan a model for her self-proclaimed values of justice and selflessness, Jordan's family also placed particular importance on education. Even though her parents grew up an era of severe racial discrimination for African Americans, the 1920s and 1930s in Texas, they still followed their own separate paths to education and ensured that their children would as well. Her mother Arlyne completed high school, and although she did not attend college, she continued her education by enrolling in typing classes to eventually move to a better job. Jordan's father did attend college but had to leave during his last year because he did not have enough money to finish. Likely because of his own inability to complete school, Jordan and her sisters Rose Mary and Bennie were encouraged to do well and attend college.

Perhaps as a hint to her future as a lawyer, politician, and renowned speaker, Jordan attended Phillis Wheatley High School in Houston, which was named for a black poet in the era of the American Revolution, another black woman remembered for her ability with words. Although it is hard to imagine Jordan ever blending in to a crowd, she claimed to have done just this when she first began high school. Her personal drive for success soon took over, however, and she participated in competitions and won awards, anything to make her stand out as different.

Even though the high school provided important opportunities for its students, such as trips to the Houston Symphony to see acclaimed African American opera singer Marian Anderson, Jordan was aware of the disadvantages faced by the black community. In contrast to her prolonged and often vocal fights for justice on the state and national level, in high school she seemed much more complacent about segregation and the effects of racial discrimination. She disagreed with segregation, but thought it would take many years to change, and in the meantime, Jordan later explained: "I decided that if I was going to be outstanding or different, it was going to have to be in relation to other black people rather than in some setting where white people were." She knew that she wanted to be different, to be a lawyer when most of her fellow students planned to be teachers, but at the time she focused on excelling in comparison to fellow black students rather than pitting herself against whites. In just a few short years, though, all of this would change.

After graduating with honors from high school in 1952, Jordan enrolled at Texas Southern University (TSU) in Houston. At this time schools in the South, including Texas, remained segregated, and because Jordan knew that she needed to attend college in Houston, her options were limited. Even though college seemed to her like an extension of high school because she remained in her hometown and was surrounded by many of the same people, she continued to work hard and get involved in new areas.

One activity that helped shape her in many ways was the TSU debate team. During the summer, the debate team often travelled to competitions across the country, but women rarely were allowed to be a part of this trip. To attend, Jordan later said that she consciously gained weight and wore plain clothing to downplay her femininity. Her tactic worked, and she was able to join the team on its trip to cities such as Chicago, Boston, and New York. As her first real time away from home and the strict rules of her family and also as her first exposure to the Northeast and its more integrated and open society, this summer was an important one for Jordan.

Always aiming to be the best, she graduated magna cum laude with degrees in history and government in 1956. With her eyes set on law school, she moved to Massachusetts to attend Boston University. Although it was difficult for her family to afford this expensive school, her parents managed to pay for her tuition and housing while her oldest sister covered the cost of her books. Both of her sisters gave her $10 a month on which to live. On this strict budget and with her father's departing words of, "Once you get there, you're there" because the family could not afford for her to come home for the holidays, Jordan began law school.

Unlike high school and college where she was surrounded by friends and fellow black students, she was one of only six women and two African American women in her freshman class of 600. She quickly realized that success would not come as easily to her as it had before because she now was competing against students from more privileged backgrounds. According to Jordan:

> So I was at Boston University in this new and strange and different world, and it occurred to be me that if I was going to succeed at this strange new adventure, I would have to read longer and more thoroughly than my colleagues at law school had to read. I felt I had to compensate for what I had missed in earlier years, I would have to work harder, and study longer, than anybody else.

This devotion to her studies and her struggle to compete equally with people who came from different backgrounds proved to be an important and lasting lesson for Jordan, one she would take with her to the state and national legislatures and one that would help her succeed throughout her life.

Prior to law school, Jordan had experienced more problems relating to racial rather than gender discrimination. Her time in Boston opened her eyes to the problems that women faced as well. The professors, who were all male, rarely called on female students in class unless they decided to hold a "Ladies Day." Probably because of this rather hostile environment, only two of the six original women in the class graduated in 1959—Jordan and the other African American woman.

Although it may seem surprising that the two black women, both from Texas, were the only women in their class to graduate, it likely is a testament to the forces that drove Jordan herself to succeed throughout her life. Jordan and the other woman entered school with the knowledge that they would have to work hard to pass the coursework. They understood they were at a disadvantage and already had encountered limitations on their opportunities as black women in Texas. This resilience likely led to their success while other women failed.

Following her completion of law school in 1959, Jordan initially wanted to remain in Boston. Not yet attuned to politics, there is no telling what the future would have held for her if she had stayed there. Fate seemed to have a different future in mind for Jordan, and she returned to Texas after she discovered that it was almost impossible to find a job in Massachusetts when she had no connections there.

Two years after she completed her law degree, Jordan found herself back in Texas in 1961. Although she soon became interested in politics, she first opened her own practice and passed business cards around town. Within a few years, she also served as the administrative assistant to the county judge in Harris County, where Houston is located. Just one of the many precedents she set in her life, Jordan was the first black women to hold this position.

In her free time, she also got involved in John F. Kennedy's presidential campaign, but did not get interested in politics herself until someone asked whether she would be interested in running for the Texas House of Representatives in the 1962 election. She could not afford the filing fee, but a friend lent her the money. Just as she prepared for class and exams in law school, Jordan read extensively on the Texas legislative system so that she would understand everything before the race began. She knew the race would be tough, but in 1962 she was just a novice in politics and did not see that the design of the voting districts in Houston made it almost impossible for an African American to win any election.

Even though she received a standing ovation at one of her speeches, just the first of many speeches and ovations in her political career, and despite the large numbers she received in votes, Jordan lost the election. She won 46,000 votes while her opponent Charlie Whitfield, a white man, won 65,000. Jordan won the vast majority of the black votes, especially in the 5th Ward, but her failure to attract the white vote made a win impossible. This, of course, was exactly what the design of the voting districts was intended to do. Surprised by the outcome of the race, because both she and Whitfield were running for the first time and because she did so well with the black population, Jordan struggled to understand the outcome: "That was very puzzling to me, and disturbing. I spent a lot of time trying to figure out what did happen in that race."

Even though she still had not come to terms with the outcome of that first race, the same friend encouraged her to run a second time and once again lent her the filing fee. Rather than wait until the election in 1964, Jordan continued to speak and visit people as soon as the 1962 election ended. She also began to understand the very political nature of politics, which she demonstrated by buying new clothes and a new car. Jordan now understood the importance of looking the part and did that in addition to her local campaigning.

Although she made a big impact during the campaign, this time she was running against an incumbent and still had to overcome the division of the voting districts. Just as in 1962, Jordan lost the 1964 election despite winning the black vote in her district. With this, she realized that winning would be impossible until the districts changed. That same year, the passage of the Civil Rights Act and a series of Supreme Court cases determined that the voting districts in Houston had to be redrawn to reflect equal representation for the people living in those districts. This meant that Jordan's district became the 11th District and now contained a population that was 38 percent black, in addition to numerous Hispanics and white workers, all groups that she won in the previous two elections.

Based on the change in voting districts, Jordan decided to run one more time in the election of 1966. Again running against incumbent Charlie Whitfield who beat her two times already, Jordan tackled a political race that quickly became about race itself. Realizing that he was in a difficult position, Whitfield focused on the dangers of what he called the "black block vote." Jordan, using her thinking and speaking skills learned on the high school debate team and honed in law school, retorted: "Look, don't tell us about black block votes. You know white folks have been block-voting for the past century. We don't have to apologize. Our time has come!" She also made it clear that she was from that part of Houston and grew up there and, thus, understand what the people needed whereas Whitfield only moved there for the elections in 1962.

Just as Jordan predicted during the race in 1966, "Our time had come!" Jordan won 64.8 percent of the votes in her district, sweeping the black votes but also attracting voters of other races as well. With this, Jordan was elected to the Senate and Curtis Graves, a black man, to the House of Representatives where they were part of a very small number of African Americans to serve in the Texas Legislature since the years of Reconstruction following the Civil War. In fact, Jordan was the first African American to serve as a Texas senator since 1883 and the first black woman to ever do so. Moreover, she also was one of the few women of any race to be involved in Texas politics and was the only woman to serve in the Texas Senate that term.

Jordan quickly took note of how the legislature operated and worked quietly in the beginning. Just as she dressed plainly to blend in with the men on her high school debate team, she made it clear to her fellow senators that she was there to be a senator, not to be a threat or to be different. Even though some people in her district complained that she was not doing anything, Jordan explained, "You don't get in there having a drink quickly. You work and you learn the rules and you keep your mouth shut until it is time to open it." Even though she was new to elected office, she understood how the system worked, and based on her law school experience, she knew how to sit quietly and learn from the experiences until it was her time.

Based on this experience, Jordan decided to run again in 1968 and won a four-year term that time. A clever politician, in 1970 she decided to run for U.S. Congress in the 1972 election year because the new congressional districts were favorable to her, making it more likely that she would win. She ended up running against Curtis Graves, the man with whom she shared the honors of being black elected officials in the legislature in Texas. A fiercely contested debate ensued between former allies, and Jordan won the 1972 election.

Even though she only served two terms for a total of six years in the Texas Senate, Jordan made a big impact on politics in the state. By persisting through repeated losses, Jordan succeeded in the Texas political climate, one dominated by white men, and helped open doors to both African Americans and women. As a senator, she lobbied for minimum-wage laws in the state and focused on increasing voter registration. She also served on the Labor and Management Relations Committee and in 1972 was unanimously elected president pro tempore of the Texas Senate. Before she left for the national political scene, the state recognized Jordan's service by naming her "Governor for a Day."

When Jordan won the election in 1972, she became the first woman from Texas to win an election to the national legislature and the first black woman from a Southern state to be elected to the U.S. House of Representatives. Just as few blacks had served in Texas politics since Reconstruction, Jordan and a man named Andrew Young, who also won an election that year, were the first two African Americans from the South to serve in Congress in the twentieth century.

These milestones aside, when she walked into the House of Representatives in the nation's capital in 1973, Jordan realized that the stage was much different. Instead of working alongside 31 Texas senators, she now was surrounded by 435 representatives from all 50 states. These overwhelming numbers would make it much harder to be noticed as a junior congresswoman and to make much of an impact. However, unlike her early time in the Texas Senate, Jordan quickly became renowned for her big presence and recognizable voice. A powerful and eloquent speaker, she was given a chance to make her mark early in her time in Washington, DC.

Having only arrived as a junior legislator in 1973, she was named to the Judiciary Committee investigating President Richard Nixon and Watergate in 1974. When they released their findings, each member of the committee gave a 15-minute address on national television. Going in order of seniority, Jordan gave the final speech. One this day of July 25, 1974, Jordan made her mark on the national stage. Because she understood where much of the population was from, she spent her time explaining the Constitution, defining the term impeachment, and identifying what exactly the President had done and why it was wrong. In doing so, she not only appealed to the viewers, but she also demonstrated her unswerving devotion to justice and the Constitution. As she explained, "I am not going to sit here and be an idle spectator to the diminution, the subversion, the destruction of the Constitution." Letters poured in from across the country with many people demonstrating their gratitude.

Because of this support, much of it coming from the African American population who previously had seen little of itself in politics, because of her belief in justice, and because of her recognition that legislation, like voter redistricting, allowed her to successfully be involved in politics, Jordan was a strong supporter of minority legislation. She understood that individual drive and success could only bring people so far. After that, change in the law was needed to bring about further equality and opportunities for minority groups.

Her first legislation, the Omnibus Crime Control and Safe Streets Act which was up for renewal in 1973, reflected this interest. The original bill, passed in 1968, included no civil rights provisions. In what became known as the Jordan Amendment, Jordan ensured that the renewed bill included a statement that said federal funds had to be used in a nondiscriminatory manner.

Beyond her involvement in minority rights, Jordan also engaged in women's interests, although on a smaller scale. She did vote for the Equal Rights Amendment and for abortion rights, but also believed that women could and would succeed without these changes. Unlike racial minority rights, which she thought needed the help of legislation to change, Jordan believed that for women it was more an issue of attitude than law. Much of this came from her own experiences—she did not lose the first two elections in Texas because she was a woman, she lost because of unfair districting and because of her race. In addition, some of the issues related to gender inequality, such as credit discrimination and the loss of contractual autonomy, never affected her because she remained single. Thus, although she supported women's rights and the legislation related to women, Jordan was more closely affiliated with issues related to racial minorities.

Because of her growing stature and in large part because of the success of her Watergate address, the Democratic Party asked Jordan to give the keynote address at the 1976 Democratic National Convention. Not one to mince words, she asked the crowd: "But there is something different tonight. There is something special about tonight. What is different? What is special? I, Barbara Jordan, am a keynote speaker." While she was a clever politician, Jordan had struggled to achieve each step in her career, recognized her success, and acknowledged her importance as a model for others to follow.

Her successful address indirectly pressured Jimmy Carter, the Democratic presidential candidate, to name Jordan to the vice presidential spot. Jordan believed that such an announcement would be unlikely and that the country, although accepting of her, was not then ready for either a black or a woman in national office: "It's not my turn. When it's my turn, you'll know."

Following the success of her first two terms, Jordan ran for re-election one more time, and in 1977 won a third term in Congress. However, at the end of that term, Jordan chose to retire from politics. In 1979 she left Washington, DC, and returned to Texas where she served as a professor in the Lyndon Baines Johnson School of Public Affairs at the University of Texas in Austin. Although she continued to be involved in politics on the side, her primary focus became teaching public affairs and ethics, which she did until her death in 1996.

Despite struggling with her health in the 1980s and 1990s, Jordan tried to remain active. Even though she left the public sphere officially, she acted as a counselor to Governor Ann Richards in Texas in the early 1990s, delivered a second keynote address to the Democratic National Convention in 1992, and served as the chairwoman for the U.S. Commission on Immigration Reform, under President Bill Clinton. For all of these actions and her continued service to her country in the name of justice, Jordan received many honors, including an induction into the National Women's Hall of Fame in 1990 and a Presidential Medal of Freedom in 1994.

Following her death at the age of 59 on January 17, 1996, from a combination of multiple sclerosis, pneumonia, and leukemia, Jordan's body lay in state at the University of Texas campus in Austin for 24 hours. Like her groundbreaking life, she continued this tradition in her death and was the first African American, man or woman, to be buried in Texas State Cemetery in Austin. As she said during her 1976 address at the Democratic National Convention, "My presence here is one additional bit of evidence that the American Dream need not forever be deferred." Rightly so, Jordan's triumphs in life and death helped inspire generations of people, not just blacks and women, to achieve their dreams, fight for freedom, and advocate for justice.

Elyssa Ford
Arizona State University

FURTHER READING

Jordan, Barbara, and Shelby Hearon. *Barbara Jordan: A Self-Portrait*. Garden City, NY: Doubleday & Company, 1979.

Margolies-Mezvinskey, Marjorie, and Barbara Feinman. *A Woman's Place . . . The Freshman Women Who Changed the Face of Congress*. New York: Crown Publishers, 1994.

Parham, Sandra, ed. *Barbara C. Jordan: Selected Speeches*. Washington, DC: Howard University Press, 1999.

Rogers, Mary Beth. *Barbara Jordan: American Hero*. New York: Bantam Books, 1998.

Sherman, Max, ed. *Barbara Jordan: Speaking the Truth with Eloquent Thunder*. Austin: University of Texas Press, 2007.

Photofest

Michael Jordan (1963–)

When sport fans and media pundits discuss the greatest basketball players of all time, Michael Jeffrey Jordan is inevitably at the top of their lists. Even U.S. President **Barack Obama,** a known basketball aficionado, selected Jordan as his choice as the greatest basketball player of all time, telling the Associated Press in 2009 that he favored Jordan over the Los Angeles Lakers' Kobe Bryant. Jordan is likewise among the most financially successful athlete-endorsers to ever pitch a product and among the world's most recognizable athletes. At the height of his basketball-playing career with the Chicago Bulls during the 1980s and 1990s, popular commentators celebrated this African American crossover star for securing fan support across diverse groups of all races, genders, nationalities, and creeds. Scholars and fans alike continue to acknowledge and debate Jordan's larger cultural significance.

There is very little debate about Jordan's lofty place in the annals of basketball history, however. His unique combination of skill, grace, speed, and power, coupled with savvy play, a relentless competitive drive, and tireless work ethic helped Jordan garner numerous individual and team accolades in his 15-year professional basketball career. During his tenure in the National Basketball Association (NBA), Jordan averaged over 30 points per game and helped lead the Chicago Bulls to six NBA championships managing to take a brief two-year retirement between a string of titles or two three-peats (1991–1993 and 1996–1998) to play minor league baseball. Jordan again had a difficult time staying away from the game after a 1999 retirement returning for a two-year playing stint in 2001 with the Washington Wizards, his final tenure as an NBA player. Since 2006 he has been part owner of the NBA's Charlotte Bobcats.

Not only is Jordan a member of the Basketball Hall of Fame in Springfield, Massachusetts as a 2009 inductee but, ESPN, the leading sports television network, named him the greatest athlete of the twentieth century. Jordan earned that honor over such legendary American athletic icons as baseball player Babe Ruth and boxing champion **Muhammad Ali.** The Associated Press placed Jordan second to Ruth on its greatest list. *Sports Illustrated* magazine named Jordan the 1991 "Sportsman of the Year" commemorating the occasion with a hologram of the superstar on its cover.

One-time Chicago Bulls coach Doug Collins noted the unique contributions of Jordan calling him "the greatest athlete who's ever played any sport: He's changed how basketball's played—that a 6–6, 200-pounder can dominate the game." Fellow basketball star Larry Bird once compared Jordan's play to deity, suggesting that the superstar was "God disguised as Michael Jordan." It is easy to understand why Jordan has earned such lofty accolades. Among his individual professional basketball accomplishments: 5 NBA Most Valuable Play (MVP) awards (1988, 1991, 1992, 1996, and 1998), 6 NBA Finals MVP awards (1991–1993, 1996–1998), 3 NBA All-Star game MVP honors (1988, 1996, 1998), membership on 10 First Team All-NBA teams (1987–1993, 1996–1998) and on 9 All-Defensive First Teams (1988–1993, 1996–1998), and won the Defensive Player of the Year award in 1988. In 1996, Jordan was selected to the NBA's 50th Anniversary All-Time Team.

Jordan also parlayed his basketball talents into a financially lucrative endorsement career. In 1984 prior to his entry into the NBA, the multinational athletic shoe and apparel company Nike signed Jordan to his first notable deal for $2,500,000 over five years. In many ways, Jordan helped to usher in a new era of lucrative salary and endorsement deals for elite athletes thanks partially to his talents and saleable image. Indeed, Nike's Air Jordan sneakers generated $125,000,000 in sales during its initial year. According to *Forbes* magazine, in 2009 Jordan still earned $45,000,000 in endorsements, several years after his retirement as a player.

With an assist from Jordan's agent David Falk, the NBA carefully marketed Jordan throughout his career, which in turn helped the league achieve a global presence. The athlete's numerous corporate sponsors also assisted in crafting his saleable pitchman persona as an affable, approachable individual. These numerous corporate sponsors include such notable U.S. financial icons as McDonald's, Coca-Cola, Chevrolet, Gatorade, and Wheaties. He has also represented MCI long-distance telephone service, Hanes Underwear, Rayovac batteries, and Bijan cologne among many others. By the end of twentieth century, Jordan had helped to generate over $10,000,000,000 in profit for numerous sponsors. Nike continues to play a key role having crafted both the famous Air Jordan shoe and Air Jordan persona through cleaver commercials, which began in 1985. These commercials highlighted Jordan's acrobatic, slam-dunking and entertaining style of play while establishing his family-friendly off-the-court image. Today, Jordan continues his association with Nike with Brand Jordan, his own signature label, which *Forbes* estimates, has earned over $1,000,000,000 in sales for Nike.

Although Jordan has achieved financial success and global visibility through sport and endorsements, he hails from fairly modest beginnings. Jordan was born to Delores and James Jordan, on February 17, 1963 in Brooklyn, New York, although his family subsequently moved to Wilmington, North Carolina. Delores Jordan worked in a bank while father James, an Air Force retiree, was employed by General Electric as a mechanic and supervisor. Jordan has four siblings, Larry, James Jr., Deloris, and Roslyn. Jordan often credits his older brother Larry for providing guidance and tough playing competition, which would help develop Michael's athletic skills.

Young Michael's first love was baseball. He excelled as a star pitcher and his team nearly earned a spot in the Little League World Series when he was 12. His prowess and interest in basketball developed later and by the end of his senior year at Laney High School Jordan averaged over 29 points, 11 rebounds, and 10 assists per game. Not only did Jordan earn a place on the McDonald's High School All-American team, but the legendary coach Dean Smith also successfully recruited him to play basketball at the University of North Carolina.

As a freshman Jordan quickly took advantage of the national spotlight as his last minute shot helped the Tarheels win the 1982 National Collegiate Athletic Association Championship title. By the time he entered the NBA draft as a junior, the talented collegiate had earned numerous awards including the "Sporting News College Player of the Year" award in 1983 and 1984 as well as the Naismith and John Wooden awards for excellence in 1984. Selected by the Chicago Bulls as the third overall choice in the 1984 professional basketball draft (behind Houston's choice of Akeem Olajuwon and Portland's choice of Sam Bowie), Jordan eventually completed his coursework and graduated from the University of North Carolina with a degree in geography in 1986.

Prior to taking to the court with the Bulls, Jordan participated in the 1984 Olympic Games, which at that time was still only open to amateurs. Jordan helped lead the U.S. team to a gold medal appropriately, at the highly commercialized Los Angeles Olympic event. In 1992, Jordan would also earn a second gold medal, this time as a professional, leading the highly marketed U.S. Dream Team, composed of top U.S. NBA players.

After successfully competing on the global stage of the Los Angeles Olympics, Jordan began his NBA career intent on helping the Bulls improve. He earned a place in the All-Star game as a first-year player thanks to fan voting and later earned Rookie of the Year honors with a 28-points-per-game average. In 1988, Jordan won the NBA's slam-dunk contest during the All-Star game festivities before his hometown Chicago fans. His most memorable dunk had Jordan leaping from the foul line covering the distance of 15 feet at an elevation high enough to meet the 10-foot-high basket with a forceful jam. In subsequent years, as his athletic and marketing legend grew, so too did the Bulls advance further and further into the playoffs, making the Eastern Conference finals in both 1989 and 1990.

Just as Jordan's professional athletic and endorsement career began to blossom, he began to date Juanita Vanoy. They were married in Las Vegas on September 2, 1989. The couple have three children: Jeffrey Michael born in 1988, Marcus James born in 1990, and Jasmine born in 1992. Whereas Jordan would often appear in commercials with children, the Jordans attempted to shield their own children from the spotlight given the intense public interest and scrutiny surrounding the basketball superstar.

Indeed, while widely admired, Jordan has also been subject to considerable criticism. Early in his career critics suggested that universal acknowledgment of his basketball greatness could only be secured if Jordan led the Bulls to the NBA title. Throughout his playing career the media also made allegations of self-centered play, greed, excessive high-stakes gambling, and marital infidelity. (The Jordans divorced in 2006.) Michael was also fired from an executive position with the Washington Wizards in 2003. The personal trials and public challenges Jordan faced also included the tragic murder of his father James in 1993.

Initial speculation over his father's death suggested a sinister link to Michael's gambling activities; however this storyline quickly faded with the arrest, arraignment, and conviction of two North Carolina men, Larry Martin Demure and Daniel Andrea Green. Jordan had a close relationship with his father and many observers speculated that Jordan's subsequent brief retirement from professional basketball on October 6, 1993 to play minor league baseball was the direct result of his grief over his father's death. Jordan denied this claim stating he would have played minor league baseball even if his father were still alive.

James Jordan's death proved that fame could not shield Michael from tragedy, however much of the early criticism directed at Jordan for selfish play abated after the Bulls won championships beginning with the 1990–1991 NBA title. Under the stewardship of Coach Phil Jackson and with key contributions from a variety of players such as Scottie Pippen and Horace Grant the Bulls beat **Earvin "Magic" Johnson**'s Los Angeles Lakers to win the NBA championship and Jordan was selected as the MVP of the finals. Jordan and the Bulls would continue their championship form beating the Portland Blazers in the 1991–1992 Finals, and the Phoenix Suns in the 1992–1993 championship series. Jordan's dominance was apparent, as he became the first player ever to win three consecutive championship MVP trophies. The icon also demonstrated a flair for the dramatic helping his team secure the 1996 title on Father's Day. Jordan explained that winning the title on Father's Day as a tribute to his late father "makes it even more special. There's no way to really describe it."

> I've missed more than nine thousand shots in my career. I've lost almost three hundred games. Twenty-six times, I've been trusted to take the game winning shot and missed. I've failed over and over again in my life. And that is why I succeed.
>
> —Michael Jordan

As the NBA Finals drew increasingly higher levels of worldwide attention, so too did admiration heighten for Jordan's expressive style of play. According to cultural critic Michael Eric Dyson, Jordan's "head moving, arms extending, hands waving, tongue wagging and legs spreading" as also captured in the Air Jordan moniker suggest grace and style. Dyson adds that these expressive body movements are comparable to other historical expressions of African American culture, including jazz and rap. Read from this perspective Jordan's ability to slam the basketball and make dynamic movements on the basketball court represents a form of cultural resistance to white power structures as his style is an expression of bodily ingenuity and creativity.

The accompanying intense focus on and marketing of his body by Nike and the NBA is additionally significant for numerous cultural reasons. Celebrations of Jordan's athleticism provide one more example of America's obsession with the physical capabilities of the male body. Even though women are involved in sport, popular representations of athletic masculinity continue to suggest and legitimize myths of male physical superiority, which is too often conflated with male social superiority.

And yet to make this statement is to acknowledge that representations of Jordan carry multiple cultural meanings, many of which are additionally complicated by race give historical and contemporary white preoccupation with the physicality of black bodies. This preoccupation has its roots in Social Darwinist thought and presumes that African Americans are physically gifted, closer to nature, and less civilized than whites. These stereotypes are not benign, as they have been used by whites to justify racist treatment from the advent of slavery to the contemporary dismantling of social welfare programs.

This interest in Jordan's physicality is clearly seen in advertisements including one of the first Nike commercials broadcasted in the spring of 1985, "Jordan Flight." The commercial features Jordan playing on a playground basketball court with the Chicago skyline in the background. The sound of jet engines revving up for flight accompanies the images of Jordan slam-dunking the basketball. The final 10 seconds of the commercial feature Jordan wearing his black and red Technicolor Nike Air Jordan shoes suspended in air with his legs wide apart as if in flight. A voice-over asks, "Who said man was not meant to fly?" This commercial suggests that Jordan represents the ultimate "natural athlete," for he can literally fly through the air.

Both Nike's and the NBA's promotions helped to reinforced beliefs about black bodies by positioning Jordan as someone who was, according to critic David Andrews, "seemingly born to dunk." In this way, Jordan's corporate sponsors both participated in and additionally encouraged a cultural preoccupation with black physicality.

The NBA's marketing machine helped to promote and capitalize on these and other representations in an effort to move away from previous associations, which had been connected to the league in the 1970s and early 1980s. During this time racist images projected the largely African American playing force of the NBA as undisciplined and deviant. Michael Jordan's All-American athletic persona helped bolster the image of the league by appeasing white audiences' fears. These fears stem from the mythical associations of urban blackness, which rest on racist stereotypes of an uncontrollable and undisciplined style of play and the stigma of assumed drug abuse.

Instead of directly confronting the pernicious belief systems underlying these stereotypes, the league instead began promoting black players such as Michael Jordan as friendly and athletic, and in ways aligned with heroism, wholesomeness, racial harmony, moral pureness, and a disciplined physicality. On the surface such attention to Jordan and other black players seems positive, and yet, this revision of black masculinity, created by white-controlled institutions such as the NBA and Nike, never displaced previous stereotypes but instead ware designed to evoke pleasure rather than fear or distain. In sum, Nike and the NBA used Jordan's talents to sell their products and ideas about athleticism and black athleticism in particular.

Jordan's own political voice is more difficult to definitively characterize. Clearly, however, his views and actions resonate differently than those of other famous black athletes from previous generations, especially athletes competing in the 1960s. These include such politically active athletes as **Tommie Smith and John Carlos** who protested racial inequality and apartheid at the 1968 Olympics as well as Muhammad Ali who spoke out against racism and what he saw as an unjust war in Vietnam. In many ways, Jordan was a willing corporate pitchman and his participation as a safe and uncontroversial salesman stands in stark contrast to the vision of African American athletes as outspoken critics of the white establishment. Jordan instead preferred to work within established institutions and serve as a role model for the ideas of racial tolerance, dedication, and achievement. Jordan's approach and the ways is which advertisers and the NBA represented him are also, in many ways, part and parcel of the political tenor of the times in which he lived.

As several sport sociologists suggest, representations of Jordan reverberate with the political project of Reaganism. This era is associated with the leadership of President Ronald Reagan, who served from 1980 to 1988. And yet, many of the central tenants promoted by Reagan continue into the twenty-first century suggesting the legacy of a broader economic and social conservative movement. The hallmark of this era is the advancement of Reaganomics, a big business agenda promoting supply-side economics, tax breaks for the wealth, global market expansion, and corporate deregulation.

This philosophy additionally faults the state for stifling economic and persona initiative through excessive taxation and social welfare programs. Promoting individualistic worldviews, supporters of Reaganomics continue to downplay structural issues such as class inequality and racism, conditions that limit social mobility. Instead conservatives frequently suggested that such social problems as unemployment, poverty, and urban decay are not the effects of social and economic forces but rather the inevitable result of the personal immorality of the poor, especially poor African Americans. Given this reasoning, advocates of pro-business agendas did more than promote an economic agenda; they actively sought to dismantle the social welfare safety net for the programs' alleged oppressive effects on personal responsibility and financial growth.

Jordan's ascendancy to global athletic icon and celebrity endorser occurred within this conservative climate. However, it is important to note that Jordan did not actively support many of the regressive social policies of the times. Indeed Jordan rarely expressed political views and instead focused on philanthropic work including the establishment of a Chicago Boys and Girls Club in his late father's name. An emphasis on philanthropy does suggest a measure of awareness that inequalities continue to impact the poor in general and poor African Americans in particular. Still the relentless promotion of Jordan's wholesome persona and ability to secure large endorsement deals resonates with the pro-business agenda of the times.

On the court, Jordan was represented as a tough-minded individual who could dominate opponents and make things happen for his team. This emphasis on rugged individualism reinforced the mantra advanced by the era's conservative voices that repeatedly suggested success is merely a matter of personal determination, not an issue affected by structures of opportunity.

Jordan's off-the-court reputation as committed to the joys of family life also played into the era's focus on the nuclear family and traditional family values as central to reinvigorating the national mood. *Rare Air: Michael on Michael*, a book with text written by Jordan and accompanied by numerous photographs offers a window into his persona as a dedicated family man. Images feature Jordan performing on the basketball court and communing at home with his own family suggesting a persona as a loving, breadwinner father and husband who is also committed to the tough macho world of sport. While these pictures include then wife Juanita and their young children Jeffrey, Marcus, and Jasmine, one photo is particularly illustrative. It features a bare-chested Jordan holding his then-infant, diaper-clad daughter Jasmine. The photograph features a noticeable contrast between Jordan's muscled body and the vulnerability of his daughter's tiny form.

Again, the broader cultural messages communicated throughout the book are complicated. For example, this book offers representations of the Jordan family bliss, images that challenge stereotypes about the black family while simultaneously reinforcing traditional gender roles. That is, as represented in *Rare Air* the engaging Jordan family suggests both black success and consumer comfort, visions which countering conservative suggestions that black families are "broken," inherently pathological, or the embodiment of what then-Vice President Dan Quayle suggested was "a poverty of values." This vision of the Jordan family also counters negative assumptions about black male athletes, as overly macho and hypersexual. And yet, one could also read these sanitized representations as the epitome of traditional gender roles, domestic tranquility, and consumer comfort—the very same privatized qualities advocated for by conservatives in post-Reagan American. Thus regardless of intent, the projection of these Jordan "family values" both challenge stereotypes of the black family just as they also participate in a broader conservative project related to U.S. families.

The global reach of the NBA and Nike, means that Jordan's iconic status continues to produce complex cultural meanings across the world. His basketball persona has traveled across the globe touching such diverse spaces as Poland, New Zealand, and across the Black Atlantic. One study suggests that for youth living in Poland, Jordan represents the promise of American success and democracy in the post-communist nation. In New Zealand, Jordan's commercialized persona has likewise helped to generate more discussion and interest in a variety of sports—not just basketball. This interest has been particularly helpful in rejuvenating participation in traditional New Zealand sporting activities. To the members of the Black Diaspora living across the world, Jordan represents black accomplishment and pride. The icon's achievements signify the possibility of and hope for a better future for people of color across the globe.

Jordan serves as a transnational symbol whose meaning varies according to local contexts and interpretations. As suggested here, his crafted public persona and reputation as a hard-working African American athlete who allegedly transcends race have also served complex and contradictory ends within the U.S. context. Indeed the dominant vision of the super salesman and accomplished athlete positions Jordan as the antithesis of persistent racist stereotypes of black men as deviant and dangerous. But Jordan's iconic status is also reflective of the tenor of the times reinforcing an ideology of rugged individualism and unleashing narratives of racial progress with claims that his success is proof that race no longer matters. These projections occurred just as more community-oriented values and social welfare practices were being demonized by conservatives via policies which disproportionately harmed people of color. In this way, elements of Jordan's persona have been mobilized to justify regressive social ends.

> I realize that I'm black, but I like to be viewed as a person, and this is everybody's
> wish. —Michael Jordan

And while the overwhelming public and media attention directed toward Jordan has abated since his retirement, Jordan still is not completely out of the spotlight as he continues working with Nike and as part owner of the North Carolina Bobcats. Given this presence, there is no doubt that new cultural meanings and associations will continue to accrue. Not only is Jordan one of the greatest basketball player of all time, but an important cultural icon who has meant so much to diverse groups of people and economic interests.

Cultural critic Michael Eric Dyson suggests that Jordan's global appeal reflects admiration for Jordan's tremendous athletic talents and saleable public persona, which additionally speak to the convergence of a variety of cultural needs, economic practices, and discourse. And yet, according to Dyson it would be impossible to offer a final analysis of Jordan's significance as the icon "does not offer a stable and uniform place within diverse and complex popular cultures. Jordan has and will continue to mean different things to different people, within different cultural contexts within diverse historical moments."

The Jordan phenomenon additionally reminds us that the meanings of sporting and advertising performances are never simple or obvious. The backlash of Reaganism serves as one salient context from which to consider the broader significance of Michael Jordan. And yet, thanks to the fluidity of the cultural process, there is no guarantee that this interpretation of Michael Jordan will remain permanently inscribed in history. Indeed, cultural and historical analysis reveals the shifting character of power relations and interpretations. Given these insights, it is clear that Michael Jordan is a complicated, instructive, and powerful African American icon who challenges us to critically engage and continuously wrestle with his broader cultural contributions and significance.

Mary G. McDonald
Miami University

FURTHER READING

Andrews, D.L. "The Facts of Michael Jordan's Blackness: Excavating a Floating Racial Signifier." *Sociology of Sport Journal* 13, no. 2 (1996): 125–58.

Andrews, D.L., ed. *Michael Jordan, Inc.: Corporate Sport, Media Culture and Late Modern America*. Albany: State University of New York, 2001.

Dyson, Michael Eric. "Be Like Mike?: Michael Jordan and the Pedagogy of Desire." *Cultural Studies* 7, no. 1 (1993): 64–72.

Halberstam, David. *Playing for Keeps: Michael Jordan and the World He Made*. New York: Random House, 1999.

Jordan, Michael, and David Halberstam. *Driven from Within*. New York: Atria, 2006.

Jordan, Michael, and W. Iooss. *Rare Air: Michael on Michael*. New York: HarperCollins, 1993.

McCallum, Jack. "The Desire Is Not There." *Sports Illustrated* 79 (1993): 28–35.

McDonald, M. G. "Michael Jordan's Family Values: Marketing, Meaning and Post Reagan America." *Sociology of Sport Journal* 13 (1996): 344–65.

McDonald, M. G., and D. L. Andrews. "Michael Jordan: Corporate Sport and Postmodern Celebrityhood." In *Sport Stars: The Cultural Politics of Sporting Celebrity*, edited by D. L. Andrews and S. J. Jackson, 20–35. London: Routledge, 2001.

Norment, L. "Michael and Juanita Jordan Talk about Love, Marriage, and Life after Basketball." *Ebony* 47 (November 1991): 68–76.

**Florence Griffith Joyner
(1959–1998)**

Florence Griffith Joyner, the reigning world record holder in both the 100- and 200-meter dashes, embodies athletic and personal excellence. A renaissance woman in her own right, Griffith Joyner is an icon of black America for more than her status as "the world's fastest woman"; she is celebrated for her ability to overcome adversity and for her talents on and off the track. Indeed, former USA Track and Field President Patricia Rico argued that Griffith Joyner,

> was a living legend. Flo Jo and track and field were synonymous. I don't think you could have one without the other. We entered a new era with Flo Jo on the scene, particularly for women. She was dynamic out there, very sophisticated. She put a new twist on women's competitive sports. (Knight)

As a confident, successful African American female, on and off the track, Florence Griffith Joyner demanded respect and earned role-model status in the United States and around the world.

Griffith Joyner earned her nickname "Florescent Jo," or "Flo Jo," because of her flashy, handmade uniforms and her unique, confident style. She was also revered as a role model for young girls who came of age in the 1980s, often called "Title IX babies." After the passage of the landmark legislation declaring equal opportunity for girls and women in education, including athletics, thousand upon thousands of young girls across the United States hit the courts, playing fields, and tracks of their communities. Flo Jo, more than any other female athlete, showed the possibility of being both competitive and athletic, glamorous and feminine. She, more than any other sports legend, influenced an entire generation of girls and women to take pride in their athletic bodies and to appreciate them for their beauty, strength, and power. Flo Jo taught a generation of Americans that a strong, fast, intelligent black woman is a beautiful thing.

Florence Delorez Griffith was born the seventh of 11 children to Robert, an electronics technician, and Florence, a seamstress, on December 21, 1959. After her parents divorced, "Dee-Dee," as she was called, and her siblings lived in a housing project in the Watts district of Los Angeles. Their mother, and grandmother Gertrude Scott, a beautician, raised the children and encouraged them to be creative and confident individuals. Tough love was a good descriptor of the two women's parenting style. Television was prohibited during the school week, so the children became big readers. Books were scattered throughout the household, and the straight-A student flourished in a home of reading and learning. Poetry was Griffith's favorite genre, and the young girl always kept a diary including her poems, writings, dreams, and desires.

Even in her childhood, Griffith proudly stood out among her peers with a strong identity and self-confidence atypical of prepubescent girls. In elementary school, Griffith owned a boa constrictor that she named Brandy because she was tired of the family dog and its fleas. Brandy grew to five feet in length, and

Griffith enjoyed saving its sheddings to paint designs on the dead skin. Her individuality made her different from her peers. Griffith also applied her artistic talents to fashion design and beauty at a young age. She designed and constructed outfits for her Barbie dolls with her mother, and earned a popular status among many of her peers because she did all the neighborhood kids' hair and nails. At the same time, conformity was not a part of Griffith's vocabulary. The young girl kept to herself and seemed to sometimes exist in her own little world, immune to ridicule. Reflecting on her childhood, Flo Jo stated while in the prime of her athletic career, "I was very quiet, always. But in kindergarten I would braid my hair with one braid straight up. I'd go all day like that, and when kids teased me, I'd just laugh with them" (Moore, "Very Fast"). The confidence and strong identity in self that developed in young Griffith, nourished by her supportive mother and grandmother, were the building blocks of the world's fastest woman.

Griffith's athletic success also began at quite a young age. She participated in sporting events sponsored by the Sugar Ray Robinson Youth Foundation in 1965 at the age of seven. In her first year of competitive athletics, Griffith won a gold medal at the Jesse Owens National Youth Games. Despite the experiences of her parents' divorce and growing up in the projects, one could already see in young Griffith the makings of a driven, special individual. Griffith, however, continued to face a series of obstacles in life; perhaps the process of overcoming adversity is what made her an Olympic champion and world record holder.

After graduating as a star scholar-athlete from Jordan High School in Los Angeles in 1978, Griffith attended California State University at Northridge to pursue a degree in business. Despite earning a 3.25 GPA in her first year, financial problems forced her to drop out and work as a bank teller. Cal State assistant track coach Bob Kersee convinced Griffith to return to the university, helped her apply for and gain financial aid, and began working with the young athlete to develop her sprinting skills in the 200-meter dash. When Kersee accepted an assistant coaching position at the University of California-Los Angeles in 1980, Griffith followed her coach even though UCLA did not offer a degree in business. Her reluctant decision to follow her athletic dreams at the expense of her desired degree in business proved difficult for Griffith. Reflecting on the transfer, in 1988 Flo Jo stated, "It kind of hurts to say this—I chose athletics over academics" (Moore, "Very Fast"). A woman who sought to develop both her mind and body, the ambivalence revealed in her comment demonstrates Griffith Joyner's goal-oriented nature and her desire to be the best in all areas of her life.

Griffith thrived as a scholar athlete at UCLA; she and her teammate, heptathlete Jackie Joyner, led a star-studded Bruin squad. In 1982, Griffith won the 200-meter dash at the inaugural NCAA women's outdoor track and field championships at Brigham Young University in Provo, Utah. Her collegiate record-setting time of 22.39 seconds ensured her a place among the world's most promising young sprinters. The following year, although failing to defend her national crown in the 200-meter by placing second to Merlene Ottey of the University of Nebraska at Kerney, Griffith competed in four events to help UCLA secure back-to-back team titles in a close race with the University of Tennessee and Florida State University. She added another NCAA gold in a different event, winning the 400-meter dash in a recording-setting 50.94 seconds. Griffith still holds UCLA school records in the 200- and 400-meter dashes.

Following the 1983 track season, Griffith and Joyner continued to train with their UCLA coaches in preparation for the 1984 Olympic Games. Both women earned silver medals in their respective events; Griffith, hampered by a hamstring injury, placed second to Valerie Brisco-Hooks. She ran a personal-best time of 22.04, but Brisco-Hook's 21.81 set a new Olympic record. The loss devastated Griffith, who made a decision to take some time off from training to work as a secretary in a bank. She also returned to two of her lifelong passions, working at night as a hair stylist and designing children's books by day. Friends and family teased Griffith, who was rumored to have gained close to 60 pounds during her break from training, but were not troubled by her sudden change in direction. Rather than moping about and feeling sorry for herself, Griffith decided to pursue her other interests and to develop her many other skills.

> There's no substitute for hard work. . . . I have the medals to prove it!
> —Florence Griffith Joyner

Unfortunately, Griffith's experience is far from uncommon in the world of elite track and field competitors. With the Olympics cycling over a period of four years, the downtime after an Olympic year proves to be difficult for many world-class athletes, especially those who participate in sports that are less popular in their respective countries. In the United States, significant popular interest in track and field only comes in Olympic years. Elite athletes find themselves struggling to continue strenuous, time-consuming training schedules while also having to work additional jobs to support themselves financially. Many individuals walk away from the sport, while others, like Griffith, return to training and competing after being encouraged by a coach or a close friend to pursue their dream of winning an Olympic gold medal. In 1986, Bob Kersee and Al Joyner, Jackie's brother and 1984 Olympic triple-jump gold medalist, convinced Griffith to return to track and field to prepare for the 1988 Seoul Olympics. That same year, Bob Kersee and Jackie Joyner married, while 20 months later Florence Griffith and Al Joyner tied the knot. The four athletes had created an American track and field dynasty.

In the moments immediately following the Olympic Trials' second round of the women's 100-meter dash, television commentators Marty Liquori and Bob Hersh were speechless. Liquori finally broke the silence as he stammered in disbelief, "It can't be! No one can run that fast!" (YouTube). Griffith Joyner's time on the scoreboard read an unbelievable 10.49 seconds. Had the timing system broken? Was the race wind-aided, with wind speeds greater than 2 meters-per-second, which would therefore make Griffith Joyner ineligible to break the world record? More importantly, did a woman really just break 10.5 seconds in the 100 meters? Impossible! As the television commentators struggled to make sense of what just happened on the rock-hard Mondo track in Indianapolis, Indiana on that hot July day, at-home television viewers watched the race rerun repeatedly and fans who had witnessed the event sat dumbfounded and awed by the spectacle. The anemometer read that the wind was less than 2 meters-per-second, declaring the race legal, and the timing system appeared to have functioned normally. After a delay, the meet officials certified the race results; Griffith Joyner had just become the fastest woman in the world, breaking Evelyn Ashford's old world record by nearly 0.3 seconds.

Perhaps Griffith Joyner's outfit and style contributed to the disbelief in the stands and among the commentators and home-viewers. Dressed in an electric purple bodysuit with one leg bare, a turquoise bikini brief, and long orange, black, and white fingernails, Griffith Joyner looked more like a cartoon image than an actual person as she stormed down the track. The second half of the race only contributed to this fantasy-like quality; while Griffith Joyner ran virtually even with her competitors over the first half of the race, she extended her lead by what seemed to be an impossible margin (over 4 meters) over only the last 50 meters. The contrast between her one purple-clad leg and her bare leg worked to accentuate her already gigantic and powerful stride-length and turnover. With her hair free and blowing in the breeze generated by her gazelle-like speed, and her costume-like uniform, Griffith Joyner appeared more superhero than human.

Her post-race interview added to her mysterious, iconic nature. Her soft, yet rich and comfortably confident voice provided a marked contrast to her flashy, flamboyant clothing style. She explained the race as if she knew in advance what the rest of the world was still struggling to comprehend, "Bobby told me to pay attention to the triple jump and if the wind was down, to go for the world record. The wind went down and I went for it" (YouTube). Downplaying the remarkable nature of her feat, Griffith Joyner, who earned the nickname "Florescent Jo" or "Flo Jo" through this flamboyant Trials performance, backed up her performance with a time of 10.61 seconds in the final; had her 10.49 record been recalled, her time in the final still would have broken Ashford's world record.

Sportswriters who reflected on Flo Jo's magnificent performance recognized immediately the momentous nature of the feat. Covering the Trials, Kenny Moore wrote the following:

> How could this converted 200-meter runner, in only her fourth serious 100 meters, take a huge .27 of a second off the world record? That's two-and-a-half times the slice Ben Johnson cut from the men's 100 record last year with

his watershed 9.83. According to projections based on past improvements, no woman was supposed to reach even 10.65 until the year 2000. (Moore, "Getup and Go," 1998)

In fact, the projections proved correct: only Marion Jones has broken 10.7 seconds in the nearly two decades since Griffith Joyner's 10.49. He also pointed out that Griffith Joyner's time was faster than both Ben Johnson's 100 meters the previous day in a qualifying round and O. J. Simpson's personal best as a member of a world record-setting relay team!

Griffith-Joyner headed to the Olympics in Seoul, Korea to compete in four events: the 100 meters, 200 meters, and as a member of both the 400- and 1600-meter relays. She earned gold in both of her individual competitions, breaking the world record in the 200 meters in both the semifinals and the finals, setting a new mark of 21.34 seconds. Her third gold came as she anchored the 400-meter relay; Griffith Joyner picked up her fourth medal, a silver, by running a leg of the 1600-meter relay. The world's fastest woman broke world records in two events in less than three months and returned to the United States packing a whole lot of Olympic hardware. Griffith Joyner also reinvigorated interest in her sport at a time when track and field's profile was sinking. Her unorthodox style and flamboyant racing outfits stole newspaper headlines and magazine covers. Reflecting on her career, Griffith Joyner described how running filled her with excitement, made her feel free, and allowed her to express herself. Her self-confidence came from the cumulative effect of learning from every race that she had run—whether she won or lost. An incredibly driven and perseverant person, willing to endure pain and overcome obstacles, Griffith Joyner achieved her goals and dreams.

Nineteen eighty-eight was the year of Flo Jo; she finished it with prestigious recognition, earning the title of Associated Press's Female Athlete of the Year, U.S. Olympic Committee's Sportswoman of the Year, and the Sullivan Award (given to the nation's most outstanding amateur athlete). Perhaps she knew something that no one else did as she was competing in the Olympic Games, as she would soon retire from the sport at the height of her career. Knowing, perhaps at a subconscious level, that she was going to win, she enjoyed every moment of every qualifying round and race, which enabled her to fully embrace the Olympic experience. Moore, writing about her performance in the 100-meter Olympic final, noted the following:

> Her smile began growing at seventy meters, even as she roared away. By 90 meters it was a glorious grin. By 95 she had her arms up celebrating. At 100 the clock stopped at 10.54. . . . With that smile she beamed out all the sensations of her joyfully relaxed mastery in a way more evocative than any eye-popping outfit. (Moore, "Go, Flo, Go")

With the benefit of hindsight, it becomes obvious that Griffith Joyner enjoyed every moment of her Olympic victories because she knew that they would be both the climax and the last moments in her competitive track and field career. Reflecting on the 1988 Olympics nearly a decade later, Griffith Joyner recollected the following in an interview:

> Twenty meters before I got to the finish line I was so overwhelmed with joy. I knew that I was going to win the gold medal because I didn't see anyone else close by. I thought, "My God! The race is about to be over and I'm going to finally win a gold medal—my first gold medal in the 100 meters." (Hatch and Hatch)

Only an elite athlete perfectly in tune with her mind, body, and spirit can have that type of awareness and clarity while in the act of making history.

In February 1989, Griffith Joyner retired from her sport, naming acting, designing, modeling, and writing as areas of interest that left her little time to train. Trying to justify why she would retire at the top of her game and perhaps frustrated by her decision, many individuals both inside and outside track and field raised drug accusations to explain both Griffith Joyner's incredible feats and her abrupt decision to retire. These individuals apparently chose to ignore the hard evidence: Griffith Joyner passed all 11 of her drug tests in the year 1988. She was clean as a whistle and always vehemently denied she had done anything unethical, citing determination, the ability to endure incredible amounts of pain, and hard work for her achievements. Griffith Joyner's reflections on her Olympic gold medal achievement illustrate her sense of accomplishment and should allay the skepticism of critics. "It was a twenty-year dream. At that moment I knew everything was worth it. I felt so happy inside that I had it won I just had to let it out" (Moore, "Go, Flo, Go"). Her strong sense of identity, self-worth, contentment, and accomplishment told her that it was time to move on to other talents in her life. She had endured 20 years of pain and hard work to achieve her dreams, and she accomplished them with style and flair.

> It was a twenty-year dream. At that moment I knew everything was worth it. I felt so happy inside that I had it won I just had to let it out.
> —Florence Griffith Joyner

Many athletes at the top of their game possess a strong sense of self and confidence in their unique identity. Griffith Joyner became the embodiment of a new ideal in American womanhood: a woman who could be both beautiful and physically fit, both feminine and powerful. With her fluorescent, revealing outfits, her long hair loose and flowing, and her three-inch artistically manicured nails, she brought style and sexuality to women's athletics. Although girls and women who participated in "feminine" sports that emphasized grace, beauty, and performance, such as gymnastics, figure skating, and cheerleading, benefited from media coverage and popular support, females who competed in traditionally male sports associated with power, strength, and aggression found coverage and support of their sports lacking. Stereotypes plagued women who competed in these sports in the United States; many were considered to be lesbians or asexual, or to have "something wrong" with them that motivated them not to conform to American ideals of womanhood. Moreover, Griffith Joyner demonstrated to girls and women of color that they could develop strong bodies and minds, and could do so with pride, confidence, and grace.

Girls and women in the United States entered sports participation in record numbers after the passage of Title IX. These athletes revised American ideals as they demonstrated that athletic success and femininity could exist together; moreover, physical fitness and a healthy lifestyle became central components of what made up the new American woman. Title IX did not provide identical opportunities to all American women, however. This legislation and the expansion of girls' and women's opportunities in sports benefited white women of privileged backgrounds more than it helped females of color and women of lower socioeconomic status. As a black female, Griffith Joyner is an icon for more than her athletic prowess; she is a role model for the girls of the United States, especially African American girls, who wish to become the best in their area of talent and to go after their dreams.

Griffith Joyner also demonstrated that female athletes need not be humble. Her confidence was not cocky or arrogant; rather, she exuded a radiance that an unfortunate number of female athletes, and women in general, lack. For example, she painted three fingernails red, white, and blue, and a fourth gold, to reinforce her goal of Olympic gold. Reflecting on her success after the Games, she boldly stated, "There's no substitute for hard work. . . . I have the medals to prove it!" ("Florence Griffith Joyner: The World's Fastest Woman"). Griffith Joyner's confidence came from her strong sense of self and pride in her identity, which were instilled in her by her mother and grandmother from birth. A goal-oriented and driven person, Griffith Joyner's confidence and self-awareness allowed her to achieve and also enjoy her successes in life.

As a volunteer and woman of service, Griffith Joyner remembered her roots and recognized her responsibility from her position of celebrity and privilege to always help others. In 1989 she became spokesperson for the American Cancer Society, the Multiple Sclerosis Foundation, and Project Eco-School. Four years later, President Bill Clinton appointed her as co-chair of the President's Council on Physical Fitness and Sports (PCPFS) with Tom McMillen, a star basketball player, Rhodes scholar, and U.S. Congressman.

During their joint tenure, Griffith Joyner and McMillen developed an adult fitness program and established the Silver Eagle Award to promote fitness among seniors. The two leaders also helped develop a three-year advertisement campaign focused on youth fitness entitled, "Get Off It!" and later, "Get Up, Get Out." Finally, Griffith Joyner and McMillen supported the decision to make available in the Spanish language all health-related materials produced by the PCPFS. The Clinton administration dramatically expanded the programs of the PCPFS, thanks in large part to the hard work and dedication of American activist-athletes Griffith Joyner and McMillen. In his eulogy of Griffith Joyner, Bill Clinton commented on the athlete's service and commitment to community. "Though she rose to the pinnacle of the world of sports," he stated, "she never forgot where she came from, devoting time and resources to helping children—especially those growing up in our most devastated neighborhoods—make the most of their own talents" (Noden).

Drawing from her significant body of experience in volunteerism and service work, in 1994 Griffith Joyner and her husband, Al, started the Florence Griffith Joyner Foundation for Disadvantaged Youth. The nonprofit organization encouraged young people to apply the lessons learned from participation in athletics to their lives in general, including school, family, friendship, and community. The Joyners and their staff worked with inner-city children to provide them with opportunities they might have lacked otherwise, just as the Sugar Ray Robinson Foundation activities in the Watts neighborhood of Los Angeles provided Griffith Joyner with opportunities during her childhood.

As a renaissance woman, Griffith Joyner demonstrated that athletes are not one-dimensional and can be successful on and off the track. After 20 years devoted to strenuous training and competitive athletics, Griffith Joyner turned to fully embrace her other talents and interests, including acting and modeling, designing, and writing. Indeed, she pursued each of these pursuits. Griffith Joyner had a holistic sense of self-improvement and developed skills that utilized both her body and her mind. She embodied a philosophy that many athletes, especially those in individual sports, strive for, a philosophy that celebrates a well-rounded lifestyle. Though she always sought out new challenges and projects, Griffith Joyner seemed even busier in retirement than she did in her years as an elite athlete. In addition to running the Florence Griffith Joyner Foundation with her husband and contributing to other volunteer organizations, she managed to write 33 children's books (one for each of her nieces and nephews) and a book on exercise and nutrition for adults, entitled *Running for Dummies*. Griffith Joyner continued to design clothing for herself, her family, friends, and for sale; in 1989 she helped design the Indiana Pacers' basketball uniforms and logo for the 1989–1990 season. She also jumpstarted her own nail company, FloJo Nails, selling nail art including paints, stencils for designs, artificial nails, and glitter.

A natural performer, Griffith Joyner recognized her true calling in retirement as she found herself pulled toward the big screen. She acted in films and television series (both in the United States and abroad), made celebrity appearances on game shows, participated in documentaries and made-for-television specials on sports, worked as a sportscaster covering track and field, and produced as well as acted in educational programs for youth. In conjunction with *Ebony* magazine and the American Medical Association, Flo Jo worked on a documentary, entitled "A Guide to Healthy Living for African Americans."

She also participated in "A Crash Course on Calcium" for the National Dairy Council, and with SmithKline Beecham Pharmaceuticals she acted in " 'Protecting Our Kids': Against Childhood Diseases through Vaccination." In perhaps her best-known educational documentary, Griffith Joyner worked with Arsenio Hall and others to produce "The Flo-Jo Workout: Mind, Body, and Spirit," which introduced young aspiring athletes to her holistic and healthy lifestyle philosophy. For Griffith Joyner, her life was seamless; there were no boundaries separating career, volunteerism, and recreation; those were simply manmade, constructed categories with artificial divisions.

After 1988 and retirement from track and field, Griffith Joyner's number-one priority became her family. Following the examples set by her mother and grandmother, she concentrated on being a mother to her first and only child, Mary Ruth, who was born in the fall of 1990. The Joyners were like three peas in a pod; a close-knit family that cherished its fortunes and dedicated itself to helping others. The Joyners also embraced their large extended family, spending time with Florence's many nieces and nephews, aunts and uncles, and brothers and sisters. Finally, for the Joyners, family also included the even-larger extended family of U.S. track and field. The Joyners fully embraced life and surrounded themselves with loved ones.

On September 21, 1998, Florence Griffith Joyner passed away in her sleep in the Joyners' Mission Viejo, California, home. The official cause of death from the sheriff-coroner's office included three causes: positional asphyxia, epileptiform seizure, and cavernous angioma of the left orbital frontal cerebrum (a brain abnormality discovered during autopsy and a signifier of repeated seizures). At the time of her death Griffith Joyner was only 38 years old. She was a legend who died young, before her body began to decay, and before other athletes could relieve her of the title of world's fastest woman. Iconic Griffith Joyner will always be remembered for her power, beauty, and incredible speed.

Today, the many memorials and articles on Griffith Joyner separate her athletics from her post-athletic talents. This dichotomous interpretation, however, does not truly describe or provide a full understanding of the woman who was Griffith Joyner. Her strong sense of self included athleticism as a central component; she continued to workout after retirement because being physically fit was a fundamental part of who she was, and because she simply enjoyed it. The world's fastest woman had no problem heading out to the local high school in a sweat suit to jog a few laps around the track, much like any other recreational runner. Griffith Joyner expressed herself through her flamboyant style and confident attitude to be true to herself, not to be unique or different, or to grab others' attention and headlines. The way she carried herself with grace, power, confidence, and dedication inspired a generation of young women to pursue their athletic aspirations, and to do so without shame or fear of sacrificing their femininity. Griffith Joyner never forgot her roots; she recognized the responsibility and opportunity her position of privilege gave her to always help others. Florence Delorez Griffith Joyner was a renaissance woman and a true champion in all aspects of her life, both on and off the track.

Victoria L. Jackson
Arizona State University

FURTHER READING

Aasang, Nathan. *Florence Griffith Joyner: Dazzling Olympian*. Minneapolis: Lerner Publications, 1989.

"Florence Griffith Joyner: The World's Fastest Woman." Estate of Florence Griffith Joyner. www.florencegriffithjoyner.com.

Knight, Athelia. "Track Star Griffith Joyner Dies at 38." *The Washington Post Company*, 1998. www.mmjp.or.jp/amlang.atc/di&legends/flojo/aboutflojo.htm (accessed October 28, 2006).

Moore, Kenny. "Getup and Go: Florence Griffith Joyner's Dramatic Garb Made Her a Colorful Blur as She Smashed the World Record in the 100 Meters at the Olympic Trials." *Sports Illustrated*, July 25, 1998. http://Sportsillustrated.cnn.com/Olympics/features/ joyner/flashback2.html (accessed October 14, 2006).

Moore, Kenny. "Go, Flo, Go: Florence Griffith Joyner Did Just That in Blazing to Victory in the 100 Meters." *Sports Illustrated*, October 3, 1988. http://Sportsillustrated .cnn.com/Olympics/ features/joyner/flashback3.html (accessed October 14, 2006).

Noden, Merrell. "FloJo Lived Her Life in Fast-Forward." *Sports Illustrated*, September 22, 1998. See http://Sportsillustrated.cnn.com/Olympics/features/joyner/flojo _noden.html (accessed October 14, 2006).

YouTube, 1988 Olympic Trials 100m, "Flo Jo" World Record and Interview. See http://www.youtube.com/watch?v=dAvBonP6JDw (accessed October 24, 2006).

Library of Congress

Martin Luther King, Jr. (1929–1968)

Martin Luther King, Jr., emerged as the most electrifying orator and most prominent figure in the largest mass struggle for human rights in U.S. history. He helped lead three hugely significant, peaceful protests in Alabama—the Montgomery Bus Boycott of 1955–1956, the Birmingham campaign of 1963, and the Voting Rights March from Selma to Montgomery in 1965. For his non-violent efforts aimed at tearing down the walls of racial segregation, he received the Nobel Peace Prize in 1964. He and other civil rights pioneers provoked Congress to pass landmark legislation: the Civil Rights Act, which barred legal segregation in public accommodations, and the Voting Rights Act, which granted African Americans the right to vote in every county of every state. During the last two years of his life, he focused mainly on the goals of eliminating poverty in the United States and stopping the Vietnam War. The federal government honors King by observing his birthday as a national holiday.

Born in 1929, King was nurtured by a loving, middle-class family in Atlanta. His father, Rev. Martin Luther King, Sr., grew up in poverty in rural Georgia, where his parents were sharecroppers. He became a preacher when he could barely read and write and, against his father's wishes, moved to Atlanta. There he married Alberta Williams, the daughter of Rev. A. D. Williams. In 1917, A. D. Williams helped found a local branch of the National Association for the Advancement of Colored People (NAACP). Two years later he traveled to Cleveland to address a national convention of the NAACP. As senior minister of Ebenezer Baptist Church, Williams welcomed his son-in-law, King, Sr., as the co-pastor of his congregation.

When King, Jr., was a child, Williams died, leaving King, Sr., to assume the helm of Ebenezer Church during the troubling years of the Great Depression. As a boy, King, Jr., witnessed poverty and soup lines on Auburn Avenue, which had been one of the most prosperous streets in any African American community. While King, Sr., and church loyalists struggled, successfully, to keep their church property from being foreclosed, King, Jr. became thoroughly immersed in African American Baptist life. Attending very long church services every week, he heard his father and guest ministers deliver hundreds of sermons and prayers. While listening to his mother play the organ, he joined the congregation in singing many spirituals, hymns, and gospel songs.

Because numerous members of its African American (and entirely male) student body were serving in the military during World War II, **Morehouse College** of Atlanta began admitting younger students, including King, Jr. There King was mentored by his professors and by Benjamin Mays, an African American who had earned a PhD from the University of Chicago and who served as President of Morehouse College. King decided to become a minister. Upon graduation, he entered a largely white environment for the first time while attending a liberal Protestant seminary outside Philadelphia. Upon receiving his seminary degree, he pursued a PhD in theology at Boston University. His dissertation amounted to a very abstract theological discussion, far removed from social concerns.

When King had almost completed his doctoral studies, he accepted the pulpit of Dexter Avenue Baptist Church of Montgomery, Alabama. Aware of larger developments in American race relations—such as the recent *Brown* decision of the U.S. Supreme Court—African Americans in Montgomery were especially frustrated with segregation in public transportation. JoAnn Robinson, E. D. Nixon, and others used the arrest of **Rosa Parks** as the spark for organizing a boycott of city buses. King was elected president of the boycott organization. Along with his friend Ralph Abernathy and other ministers, King ignited crowds at nightly meetings, inspiring listeners to avoid city buses for an entire year. He claimed that both the Bible and the U.S. Constitution demanded the end of centuries of racial exploitation of African Americans. When white supremacists bombed his front porch with his wife, Coretta Scott King, and their baby inside the home, he urged a large crowd of angry and armed blacks to discard their weapons and continue their nonviolent protest. Fortified by an intense religious experience in his kitchen, he welcomed support for the boycott while accepting speaking invitations around the nation. Eventually the U.S. Supreme Court vindicated the Montgomery Bus Boycott by declaring that segregation on buses violated the Constitution.

In 1960, King returned to Atlanta to co-pastor Ebenezer Church with his father. Within a few days, thousands of college students challenged segregation by staging sit-ins to integrate Southern lunch counters. Encouraged by **Ella Baker**, a veteran organizer for the NAACP, the lunch-counter activists formed the Student Nonviolent Coordinating Committee (SNCC). In 1961, led by James Farmer, the Congress of Racial Equality (CORE) sponsored Freedom Rides to integrate interstate buses. In Alabama, white supremacists bludgeoned many of the Freedom Riders, sending them to the hospital. In danger of being outflanked by SNCC and CORE, King somewhat reluctantly agreed to participate in demonstrations in Albany, Georgia. But, despite exuberant songfests and enthusiastic speeches and marches, the Albany campaign fizzled in 1962. During that same year, however, James Meredith, despite fierce resistance from white racist mobs, triumphed in his audacious quest to integrate the University of Mississippi.

After stark failure in Albany, King, Abernathy, Fred Shuttlesworth, James Bevel, and Wyatt Walker began to plan far more carefully for a campaign to integrate downtown stores in Birmingham. King's Southern Christian Leadership Conference (SCLC) targeted Birmingham for two reasons. First, Shuttlesworth had proven himself an especially capable and fearless local leader. Second, Birmingham was a stronghold of segregation. SCLC strategists figured that, if they could succeed in Birmingham, that victory would reverberate throughout the South and the nation. But danger lurked. White racists had bombed Shuttlesworth's home and so many other African American houses that blacks often dubbed the city "Bombingham." None of the bombers had been arrested.

When nonviolent marchers appeared on the streets in spring 1963, Eugene "Bull" Connor and other white officials in Birmingham greeted them by unleashing sharp-toothed police dogs and powerful fire hoses. After success-fully courting arrest, King wrote "Letter from Birmingham Jail." Modeling his letter after the epistles of Paul, he responded to eight local clergy who, objecting to racial demonstrations, had urged caution and moderation. Detail-ing the suffering of African Americans, he attacked segregation as immoral and unconstitutional and criticized churches for tolerating it. He also explained that he violated racist laws on purpose and gladly suffered the pen-alties that authorities imposed, including time in jail. Because his lawbreaking served to dramatize the inequities of the law, he argued, he was actually affirming the Constitution and the rule of law. In addition he celebrated the work of such "creative extremists" and protestors as the Hebrew prophet Amos, Shadrach, Meshach, Abednego, Socrates, Jesus, Paul, early Christians in Rome, Martin Luther, Abraham Lincoln, German opponents of the Nazis, and anti-Soviet Hungarians. All these "extremists," he argued, had advanced humanity by challenging the status quo. Eventually, he contended, the entire South would recognize such nonviolent agitators as James Meredith as its "real heroes." "Letter from Birmingham Jail" gained a large, immediate national audience and is now widely treasured as one of the most important of all American essays.

After King's release from jail, James Bevel, troubled by the caution of many African American adults in Birmingham, prompted high school students and even young children to swell the ranks of marchers. Recording images of police violence against nonviolent demonstrators were television camera crews, whose videos appeared on nightly news programs, and Charles Moore, whose expertly framed photographs of the same violence appeared in large-circulation magazines. Many whites in the North, Midwest, and West recoiled in horror when they witnessed images of police brutality in Birmingham. Prodded by Attorney General Robert Kennedy, business leaders in downtown Birmingham negotiated with SCLC, and the parties eventually reached an agreement. King called a press conference to announce a great victory.

Later in 1963, **A. Philip Randolph** and **Bayard Rustin** organized a massive March on Washington as a protest for racial justice. Remembering Marian Anderson's famous outdoor concert at the Lincoln Memorial in 1939, they selected the same spot for another major rally. In private, Pauli Murray objected to the absence of women amid the parade of speakers; Randolph and Rustin rejected her plea. Unaware of this disagreement, approximately 250,000 protestors gathered in front of a gigantic marble statue of Lincoln to hear often droning speeches by male civil rights leaders. Mahalia Jackson, a renowned gospel singer, finally aroused the crowd by belting out a spiritual. Behind the scenes, the administration of President John Kennedy succeeded in censoring the militant speech of John Lewis of SNCC. But the public witnessed a very large, well-orchestrated rally that occurred without incident.

King capped the proceedings by delivering "I Have a Dream," one of the most famous American speech of the twentieth century. "I Have a Dream" follows the Promise/Failure/Fulfillment pattern of the African American jeremiad, a form of oratory developed by **Frederick Douglass, Ida B. Wells-Barnett,** and many others. Articulating the promise of democracy, King quoted Hebrew prophets, Thomas Jefferson, and Lincoln. King observed that 1963 marked the one hundredth anniversary of Lincoln's Emancipation Proclamation. Yet, despite the promises, he lamented, African Americans had yet to achieve freedom. He outlined the terrors, suffocation, and indignities created by white racism. Then he yearned for the fulfillment of the Biblical and patriotic promises, which, he remarked, would foster harmony and friendship throughout the nation. He concluded by borrowing and adapting the "Let freedom ring" refrain from a speech that Archibald Carey, an African American minister in Chicago, had delivered in 1952.

Shortly after the exhilarating triumph of the March on Washington, four African American girls in Birmingham were murdered by a bomb that exploded on Sunday morning at their church. King supplied a eulogy for three of the girls. Then tragedy struck again as President John Kennedy, who had recently proposed a momentous civil rights bill, was assassinated, prompting a period of national mourning and reflection. Provoked by the Birmingham crusade, the March on Washington, and the entire Civil Rights Movement, President Lyndon Johnson massaged Congress until it passed Kennedy's bill. This law, the Civil Rights Act of 1964, mandated the racial integration of all hotels, motels, restaurants, cafes, libraries, bowling alleys, golf courses, and other public venues throughout the United States.

In early 1965, following a momentous summer of civil rights activism in Mississippi, mainly organized by SNCC, King joined Amelia Boynton and other local agitators who were campaigning in Selma for the right to vote. Despite considerable friction between youthful SNCC militants and the church-based SCLC, John Lewis of SNCC and Hosea Williams of SCLC led nonviolent marchers across the Edmund Pettus Bridge. Wearing gas masks and riding horses, police officers assaulted the demonstrators with nightsticks and tear gas. Recorded by television cameras, the police attack saddened the nation and was soundly condemned by many members of Congress. In the aftermath of "Bloody Sunday," King, following a suggestion from James Bevel, invited clergy and other sympathizers to fly to Selma for a 50-mile march to Montgomery. To the chagrin of Governor George Wallace, a federal judge sanctioned the march. When the hikers completed their trek, others arrived in Montgomery as 50,000 people materialized in front of the state capitol to applaud King's speech. In that address, King explained that the marchers from Selma walked side by side with Biblical Hebrews, who tramped around the walls of Jericho, and with Southern slaves, who escaped bondage by walking to the North—all in search of freedom. Assuring his listeners of God's support for their struggle, he ended by quoting stanzas of "The Battle Hymn of the Republic," an anthem that abolitionist Julia Ward Howe penned during the Civil War.

Responding to "Bloody Sunday" and the Selma-to-Montgomery March, President Johnson delivered a nationally televised speech in which he urged Congress to pass the Voting Rights Act. By approving that law, Congress authorized the dispatch of federal officials to ensure that African Americans could, for the first time and without any impediment, vote in the South. Throughout these years, King did not confine himself to leading demonstrations. He engaged in an oratorical marathon as he crisscrossed the nation virtually every week to deliver hundreds of sermons and speeches. He produced memorable phrases in rolling cadences that engaged listeners in the kind of call-and-response interaction that typifies black Baptist preaching. Also, like slaves and later generations of African Americans, he interpreted the Biblical Exodus as an ongoing drama. Whereas slaves regarded Abraham Lincoln or **Harriet Tubman** as a new Moses, King interpreted Gandhi as a Moses and explained the Civil Rights Movement as another chapter in the Exodus narrative.

King often borrowed and adapted illustrations, literary quotations, and other content from such well-known, liberal, white Protestant ministers as Harry Emerson Fosdick, J. Wallace Hamilton, and George Buttrick. King also mirrored and updated material from Benjamin Mays, Howard Thurman, and other luminaries in the African American pulpit. Like many other Christian preachers, King treated the language of sermons as a shared treasure, not private property. Into well-framed white sermons that seldom mentioned race, he constantly injected appeals for racial equality. Frequently leaning on prophets from the Hebrew Bible, he cited a line from Amos—"Let justice roll down like waters and righteousness like a mighty stream"—more often than any other passage of scripture.

Despite what many people think today, King never limited himself to the topic of race. Arguing that social practices do not occur in isolation, he often explicated the intertwining "triple evils" of poverty, racism, and war. During the later years of his life, especially, he often claimed that Americans could only solve racism by *simultaneously* addressing poverty, racial inequity, and war. Despite his idealistic agenda for wholesale reforms, King persuaded many white moderates, partly because Black Nationalists, especially **Elijah Muhammad** and **Malcolm X**, appeared more threatening than King. Concentrating his efforts in the urban North, Malcolm X recruited large numbers of disaffected poor people into Elijah Muhammad's Nation of Islam (NOI). Disdaining Christianity, members of the NOI sought economic self-sufficiency and complete separation from whites. In stinging tones, Malcolm X insistently denounced whites as evil predators on the black community. Refusing to embrace nonviolence, he urged African Americans to seek freedom "by any means necessary."

Clinging to Christian nonviolence, King now faced much more difficult political terrain. J. Edgar Hoover, the Director of the FBI, marshaled the resources of the FBI to oppose the African American struggle for equality. He authorized spying on both Malcolm X and King, attempted to smear King's reputation, and once sent King a note asking him to commit suicide. In addition to harassment from the FBI, King also received regular death threats. Further, some of the youthful agitators of SNCC (especially black males) had become disenchanted with nonviolence. In reaction to the murders of colleagues and their own beatings and jailings in Mississippi and Alabama, many of them began to articulate a form of Black Nationalism that in some ways resembled the views of Malcolm X. After the assassination of Malcolm X in 1965, **Stokely Carmichael,** the new leader of SNCC, attracted national attention by advocating "Black Power" and revolution.

In 1966 King confronted further difficulties when he ventured to Chicago to push for open housing. During one of his demonstrations, blue-collar whites threw bricks at the peaceful marchers, and one landed on King's head as tear gas filled the air. This incident, however, attracted far less national sympathy than had similar events in the South. Defeated by Richard Daley, the wily mayor of Chicago, King left town with only an empty agreement.

Although King disagreed with U.S. foreign policy, he initially hesitated to criticize the war in Vietnam. Like everyone else, he realized that the war effort was orchestrated by President Johnson, the same president who had successfully promoted watershed laws for civil rights. Finally, in 1967, ignoring the advice of his father and close advisors, King blasted U.S. policies in Southeast Asia. This speech, which featured a detailed analysis of politics and war in Vietnam, offended and alienated not only President Johnson, but also many of King's black and white allies and much of the national press. Strong and widespread criticism, however, did not deter King. He continued to denounce the war in various orations, including one delivered at a gigantic anti-war rally in New York City.

King devoted much of 1967, though, to organizing a large, multi-racial Poor People's Campaign that would summon thousands of protestors to Washington, DC. He thought the demonstrators could prod Congress to develop federal programs that would ameliorate poverty. Mindful of recent, large-scale race riots in such cities as Los Angeles, Detroit, and Newark, many predicted that the campaign would fail badly. Even some of the board members and some staff of SCLC doubted the practicality of the plan and urged King to drop it. But King insisted on the necessity of the Poor People's Campaign.

While King was organizing that effort, James Lawson, a nonviolent activist and old friend, called him from Memphis in early 1968. Lawson explained that, though ignored by the national media, over a thousand African American garbage workers had gone on strike. Led by T. O. Jones, they objected to pitifully small wages and horrifying working conditions on what some decried as the urban version of a slave plantation. Resisting the demands of the garbage workers, Mayor Henry Loeb and many other whites in Memphis staunchly opposed labor unions. Memphis police angered African Americans by spewing a harsh chemical spray, known as mace, onto the faces of Lawson and other nonviolent ministers. Ignoring objections from his staff, King flew to Memphis to address a large rally in the spacious sanctuary of a Pentecostal church. Uplifted by the jubilant crowd, King agreed to return to Memphis.

When King arrived again in Memphis, he headed a march that turned violent when youthful black militants, plus an assortment of hooligans, began smashing windows and looting. Although James Lawson urged calm, chaos ensued. While King's aide coaxed him into a randomly passing car, police wielded their nightsticks on the marchers, pummeling both the window breakers and polite, middle-aged churchgoers. After chasing demonstrators down the street and into a church, police barged into the church, continuing to beat the marchers and staining the interior walls with canisters of tear gas.

Once-friendly public officials and a once-friendly press corps now buried King under an avalanche of criticism. Acutely depressed, he slipped off to Atlanta for a few days. After calming himself, he returned to Memphis. A huge downpour and his own exhaustion prompted him to dispatch Abernathy to speak to trash collectors and their supporters at the Pentecostal church. An ebullient throng, however, prompted Abernathy to telephone King and ask him to appear.

As rain punished the roof and thunder sounded, King entered the pulpit and spoke. In his address, "I've Been to the Mountaintop," he defined the garbage workers' strike as an event that reiterated the meaning of the Exodus, the Protestant Reformation, and the Emancipation Proclamation. In the manner of a Biblical prophet, he attacked Mayor Loeb as a Pharaoh and decried the Memphis newspapers. He implied that the unlettered garbage workers understood the Constitution far better than a federal judge in the city. He also advocated a boycott of Coca-Cola, Sealtest Milk, and other white-run businesses. Blacks should withdraw their funds from downtown banks, he declared, and deposit the money in a black-run bank. He praised the garbage workers for their difficult labor.

Further, he urged a city-wide strike that would paralyze the schools and the entire economy of Memphis until the trash collectors receive justice. In cascading phrases, he recalled his near-assassination in Harlem several years earlier. He also expressed gratitude that he had survived to deliver "I Have a Dream" and to lead a great movement in Birmingham and Selma. He concluded by comparing himself to an aging Moses atop Mount Pisgah who was able to see the Biblical Promised Land, but not to enter it. By this time, his ecstatic audience had reached a state of near pandemonium. Amid shouts of joy, and in a loud crescendo, he promised that the African American people would arrive at the Promised Land. He concluded by quoting the opening lyrics of Howe's "The Battle Hymn of the Republic": "Mine eyes have seen the glory of the coming of the Lord!" Then, turning from the pulpit, he almost fell into Abernathy's arms. Amid the tumult, some listeners wept, as did King.

After staying up most of the night, King slept late the next day; bantered with his aides; telephoned his mother; and, grinning, started a boyish pillow fight with his friend Andrew Young. Early that evening, while standing on a motel balcony, preparing to leave for dinner, King was killed by a rifle shot. Several days later, thousands of people tried to jam their way into Ebenezer Church to attend King's funeral service. At his graveside in Atlanta, Benjamin Mays delivered a calm and eloquent eulogy.

Keith Miller
Arizona State University

FURTHER READING

Fairclough, Adam. *To Redeem the Soul of America: The Southern Christian Leadership Conference and Martin Luther King, Jr.* Athens: University of Georgia Press, 2001.

Garrow, David. *Bearing the Cross: Martin Luther King, Jr., and the Southern Christian Leadership Conference.* New York: Harper Perennial, 2004.

King, Martin Luther, Jr. *A Call to Conscience: Landmark Speeches of Martin Luther King, Jr.* Edited by Clayborne Carson et al. New York: Warner Books, 2002.

Kotz, Nick. *Judgment Days: Lyndon Johnson, Martin Luther King, Jr., and the Laws That Changed America.* New York: Houghton Mifflin, 2005.

Miller, Keith D. *Voice of Deliverance: The Language of Martin Luther King, Jr., and Its Sources.* Athens: University of Georgia Press, 1998.

Rieder, Jonathan. *The Word of the Lord Is upon Me: The Righteous Performance of Martin Luther King, Jr.* Cambridge, MA: Harvard University Press, 2008.

AP/Wide World Photos

Spike Lee (1957–)

Spike Lee, the eldest child of William James Edward Lee III and Jacquelyn Lee, was born Shelton Jackson Lee in Atlanta, Georgia on March 20, 1957. Spike Lee is a filmmaker known for his unique cinematic style and his keenness to explore race relations within his films. He is a writer, producer, director, actor, author, entrepreneur, and professor. One of Lee's most distinguishing qualities is his mastery of the art of storytelling which allows him to make critically acclaimed feature-length films, documentaries, television miniseries, music videos, and commercials. Spike Lee is also credited with providing many African Americans opportunities both in front of and behind the camera.

Spike, a nickname given to him by his mother because of his fiery character, is the eldest of the five Lee children. He has been exposed to the arts throughout his life. His father, Bill Lee, an upright bassist, relocated the family to Brooklyn, New York, to connect with the 1960s jazz scene. His mother, a former school-teacher, took Lee to see musicals and plays. Despite these artistic influences, Lee was consumed by the world of sports and aspired to be a professional base-ball player. While not extinguishing his passion for sports, he conceded to the reality of his limited athletic ability and headed to **Morehouse College** in Atlanta in the fall of 1975.

At Morehouse he met Monty Ross who would become co-producer of seven of Lee's films. Their bond was rooted in a mutual interest in black politics and movies. With a $1,000 grant from the City Bureau of Cultural Arts in Atlanta they shot *Black College: The Talented Tenth*. Following the screening of the film, Lee wrote another screenplay called *It's Homecoming*, which would eventually become the script for his second feature film *School Daze*.

The summer of 1977 was beset with events that set the course for Lee's life. Foremost, he grieved at the loss of his mother to liver cancer. The sudden passing of his mother impacted Lee deeply. Lee refers to receiving the news of his mother's passing as, "the worst words a human can hear" (Aftab, 10). He returned to New York for her services and to spend the summer before returning for his junior year of college.

Upon his return home to New York he was given the gift of a Super-8 camera. Ironically, a problem occurred with the "grid" causing a blackout for twenty-five hours in New York City on July 13. He used is Super-8 camera to shoot footage of the looting in Harlem during the blackout which became the basis for another short film, *Last Hustle in Brooklyn*. Going into his junior year at Morehouse he had not selected a major yet. During the summer of 1977 he made the decision to major in Mass Communications and pursue a career as a filmmaker.

The idea of Lee becoming a filmmaker was seen by his peers and mentors as a long shot. At this time in history there were few black filmmakers of note; early twentieth-century film pioneer, Oscar Micheaux, renowned photographer Gordon Parks and independent film maverick Melvin Van Peebles. **Sidney Poitier** (*Uptown Saturday Night/Let's Do It Again/A Piece of the Action*) and Michael Schultz (*Cooley High/Car Wash*) were the only two blacks actively making feature films for major studios in the 1970s. Despite this seemingly bleak reality, Lee continued to lay the foundation for his career after graduating from Morehouse in 1978.

Following a summer internship at Columbia Pictures, Lee began graduate film studies at New York University (NYU). At NYU, he met fellow graduate student Ernest Dickerson, who would eventually serve as the cinematographer for six Spike Lee films. As a graduate student, Lee made *The Answer*, *Sarah*, and *Joe's Bed-Stuy Barbershop: We Cut Heads*. *The Answer* was a silent film Lee made as a rebuff to D. W. Griffith's classic yet overtly white supremacist film *Birth of A Nation*. *Sarah* was a film he made at the request of his grandmother, Zimmie Shelton, who financed his undergraduate, graduate education, and early independent films. *Joe's Bed-Stuy Barbershop: We Cut Heads* won Lee the Student Academy Award in 1983.

He was prepared to be welcomed with open arms by the film industry following the critical acclaim of *Joe's*. He secured representation from the William Morris agency and waited for the phone to ring. When he did not receive any phone calls from studios nor acclaimed filmmakers he began to search for ways to stay active. He met up-and-coming actor Laurence Fishburne and cast him to star in a music video for the Grandmaster Flash and the Furious Five record, *White Lines*. Laurence Fishburne portrayed a cocaine-sniffing pimp. Sugar Hill Records rejected the video, however it was included on a compilation DVD a decade later.

Lee then set out to make *The Messenger*. *The Messenger* was a semi-autobiographical film focusing on a bicycle messenger who takes issue with his father's new wife after the death of his mother. The story line parallels Lee's discontent with his father after the passing of his mother. Lee took issue with his father for moving his new wife, a white Jewish woman, into the family home. The film was to star Giancarlo Esposito and Laurence Fishburne. Due to financial constraints, the film never made it out of pre-preproduction.

One of the key lessons taken from the failure of *The Messenger* was to scale back and make his first feature length film less ambitious. He also decided to make a film possessing mass appeal, and he figured a sexual theme would be a bigger draw. Lee wanted to put a twist on the dating phenomenon where men would have multiple sex partners yet were jealous if one of their girlfriends slept with someone else. In October 1984 Lee began writing the script for a film about a young Brooklyn woman with multiple sexual partners who are attempting to force her to choose one of them to date exclusively.

Lee burst onto the public radar screen in August of 1986 with his debut film *She's Gotta Have It*. The film was independently financed with a $175,000 budget and grossed $8 million at the box office. With such a return on a film written, produced, directed, and starring an all-black cast, Lee caught the attention of major film studios. Lee was active both behind and in front of the camera as he played the role of the hip-hop bike messenger Mars Blackmon. It also placed his 40 Acres and a Mule Filmworks company on the map.

The name 40 Acres and a Mule is a historical reference to an order issued following the U.S. Civil War. Special Field Orders, No. 15 was issued by Union General William Sherman to provide each freed family with 40 acres of land and a mule to assist with land cultivation. The orders specifically limited the land to be granted in the islands of the Carolinas and in parts of Georgia and Florida. The newly freed Africans interpreted these orders as an opportunity to build a foundation following Emancipation and the news of "40 acres and a mule" spread throughout the South. The orders were only in effect for one year and have been interpreted as a broken promise to African Americans. Lee's choice of name for his company is designed to remind us of those sentiments.

Intent on staying true to his New York roots, Lee chose to locate his production headquarters in the Fort Greene section of Brooklyn. By using this renovated firehouse as his home base he was placing a legitimate institution in the heart of a predominantly black community. As with the naming of the company, the selection of the location of its offices was a statement.

Having generated a buzz and firmly planted his company, Lee began to rework the script of *It's Homecoming*. He was eager to return to filmmaking. Before he could begin work on his next project, he was summoned by Nike to shoot a series of commercials with an up-and-coming basketball player named **Michael Jordan**. Lee donned the character of Mars Blackmon for the commercials. In *She's Gotta Have It*, Mars Blackmon plead to the lead character Nola Darling, "Please baby, please baby, baby, baby, please." In the Spike and Mike ads he insisted to Jordan, "It's gotta be the shoes" to explain Jordan's exemplary basketball skills. The commercials were a hit and broadened Lee's fan base.

Lee began shooting his first studio-backed film *School Daze* in 1987. He had transformed the script of *It's Homecoming* into a musical addressing issues faced by college students attending the fictitious historically black Mission college. He was given a $6 million budget, a far cry from the $175,000 budget for his first feature. *School Daze* was shot mostly on location at Morris Brown. Lee's alma mater, Morehouse recanted on its commitment to allow shooting *School Daze* on their campus because he refused to allow them to approve the script prior to shooting. The film would go on to gross $14 million, however critics lambasted the film for its ambitious music and dance sequences and portrayal of women.

Beyond the commercial success and scathing criticism *School Daze* received it also served as the prototype for Lee's commitment to employing talented African Americans for his productions. He already had Ernest Dickerson, Monty Ross, his sister, actress Joie Lee, his father Bill Lee, composer, and Ruth Carter, costume designer, as a part of his 40 acres team. He now added set designer Wynn Thomas and casting director Robi Reed. In front of the camera *School Daze* served as the big break in the acting careers of Samuel L. Jackson, Tisha Campbell, Kadeem Hardison, Jasmine Guy, Roger Guenveur Smith, Bill Nunn, and Kasi Lemmons.

Do the Right Thing, Lee's third feature film served as his proving ground as a filmmaker. *Do the Right Thing* chronicles the activities on a Brooklyn city block on the hottest day of the summer of 1989 as tensions rise fueled by issues of age, race, and class. Lee stars as Mookie, a local pizza delivery guy who lives with his sister and is an absentee father. The film climaxes when a local resident, Radio Raheem is killed by police officers as they attempted to quell a melee taking place at the local pizzeria. The film grossed $28.5 million at the box office and Lee received an Academy Award nomination for the screenplay.

As with most Spike Lee Joints (a moniker he uses for his productions) *Do the Right Thing* tackled sociopolitical matters. Police brutality, gentrification, racism, absentee parenting, unemployment, and the generation gap took turns in this merry-go-round of social commentary. Another constant presence in the film was the rap song "Fight the Power" composed and performed by Public Enemy. Lee also shot a video for the song in Brooklyn depicting a protest march. This music video would serve as a key promotional tool for the film and another notch in his growing music video directing belt.

Lee had already directed several music videos at this point in his career. He directed the music videos for **Miles Davis**'s "Tutu," Branford Marsalis's "Royal Garden Blues," go-go band E.U.'s "Da Butt," Phyllis Hyman's "Be One," and Anita Baker's "No One in the World." Lee would direct several other music videos in his career, most notably Naughty by Nature's "Hip Hop Hooray," Arrested Development's "Revolution," Prince's "Money Don't Matter 2 Night," and Michael Jackson's "They Don't Care About Us."

Lee's fourth feature film, *Mo' Better Blues*, became the first of four movies Lee would direct starring actor **Denzel Washington**. Lee admired Washington's theatrical work in *A Soldier's Play* and his portrayal of South African freedom fighter Steve Biko in *Cry Freedom* (1987). The pair would team up for *Malcolm X* (1999), *He Got Game* (1999), and *The Inside Man* (1999). Washington joined the long list of individuals who could credit Lee with providing a boost to their careers; *Mo' Better Blues* was Washington's first role as a leading man. The film cost $10 million to make and grossed $25 million at the box office.

Mo' Better Blues marked the end of a working relationship between Lee and his father Bill Lee. Although the two have a contentious relationship, Bill Lee had served as the composer for his son's films beginning with *Joe's Bed-Stuy Barbershop*. Bill Lee was a jazz purist and balked at using electronic instruments and other technological enhancements when recording music. This posed some challenges as the 40 Acres family sought to connect with the younger audience through both the visual presentation of their films but also with the musical compositions. Jazz trumpeter Terence Blanchard assumed the role as composer for Spike Lee's Joints from that point on.

Mo' Better Blues was followed by *Jungle Fever*, a movie confronting interracial relationships with the devastation the African American community was experiencing as a result of the crack epidemic serving as the subplot. Budding actor Wesley Snipes took the lead role and the film introduced audiences to a model turned actress named **Halle Berry**. Having established himself as a seasoned filmmaker, he set his eyes on making a biopic about one of his biggest influences, **Malcolm X**.

Prior to the filming of *Malcolm X*, Lee gave Chicago Bulls star shooting guard Michael Jordan a promotional baseball cap with a huge "X" on the front. The cap became a must-have item for celebrities and urban youth alike. Lee had already established a retail-clothing store, *Spike's Joint* in Fort Greene Brooklyn to sell merchandise associated with 40 Acres and a Mule. Lee's knack for generating merchandising capital had begun early in his career with the promotion of *She's Gotta Have It*. He continued to capitalize on his ability to connect with consumers and became a key player in a yet-to-be-developed urban market. Lee was also very deliberate about marketing the soundtracks to his films. One of his entrepreneurial endeavors also included the short-lived record label, 40 Acres and a Mule Musicworks.

I know history.... And I know the history of Hollywood and its omission of the one million African-American men and women who contributed to World War II. Not everything was John Wayne, baby.

—Spike Lee

Malcolm X was an ambitious undertaking. Lee and Dickerson decided the film should be an epic, running over three hours. Shooting took place in New York, Cairo, South Africa, and Saudi Arabia. Denzel Washington was entrusted with portraying the transformational, charismatic, and witty Black Nationalist leader who was slain in 1965. Spike Lee's *Malcolm X* aimed to show Malcolm X at four key phases of his life; as the street hustler, Detroit Red, the convict, the Nation of Islam minister, and the mature Black Nationalists/Sunni Muslim leader El Hajj Malik El Shabazz. Lee and the 40 acres crew had to contend with pressure from Black Nationalist organizations, Warner Brothers studios, and the bond company. Warner Brothers and the bond company stopped financing the film during post-production and Lee solicited the financial support of **Bill Cosby, Oprah Winfrey, Earvin "Magic" Johnson,** Tracy Chapman, Prince, Peggy Cooper-Cafritz, Michael Jordan, and Janet Jackson to complete the film as envisioned.

Following *Malcolm X*, Lee's feature film credits include *Crooklyn* (1994), *Clockers* (1995), *Girl 6* (1996), *Get on the Bus* (1996), *He Got Game* (1998), *Summer of Sam* (1999), *Bamboozled* (2000), *25th Hour* (2002), *She Hate Me* (2004), *Inside Man* (2006), and *Miracle at St. Anna* (2008). Although his films vary in subject matter, he has a visual and storytelling style, which certifies his films as Spike Lee Joints. There is an omnipresence of sports references within his films; his moving camera-dolly shot, which create a floating effect for the actor while running or walking, and a powerful musical score.

Lee's artistry is not limited to the world of fiction, as he has established himself as an accomplished documentarian. His documentary films include *4 Little*

Girls (1997), *Jim Brown: All-American* (2002), *When the Levees Broke: A Requiem in Four Acts* (2006), and *Kobe Doin' Work* (2009). *4 Little Girls* and *When the Levees Broke* confronted tragedies that befell the African American community, the 1963 bombing of the16th Street Baptist Church and the aftermath of Hurricane Katrina in New Orleans in August 2005, respectively. *Jim Brown* and *Kobe* allowed Lee to practice his craft of filmmaking while engaged with his first love of sports by profiling football great and community activist Jim Brown and Los Angeles Lakers star shooting guard Kobe Bryant.

Lee has also lent his filmmaking talents to concert films. He has directed the one-man shows *Freak* (1998) starring John Leguizamo and *A Huey P. Newton Story* (2001) featuring Roger Guenveur Smith. *Pavarotti & Friends for the Children of Liberia* (1998) and *Pavarotti & Friends for Guatemala and Kosovo* (1999) were also filmed under Lee's direction. Lee was also tapped to lend his touch to the Broadway musical show *Passing Strange* (2009). His most popular concert film is *The Original Kings of Comedy* (2000) starring comedians Steve Harvey, D. L. Hughley, Cedric the Entertainer, and Bernie Mac.

From the beginning of Lee's career he has been critical of the entertainment industry with regards to African American people. While promoting his film *Miracle at St. Anna* at the Cannes film festival in 2008, Lee commented on the lack of African American servicemen in actor/director Clint Eastwood's two films about Iwo Jima. When Eastwood responded stating that Lee should "shut his face," Lee had the following response:

> If he wishes, I could assemble African American men who fought at Iwo Jima and I'd like him to tell these guys that what they did was insignificant and they did not exist. I'm not making this up. I know history. I'm a student of history. And I know the history of Hollywood and its omission of the one million African American men and women who contributed to World War II. Not everything was John Wayne, baby.

His criticisms are not only directed at individuals who leave black people out of films. In an interview on the cable television show "Our World with Black Enterprise" Lee commented on the lack of progressive images of African Americans on television as follows:

> Each artist should be allowed to pursue their artistic endeavors, but I still think there is a lot of stuff out today that is coonery and buffoonery. I know it's making a lot of money and breaking records, but we can do better. . . . I am a huge basketball fan, and when I watch the games on TNT, I see these two ads for these two shows (Tyler Perry's "Meet the Browns" and "House of Payne"), and I am scratching my head. We got a black president, and we're going back to Mantan Moreland and Sleep 'n' Eat?

Lee has not been one to only respond with commentary. He has leant his services as executive producer and producer to several films he wanted to see be made. Some of the films of note are *Drop Squad* (1994), *New Jersey Drive* (1995), *Tales from the Hood* (1995), *The Best Man* (1999), and *Love & Basketball* (2000). Many of these films were written and directed by up-and-coming African Americans and featured predominately black casts. This role as a producer not only serves to provide opportunity to emerging talent but also is also reflective of Lee's dynamic ability to work in various creative capacities.

Continuing his enterprising ways Lee launched SpikeDDB. The company is a joint venture between Lee and DDB Worldwide Communications Group, Inc. A full service consumer-advertising firm that combines the resources of one of the country's largest agencies, DDB Worldwide with Lee's insights, understanding, and direction to the urban market. Founded in 1998 SpikeDDB clients include Nike, Chanel, Pepsi, Frito Lay, Essence Communications, Mountain Dew, ALLTEL, New Era, and Royal Caribbean.

Beyond his work Lee has bolstered his celebrity status with his omnipresence at the New York Knicks basketball home games. His legendary encounter with Indiana Pacers' forward Reggie Miller during a 1994 playoff game made newspaper headlines. Lee's notoriety as a celebrity fan landed him a publishing deal as the subject for the book *Best Seat in the House* written by sportswriter Ralph Wiley. The book chronicles Lee's life-long love affair with basketball, generally, and the Knicks specifically. Lee credits his well-documented affinity with the sport for being allowed to make *Kobe Doin' Work*. When asked if only he would have been able to create such a film, he replied:

> The only reason why Phil Jackson, Kobe and Dr. [Jerry] Buss gave me access is because I love the game, I have a great knowledge and I know what I'm talking about. If Joe Blow off the corner came to them and he's never been a well-known filmmaker it would have been hard. Because they are not going to trust someone who doesn't know anything about the game. You have to have some credibility.

Lee has admittedly had challenges balancing his adoration of sports with his role as a husband and father. He married lawyer Tonya Linette Lewis on October 2, 1993. They have two children, a daughter named Satchel (named after the famed Negro Leagues pitcher Leroy "Satchel" Paige) and son, Jackson. With a tinge of embarrassment upon reflection Lee states, "I'm ashamed to say on both pregnancies I left Tonya in the hospital with a newborn baby to go to a stupid-ass Knicks game. I'm not proud of it, but I did do that" (Aftab, 171).

Lee's body of work ranges from feature films, television commercials, music videos, and documentaries spanning over a 27-year career. His alma mater New York University has provided Lee an avenue to pass on his accumulated wisdom to its film students. Since 2003 he has served as the Artistic Director of the Graduate Film Program and the Amy and Joseph Perellla Chair at

NYU's Tisch School of the Arts. He instructs the third year Masters Series; Directing Strategies.

After over a quarter of a century as a filmmaker and entertainment icon, Lee still has high aspirations for his career. For over a decade, he has been lobbying, to no avail, for major studio backing of two biopic films about sports heroes, **Joe Louis** and **Jackie Robinson**. Studios have not been sold on the profitability of these films. His films have been critically acclaimed, thought provoking, and artistic yet, not blockbusters by Hollywood standards. Until his 2006 collaboration with Denzel Washington, *Inside Man*, none of his film had grossed over $100 million.

Being the fiery, uncompromising auteur he is, Lee continues to work and inspire despite the lack of support for his sports epics. He fills his calendar with more than 60 speaking engagements a year, directing television commercials, and instructing his students at NYU. A documentary on the life of Michael Jordan and *Inside Man 2* are due for 2010 releases. Lee currently lives in New York City with his wife Tonya and their two children.

Lasana O. Hotep
Arizona State University

FURTHER READING

Aftab, Kaleem. *Spike Lee: That's My Story and I'm Sticking to It*. New York: W.W. Norton, 2005.

Jones, Lisa, and Spike Lee. *Do the Right Thing*. New York: Fireside, 1989.

Lee, Spike. *She's Gotta Have It: Inside Guerilla Filmmaking*. New York: Fireside, 1987.

Lee, Spike. *Uplift the Race: The Construction of School Daze*. New York: Fireside, 1988.

Lee, Spike, and Ralph Wiley. *By Any Means Necessary: The Trials and Tribulations of Making Malcolm X*. New York: Hyperion, 1992.

Massood, Paula. *The Spike Lee Reader*. Philadelphia: Temple University Press, 2008.

Wiley, Ralph, and Spike Lee. *Best Seat in the House: A Basketball Memoir*. New York: Crown, 1997.

Hulton Archive/Getty Images

Joe Louis (1914–1981)

Joseph Louis Barrow was born on May 13, 1914, in Chambers County, Alabama. Nicknamed the "Brown Bomber," Joe Louis is recognized as one of the greatest fighters in the history of professional boxing. Louis held the heavyweight championship from June 22, 1937 until his initial retirement at age 34 on March 1, 1949. Louis's nearly 12 years as champion and 25 title defenses both stand as records in the heavyweight division. Joe Louis is arguably the first African American athlete to truly transcend racial boundaries and become a hero to all Americans. His June 22, 1938 first-round technical knockout (TKO) victory over former champion Max Schmeling, a fighter whom German dictator Adolf Hitler used as a propaganda tool to demonstrate the innate superiority of Aryan peoples, is arguably the most politically and culturally significant fight in the history of boxing. Louis's prowess in the ring, his defeat of a Nazi icon, and the dignified manner in which he comported himself made him one of the most beloved figures in the history of American sport.

Joseph Louis Barrow (referred to simply as Louis hereafter) was born into dire poverty in Lafayette, Alabama, the county seat of Chambers County, on the far eastern side of the state. At the time of Louis's birth, approximately 1,600 people lived in the community. His family worked as tenant farmers in Chambers County's lush cotton fields. Louis was the seventh of Munroe Barrow and Lillie Reese Barrow's eight children. Munroe had a mixed white and black racial heritage while his wife had a mix of African American and Cherokee lineage. Munroe Barrow was only a part of his son's life for a very short time. He had suffered from mental illness for a number of years. Between 1906 and 1916, he bounced in and out of a number of state mental health institutions. In 1916, he was institutionalized permanently at the Searcy Hospital for the Negro Insane in Mount Vernon, Alabama. Louis never saw his father again, though Munroe Barrow lived until 1938 unaware of his son's success as a fighter. In the late 1910s, the Barrow family had been misinformed that Munroe Barrow had died while institutionalized. After hearing of her institutionalized husband's death, Lillie Reese Barrow remarried in 1920. She married Pat Brooks, a Chambers County construction worker who shared her pious Baptist religious convictions. Brooks brought financial stability to the large family with his steady income and steady behavior at home. The Brooks-Barrow family's standard of living remained at a subsistence level, but this differed from the even more dire poverty of many of their neighbors.

Following a 1926 late-night encounter with the Ku Klux Klan, Brooks decided to move his family to the industrial north to avoid violence at the hands of the terrorist organization. Brooks settled his family in the burgeoning industrial metropolis of Detroit. Like hundreds of thousands of other African American migrants during the Great Migration, a combination of push factors, particularly poverty and the violence toward black Americans in the Jim Crow South, and pull factors, including the economic opportunities in the industrial north, encouraged families to move to cities such as Detroit.

Brooks secured a large older home for the family on Macomb Street in the city's Black Bottom neighborhood. Brooks and the older Barrow children found employment in the city's plentiful industrial sector. Joe Louis, like his older siblings, began working at Ford's massive River Rogue plant when he turned 17. Louis had attended the Bronson Vocational High School prior to working at Ford.

Louis's boxing career began in the backyard of their Macomb Street home during his adolescence. Louis and the other Barrow boys took on neighborhood kids in impromptu boxing matches in an improvised ring just out of their mother's line of vision in the kitchen. Lillie Barrow-Brooks preferred the idea of her son taking up an instrument as a leisure activity. Louis took violin lessons, but his interest in boxing far outweighed his interest in classical music. Early in his teens, he started ditching his violin lessons and used the money to rent a locker at the Brewster Recreation Center where he honed his skills as a fighter. His mother soon became aware of the ruse.

Louis began his amateur career under the tutelage of Atler Ellis in 1932 at age 17. Around this time, he dropped "Barrow" from his name and went by "Joe Louis." Ellis believed the hard-hitting light-heavyweight would be best served as an overall boxer by fighting challenging opponents early on in his amateur career. In his amateur debut, he faced Johnny Miller, a highly regarded light-heavyweight who went on to make the 1932 U.S. Olympic boxing team. Miller knocked Louis out in the second round. Ellis and Louis learned a great deal from the fight. They recognized that Louis needed better hand speed to succeed against top ranked opponents. He began training with middleweights and welterweights to work on this aspect of his fight game. The new training regimen worked. Louis knocked out (KO) his next 14 opponents.

Louis suffered a pair of losses on decisions to elite light heavyweight fighters in 1933 before entering that year's novice Detroit Golden Gloves tournament. He cruised into the championship match, easily defeating most opponents. In the Championship fight, he won a decision against Stanley Evans, one of the fighters who had defeated him earlier that year. He went on to win a tournament of Golden Gloves Champions in Chicago later in the year. Louis culminated his amateur career in 1934 by winning the national American Athletic Union (AAU) light heavyweight championship in St. Louis.

Following his remarkable success in the amateur ranks, Louis embarked on a professional career in late 1934. He followed the advice of his trainer Ellis and moved up to the heavyweight division. Not only did it carry larger prize purses, but a fighter with the hand speed of Louis would be an anomaly in the division. Louis had long teetered weight-wise on the brink of the heavyweight division, so the decision to move up in weight class was easy for him. Louis's choice of manager proved more controversial. He opted to hire a black promoter, an unprecedented move among even black prize fighters. Louis signed on with John Roxborough, a wealthy Detroit numbers racketeer. Roxborough convinced Louis that white managers were not interested in bringing black fighters into title contention. There had not been a black heavyweight champion since **Jack Johnson** had been defeated by Jess Willard in 1915. Roxborough promised Louis that he would focus his efforts on securing the fighter the best possible fights and the best possible purses. Louis agreed to work with Roxborough, in spite of his notorious background.

Roxborough put Louis to work with a Chicago-based trainer named Jack Blackburn, a former lightweight contender who had a great deal of experience working with new professional fighters. Louis relocated to Chicago to work with Blackburn at the Trafton Gym on Randolph Street. Roxborough formed a partnership with Chicago nightclub owner, boxing promoter, and numbers runner Julian Black. Black scheduled a group of fights between Louis and a series of journeyman Chicago area heavyweights. Despite their connections to gambling, Louis's managers demanded the fighter stay away from gambling as well as drinking and carousing. They demanded he never participate in a fixed fight or gloat over a fallen opponent. They demanded that Louis never have his picture taken alone while in the company of a white woman, for fear that the media would compare him to Jack Johnson, who married a white woman during his tenure as heavyweight champion. Johnson's marriage to a white woman led to his legal troubles and the end of his reign as champion. Roxborough and Black realized that in the white-dominated world of boxing, an up-and-coming black fighter would be held to a different ethical standard. They believed Louis would only get a title shot if he carried himself in a dignified manner. Throughout his career, Louis was lauded for his clean living in the midst of a sport notorious for its frequent corruption.

Louis debuted as a professional fighter on Independence Day 1934 against Jack Kracken. "The Brown Bomber" decked Kracken, knocking him out in the first round. One week later, he disposed of Willie Davis in three rounds. Louis steamrolled through his opponents until his sixth professional bout, a homecoming fight on September 11, 1934 against a 17–1 Canadian brawler named Alex Borchuk. Louis stopped Borchuk in round four via TKO, but in the second round Borchuk landed a vicious right to Louis's face that knocked out one of his front teeth. Louis won six more fights in 1934, concluding the year with a third round KO of Lee Ramage. While training for the fight, Louis became acquainted with a secretary named Marva Trotter. The pair became romantically involved. They married on September 24, 1935, hours before Louis's fight against former champion Max Baer.

In his 15th professional fight, Louis faced off against Ramage in a February 21, 1935 rematch in Los Angeles. Louis again pounded Ramage into submission, winning by way of knockout in the second round. Mike Jacobs, a promoter and insider in the New York City fighting scene, introduced himself to Louis and his management following the fight. Jacobs formed a business relationship with the Louis team. He used his influence to hype Louis's next fight against veteran pugilist Natie Brown in Detroit to the New York media. Louis won a hard-fought 10-round decision against Brown. The New York fight press panned Louis's performance, but the attention from the fight helped Jacobs land his 17–0 fighter a match with former heavyweight champion Primo Carnera.

Primo Carnera remains the largest man to hold the heavyweight championship. The Italian fighter stood nearly six foot six and weighed almost 280 pounds. He won the heavyweight championship by KO'ing Jack Sharkey in the sixth round on June 29, 1933. Rumors that Carnera's fights were frequently fixed on the slow handed Italian's behalf emerged soon after he became world champion. Max Baer stopped Carnera in round 11 in June 1934 to take hold of the heavyweight title. The June 25, 1935 fight against Louis in New York City served as a comeback for Carnera, who was seeking an opportunity to regain the heavyweight title.

The Carnera-Louis fight took place in the aftermath of Fascist Italy's invasion of Ethiopia. The press did not miss out on rendering the fight metaphorically, as a battle between a black fighter and the world's most-well-known Italian athlete. Louis destroyed the former champion in front of 60,000 fans at Yankee Stadium, many of whom cheered on Carnera. From the opening bell, Louis dominated the fight, opening several cuts on Carnera's face in round one. Louis never allowed the burly Italian fighter to get close to him. He floored the exhausted Carnera twice in round six, prompting the referee to stop the fight. The victory earned Louis unprecedented exposure and widespread acknowledgement that he was a top contender for the heavyweight title. The Carnera fight earned Louis a purse of $44,500, the majority of which went to Jacobs, Roxborough, and Black.

In September 1935, Louis fought former champion Max Baer in front of 95,000 fans again at Yankee Stadium. Louis pummeled Baer, stopping him in four rounds. The victory over Baer made Louis the number-one contender for the heavyweight title. Louis disposed of Paulino Uzcudun and Charley Retzlaff in quick KO victories to improve his record to 23–0 before facing off with former heavyweight champion Max Schmeling. Promoters portrayed the June 19, 1936 fight as a tune-up for the young contender against an over-the-hill opponent. Louis took a more relaxed attitude toward training for the fight, taking up golf while in fight camp. Schmeling surprised the 90,000 fight fans at Yankee Stadium by taking control of the fight in the early rounds. He exploited Louis's tendency to drop his left hand after jabbing. In the first three rounds, Schmeling stunned Louis with intense volleys of counterpunches to every attempt by the young contender to go on the attack. In round four, Schmeling landed a devastating right cross to Louis's jaw, dropping him for the first time in his career. Louis got up but continued to be overwhelmed by Schmeling's assault on Louis's newly susceptible defenses. Schmeling finally knocked out Louis in round 12 with another right to the jaw. Though never politically affiliated with the Nazi Party, Schmeling received a hero's welcome from the Nazi Regime upon his return home to Germany. Hitler and Goebbels claimed that Schmeling's victory over the world's top-ranked black heavyweight offered proof of Aryan racial superiority.

Rather than stewing over his loss to Schmeling, Louis returned to the ring quickly to regain his momentum for a title shot. Less than two months after the Schmeling fight, Louis stopped former champion Jack Sharkey in three rounds at Yankee Stadium. Louis concluded 1936 with three more quick knockouts against Al Ettore, Jorge Brescia, and Eddie Simms. Concurrently, Mike Jacobs negotiated with the camp of new heavyweight champion James J. Braddock for a June 1937 title fight. The Braddock camp drove a hard bargain, but Jacobs convinced them to offer Louis a title shot instead of Schmeling. The fight proved particularly lucrative for Braddock, who earned over $300,000 for the bout.

Louis (30–1) faced off against James "Cinderella Man" Braddock (50–25–7) for the heavyweight championship at Comiskey Park in Chicago on June 22, 1937. In round one, the crafty Braddock worked his way inside on the lanky Louis and nailed him with a right uppercut which dropped "The Brown Bomber." Louis hopped right up from the surprising blow and quickly took control of the fight. He opened up cuts on Braddock's face in round three and went to work on barraging him with a continual flurry of blows. Following round seven, doctors nearly stopped the fight as a result of the serious bleeding around Braddock's eye. "The Cinderella Man" answered the bell for round eight. Louis went right after his wounded opponent, felling him with a right cross just over a minute into the round. Braddock lay motionless in the ring for a count of 10. Louis had become the first black heavyweight champion of the world in more than 20 years. Black Americans across the country listened to the fight on the radio and celebrated in the streets following Louis's victory. Throughout his reign as champion, Louis remained an iconic figure in the African American community. His prowess in the ring, his personal comportment, and his willingness to give his time and money to antipoverty and youth organizations made him one of the most widely revered athletes in Depression Era America.

Nine weeks after winning the world title, Louis defended the belt against British champion Tommy Farr. "The Brown Bomber" won a controversial unanimous 15 round decision against the solidly chinned Welshman. Neither fighter fell during the bout, but Louis later admitted that Farr hurt him on two occasions during the fight. A smattering of boos emanated from the crowd at Yankee Stadium following the decision. Louis took some time off following his rocky initial defense, waiting until February 1938 to make his second title defense. Louis knocked out Nathan Mann in three rounds. He followed up that victory with a fifth round KO of Harry Thomas on April Fools' Day in Chicago.

The much-hyped rematch between Max Schmeling and Joe Louis took place on June 22, 1938, at Yankee Stadium. As Europe teetered on the brink of war, the Louis-Schmeling fight took on a great deal of symbolic importance. Louis symbolized all of the ideals the United States had aspired to, but never quite lived up to, throughout its history: its respect for personal freedom, its willingness to take in people from around the world, the economic opportunities it provided people from all social classes. Schmeling, conversely, symbolized an aggressive, tyrannical regime built upon notions of racial superiority. A robust multi-racial, multi-class consensus developed in support of Louis in the build up to the fight. Louis was, to appropriate the overused moniker, "The People's Champion."

Louis-Schmeling II had coast-to-coast and trans-European radio coverage. Seventy thousand fans piled into Yankee Stadium for the fight. Fans booed Schmeling mercilessly as he made his way to the ring. Some pelted him with bottles and cigarette butts. When the ring announcer called out Louis's name, a roaring, five-minute ovation radiated from the crowd. The actual Louis-Schmeling rematch lacked the drama of its intense build-up. The well-primed Louis went on the attack immediately, nailing Schmeling with a series of body shots which his handlers complained were kidney punches. Louis dropped Schmeling 90 seconds into the fight. Schmeling rose from the mat, but Louis knocked him down again with a swift right cross to the jaw. The German wobbled back to his feet again. Louis hammered him with another right, leaving Schmeling reeling for a third time. At 2:04 of the first round, Schmeling's corner threw in the towel. Louis's First Round TKO of Max Schmeling provided a thunderous second to Jesse Owens's four gold medals at the 1936 Berlin Olympics, proof of the fallacy of Aryan athletic superiority.

Louis continued his dominance of the heavyweight division in 1939, knocking out four consecutive challengers. He defended his belt four times in 1940, including a pair of brawls with South American Heavyweight Champion Arturo Godoy. Godoy and Louis battled for 15 rounds at Madison Square Garden in February 1940. Louis slipped away with a split decision victory. In the rematch that June, Louis battered Godoy for eight rounds until the referee stopped the fight. Louis defended his title on seven occasions in 1941, including his remarkable come-from-behind knockout victory against light-heavyweight champion Billy "The Pittsburgh Kid" Conn. The more agile Conn dominated the fight for 12 rounds. Conn stuck to the stick-and-move playbook, frustrating Louis' attempts to turn the fight into a donnybrook. "The Pittsburgh Kid" stunned the sell-out crowd at the Polo Grounds in New York by going toe-to-toe with Louis in the 13th round. After the fight, Conn said his desire to knockout Louis led to his change in strategy. Louis responded to Conn's new strategy by mauling his undersized opponent. With two seconds remaining in round 13, referee Eddie Joseph counted Conn out after Louis dropped the light-heavyweight with a big right hand.

The Japanese attack on Pearl Harbor brought the United States into World War II. Joe Louis enlisted in the U.S. Army in January 1942. Louis wanted to serve in combat, but the U.S. Army used his celebrity as a means of boosting morale among GIs. He toured Europe and Asia, putting on dozens of exhibition fights for Allied troops. Louis also appeared in a wide range of recruitment materials, including posters, pamphlets, and propaganda films. During the war, Louis defended his title rarely, twice in 1942 and once in 1944.

During the war, Marva Trotter Louis gave birth to the couple's first child, Jacqueline in 1943. Marital problems soon strained the couple as Joe Louis's affairs while stationed abroad came to his wife's attention. The couple divorced in March 1945, but soon reconciled. Their second child, Joseph Louis Barrow, Jr. was born in 1947. Conflict between Joe and Marva Louis reemerged soon after their son's birth. This time, financial troubles sparked the conflict. While Louis had earned millions of dollars over the course of his fighting career, his management had taken the lion's share of the money. A combination of Louis's generosity and poor tax advice left the fighter in serious debt. Moreover, he owed several hundred thousand dollars to the Internal Revenue Service (IRS). Financial problems plagued the perennially cash-strapped Louis for the remainder of his life. Marva and Joe Louis divorced for the second time in 1949.

Thirty-two-year-old Louis resumed his reign as heavyweight champion following his 1946 discharge from the U.S. Army. He earned the rank of sergeant and the Legion of Merit for his service to his country. On June 19, 1946, Louis dominated Billy Conn in a rematch of their 1941 fight. Louis TKO'ed Conn in the eighth round. Tami Mauriello posed little challenge to Louis in their September 18, 1946 title bout. Louis knocked him out in the first round. "The Brown Bomber" did not defend his title again for more than a year. In December 1947, he squared off against a journeyman 33-year-old fighter named Jersey Joe Walcott. The lightly regarded Walcott engaged Louis aggressively in the opening round. He stunned Louis with a right cross which briefly sent the champion to the mat. Louis tried to stay away from the aggressive challenger in the early rounds, but in round four Walcott unloaded on the champion and sent him to the canvas for the second time. In subsequent rounds, Louis clawed his way back into the fight, but Walcott, entering the final three rounds, believed he was securely ahead on the scorecards. Walcott spent the 13th, 14th, and 15th rounds outside of Louis's reach. Boxing experts believed this strategy cost Wolcott the fight as Louis scored enough points in the final rounds to score a split decision victory over the challenger. The Madison Square Garden audience booed the decision.

Plans for a Louis-Walcott rematch got underway soon after the controversial decision. On June 25, 1948, a sold-out Yankee Stadium crowd watch Louis avenge his poor performance in their previous fight by knocking out Walcott in the 11th round. The rematch proved a hard fight as well. Walcott knocked Louis down in round three, but Louis soon took control of the fight. Louis's second victory over Jersey Joe Walcott was his 25th title defense, a record in the heavyweight division. On March 1, 1949, Louis retired after nearly 12 years as champion, a record as well. The champion cited his evidently deteriorating skills as the reason for his retirement.

Financial woes lured Louis back into the ring less than 18 months later. Louis received a large payday to face off with new heavyweight champion Ezzard Charles. Charles, "The Cincinnati Cobra," showed a great deal of power and hand speed as he overmatched Louis in their September 27, 1950 fight. He defeated Louis easily by a unanimous decision. Louis continued fighting in 1950 and 1951, scoring eight consecutive victories and eight large paydays against primarily mediocre opponents. Most of his victories came by way of decisions in 10-round fights. On October 26, 1951, Louis made his final appearance as a professional fighter against new heavyweight champion Rocky Marciano at Madison Square Garden. The 37-year-old Louis never stood a chance in the fight. Marciano overwhelmed the former champion from the opening bell, finally knocking him out in the eighth round. Louis continued to compete in exhibition fights for the next few years. He even tried his hand at professional wrestling in the late 1950s and 1960s.

Retirement proved difficult for the former champion. Louis lent his name to several business ventures, all of which proved unsuccessful. He developed a substance abuse problem in the late 1960s which nearly cost him his life. In later years, Louis took on the role of elder statesman in the boxing world, refereeing championship bouts and serving as a spokesman for the sport. In the midst of his personal turmoil, Louis took solace in his family. He married for a fourth time in 1959 to Martha Jefferson. The couple remained married until Louis's death on April 12, 1981. Louis remained a prominent public figure for decades after his retirement, a respected former champion whose success in the ring and compassion for humanity outside the ring overshadowed his personal and financial troubles. Nearly three decades after his death, Louis is remembered as a groundbreaking athlete, a patriot, and a man who carried himself with dignity in spite of all the struggles he faced during his lifetime.

Clayton Trutor
Boston College

FURTHER READING

Bak, Richard. *Joe Louis: The Great Black Hope*. New York: Da Capo, 1998.

Barrow, Joe Louis, Jr., and Barbara Munder. *Joe Louis: 50 Years an American Hero*. New York: McGraw-Hill, 1988.

Louis, Joe. *My Life*. New York: Ecco, 1997.

Margolick, David. *Beyond Glory: Joe Louis v. Max Schmeling, and a World on the Brink*. New York: Vintage, 2006.

Myler, Richard. *Ring of Hate: Joe Louis v. Max Schmeling: The Fight of the Century*. Baltimore: Arcade Press, 2006.

Malcolm X (1925–1965)

Malcolm X, known also as El-Hajj Malik El-Shabazz, was one of the most prominent of African American leaders during the era of civil rights protests in the 1950s and 1960s. At the height of his renown, Malcolm X could claim scores of thousands of followers. He also received widespread acclaim internationally especially from leaders of the then newly independent nations of Africa. He struck a responsive chord both in his message of black pride and dignity and of his embodiment of uncompromising challenges to the various forms of racism existing in American society.

Malcolm X's audience was primarily composed of the alienated black communities of the Northern cities of the United States for whom the message of nonviolent protests preached by the Rev. **Martin Luther King, Jr.**, was found to be wanting. For Northern urban blacks, Martin Luther King's doctrine of nonviolence was unconvincing in view of their daily experiences with the institutionalized forms of racism in the United States such as substandard schools and uncaring teachers, foreclosed employment opportunities, entrapments in vice and petty crime, and constant encounters with racial profiling and police brutality. Malcolm X stood out in contrast to King and civil rights protest leaders in his rejection of the pacifist and integrationist goals of the Civil Rights Movement.

Malcolm X was a gifted public speaker. He excelled at debate at any level. He was comfortable engaging opponents with whatever their intellectual credentials and in any forum, from a street corner in Harlem in New York City to a lecture hall at Harvard University. His audiences marveled at the skill of someone whose formal education extended to no further than the eighth grade. Malcolm was particularly adept at exposing the weaknesses in the arguments of black leaders who held closely to the goal of integration, or the simple abolition of the legal barriers against black entry into the otherwise prohibited areas of U.S. society. Above all, Malcolm X projected a sense of unfailing integrity in his denunciations of racism in the United States. This integrity was grounded in the spiritual dimension which Malcolm X acquired first as a minister in the Nation of Islam and subsequently in his conversion to the orthodox faith of Islam.

Malcolm X's relentless protests against racism in the United States inspired several other noteworthy leaders in the struggle for civil rights, black pride, and human rights both domestically and internationally. His inspiration touched especially a younger generation of black activist in the Black Power phase of African American activism. Among these young leaders were **Kwame Ture** (formerly **Stokely Carmichael**), and H. Rap Brown, both of the Student Nonviolent Coordinating Committee (or SNCC), and **Huey P. Newton and Bobby Seale**, and Eldridge Cleaver, founders of the Black Panther Party. Also, inspired by Malcolm X was the creation of the African American nationalist group, the Republic of New Africa. Beyond the United States other prominent figures of African descent, such as the Cuban dissident, Carlos Moore, and the South African Black consciousness leader, Steve Biko were heavily influenced by him. In addition artists of note have captured Malcolm's life in several art forms including poetry by Margaret Walker and Gwendolyn Brooks, a film by director **Spike Lee**, and an opera by composer Anthony Davis. Malcolm X's autobiography, co-authored with **Alex Haley**, remains an important contribution to American literature.

Much of what explains Malcolm's place in the history of African Americans is the circumstances of his life. Malcolm rose from destitute poverty and a life ensnarled in criminality to become a moral and political leader of considerable force. Malcolm was born in an environment of race consciousness. His father, Earl Little, was a representative of **Marcus Garvey**'s Universal Negro Improvement Organization. Earl's open race pride incurred enmity among his white neighbors. This enmity was the cause of relocating his family from Omaha, Nebraska, where Malcolm was born on May 19, to Lansing, Michigan. After moving the family to Lansing there was no abatement of the racial animosity directed at Earl. His family's house came under a fire bomb attack. Earl subsequently was found lain across a set of trolley tracks, killed presumably by elements of the Ku Klux Klan.

Malcolm's widowed mother, Louise, succumbed to the pressures of holding a family of eight siblings together. The family's impoverished state and his mother's pride eventually forced Mrs. Little to be institutionalized. As a result, her children were declared wards of the state. Each of Malcolm's siblings was assigned to various white foster parents. In these circumstances Malcolm began to be aware of the extent that white paternalism was an integral ingredient of racism. It could be as pernicious as the racism of outright hostility suffered by his father. One particular experience which Malcolm recalled is an encounter with a teacher at the predominantly white grade school that Malcolm attended. The teacher whom Malcolm regarded as one of his favorites counseled Malcolm with brutal frankness not to pursue a dream of becoming an attorney. It was this childhood encounter which defined for Malcolm the rigidities of the American caste system.

Malcolm could speak with such tremendous authenticity about black urban life because he felt a strong attraction to it. Soon after leaving Lansing for Boston, where he went to live with his half sister, Ella, he experienced a sense of adolescent awakening with the discovery of black ballrooms, jazz celebrities, and flamboyant hustlers. Boston was a world away from the slender black cultural milieu of Lansing.

Malcolm preferred the life of the hipster over that of Boston's snobbish black middle class. In effect, he saw just two alternatives open to him. He rejected the middle-class way of life (which Ella, wanted him to aspire to) for its perversity in claiming a false superior status far out of keeping with the menial positions that the members of that class actually possessed. The hipster's life on the other hand provided the more tangible status of a hipster's reputation which was gained from the wits employed in predatory deceptions of victims in a hipster's con games or the canny use of threats against rivals.

One mark of Malcolm's hipster's reputation was his being accorded the nickname of "Detroit Red."

Malcolm engaged in every manner of hustles, from banking numbers (illegal gambling), to steering "Johns" to specialty prostitutes, to pushing drugs (marijuana and cocaine). Income from these activities fueled Malcolm's own drug-soaked existence. All were the mainstays of the hipster's life of emersion into any sort of illicit activity. And above all, deception and threat were the amoral assumptions that guided Malcolm's hipster's life.

Malcolm's life would eventually end in the final fate of a hustler. In Boston he and his crew of associates, including Malcolm's white girlfriend, were apprehended for committing a series of burglaries in the Cambridge area. Malcolm's conviction was fraught with racial significance. He was made aware that his particular sentence had been set at the maximum because he had involved white women of arguably decent reputation in the commission of the crimes. Malcolm was remanded to the Charlestown State Prison for a 10-year term (of which he served seven years). He was 21 years old.

Despite its institutional assaults on the human spirit, the Charlestown Prison provided Malcolm with several means for embarking on a remarkable transformation in his life. Malcolm rediscovered his dormant intellectual talents with the help of an older inmate who had taken an interest in him. He also renewed contact with his siblings. One of them, his younger brother, Reginald, revealed to him a new religion that he urged Malcolm to consider. It was a religion that placed black people at the center of creation and of the cosmic moral conflict between good and evil. This new religion was the Nation of Islam (NOI).

A certain phrase conveyed to him by his brother Reginald gave him pause. It was Reginald's declaration of one of the tenets of this new religion, that "all Whites were devils." As Malcolm tells it in his autobiography, he slowly came to the realization of the radical nature of this statement. It could easily be applied to those whom he encountered in his hipster's world, the police who were the natural enemies of the black hustler, the white Johns, or clients of the black prostitutes who fed a constant degradation of black women, and the judge who had tipped the scales of justice against him out of racial animus. Malcolm then realized that this claim could also be leveled at the whites of presumed good intentions whom had also caused him injury. These included the white foster family who had taken him in Michigan and who treated him more as a family pet, and the teacher, who had counseled him to acquiesce to the U.S. racial caste system. He embraced this new religion in a handwritten letter sent to the religion's founder, the Hon. **Elijah Muhammad.**

Prison provided still another platform for his transformation. It was Ella who pressured the authorities in having Malcolm transferred to a new experimental prison. The prison operated on the premise that prisoners could be rehabilitated in a setting resembling a college campus in which prisoners were encouraged to pursue a life of the mind. The Norfolk Prison Colony offered classes led by volunteer professors from Harvard University and provided access to an extensive library. Malcolm took to this new environment enthusiastically. He excelled especially in the prisoners' weekly debates. He also made full use of the library. Malcolm read widely. Among the works that comprised his extensive reading list were Will and Ariel Durant's *The Story of Civilization*, H. G. Wells's *An Outline of History*, **W. E. B. Du Bois**'s *The Souls of Black Folk*, Harriet Beecher Stowe's *Uncle Tom's Cabin*, and the works of J. A. Rodger. Malcolm also read works on Nat Turner, Mohandas Gandhi, and above all on European imperialism in Africa and Asia. Malcolm's reading was so prodigious that his trademark image of his glaring through half-framed glasses stems from the astigmatism he acquired from his clandestine reading bouts after the prison lights were dimmed at night.

Malcolm rushed head on into the Nation of Islam with the enthusiasm of a recent convert. He rose rapidly through the ranks of the Nation. In short order he was named the Minister of perhaps the most strategic of the Nation's mosques, the Mosque # 7 in Harlem, New York. His charisma, his organizational skills, and his ability to explain the Nation's theology, grounded in the premise of a lost-found race being rescued from degradation by its leader the Hon. Elijah Muhammad, contributed to the phenomenal growth of the Nation from a few thousands to tens of thousands in a short time.

One incident secured Malcolm's reputation as a leader of considerable skill in confrontational situations. The incident involved an instance of police brutality in which a member of Malcolm's congregation was severely beaten by the police on a Harlem street corner. In response to the incident Malcolm organized an assembly of mosque members, and arranged them in disciplined military fashion just outside of the police station where the victim had been taken. When the police were made aware of Malcolm's phalanx standing in close proximity, and fearing being drawn into an uncontrollable situation, the police then acquiesced to Malcolm's demands for the victim's release. With a silent signal Malcolm dismissed his followers. One senior official witnessing the event remarked of Malcolm's presence: "No one should have that much power." (*Autobiography of Malcolm X*, 335–336). The confrontation heightened Malcolm's stature considerably across the Harlem community and beyond.

Malcolm's national prominence grew almost simultaneously with the ascendency of the Civil Rights Movement led by Martin Luther King and others. This situation posed a dilemma for him. In his role as a national spokesperson for the Nation, Malcolm was being called on to define his own position with respect to civil rights protests. His position as a chief minister in the Nation of Islam compelled him to follow the injunction of Elijah Muhammad not to become involved in "the politics of the devil." However, following the dictates of the Nation made of Malcolm a passive and silent witness to one of the largest events of the time, the 1963 March on Washington. Malcolm felt a sense of isolation from the unfolding of historical process of tremendous proportions. Malcolm urged Elijah Muhammad to allow greater involvement in the civil struggles to no avail.

Another set of circumstances, however, resulted in pushing Malcolm away the Nation of Islam irrevocably. Since his conversion Malcolm and Elijah Muhammad enjoyed a close relationship. Malcolm accorded deference to Elijah Muhammad akin to a disciple to his prophet. An irreconcilable breach came between them, nevertheless. The source was rumors about Elijah Muhammad's personal life. These rumors suggested that the prophet himself had sired several children out of wedlock. When Malcolm verified the rumors for himself, he made his psychological break with the prophet. Nevertheless, he maintained his position in the Nation until he was officially censured by Elijah Muhammad in 1963for a statement Malcolm made regarding the assassination of President John Kennedy, describing the act rather coldly as "chickens coming home to roost." From then on Malcolm ceased being a faithful disciple in the Nation. The official break occurred in April 964 when Malcolm set out on his own road of independence from Elijah Muhammad.

As his breach with Elijah Muhammad widened, Malcolm embarked on his most significant transformation. He would reject the narrow constraints which the Nation of Islam imposed on his thinking. He would instead search for new models for framing the direction of the black struggle for justice. In effect, Malcolm moved on to attempt to place his own stamp on the civil rights revolution. He would accomplish this by offering fresh thinking that was neither of the stripe of the Nation of Islam nor of the more conventional integrationist approach of the major civil rights groups.

Malcolm would formulate his post-Nation paradigm for the black struggle for justice along three lines. These were Black Nationalism, Pan-Africanism, and Revolutionary violence. Black Nationalism included at least two dimensions: black unity and community control. Malcolm extended himself beyond the parochial confines of the Nation of Islam by reaching out to all other positive forces for change. Black Nationalism was envisioned as a vehicle for fostering solidarity among African Americans across parochial religious, partisan, and regional lines. Solidarity, according to Malcolm was the first step in building a sense of pride and strength enabling blacks to confront the white power structure on something close to an equal footing.

Black Nationalism also involved assuming control of community institutions and resources. Black control was necessary in confronting the most visible faces of the U.S. power structure. These were the elected officials, social service agents, teachers, police, and merchants whose contact in the community ended with the working day. They all possessed a psychological distance from the community that prevented them from mustering the kind of sympathy and understanding needed for coming to terms with the complex problems that the community faced.

Malcolm's articulation of Black Nationalism raised a crucial question. What room did it leave for well-meaning whites to take part in ameliorating the conditions in the black community? Regarding this question, Malcolm did experience a change of heart during his pilgrimage to the holy city of Mecca in 1964.

On the pilgrimage he shared in the interracial religious communality of the Muslim faithful from a variety of nations. He could not simply dismiss or condemn his other Muslim brothers and sisters outright if they were white, as he might have done if he were still a disciple of the Nation of Islam. While this experience opened him to the possibility of acknowledging the sincerity of American whites, he still insisted that they could not be incorporated into his program of Black Nationalism. Whites, in Malcolm's view, still had the obligation of proving their sincerity. The test of it was one, Malcolm suspected, few could pass.

Another of Malcolm's significant contributions to the way that the U.S. civil rights struggle was framed was in placing the U.S. civil rights struggle into a wider international context. Malcolm came away from his visits in 1964 to the several newly independent nations of Africa with the sense of both a cultural as well as a political connection with those nations. He had been received as a virtual head of state and astutely observed that there existed noticeable similarities between the anti-colonial struggles and those of the U.S. Civil Rights Movement.

He added to his reformulation of the American struggle a call to revive the sensibilities of Pan-Africanism which had lain dormant in the consciousness of African Americans since the demise of the Marcus Garvey movement in the 1920s. Malcolm devised an innovative strategy emerging from this Pan-African awareness. He proposed linking the U.S. movement to the newly independent nations of Africa through a UN resolution, spearheaded by the African nations, calling on a UN condemnation of the United States for its civil rights record. His proposal would expose the United States to a diplomatic embarrassment in the face of the cold war ideological competition between Russia and the United States. While Malcolm tried to capitalize on the good will shown him on his visits he was never able to persuade the new nations to fully confront the U.S. super power in this fashion. Nevertheless, Malcolm pressed for this proposal until his death.

Malcolm's design for reframing the black American struggle of the mid-twentieth century was outward looking. As his Pan-African impulse indicates Malcolm wished to place the struggle into an international context. Quite naturally, Malcolm set his sights on one particular set of contemporaneous events where common elements might be found to exist between the situation of black Americans and a larger world. The set of events that he identified in this manner was the wave of post–World War II anti-colonial struggles in Africa and Asia. Shared in common was European exploitation supported by white racism. This focus led Malcolm to reflect on the ability of importing the paradigm of the anti-colonial struggle, namely revolutionary insurgency and violence, into the U.S. context.

Malcolm spoke publically about recasting the U.S. struggle in terms of revolutionary insurgency. He made open references to the insurgencies in Algeria and Kenya, for example, in his speeches. He went further in articulating the issue of violence in apocalyptic terms, the magnitude of which invariably frightened the whites in his audience. Violence in Malcolm's thinking was an inevitable outcome of the unanswered brutalities suffered by black Americans. To bolster his case Malcolm could refer to incidents that were seared into the consciousness of the United States such as the recent killings of four African American girls in Birmingham, Alabama. Malcolm, however, believed that retributive justice through violence should be measured and not used indiscriminately. He made clear that his advocacy of "gun clubs" should not be regarded as incitements, but rather as cautions to those who would use violence against those thought to be defenseless victims.

Malcolm's reflections on violence were inchoate. His pending death in 1965 left little time to articulate a fully systematic statement on the subject. However, His views are consistent with his efforts at recasting the black movement in internationalist terms.

Malcolm's innovation to internationalize the Civil Rights Movement and his exhortations to black unity faltered in their implementation. Efforts to create an organizational base for his post-Nation advocacy remained inchoate. His Organization of Afro American Unity (OAAU) failed to emerge as a mass movement in its own rights.

Personal preoccupations seriously hampered work on these new ventures. His break with the Nation of Islam was the major cause of these preoccupations. Since his formal announcement of the break in April 1964 (and at the same time the creation of the Organization of Afro-American Unity), Malcolm lived in the shadow of the break's psychological consequences. Malcolm had good reason to suspect that the Nation would extract a high cost for his presumed apostasy. He had witnessed his brother Philbert's mental breakdown after his excommunication from the Nation. Moreover, Malcolm sensed the extent to which the vindictiveness of Elijah Muhammad could be converted into actual threats on Malcolm's own life.

Apostasy was regarded as the worst and unforgivable offense in the Nation. This was the psychological environment, of constant and almost minute-to-minute sudden death threat that gripped Malcolm's last several months. Malcolm did find some relief from this constant tension in an invitation extended to him by **Muhammad Ali** for Malcolm and his family to be Ali's guest at his training camp in Florida as Ali prepared for an upcoming fight with Sony Liston. Nevertheless, one incident was especially unsettling. On February 13, a fire engulfed Malcolm's home in Queens, New York. He, his wife Betty, and their four daughters managed to escape unharmed. There was little doubt that the fire had be set by a bomb thrown by embittered members of Mosque #7, the mosque which Malcolm had previously led so brilliantly. This incident demonstrated the lengths to which the Nation would go to carry out its vendetta against Malcolm.

It was in this period of unsettling concern with his own safety and that of his family that Malcolm also attempted to work out in a more detailed way the organizational design of his broader vision of African American struggle. The creation of the Organization of Afro-American and African Unity was a step in this direction. However, as Peter Goldman has pointed out, Malcolm's new moves provoked more doubts about what he proposed accomplishing in concrete ways. Making his intentions even more ambiguous was his approximation, however slight, to the civil rights leaders, such as Martin Luther King, whom he previously had vilified. Malcolm went so far on one occasion as to share the stage at a protest rally with King's wife, Coretta Scott King. Also, his strategy of gaining a UN censure against the United States met with tepid response among the African diplomats whom Malcolm looked to for support. Malcolm had miscalculated the extent that the newly independent nations were willing to take on a super power such as the United States in a forum such as the United Nations that they had only recently entered.

The inchoate nature of Malcolm's program in his final days has led to an array of interpretations about what he might have developed had he lived long enough to continue to evolve. Eric Michael Dyson's synthesis of these interpretations is evidence of the attempts of succeeding generations to come to terms with Malcolm's complexity. He certainly inspired Black Nationalism and the disciplined use of violence under certain circumstances. These were the facets of Malcolm's vision taken up eventually by the student protest movement under Stokely Carmichael (Kwame Ture) and others. His sense of nationalism, reframed as "Black Power," also, underpinned the first massive entry of African Americans into electoral politics. Some have even suggested, as George Breitman has, that Malcolm was moving toward an openly Marxist view of the black struggle. Peter Goldman, on the other hand, has disputed Brietman's view. In any case, Malcolm's continual transformations were cut short in a hail of assassins' bullets on February 21, 1965, as he addressed an audience of followers at the Audubon Ballroom on the upper west side of Manhattan. He was 39 years old.

Assessing Malcolm's legacy remains a daunting task. The complexity of Malcolm's transformations makes it difficult to set down in succinct terms what precisely that legacy has been. He certainly was a charismatic force who inspired the mobilization of masses of African Americans. He also altered the ideological face of the black struggle by insisting that it be placed in an international context. However, what endure in even greater measure are the qualities of leadership that warrant emulation. He exercised leadership with an unwavering integrity in not compromising with the forces which perpetuate injustices. And, he insisted on affirming the dignity of African Americans against the powerful elements of a society that would deny the assertion of that dignity. These are the aspects of character which Ossie Davis summed up in his obituary for Malcolm. Malcolm, Davis declared, was "Our Shinning Black Prince" (Eulogy, xi–xii).

Michael Mitchell
Arizona State University

FURTHER READING

Breitman, George. *The Last Years of Malcolm X*. New York: Pathfinder Press, 1976.

Clarke, John Henrik, ed. *Malcolm X: The Man and His Times*. Trenton, NJ: Africa World Press, 1969.

Dyson, Michael Eric. *Making Malcolm: The Myth and Meaning of Malcolm X*. New York: Oxford University Press, 1995.

Goldman, Peter. *The Death and Life of Malcolm X*. New York: Harper and Row, 1973.

Wolfenstein, Eugene Victor. *The Victims of Democracy: Malcolm X and the Black Revolution*. New York: Guilford Press, 1993.

X, Malcolm. *The Autobiography of Malcolm X*. London: Penguin Press, 2001. Originally published 1965.

X, Malcolm. *Malcolm X Speaks*. New York: Grove Press, 1965.

Joseph Lavenburg, National Geographic Society, Collection of the Supreme Court of the United States

Thurgood Marshall (1908–1993)

Thurgood Marshall was one of the most influential lawyers in the United States in the twentieth century. As a litigator and strategist with the National Association for the Advancement of Colored People (NAACP) Legal Defense and Educational Fund (LDF), Marshall helped craft and implement much of the civil rights campaigns in the nation's courts that from the 1930s to the 1960s laid siege to and eventually overturned the law and practice of Jim Crow racial segregation. As plaintiffs' lead counsel, he won the landmark *Brown v. Board of Education* (1954) case in which the Supreme Court of the United States declared that "in the field of public education, the doctrine of 'separate but equal' has no place" (347 U.S. 483, 495). That signaled an accelerating end to legal segregation. In 1967, Marshall became the first black justice on the Supreme Court of the United States, where he remained a steadfast champion of equal protection of the law for all.

Named Thoroughgood at his birth on July 2, 1908, in Baltimore, Maryland, Marshall reportedly changed his name in elementary school. Illustrating early impatience for which he would be noted later, he cut one-third of the 12 letters and wrote his personal name simply as "Thurgood." Marshall's parents, the schoolteacher née Norma Williams and the porter-steward-waiter William Canfield Marshall, accepted their second son's asserting himself as another sign of his being special. He clearly differed from their first son, who carried his father's name, William. Born on September 15, 1905, he was not a junior, however. His parents believed in individuality. They gave baby William the middle name Aubrey, and that was what the family called him, "Aubrey." They gave their second son the name his once enslaved great-grandfather reportedly gave himself on enlisting in the U.S. Army during the Civil War. The man who named himself Thoroughgood tapped old traditions. He crafted his own name to sign himself as a completely favorable and reliable character, as thoroughly good. On impulse or instinct, his great-grandson early cut his own way into that heritage.

Young Thurgood proved less than thoroughly good. In later life, he often contrasted his boyhood behavior with that of his older brother who was a well-behaved "A" student always on the good side and who ultimately delighted his parents by becoming a physician. While his brother did as he was told and stayed in the front yard in easy earshot of his mother's calls, Marshall described himself as being off adventuring in back alleys with roughnecks and rowdies. At school, Marshall appeared in trouble from the start. He was a cutup. An inveterate prankster and merciless teaser, he was perpetually involved in mischief. At Baltimore's Elementary School No. 103 on Division Street, reputedly the segregated city's best black primary, Marshall's teachers learned to seat him in the front row where they could keep an eye on him.

At Baltimore's Colored High and Training School (later renamed Frederick Douglass Senior High School), where Marshall entered ninth grade in 1921, he became a fixture in detention. Sent to the basement for punishment, Marshall found himself forced to copy and recite sections of the U.S.

Constitution. He later often reminisced with a chuckle or wry smile that he knew the entire Constitution by heart before he graduated.

Although he gave his books only glancing attention, Marshall did well enough in school. His parents would have it no other way. His mother was a teacher, after all. So were her mother and sister. Education held high priority in their lives and in the Marshall household. While his mother was directly insistent, his father was more indirect, yet no less insistent. Marshall's father preferred example to dictate. He continually engaged Marshall in debate and discussion, urging his son to articulate reasoned positions. Banter dominated their exchanges, but the practice at formal argument served the younger Marshall well.

At his mother's prodding, Marshall graduated from high school a semester early and went to work to earn college tuition money. Paying for two boys in college at the same time was more than Marshall's parents could do. At his high school graduation, his parents were almost a full year behind on his brother Aubrey's payments as a pre-medical student at Lincoln University outside Philadelphia, Pennsylvania. Although pleased enough with his qualifications to admit Marshall when he applied to start in the fall of 1925, Lincoln administrators expressed concerns about the student's unpaid $330.50 balance.

Benefiting from his father's connections, Marshall signed on full time in February 1925 as a Baltimore and Ohio Railroad (B&O) dining car waiter. By September, he had tuition money in hand and went off to Oxford, Pennsylvania, to join his brother, then entering his senior year at what some dubbed "the black Princeton." Similarities of shared Presbyterian origin, academic aspirations, and social striving vaguely connected Lincoln (founded in 1854 as the first institution for blacks to earn college degrees) with the famed Ivy League school founded 100 miles northward in New Jersey in 1746.

In college, Marshall exerted himself to study about as much as he had in high school. Again, he earned more than passable grades. Studying was not his priority, however. He preferred the high life. He was ever ready for a hearty laugh, good party, or trick-filled card game. He especially enjoyed pinochle. Tall and tan with wavy hair and witty words, he was also a ladies' man.

Marshall pledged the Alpha Phi Alpha fraternity, and his enthusiasm for hazing nearly got him expelled. Only quick thinking of his older pal **Langston Hughes**, the later renowned writer, saved the day. But Marshall did not escape his antics unscathed. In spring 1928, he snagged his groin while trying to jump aboard a moving truck. The accident cost him a testicle. The barbed humor he so often turned on others, turned his nickname from "Legs," deriding his gangly six-foot frame, to "One Ball."

The mishap forced Marshall to miss a semester at college. The experience sobered him. On returning to Lincoln in fall 1928, he got serious. He cut his partying, particularly after 17-year-old University of Pennsylvania first-year student Vivian "Buster" Burey captured his attention. They married in June 1929 in a social register gala at her church, Philadelphia's First African

Baptist, which dated back to 1809 as one of the nation's oldest and most eminent black congregations.

Marshall now had real responsibilities. He had a wife and hoped for an enlarged family. He had plans to make and things to do for more than himself. He turned to serious studying. Friends remarked at his change. He graduated from Lincoln in January 1930 with a Bachelor of Arts degree with honors. When filling out his application to Lincoln as a 16-year-old, Marshall entered "lawyer" in responding to a question about his "life plans." As he had when graduating from high school with a semester's gap before the start of the next academic year, Marshall went to work full time. With his college degree in hand, he aimed to earn law school tuition and living money for himself and his wife. Again, his father's connections paid off nicely, but not with B&O dining cars, where Marshall worked after high school.

During his years at Lincoln, Marshall worked baking bread in the campus cafeteria. Summers he worked also in food service, but not on campus and not in the kitchen. He waited tables at the Gibson Island Club, an exclusive whites-only country club 30 miles outside Baltimore, where his father served as head steward. He set up Marshall as a club waiter in the summer of his first year at Lincoln. The pay was good, and Marshall returned every summer during college. He returned again in January 1930. With the 1929 stock market crash signaling the decade-long economic downturn of the Great Depression, Marshall happily donned his white waiter's jacket for steady wages and tips.

Marshall had his heart set on entering the University of Maryland Law School (UMLS) in fall 1930. Located in downtown Baltimore, it was his hometown law school. Established in 1816 (although without regular instruction until 1824), UMLS had a venerable pedigree and high prestige extending throughout the state and region, including 40 miles southeast to the U.S. capital. It counted the bulk of the local legal community among its alumni. Moreover, as a public law school, it offered cheap tuition. UMLS was the place to start a promising legal career in Baltimore, such as Marshall envisioned.

UMLS demanded a qualification Marshall lacked, however: he was not white. In an earlier era, UMLS grudgingly had admitted a rare black student. It had graduated two. But since the heyday of Jim Crow in the 1890s, UMLS had admitted no blacks. Local black lawyers advised Marshall to forget UMLS. No way was he getting in there. Jim Crow barred his admission. If he wanted to be a lawyer, as he declared, then he needed to go elsewhere.

He did. In moving on, however, Marshall never forgot how segregation sapped his dream. Yet he refused to be denied. He was determined to be a lawyer. Bitterly turning down the road, Marshall headed to the Howard University School of Law (HUSL) in Washington, DC. Beginning instruction in its law department in 1869, HUSL sat in sharp contrast to UMLS. The Baltimore school stood high and the DC school low in legal circles. Nevertheless, each offered entry to the bar. And from Marshall's perspective the two shared another important thing: cheap tuition.

Low as HUSL's costs were, Marshall came up short of money to move to Washington, DC and matriculate at Howard on schedule. He considered deferring his start for a year to earn more money. His mother refused to let him. She pawned her engagement and wedding rings to get him the added cash he needed to start law school in September 1930, waking daily at 5 a.m. to commute from his parents' Baltimore home to DC. Marshall entered HUSL on the cusp of its emerging into legal limelight. Staging the change was the school's new dean, Charles Hamilton Houston. The 35-year-old, *cum laude* Harvard Law School graduate greeted Marshall and his 35 fellow first-year students with a no-nonsense ultimatum. Insisting on nothing less than excellence, Houston demanded dedication to the law. Gone were the days of part-time attendance at HUSL. Marshall and his fellow 1Ls sat in HUSL's first full-time day class.

Houston took no prisoners. He grabbed Marshall's heart and mind that first day. Marshall later recalled determining to make the grade as he listened to Houston's challenge. He considered he had too much riding to fail. Houston became an immediate exemplar and later a mentor for Marshall. Houston graduated in the top 5 percent of his class and became the first black to earn a spot on the *Harvard Law Review* editorial board. He fixed Marshall's eyes on achievement. Houston almost gleefully told HUSL students that the devil should take the hindmost. He accepted only the best and, in 1931, drove HUSL into the ranks of American Bar Association accreditation and membership in the Association of American Law Schools.

Houston boldly declared his aim to make HUSL the "West Point of Negro leadership." He fully intended the reference to the U.S. Military Academy founded in 1802 at West Point, New York. He envisioned a war against American apartheid, and he saw himself in the business of training battlefield commanders. Marshall enlisted eagerly. He won a place as the student assistant in the law library, and he dug deeply into the law books. The pay reduced his money worries, and the reading and research honed his skills and whet his appetite for more. The occasional student from high school and college became a dedicated student of law. He graduated in June 1933 first in his HUSL class.

Marshall's law degree opened no doors immediately. Segregation shut most law practice opportunities to him. The professional bellwether American Bar Association then rejected blacks for membership. Major law firms were whites-only enterprises. The few black lawyers practicing rarely had room for any other hands.

So Marshall returned as a waiter to the Gibson Island Club. With his father in charge and money not so pressing, he could set his own schedule. When HUSL Dean Houston asked him to go on a tour of black elementary schools in the South as a follow-up to a 1931 NAACP study proposing court challenges to wretched conditions segregation imposed on blacks, Marshall jumped at the chance. Marshall and his mentor took turns driving by car from Washington, DC to New Orleans, Louisiana, and back. They slept in private homes and ate there or in the car, as Jim Crow closed hotels, motels, and restaurants to them. But that was not the worst of it.

The abysmal school conditions shocked Marshall. He saw buildings barely standing in backward settings where blacks had virtually nothing. His eyes beheld horrors he had heard of and read about but had not known to this depth firsthand. More than repulsing him, the conditions impelled him to determine to do whatever he could to abolish inequities and injustices. Marshall had an option. Dean Houston had recommended Marshall to his own former teacher, the distinguished U.S. legal scholar and educator Roscoe Pound, dean of Harvard Law School. Pound was impressed enough to offer Marshall a scholarship for advanced legal study at Harvard, an opportunity afforded few.

Choosing between the distinct honor of going to Harvard or going to work, Marshall chose to go to work. He took the Maryland bar examination for admission to practice there, passed it, and got his law license on October 11, 1933. Marshall opened an office in Baltimore's downtown Phoenix Building on Redwood Street. He soon enough got experience aplenty in lawyering, taking whatever cases came his way, from criminal charges, including murder and rape, to civil complaints from divorces to personal injuries. Yet his first year receipts ran $3500 less than his bills.

With his paying clients few and scattered, Marshall had time to continue work with his mentor Houston on fact-finding for an NAACP assault against the South's segregated elementary public schools. The two grew into a partnership. Marshall continued to learn and Houston continued to teach as they developed a hand-in-hand collaboration. Marshall became a respected regular in Baltimore's courts. In April 1935, he filed what became his first major case. With special personal satisfaction, he sued Raymond A. Pearson and other officers and members of the University of Maryland Board of Regents in Baltimore City Court for a writ of mandamus on behalf of Donald G. Murray, challenging as unconstitutional UMLS's bar to admitting blacks. Working with Houston, who had become NAACP chief counsel, and with help from another of his HUSL professors, William H. Hastie, Marshall won.

Maryland's highest court affirmed Marshall's victory in *Pearson v. Murray* (1936). Writing for a unanimous Court of Appeals, Maryland Chief Justice Carroll T. Bond explained that:

> The State has undertaken the function of education in the law, but has omitted students of one race from the only adequate provision made for it, and omitted them solely because of their color. If those students are to be offered equal treatment in the performance of the function, they must, at present, be admitted to the one school provided. (169 Md. 478, 488)

The victory based on the Fourteenth Amendment's Equal Protection Clause buoyed Marshall. His and others' hopes rose for the NAACP's developing strategy to improve public school conditions and opportunities for blacks. The plan aimed to use as leverage the accepted legal rule of "separate but equal," adopted from the U.S. Supreme Court's 1896 decision in *Plessy v. Ferguson*. It aimed to force segregated public school systems, such as Maryland's, either to open facilities to blacks—such as the court ordered UMSL to do for Donald G. Murray—or to equalize facilities.

Marshall's next big case showed the continuing difficulties in assaulting racially segregated public schools in the 1930s. Baltimore County, surrounding Marshall's hometown, maintained no public high school for blacks. Still flush from his success in *Murray* and working with his NAACP allies, Marshall sued the Baltimore County school board and David W. Zimmerman, the principal of its all-white Catonsville High School, not 10 miles from the city center, to gain entry for black 13-year-old Margaret Williams.

Williams v. Zimmerman (1937) flopped. Judge Frank Duncan on the Circuit Court for Baltimore County barely heard Marshall's arguments at trial, and Maryland's Court of Appeals offered no succor as it had in *Murray*. The evidence showed nothing sufficient to violate the separate-but-equal mandate but simply "differences of only a minor importance," Maryland's high court ruled (172 Md. 563, 570). Marshall took the *Williams* setback in stride, for at about the same time he won a separate victory gaining an out-of-court settlement with Maryland's Montgomery County school board to equalize black and white teachers' pay. He was moving with broader vision, for in October 1936 he had signed on full-time to assist his mentor Houston as NAACP counsel in New York City.

Moving to NAACP headquarters at 69 Fifth Avenue in Manhattan, Marshall entered full partnership with his mentor Houston. They pressed their argument that state laws and practices of racial exclusion and so-called separate but unequal treatment violated the Fourteenth Amendment. They won the U.S. Supreme Court's agreement in April 1938. In the per curiam opinion in *Hale v. Kentucky*, the nation's high court declared "systematic and arbitrary exclusion of Negroes from the jury lists solely because of their race or color . . . [constituted] a denial of the equal protection of the laws" (303 U.S. 613, 616).

In December 1938, Houston and other NAACP lawyers used Marshall's Maryland victory in *Murray* to win Lloyd Gaines's admission to the all-white School of Law at the University of Missouri. The U.S. Supreme Court in an opinion by Chief Justice Charles Evans Hughes ruled in *Missouri ex rel. Gaines v. Canada* that Gaines "was entitled to be admitted to the law school of the State University in the absence of other and proper provision for his legal training within the State" (305 U.S. 337, 352).

Marshall was helping to pave the groundwork leading to the Supreme Court's momentous decisions in *Brown v. Board of Education* in 1954 and 1955. He found himself in charge of the NAACP's legal office at the end of 1938, when Houston relinquished the helm. And in March 1940, when the LDF incorporated as a separate legal entity to comply with federal tax rules,

Marshall became the LDF's first director-counsel and made it the prototype organization for public interest litigation.

Marshall orchestrated a broad attack against Jim Crow. He pressed two salients: voting rights and public schools, but he neglected no opening in any area. Battling against all-white primary elections as a weapon to disfranchise blacks, he continued the fight the NAACP had waged since 1921 in Texas. In April 1944, he won. In *Smith v. Allwright*, the U.S. Supreme Court outlawed black exclusion at party primary elections. It ruled all-white primaries violated the U.S. Constitution's guarantee of the right to vote regardless of race. In *Morgan v. Virginia* (1946), Marshall moved the Supreme Court to invalidate state segregation laws affecting interstate transportation as an "undue burden on commerce." And in *Sweatt v. Painter* (1950) and *McLaurin v. Oklahoma* (1950), he again prevailed, as the Court directed the previously all-white University of Texas Law School to admit the black Heman Marion Sweatt and the University of Oklahoma to admit the black George McLaurin to postgraduate study in education.

The series of connected class-action suits against segregated public schools in Delaware, Kansas, South Carolina, and Virginia that Marshall argued in the consolidated landmark victories in *Brown v. Board of Education* in 1954 and 1955 crowned him with the popular moniker "Mr. Civil Rights." Including those, Marshall won 32 of 35 cases he argued before the nation's highest court in the 1940s and 1950s. His skill as a constitutional lawyer helped to move the Court and the nation to end legal support for race discrimination.

Amid his great public triumph, Marshall suffered grief. The wife of his youth, Vivian "Buster" Burey Marshall, died on February 11, 1955, her 44th birthday, after being painfully sick for more than a year and hospitalized with cancer. Over the 25-year marriage, she may have had as many as five miscarriages. She bore no children, to both her and Marshall's great sorrow. Her death left him depressed. Within the year, Marshall married NAACP secretary Cecelia "Sissy" Suyat. A Hawaiian of Filipino heritage, she sparked renewed life in him in 1956 with the birth of their first child, a son, Thurgood Jr. In July 1958, they had a second son, John. Realizing a long-cherished hope of an expanded family, Marshall basked in private and public.

In addition to kudos in the United States, Marshall's skill and clear commitment to the rule of law garnered him international attention. On the cusp of decolonization in Africa, the United Nations and other organizations with international interests asked Marshall's advice on building legal structures for newly independent nations on the continent. The United Kingdom solicited his advice for its former West African colony that, in March 1957, emerged as Africa's first decolonized, independent state, Ghana, with Marshall's fellow Lincoln University alumnus, Kwame Nkrumah, as its leader. Marshall also offered advice in the British-administered East African area that in 1961 became independent Tanganyika (later Tanzania). Marshall's deepest influence in Africa came in Kenya. During a prolonged visit in 1960 and shuttling between London and Nairobi, Marshall crafted a bill of rights and eased constitutional negotiations between Kenyan leaders, such as Jomo Kenyatta and Tom Mboya, and British colonial administrators ahead of independence in December 1963.

The experience in Africa confronted Marshall with cultural differences in defining, evaluating, and implementing democratic self-government in multiracial states where, unlike in the United States, blacks formed the majority and whites the minority. Also, it put him on the line to confront as he had not had to before the clash between the deliberative, developmental processes of the rule of law that too often appeared ponderous to the public against insistent calls to violence as an immediate solution to historical and lingering problems.

Marshall would use the lessons at home. He expected opposition to implementing the *Brown v. Board of Education* decisions. He early counseled against wild hopes of instantly eliminating segregation. Yet his own vision proved exuberantly optimistic. Many, if not most, Southern whites refused to yield generations-old practices. They protested furiously. Virginia former governor and conservative Democrat U.S. Senator Harry F. Byrd, Sr. and others organized their backlash into the Massive Resistance movement. From 1956 to the early 1960s, Massive Resistance erected and encouraged state and local legislative impediments to desegregating public schools. The battle lines became entrenched as a countervailing Civil Rights Movement pushed to outlaw Jim Crow policies and practices. Marshall's work as a public interest litigator had opened doors to a fresh United States.

After 21 years as NAACP LDF director and counsel, Marshall resigned in 1961 to sit as a judge on the U.S. Court of Appeals for the Second Circuit. In geography, it was not a big move. The court sat in New York City, not far from the LDF offices in Manhattan. In legal circles, the move was huge. Black federal judges were rare in September 1961 when President John F. Kennedy nominated Marshall. No black had ever sat even at the entry, trial level federal bench in the continental United States until August 1961, when President Kennedy nominated James B. Parson to be a U.S. District Court judge. Marshall's HUSL professor and NAACP colleague William H. Hastie had become the first black federal judge in U.S. history in 1937. But he sat on the territorial court designated the U.S. District Court for the Virgin Islands. In October 1949, Hastie scored another first. He rose to sit on the federal bench just below the Supreme Court, when President Harry S Truman appointed him a judge on the U.S. Court of Appeals. Hastie sat in the Third Circuit based in Philadelphia, Pennsylvania.

Sitting on the Second Circuit bench from 1961 to 1965, Marshall again displayed his capacity as a workhorse. He wrote more than 150 decisions. The Supreme Court never reversed even one of the 98 decisions Marshall wrote for the majority on circuit. He proved particularly frank and forward in writing to protect those he saw as especially vulnerable. He vindicated the rights of immigrants, for example, and he insisted on fairness in criminal prosecutions and on taking seriously the Fourth Amendment's declaration of "The right of the people to be secure in their persons, houses, papers, and effects, against unreasonable searches and seizures."

In 1965, President Lyndon B. Johnson called Marshall back to the other side of the bench. Asking him to return to being a litigator, the president appointed the judge U.S. solicitor general. Heading the office that conducted and supervised federal litigation in the Supreme Court, Marshall argued and won 14 of 19 cases in his approximately two years as the government's chief courtroom lawyer.

In June 1967, President Johnson asked Marshall again to move to the other side of the bench. He nominated him to sit on the nation's highest court. With the Senate voting 69 to 11 to confirm him on August 30, 1967, Marshall became the first black member of the Supreme Court of the United States.

On the high bench, Justice Marshall persisted in speaking for persons the law too often left unheard. He had always been an advocate for the people. He remained so on the bench. He always viewed law as a tool, not as an ideal or object sufficient in itself. Its significant substance was not technicalities. It was not to be the hostage of specialists. Its promise lay in serving more than the few. Law in Marshall's view existed to serve a single purpose: Justice.

Marshall judged law in terms of real-world effects. In detail and direction, he sought to craft meaningful decisions that delivered sensible solutions to practical problems. He showed that almost immediately. In June 1968, during his first full term on the Court, his opinion in *Powell v. Texas* counseled against taking any position that "goes much too far on the basis of too little knowledge" (392 U.S. 514, 521). Treating a chronic alcoholic's criminal responsibility in the context of the Eighth Amendment's Cruel and Unusual Punishment Clause, Justice Marshall adopted what he viewed as the most reasonable position given the available alternatives.

Marshall never shied from advocating radical social transformation. He spent his career at the NAACP pushing such change. He saw himself working as a social engineer. His mentor Charles Hamilton Houston had drummed that vision into him at Howard University Law School, and he persisted in its counsel of pragmatism. Whether as advocate or as judge, he moved to get things done. Even on the bench when he insisted on procedural rules he emphasized their sole legitimate purpose was to promote substantive goals. Results mattered most to him. First, last, and always, he was a legal realist.

Justice Marshall labored to make the U.S. Constitution work for everyone in the United States. His dissents in *Dandridge v. Williams* (1970) and *San Antonio Independent School District v. Rodriguez* (1973) articulated a sliding scale theory of constitutional protection to have the nation's courts weigh the totality of circumstances, not only technicalities, in deciding how to move America's rhetoric of fundamental rights from paper propositions to functioning realities. He argued persistently against abusive power. Vindicating the rights of the weak delivered true justice, more than confirming the rights of the powerful, in his view. He resolutely required police and prosecutors to adhere strictly to the rights of criminal suspects. He opposed the death penalty. He backed women's rights and broad affirmative action, as indicated in his dissent in *Regents of the University of California v. Bakke* (1978). He always opposed arbitrary governmental discrimination.

On the nation's high court, Justice Marshall pushed his fellow justices to be mindful of law's duty to attend to human needs. He seldom muted his voice. He became one of the Court's great dissenters. As the character of the Court turned increasingly conservative in the late 1970s and 1980s, he found himself consistently in the minority. Critics dubbed his views ultra-liberal. He persisted in fighting what he saw as the good fight. Chronic heart trouble, failing eyesight, obesity, and other ills forced Thurgood Marshall to retire from the Court effective October 1, 1991. He died of heart failure at Bethesda Naval Hospital in Maryland on January 24, 1993. Various tributes acknowledged him as a civil rights giant.

Thomas J. Davis
Arizona State University

FURTHER READING

Dudziak, Mary L. *Exporting American Dreams: Thurgood Marshall's African Journey.* Oxford: Oxford University Press, 2008.

Tushnet, Mark. *Making Civil Rights Law: Thurgood Marshall and the Supreme Court, 1936–1961.* New York: Oxford University Press, 1994.

Tushnet, Mark. *Making Constitutional Law: Thurgood Marshall and the Supreme Court, 1961–1991.* New York: Oxford University Press, 1997.

Tushnet, Mark., ed. *Thurgood Marshall: His Speeches, Writings, Arguments, Opinions, and Reminiscences.* New York: Lawrence Hill Books, 2001.

Williams, Juan. *Thurgood Marshall: American Revolutionary.* New York: Times Books/Random House, 1998.

AP/Wide World Photos

Hattie McDaniel
(1893–1952)

An award-winning entertainer and actress, Hattie McDaniel was born in Wichita, Kansas, on June 10, 1893. Many biographies list McDaniel's birth year as 1895 because she often lied about her age, but the Kansas State Census confirms her birth year as 1893. In 1940, McDaniel became the first African American to win an Academy Award for her 1939 role as "Mammy" in *Gone With the Wind.* McDaniel won this award during a period in U.S. history when opportunities for African Americans in the film industry were extremely limited. This was not the only first for Hattie McDaniel; she was also the first African American woman to sing on the radio. McDaniel was also a comedienne and stage actor. McDaniel's life was fraught with tension and throughout her career she found herself walking a fine line between the expectations of both the white film industry and African Americans who saw her consistent decisions to play "Mammy" roles as a betrayal to the race. Nevertheless, Hattie McDaniel, through her success in the film industry, was able to give back to her family and to her community and became well-known as a local philanthropist. Literally pulling herself up from her own bootstraps, Hattie McDaniel desired not simply to make it as a successful entertainer. Above all, she hoped to be "a credit to [her] race and the motion-picture industry" (quoted in Watts, 2005, 179).

Although Hattie McDaniel, the youngest of 13 children (only 7 survived into adulthood), was born in Wichita, Kansas, the family moved often because of limited opportunities for African Americans. They finally settled in Denver, Colorado. Henry McDaniel, her father, was wounded fighting against the Confederate Army in the Civil War. Because of his injuries, he was unable to contribute substantially to the family's household income. After petitioning the federal government for 18 years, in 1902 Henry McDaniel was finally awarded a meager $6 a month pension that barely helped to cover the family's basic needs plus Henry McDaniel's increasing medical expenses. Like many African American women during this time period, Susan McDaniel, Hattie's mother, was employed as a domestic, often working in the homes of whites as a cook, nanny, or maid. As a result of low wages and dismal prospects for African Americans, the McDaniels raised their children in perpetual poverty. Determined to rise above these conditions, the McDaniel children looked to the entertainment industry as an avenue to change the economic situation in which they found themselves.

McDaniel's decision to become an entertainer was not farfetched given the musical and theatrical background of her family. Although McDaniel's mother and father, Henry and Susan, were musicians, it was the influence of McDaniel's older brothers and sisters that propelled young Hattie into the entertainment industry. McDaniel's older brothers and sisters, Otis, Sam, and Etta tried to supplement the family's meager income by cashing in on their musical and theatrical talents on street corners in Denver. Eventually, Otis and Sam McDaniel formed a group called the Cakewalk Kids. This group performed at events in the local African American community. At age six, Hattie McDaniel already knew that she wanted to be an actress. She once said,

"I always wanted to be before the public … I'm always acting. I guess it's just the ham in me" (quoted in Watts, 2005, 31). A year later, at the age of seven and aware of the family's desperate need for money, Hattie McDaniel joined her brothers and sisters, without their parent's permission, in performing at a local carnival. Amazing the crowd, Hattie McDaniel earned $5 for a week's worth of performances and learned that the show business industry could be a very lucrative way to help out her family. After this initial performance, McDaniel performed with her brothers and sisters quite frequently and eventually proved to be a successful solo amateur entertainer.

McDaniel would later describe one of her performances in the pivotal year of 1908 as a "life-altering experience." Sponsored by the Women's Christian Temperance Union, McDaniel entered an oratory contest in which she performed a poem entitled "Convict Joe." Claiming she won first place in the competition, McDaniel remembered this experience as particularly meaningful. Her stirring performance would be indicative of her later success.

Later that year, McDaniel joined the Mighty Modern Minstrel troupe under the leadership of J. M. Johnson. As a result of her performance with the Mighty Modern Minstrels, McDaniel was selected to perform with a New York group performing in Denver called the Red Devils. As an entertainer with these shows, McDaniel sang, danced, acted, and performed comedy routines. Although the crowds loved her, these vaudeville performances did not always prove to be as profitable as she expected. As a woman and an African American, McDaniel found herself doubly constrained. Men were usually favored for most roles and whites acting in blackface were preferred even when there were willing African American entertainers. Despite all of this, McDaniel continued to work hard in her chosen profession and even created opportunities for African American women.

On January 19, 1911, McDaniel married Howard Hickman. Hickman was an entertainer like McDaniel and was known as a very accomplished pianist—so much so that he was the first African American in Denver hired to accompany silent films. Due to both of their connections in the entertainment industry in Denver, it is likely that the couple met because they traveled in the same circles.

In 1914, McDaniel-Hickman, and her sister Etta Goff established the McDaniel Sisters Company which featured all female cast members. The McDaniel Sisters Company female minstrels were sought after in Denver, Colorado, and they performed all over the city. Eventually, they became a weekly fixture at a major venue for African Americans in the city, Eureka Hall. Having been resigned to the sidelines, McDaniel-Hickman used this company as an opportunity to showcase the talents of African American women and combat stereotypes that saw African Americans artists as capable of only performing certain roles.

McDaniel-Hickmans's company was so important not only because it provided crucial employment opportunities for African American actresses, but also because with each performance McDaniel-Hickman tried to critique the stereotypes that persisted about African American female performers. During this period, the available roles for African American women actresses mirrored their actual employment opportunities. Onstage, African American women were usually resigned to playing polite servants who responded to the every whim of their white employers. Seemingly like real life, white directors desired that African American actresses follow directions without questions and without asserting their own sense of style. McDaniel-Hickman's company reinvented the mammy role by parodying it to such an extent that her audiences knew that she felt the expectations white society prescribed to African Americans were ludicrous, silly, and ignorant.

By the time McDaniel-Hickman turned 21, she was well-known in her community for her talent as an actress and comedienne. Experiencing much success in her performing arts career, McDaniel-Hickman's personal life suffered a severe blow when her husband died on March 3, 1915 from complications of pneumonia. As was customary of the time, McDaniel-Hickman canceled all of her upcoming performances—including one scheduled for the next night—and entered a year of mourning. She moved back home with her parents and did not participate in the entertainment industry.

After the customary year of mourning, McDaniel emerged from her absence ready to resume her career. She began by organizing a memorial in remembrance of her husband as well as announcing that she would perform in a new play entitled *Spirella Johnson from Memphis, Tennessee*. Although *Spirella Johnson* was a huge success, after this opportunity there were few other acting opportunities for African Americans in the city of Denver so McDaniel began incorporating blues songs into her performances to make herself more marketable. By 1922, McDaniel had met and married her second husband, Nym Lankford. This relationship was not the best and eventually McDaniel and her husband became estranged. Continuing on with her career, in 1924, McDaniel successfully auditioned for a role with the Pantages vaudeville circuit that toured cities in the United States and Canada such as Minneapolis, Saskatoon, Calgary, Seattle, San Francisco, Los Angeles, San Diego, Denver, Omaha, Memphis, and others. After her tenure with the Pantages vaudeville circuit, McDaniel moved to Chicago because although her performances were very successful, once they ended, she could still only find work as a maid or cook.

Moving to Chicago proved to be a smart decision because McDaniel was able to audition for the African American vaudeville circuit via the Theater Owners Booking Association (TOBA). Although the work was unpredictable at best, McDaniel was able to make her face known and meet some of the most famous African American entertainers in the industry such as Bill "Bojangles" Robinson, Ethel Waters, and Bessie Smith. During this time, McDaniel also worked on her blues career more and by 1928 had recorded songs with the popular OKeh Records.

In 1931, McDaniel moved to Los Angeles and with her brother Sam's help, was able to get work singing at the Tivoli Theater. Work was extremely hard to come by as the country was still reeling from the effects of the Great Depression.

Affected by the Depression, it wasn't long before the TOBA had to close due to inability to make profits. And although several of McDaniel's entertainer siblings lived in the city, none of them really had much success except for Sam McDaniel. He had a spot on a radio show and he had even earned some speaking parts in some films.

Seeing no other way to continue her acting work but through films because of the collapse of the TOBA, McDaniel made an appointment with Charles Butler—the African American gate keeper to the silver screen. After McDaniel submitted her acting resume, measurements, and a headshot, she waited for a phone call to audition for a film. She wouldn't have to wait long and soon she had earned a position as an extra. Hattie McDaniel, slowly and patiently, worked her way up the film industry ladder. At the same time she was building her film career, she had joined her brother Sam on his radio show, the *Optimistic Donuts*. This made her the first African American woman to sing on the radio. McDaniel did so well that she was given her own show called *Hi Hat Hattie and Her Boys*.

Eventually, McDaniel would devote herself more and more time to her film career. As a result, she was cast for a significant role in *Judge Priest* in 1934. From 1934 to 1937, McDaniel was extremely busy as she worked for an average of 14 films a year, acting in such films as *Babbit* (1934, Warner Brothers); *Imitation of Life* (1934, Universal); and the *Merry Wives of Reno* (1934, Warner Brothers); *Okay Toots* (1935, MGM); *The Postal Inspector* (1936, Universal); and *True Confession* (1937, Paramount). By this time, McDaniel was well established on the silver screen and known to add her own flair to the roles she played, if given the chance.

In 1936, Margaret Mitchell published the novel that would eventually thrust McDaniel into the Hollywood spotlight and solidify her place in film history— while also causing disdain from many African Americans communities. The novel *Gone With the Wind* debuted in 1936 and after six months sold six million copies. Centered on the life of a white family living through the Civil War and Reconstruction, *Gone With the Wind* appeared on the Bestseller List and eventually won a Pulitzer Prize for fiction in 1937. *Gone With the Wind* chronicles the life of protagonist Scarlett O'Hara, a Southern Belle whose father owned a plantation before and during the Civil War. Exploring her romantic endeavors and the transformation of her life because of the Civil War, the story is also a commentary on Southern life and its treatment of African Americans. Nothing highlighted this more than Scarlett O'Hara's interactions and comments about the African Americans she encountered in her life—mainly enslaved people her family had owned and her own nurses and maids. O'Hara is once noted for thinking, "How stupid negroes were! They never thought of anything unless they were told." There was one character, however, that defied O'Hara's assessment of African Americans— Mammy. Rhett Butler, another main character in *Gone With the Wind*, calls the Mammy character the real "head of the household" and indeed, Mammy is outspoken, witty, and often chastises Scarlett O' Hara. Because she was O'Hara's nurse from birth, her behavior is seemingly more acceptable.

Seeing the enormous popularity that *Gone With the Wind* was garnering, MGM's David Selznick purchased the film rights to the novel during the summer of 1936 for $50,000—a very expensive sum of money at the time. He immediately began working on the film version and especially on finding the perfect cast. The casting call went out and not only was there a flurry of auditions for the white characters, but there was also popularity within the African American community for the leading female character—Mammy. Many African American actresses auditioned such as Georgette Harvey from George Gershwin's *Porgy and Bess* and the popular Louise Beavers from *The Imitation of Life*. Also, First Lady Eleanor Roosevelt sent her personal maid—Elizabeth McDuffie—with a letter of recommendation.

Though these African American actresses knew this would be great for their careers, auditioning for the movie was also contentious. Although the Mammy character was outspoken and sassy, the novel *Gone With the Wind* was also well-known for its demeaning depictions of African Americans. Many in the African American community felt that the film would do the black community a disservice. David Selznick, however, promised "the black Press that the story would receive careful treatment and that he would seek 'the best possible cast' " (Watts, 2005, 148). Satisfied with this pledge from Selznick, some black Press members began to throw their support behind an underdog in the audition pool—Hattie McDaniel.

Many didn't consider McDaniel at first because although she usually played maids on the silver screen, her take on these roles always leaned toward the comedic side. Margaret Mitchell's Mammy was a more serious character than McDaniel had ever played. Because of this, she was considered the underdog in the audition pool for Mammy. Despite this—Hattie McDaniel was chosen for the role and she accepted it. This was probably one of the best and most complicated decisions she made in her life. Her portrayal of "Mammy" was so wonderful that she won an Academy Award—the first African American woman to win an Oscar—but she was also criticized heavily by the African American community because despite Selznick's promise, many African Americans, especially the leadership of the National Association for the Advancement of Colored People (NAACP) and members of the black Press, felt that Hattie McDaniel's portrayal of "Mammy" did nothing to improve how African Americans were depicted in the film industry. Earl Morris, a journalist employed by the *Pittsburgh Courier* issued a particularly biting remark about McDaniel's work in *Gone With the Wind* when he wrote: " 'We feel proud over the fact that Hattie McDaniel won the coveted role of Mammy. . . . It means about $2,000 for Miss McDaniel in individual achievement . . . [and] nothing in racial advancement' " (as quoted in Watts, 2005, 156).

McDaniel, however, did not see it this way. She felt that although she was still relegated to Mammy roles on the silver screen, that some work was better than no work and that she was paving the way for future African American actresses. McDaniel felt that she could add some of her own flair to the role and prove that although African American women were resigned to play maids and servants on the screen, they could play these roles with dignity. Additionally, during the filming of the movie, McDaniel refused to deliver any lines with the racial epithet "nigger," which was quite a stand since, at that time, this slur was a common term used to refer to African Americans. McDaniel, in ways many times unrecognized by those who criticized her, tried to make progress on behalf of the African American community.

Gone With the Wind premiered in Atlanta, Georgia, on December 15, 1939. The premiere included three days of festivities including a parade, receptions, and a costume gala. Because of prevailing Jim Crow laws, McDaniel and the other black cast members were prohibited from attending any of the festivities. White cast member Clark Gable threatened to boycott because of this but eventually attended after being convinced by McDaniel. Although the movie premiered in 1939, it was released to a limited number of theaters until 1941 when it opened everywhere. Overseas, it was a huge hit and it played in London for four years straight.

Although many in the African American community disagreed with McDaniel's role in *Gone With the Wind*, others felt McDaniel was spectacular and petitioned David Selznick by writing letters to nominate McDaniel for an academy award. Other black organizations such as the Sigma Gamma Rho Sorority supported McDaniel's nomination. Additionally, the *Los Angeles Times* had praised her performance in December 1938. Unable to ignore these petitions, David Selznick did nominate McDaniel for an Oscar for Best Supporting Actress. McDaniel's win that year was not an easy task, for several actresses in other high grossing movies were nominated for the same category.

On the night of the Academy Awards, Hattie McDaniel arrived at the Los Angeles Ambassador Hotel and although she would eventually win the Academy Award, segregation prevailed and she was not seated with any of her cast members from *Gone With the Wind*. Though segregation prevailed, no one could deny the importance and excitement of the moment especially when Fay Bainter, 1938's Best Supporting Actress, announced " 'It is with the knowledge that this entire nation will stand and salute the presentation of this plaque . . . that I present the Academy Award for the best performance of an actress in a supporting role during 1939 to Hattie McDaniel' " (as quoted in Watts, 2005, 179). And, even the African American community, split though it was over McDaniel's role in the movie, had to pause and celebrate the meaning of this moment. Hattie McDaniel, ever aware of the remaining conflict and her necessity to straddle two worlds accepted her award by saying, " 'It makes me feel very humble, and I shall always hold it as a beacon for anything I may be able to do in the future . . . I sincerely hope that I shall always be a credit to my race and the motion-picture industry' " (as quoted in Watts, 2005, 179).

Ending her acceptance speech on a tearful note, McDaniel said she could not truly express how she felt so she thanked the audience and left the stage.

After McDaniel's success with *Gone With the Wind* and her receipt of the Academy Award, unfortunately her career did not continue to take off. She signed an exclusive contract with MGM that prohibited her from taking roles with other companies. This effectively caused a break in her work because although she signed with MGM, she wasn't exactly their highest priority actress. As such, though she was salaried, she was not actually working and her film average went from 14 in prior years to 3 or 4 during the early 1940s.

McDaniel, however, continued to take the roles that she could and although she had won the Academy Award, the mostly white-run film industry still did not improve roles for African Americans. This led to an even more bitter conflict with the NAACP because the organization practically blamed African American actors and actresses for the depiction of blacks in films. They argued that if these actors and actresses would not accept these roles then the film industry would have no choice but to change the roles. Black actresses and actors, however, felt that if they did not accept these roles then the black actor/actress would disappear altogether. Additionally, accepting these roles was a matter of food and shelter for most of these workers—entertainment was a job and the NAACP did not pay wages to actors and actresses who decided to boycott the film industry. McDaniel was ensconced in this debate and because she was one of the most visible actresses during this era, felt the brunt of the criticism.

No matter the criticism, McDaniel still desired to be a credit to her race. In 1942, McDaniel purchased a home in Los Angeles' West Adams "Sugar Hill" neighborhood. Other African American actresses and actors bought homes in this neighborhood as well. White residents of the neighborhood, tried for seven years, to draw up and enforce a restrictive covenant that would force African Americans out of the neighborhood. McDaniel led residents of the West Adams neighborhood in a lawsuit that sought to end restrictive covenants.

On December 5, 1945, the case went to trial and surprisingly Superior Court Judge Thurmond Clarke ruled restrictive covenants unconstitutional, allowing African American residents of the West Adams neighborhood to keep their homes and paving the way for the end of residential segregation based on race. Meanwhile, McDaniel had married for the third time in 1941. By the end of the lawsuit that allowed her to keep her home, McDaniel was in court again, this time to divorce her husband Lloyd Crawford. She testified that she desired a divorce because Crawford was jealous of her career, that he did not contribute to the household, and that he was abusive. Her divorce was granted and McDaniel moved on.

Two years later, McDaniel took an opportunity to go back to radio—an area in which she was extremely talented. This time, McDaniel auditioned for her own show on a major radio network—CBS. McDaniel auditioned for the role of Beulah—a role originally played by a southern white actor, Marlin Hurt—in the radio show *Beulah*. The main plot of the *Beulah* centered on Beulah's efforts to get her boyfriend to propose to her. Beulah was an African American woman who, of course, worked as a domestic. The show also highlighted interactions Beulah had with her white employers. McDaniel took the role to new heights, allowing CBS and the show's sponsor, Proctor and Gamble, to promote the show in new ways on TV and in visual marketing campaigns. Although McDaniel received much success performing as Beulah, she still received condemnation from the NAACP and African Americans who felt that McDaniel was, once again, perpetuating damaging and demeaning stereotypes about African Americans. This time McDaniel countered by accusing her detractors of trying to ignore the plight of most African Americans in the United States who were still employed in the most menial positions. Additionally, she argued that with the money she earned from the *Beulah* show—the most and steady salary she had ever been paid—she was able to help the African American community and give back to those in need.

On June 11, 1949, Hattie McDaniel married for the fourth and final time, this time to an interior decorator, Larry Williams who was 13 years younger than her. They married in Yuma, Arizona and as soon as they arrived back in Los Angeles problems began. McDaniel asked Williams to sign a legal agreement that would not allow him to claim any of her assets if the marriage did not last. The marriage would not last long as Williams and McDaniel argued constantly. They separated in October 1949 and by December 1950, divorced.

All throughout her life McDaniel suffered various health problems that stemmed from her hectic life and schedule, stress, and inability to manage her weight. In 1951, McDaniel suffered a stroke and was officially diagnosed with advanced heart disease and diabetes. What doctors failed to diagnose was the breast cancer that McDaniel would eventually succumb to on October 26, 1952. On November 1, 1952 over 3,000 mourners would arrive to the People's Independent Church to remember the life of Hattie McDaniel.

McDaniel worked her entire life in the entertainment industry not only to provide for herself and for those she cared about, but also to break barriers in the entertainment industry. She was supremely talented and succeeded in multiple industries including stage, film, and radio. Although she tried her hardest to be a credit to her race, it seems that all she could garner was criticism for her chosen profession. McDaniel did not let this deter her, however. She will be forever known for her being the first African American to win an Academy Award. In 2002, American Movie Classics (AMC) produced the film *Beyond Tara, The Extraordinary Life of Hattie McDaniel*, which chronicled her life. *Beyond Tara* won a Daytime Emmy Award in 2002. Also, in 2006 McDaniel was inducted into the United Postal Service's Black Heritage Series making her the first African American Academy Award winner to be honored with a stamp. Although McDaniel's life was filled with tension and tragedy, she also experienced much triumph and success—all because she would rather play a maid than be one.

Crystal Marie Moten
University of Wisconsin-Madison

FURTHER READING

Hopper, Hedda. "Hattie Hates Nobody." *Chicago Sunday Tribune*, 1947.

Jackson, Carlton. *Hattie: The Life of Hattie McDaniel*. Lanham, MD: Madison Books, 1990.

Mitchell, Lisa. "More Than a Mammy." *Hollywood Studio Magazine*, April 1979.

Salamon, Julie. "The Courage to Rise Above Mammyness." *New York Times*, August 6, 2001.

Watts, Jill. *Hattie McDaniel: Black Ambition, White Hollywood*. New York: Harper-Collins, 2005.

Young, Al. "I'd Rather Play a Maid Than Be One." *New York Times*, October 15, 1989.

Zeigler, Ronny. "Hattie McDaniel: '(I'd) ... rather play a maid.' " *N.Y. Amsterdam News*, April 28, 1979.

AP/Wide World Photos

Morehouse College

Morehouse College, located in Atlanta, Georgia, is the only private, entirely male, historically black, four-year liberal arts college in the United States. It is one of three traditional men's colleges in the United States that continues to be a single-sex institution today. Morehouse's 3,000 students enjoy a 61-acre campus and a student-faculty ratio of 16 to 1, with 100 percent of the school's tenure-track faculty hold tertiary degrees. The College exists as a part of the Atlanta University Center (AUC) that includes Morehouse School of Medicine, Interdenominational Theological University Center, Clark Atlanta University, and **Spelman College**, a women's college located in close proximity. Morehouse is one of two black colleges in the United States to produce a Rhodes Scholar, the other being Howard University, and many black leaders, including Nobel Peace Prize winner **Martin Luther King, Jr.**, have graduated from this fine institution of higher education.

Reverend William Jefferson White and Edmund Turney founded Augusta Institute in 1867, the college that would later be renamed Morehouse. Turney, a former enslaved man and the organizer of the National Theological Institute for educating freedmen in Washington, DC, and White were also assisted by the Reverend Richard C. Coulter, another formerly enslaved man from Augusta, Georgia. With the mission of educating African American men in theology and education, classes were held in the basement of Springfield Baptist Church, the oldest independent black church in the United States. The creators of Augusta Institute determined to prepare black men to enter the ministry and teaching professions.

The institution's first president was Reverend Dr. Joseph T. Robert, a white man and the father of Brigadier General Henry Martyn Robert, the author of *Robert's Rules of Order*. In the years following the end of Reconstruction in the late 1870s, the institute moved from one church basement to another, ending up at the Friendship Baptist Church in Atlanta. In 1879 the Augusta Institute was renamed the Atlanta Baptist Seminary. Within the next 10 years the school relocated twice more. In 1885, Dr. Samuel T. Graves became the second president, and moved the seminary to a location that would expand to become its present location, on four acres of land donated by John D. Rockefeller in the West End area of downtown Atlanta. Five years later, Dr. George Sale became the seminary's third president, and in 1897 the school became Atlanta Baptist College. The turn of the century ushered in a long period of formidable growth and identity formation for the college. In 1906, the college gained its first African American president, Dr. John Hope, the school's fourth president. Dr. Hope played a critical role by improving the institution's enrollment numbers, quality of faculty, and academic stature. He envisioned an academically rigorous college that would be the antithesis to **Booker T. Washington**'s educational model of agricultural and industrial training for African Americans. Hope, like **W. E. B. Du Bois**, believed that simply educating African Americans to become working professionals was not the correct way to achieve an educated mass. Through his leadership,

Hope fostered the development of an intellectual atmosphere similar to that of his alma mater, Brown University. Hope's leadership shaped the institution into a college that, by the twenty-first century, had gained international recognition and numerous accolades, both within the academic community and from the larger society.

Morehouse College took its current name in 1913, to honor Henry L. Morehouse, corresponding secretary of the Northern Baptist Home Missions Society. Morehouse joined Clark College and Spelman College in 1929 in a cooperative agreement, which formed the foundation for the later expansion of the association to form the Atlanta University Center. Two years later, Dr. Samuel H. Archer became the fifth president of the college. In a move to forge a more visible identity for Morehouse and to instill stronger school spirit, Archer selected the school colors, maroon and white, to reflect his own alma mater, Colgate University.

Dr. Benjamin Elijah Mays became Morehouse's sixth president in 1940, and continued the work of his predecessors to improve the college. Mays, who would mentor Martin Luther King, Jr. from the time he became a student at Morehouse until his untimely death, presided over Morehouse's growing domestic and international enrollment, continuing to enhance the college's reputation. Mays's intelligence, leadership, and excellent rhetorical skills proved instrumental in shaping the character of and intellectual disposition of Morehouse's students. One of his most ambitious goals, to acquire a Phi Beta Kappa chapter at Morehouse, happened in 1968, after his presidency but thanks to the momentum generated by his efforts. Mays improved the quality of Morehouse's faculty, raising the number of professors holding doctoral degrees to almost 50 percent. During Mays's tenure that spanned the first seven years of the 1960s, the peak years of the Civil Rights Movement, Morehouse students were actively involved in the struggle in Atlanta and elsewhere across the United States. Thanks to Mays's presidency and to students' involvement in the Civil Rights Movement, Morehouse earned global recognition.

Mays held a prominent position in the Christian ministry as a strong proponent of U.S. education. His outstanding leadership and service as a teacher, preacher, mentor, scholar, author, and activist made him a respected leader of the Civil Rights Movement. Born August 1, 1894 near Epworth, South Carolina, he graduated Phi Beta Kappa from Bates College in Maine in 1921. After receiving his bachelor's degree, he served as pastor of Shiloh Baptist Church for two years in Atlanta. Recruited by John Hope, Mays initially joined the faculty as a mathematics teacher and debate coach. He obtained a master's degree in 1925 and the following year married Sadie Gray, a teacher and social worker. In the mid-1930s, in the middle of the Depression he became dean of the School of Religion at Howard University, and earned a PhD from the University of Chicago. Mays served as dean until 1940, when he took over the presidency at Morehouse.

Mays's most noted forum at Morehouse was Tuesday Morning Chapel in historic Sale Hall. He challenged students to achieve excellence in scholarship and in life, and inspired many young black men, including Martin Luther King Jr., who remembered Mays as his "spiritual mentor" and "intellectual father." Upon his retirement, Mays served as president of the Atlanta Board of Education from 1970 to 1981. Throughout his educational career, he published nine books and nearly 2000 articles, and received 56 honorary degrees, including a degree awarded posthumously from Columbia University. Mays's wife Sadie died in 1969, and he passed away in 1984 leaving the legacy of a distinguished career in academia.

In 1967, Dr. Hugh M. Gloster became the seventh president of Morehouse and the first alumnus of the institution to serve in that capacity. During Gloster's tenure Morehouse gained the Martin Luther King, Jr. International Chapel, a dual-degree in engineering program that partnered the college with several southeastern universities, and in 1975 the Morehouse School of Medicine, which became independent from Morehouse College in 1981.

Morehouse School of Medicine was established with the tripartite mission of improving the health and well-being of individuals and communities, increasing the diversity of the health professional and scientific workforce, and addressing primary healthcare needs through programs in education, research, and service. All three components of the mission targeted people of color and the underserved urban and rural populations in Georgia and the nation.

The Morehouse School of Medicine projects an image as the leading community-focused, research-driven, student-centered medical school in the United States. The medical school has gained recognition in four key areas. First, its pre-eminence in the conduct of research that results in tangible community solutions and improved patient care, contributing to the elimination of health disparities. Second, Morehouse is celebrated for its model educational environment that nurtures and supports the achievement of academic excellence. Third, the medical school has earned recognition for developing models and creating practices of integrative, culturally competent, and community-empowered health and healthcare. Finally, the school has made significant contributions to the diversity of the healthcare and scientific workforce, the development of leadership committed to improving the health of vulnerable populations, and efforts to reform the nation's healthcare system.

Under the stewardship of another alumnus, Leroy Keith, Jr., Morehouse expanded its campus through the erection of a number of new campus buildings. In addition to campus improvements, Keith's presidency also enjoyed the awarding of the first Rhodes Scholar to a graduate from a historically black college or university (HBCU) in 1987.

Wiley Purdue became acting president of Morehouse in 1994. Under Purdue's leadership, Morehouse took part in hosting participants in the 1996 Summer Olympics Games, held in Atlanta. Morehouse constructed an arena that hosted basketball games. When millions of viewers tuned in to watch the U.S. "Dream Team" and other basketball teams, Morehouse gained international exposure. In 1995, Walter E. Massey, another Morehouse alumnus, had become the college's ninth president in 1995. He continued to expand the school's programs and infrastructure, built the Leadership Center, and renamed the Center for International Studies, that had been established in 1993, the Andrew Young Center for International Affairs.

Morehouse also produced two additional Rhodes Scholars during Massey's presidency, and the college secured major gifts from philanthropists such as **Oprah Winfrey**, whose donations topped $12 million over a 12-year period during the late 1990s and early 2000s. The students who were selected as Rhodes Scholars were among a large number of Morehouse men who have been honored for their distinguished achievements in their chosen fields, the most notable of which is Martin Luther King, Jr., who received the Nobel Peace Prize in 1964. The venerated list of Morehouse graduates include Lerone Bennett, Jr., who edited *Ebony* Magazine for more than a half century; Calvin O. Butts, III, pastor of Harlem's Abyssinian Baptist Church since 1989; Robert E. Johnson, associate publisher and executive editor of *Jet* Magazine; Bill Nunn, a celebrated actor; David Satcher, U.S. Surgeon General from 1998 to 2002; Louis W. Sullivan, U.S. Secretary of Health and Human Services during the George H. W. Bush presidency and co-founder of Morehouse's School of Medicine; Howard Thurman, a lauded theologian and civil rights leader in the mid-twentieth century; Samuel L. Jackson, an Academy Award-nominated actor; **Spike Lee**, an Academy Award-winning filmmaker and director; Edwin Moses, an Olympic athlete who won gold medals for hurdles in 1976 and 1984; and Maynard Jackson, major of Atlanta in 1974–1982 and 1990–1994. By the early twenty-first century, Morehouse students were admitted from the top of their secondary school classes, and three-quarters of the entering student population were involved in some community service or volunteer endeavor, which supports the reputation that Morehouse upholds.

One of Morehouse's articulated objectives is to produce graduates who lead lives of purpose, leadership, and service. This mission begins in the AUC, where schools in the consortium allow cross-registering for courses and often share social activities, such as the annual Spelman-Morehouse Christmas concert put on by the glee clubs from each school, respectively. The AUC is organized around the principle that each school shares a common commitment to the African American community. Member schools share a library, the Robert W. Woodruff Library, and a shuttle for student transport to and from public transportation stations, the library, and the various campuses.

Morehouse is composed of three major sections, and is academically competitive, with faculty members who are leaders in their respective fields. The college's three core academic sections are business and economics, humanities and social sciences, and science and mathematics. Recent faculty achievements include the psychologist Sinead Younge's work on HIV, *Searching for a Balm in Gilead: The HIV/AIDS Epidemic and the African American Church*, and David Wall Rice's *Balance: Advancing Identity Theory by Engaging the Black Male Adolescent* (2008).

Despite its storied history, Morehouse has had its share of controversies, especially during the last decade. By the second half of the twentieth century, Morehouse had become a premiere institution of higher learning. Despite its reputation and numerous accolades, many accused its students, staff, faculty, and alumni of embracing a retrograde sense of superiority, and social and intellectual aloofness that undermined the ability of the college's graduates to effectively address many of the socioeconomic problems that plague black America. Morehouse hit its most recent media peak in 2008, when Joshua Packwood became the first white valedictorian to graduate from the historically black college in the school's 141-year history.

Packwood, who maintained a 4.0-grade point average, after turning down a full scholarship to Columbia University to attend Morehouse, surrounded himself with black friends, only dated women of color, was elected dorm president and to class council during his freshmen year. Despite this, he was subjected to a firestorm of criticism when word got out that he might become the next valedictorian. Some of his classmates, even friends, were admittedly chafed. Still, the majority of Morehouse students told CNN that he earned his accolades and they stand behind him and his accomplishments. Some say, if anything, Packwood's academic success should serve as a lesson to his fellow students.

> "I think that it should be a wake-up call to an all black campus," says [Mr.] Muhammad. "At Morehouse we're supposed to be at the top as black men. We only have a few white students and to see a white student rise to this—is something unsettling to me because it shows that we need to work harder." (CNN, May 29, 2008)

Campus administrators say that black or white, Packwood's experience is consistent with the school's mission: to produce future leaders.

> "I think some of our alumni are a little nervous about a white student graduating from Morehouse with all of its rich history for producing African-American male leaders. But I don't think it's contradictory at all," says Sterling Hudson, the dean of admissions. (CNN, May 29, 2008)

Overall, Packwood says his experience is the best proof of Morehouse success, because the school was able to produce a white valedictorian, against the odds. He's eager to quote the school's most notable alums. "What Morehouse stands for at the end of the day, and what Dr. King epitomized, it's not about black or white, it's about the content of [a person's] character," says Packwood. "It's about me, representing Morehouse in that light—not as a white man or a black man" (CNN, May 29, 2008).

In 2009, Morehouse instituted a controversial dress code that angered many supporters of the elite HBCU, once again bringing Morehouse into the media's stream of controversy. The dress code, officially called the Morehouse College "Appropriate Attire Policy," banned the wearing of women's clothes, makeup, high heels, and purses as part of a new crackdown on what the institution called inappropriate attire. William Bynum, Morehouse's vice president for Student Services, indicated that he discussed the new dress-wearing ban policy with Morehouse's campus gay organization. The policy also bans wearing hats in buildings, pajamas in public, do-rags, sagging pants, sunglasses in class, and walking barefoot on campus.

However, it is the ban on cross-dressing that inspired heated debate and brought national attention to the small historically black college. The dress-wearing ban was aimed at a small part of the private college's student body, argued Bynum. "We are talking about five students who are living a gay lifestyle that is leading them to dress a way we do not expect in Morehouse men," he maintained (CNN, October, 17, 2009).

Before the school released the policy, Bynum said, he met with Morehouse Safe Space, the campus' gay organization. "We talked about it and then they took a vote," he said. "Of the 27 people in the room, only three were against it" (CNN, October, 17, 2009). There were positive responses along with some criticism throughout the campus, he argued. Senior Devon Watson said he disagreed with parts of the new policy, especially those that tell students what they should wear in free time outside of the classroom. "I feel that there will be a lot of resentment and backlash," Watson said. "It infringes on the student's freedom of expression."

Senior Tyrone McGowan said he has mixed feelings about parts of the policy. "But," he stated, "I have been inspired by the conversation it has created. We have to find a way to create diverse leaders from this college. I don't want this to place all of us in one box." Those in violation of the policy will not be allowed to go to class unless they change. Chronic dress-code offenders may face suspension from the college. Bynum said the policy comes from the vision of the college's president, who wants the institution to create leaders like notable graduates Martin Luther King Jr., Samuel L. Jackson, and Spike Lee. Senior Cameron Titus applauds the change. "The policy is just saying that you have to show more respect in how you dress and there are things that are just not acceptable at Morehouse," Titus proclaimed. "We have a legacy that we are trying to uphold" (CNN, October, 17, 2009).

In the twenty-first century, Morehouse has continued to advance. The student body is composed of nearly 3,000 men from more than 40 states and 18 countries. Morehouse College offers organized and informal co-curricular activities including 78 student organizations, varsity, club, and intramural sports, and student publications. Perhaps among the most notable of

Morehouse's current students is Stephen Stafford II, a home-schooled student who matriculated at age 11 and is scheduled to graduate when he turns 16 in 2012.

The Morehouse College Marching Band is known for their halftime performances which combine dance and marching with music from various genres, including rap, traditional marching band music, and pop music. They performed at Super Bowl XVIII, the *Today Show*, and at Atlanta Falcons home games. Known as the "House of Funk," they march alongside the Maroon Mystique Color Guard (flag spinning) squad and Mahogany-N-Motion dance team.

In 2005–2006, the Morehouse College Mock Trial Team became a member of the American Mock Trial Association (AMTA). It obtained an "Honorable Mention" award in their first appearance at the American Mock Trial Association National Championship Tournament in 2006. The school is one of only four competing teams to come from an HBCU and is also the only all-male team in the AMTA. In 2006, 2007, 2008, and 2009, Morehouse won their regional championship competitions, thereby receiving direct trips to the AMTA national championship competitions in Iowa, Florida, and Minnesota, respectively.

In sports, Morehouse College has developed and expanded as well. The college is affiliated with the Southern Intercollegiate Athletic Conference (SIAC) and the National Collegiate Athletic Association (NCAA) Division II. Its mascot is the Maroon Tiger, maintaining the maroon and white colors selected by Archer, the school's fifth president. Morehouse competes in football, baseball, basketball, cross country, tennis, track and field, and golf. The Morehouse Tigersharks was once a powerhouse swim team. From 1958 to 1976 the swim team had 255 wins and only 25 losses, with over 15 SIAC championships, making it the most successful sports team in Morehouse history. It even defeated Emory University and Georgia Tech in dual meets in different seasons. The team appeared in *Jet* and *Ebony* magazines, *Black Sports*, and *Sports Illustrated* throughout the 1960s and 1970s, and today is being considered as honorary inductees into the International Swimming Hall of Fame in Ft. Lauderdale, Florida. Actor Samuel L. Jackson was once the team statistician and was an apprentice swimmer. Some of the swimmers had competed in NCAA and NAIA competition at various times throughout the team's history. The team was disestablished in 1976 and the funds were transferred to build the Morehouse School of Medicine.

In 2006, the institution also succeeded in a well-publicized last-minute campaign to obtain the papers of its most celebrated alumnus, Martin Luther King, Jr. Those papers are now housed in the Robert W. Woodruff Library. Professor Clayborne Carson, a leading historian and public intellectual, was hired by Morehouse in January 2009 to be the Martin Luther King Jr. Distinguished Professor and executive director of the Morehouse College Martin Luther King Jr. Collection. Carson will oversee more than 10,000 pieces of King papers, memorabilia, and artifacts, will be responsible for mapping the vision and direction for the Collection, including developing programming for scholarly access and public education. One of his most important roles, however, will be to mentor future King scholars. Morehouse is now under the leadership of its tenth and current president, Robert Michael Franklin, who was inaugurated in 2007. Franklin, along with a mass of distinguished faculty, staff and students, will continue to maintain and promote the rich cultural heritage of Morehouse's reputation and tradition as demonstrated and manifested through the lives and legacy of its most distinguished graduate.

Matthew C. Whitaker
Arizona State University

FURTHER READING

Brawley, Benjamin. *History of Morehouse College, Written on the Authority of the Board of Trustees*. College Park, MD: McGrath, 1917.

Butley, Addie Louise Joyner. *The Distinctive Black College: Talladega, Tuskegee, and Morehouse*. Metuchen, NJ: Scarecrow Press, 1977.

Mungin, Lateef. "All-Male College Cracks Down on Cross-Dressing," CNN.com. http://www.cnn.com/2009/US/10/17/college.dress.code/ (accessed March 5, 2010).

Rosenblatt, Dana, and Don Lemon, "White Valedictorian: A First for Historically Black Morehouse." *Black* in *American 2*, Online. CNN.com: http://www.cnn.com/2008/ US/05/16/white.valedictorian/index.html (accessed March 5, 2010).

Wilson Mbajeke, Carolyn. *The Future of Historically Black Colleges and Universities: Ten Presidents Speak Out*. Jefferson, NC: McFarland, 2006.

Olga Besnard

Toni Morrison (1931–)

Speaking at Princeton University, Toni Morrison delivered a paper to members of the Center for Human Values, wherein she observed that "we teach values by having them" (Morrison, 195). This seemingly straightforward remark, emblematic of her ability to be simultaneously obvious and obscure, embodies Morrison's broader aesthetic regarding artistic production—an aesthetic that allows for the seamless combining of art and politics. As evinced from not only her highly successful novels, both critically and commercially, but also from her work as professor, essayist, and editor, the breadth and depth of Morrison's contributions to American letters rightly establishes her as one of the architects of contemporary American literature.

Morrison, born Chloe Anthony Wofford on February 18, 1931, grew up in Lorain, Ohio, as the second of four children. Both of her parent's families, like many black families at the turn of the century, moved North to escape the cruelties of segregation and sharecropping, only to find a different sort of inequality. Regardless, her ancestor's migration represents the first of many instances in Morrison's full life that inform the woman she is today. To know only her novels is to know only a part of her.

Prior to settling in Ohio, Ardelia Willis and John Solomon Willis, Morrison's maternal grandparents, migrated from Alabama to Kentucky with 12 children. Her grandfather, who with his sister's aid taught himself to read and play the violin, inherited 88 acres of land only to lose it to "legal predators"—land that came from his Native American mother. While in Kentucky, the Willis's discovered their girls were teaching their white teacher long division. Her maternal grandmother's desire to see her children properly educated was a key factor in the relocation further north to Lorrain, Ohio. In an essay published in the *New York Times*, titled "A Slow Walk of Trees (as Grandmother would say), Hopeless (as Grandfather would say)," Morrison writes of the distinct visions for the future each of her grandparents held, one of "hope" and one of "hopelessness." And, as Morrison is want to do, she blurs this apparent dichotomy throughout her oeuvre, merging the boundaries between these worldviews into something both honest and nuanced.

Morrison's attempt to reconcile these two disparate worldviews certainly stems from more than just her grandparents' conflicting philosophies. Her father, George Wofford, moved north from Georgia, where the racial violence he grew up with not only shaped his view of white America but also led him to communicate early on to his daughter her own sense of self and value. He worked three jobs to support his family, chief among them was his work as a ship welder. Her mother, Ramah (Willis) Wofford, a high school graduate, modeled the importance of education to her daughter, still referred to then as Chloe. The determination of both parents enabled a young Chloe, employed as a maid, to observe: "I never considered the level of labor to be the measure of self or placed the security of a job above the value of a home" (Morrison, 17). Indeed, Morrison's ability to look beyond what one does into who one is stands as a hallmark of her fiction—one that works to both enlighten and challenge readers.

Subsequently, Morrison was raised in Lorrain, Ohio, a small, blue-collar Midwestern town consisting of a diverse population, including European immigrants, Mexicans, and Southern blacks. In Lorrain, Morrison attended an integrated school and grew up with both white and black children. Despite the diversity, the line between black and white persisted, and Morrison, from a young age, perceived a difference in "the life of the spirit or the mind" (Taylor-Guthrie, 172). As such, she recalls two educations: her school education and the "life" education she received from her culture. Both educations seemed to have stuck.

Part of her "life" education came in the form of storytelling, in particular, ghost stories. Morrison remarks that her father told the best stories. Even more importantly, the ghost stories were, in part, told in a manner in which the storytellers believed in what they were saying. As such, the supernatural, for Morrison, became both tangible and real. Adding to this perception, her grandmother would often inquire as to the content of her dreams. Upon hearing the tale, her grandmother would look them up in her dream book and translate the dream into a three-digit number that would be used in a numbers game. The blending of the real and imagined resurfaces throughout Morrison's fiction, resulting in a trope some have called magical realism, a term wrought with contention, and more often applied to South American writers such as Jorge Luis Borges and Gabriel García Márquez.

Morrison's "school" education shaped her development as well; Morrison herself read widely across borders and genres while in school, where she developed a love for reading. She poured through classics, among them works by Jane Austen, Leo Tolstoy, and Gustave Flaubert. In addition, her schooling provided her with four years of Latin. She would graduate with honors from her local high school in 1949. Because of her academic success, and her parent's hard work, Morrison headed East to Howard University in Washington, DC, where she would become the first college graduate from her family. Her love for reading translated into an English major and Classics minor. It was also at this time she adopted a modified version of her middle name, from Anthony to Toni, as many had trouble pronouncing her given name.

Morrison's childhood, while certainly not void of racial tensions and realities, differed greatly from the realities of the South. Lorrain, Ohio, certainly not void of inequalities, housed the more subtle forms of often-unspoken tensions and indirect discrimination. During college, while a member of the Howard University Players, Morrison experienced firsthand what her ancestors moved North to escape, as her group traveled throughout the Deep South. Motivated by what she experienced, and shaped by the determination of her parents and grandparents, Morrison not only graduated from Howard University with a BA in English in 1953, but she also pursued a Master's degree from Cornell University in Ithaca, New York, which she obtained two years later in 1955.

The culmination of Morrison's undergraduate and graduate endeavors led to an appointment teaching introductory English at Texas Southern University in Houston—an appointment that would prove vital to her professional and personal development. It was during her time in Texas that Morrison first began to think about black culture as a subject. While at Howard, professors balked at her idea of examining the black characters in Shakespeare; whereas teaching for only a year and a half in Texas, Morrison experienced a school that not only supported her research endeavors but also celebrated black history week. During her experience, Morrison increasingly became aware of the growing black Press, and her vision of black culture as connecting solely to her familial experience into a broader examination of the black experience in the United States began to take hold.

Her time in Texas, however, was brief. Upon returning to her alma mater as a member of the faculty at Howard University, Morrison met Harold Morrison, a young Jamaican architect. They were married in 1958; they would have two sons, Harold and Slade. During her tenure, teaching as she was during the beginning of the civil rights era, Morrison encountered several key future members of the movement, including poet/dramatist Amiri Baraka (known then as LeRoi Jones) and Andrew Young, who in addition to later working with **Martin Luther King, Jr.** would go on to become mayor of Atlanta, Georgia.

During this formative period for both Morrison and the country as a whole, in addition to teaching her classes and raising her firstborn, Morrison joined a small writers group. It was in that group that she wrote a short story, well received by its members, about a young girl who prayed to God for blue eyes. This story, inspired by someone she knew and greatly informed by her experiences growing up in Lorrain, Ohio, was put away. During this time, her marriage deteriorated; Morrison, while pregnant with her second son, left her job at the university. She took her son on a trip to Europe. Upon her return, she divorced her husband in 1964 and was hired as an associate editor with Random House in Syracuse, New York.

While living and working in Syracuse, raising two sons on her own, Morrison returned to the short story her writing group had read. In her limited free time, she developed the story and decided to turn it into a novel. After three years as an associate, Morrison accepted a position as senior editor at Random House in New York City. In her position as editor she worked with such prominent figures as **Muhammad Ali** and **Angela Davis**. She also began sending out her now finished novel. And in 1970, *The Bluest Eye* was published to critical, if not commercial, success.

The Bluest Eye is a story of a young black girl, Pecola Breedlove, who prays to God for blue eyes. The book itself is told primarily through the eyes of Claudia MacTeer, a young girl the same age as Pecola. Morrison, however, adds several layers to her text, including entire sections narrated by secondary characters, including both of Pecola's parents. The story takes place in a small Midwestern town populated by a multitude of characters, all of whom, like performers in a jazz band, are given their chance to add their interpretation to the story. Despite the seemingly expansive structure, the heart of the book remains tied to Pecola

Breedlove and her desire for blue eyes. The myriad of subjects Morrison touches upon resurface again and again throughout her novels.

Shorty after the publication of her first novel, Morrison received an appointment (1971–1972) as an Associate Professor of English at the State University of New York, while simultaneously continuing to work at her position at Random House. It was at this time that she edited *The Black Book*, a book of primary sources detailing over a hundred years of black history, including newspaper clippings, diary excerpts, and countless firsthand accounts from "regular" people. Morrison, who later called the book a "true labor of love," draws inspiration from the book for many of her fictional endeavors.

Morrison's second novel, *Sula*, was published in 1973. The book details the friendship of the titular character and her best friend, Nel Wright. Similar to her previous effort, the narrative unfolds through various perspectives and balances the central story of the two women with that of the community as a whole. However, while *The Bluest Eye* took place in the real town of Lorrain, *Sula* takes place in the fictional town of Medallion. *Sula* illustrates Morrison's deliberate focus upon the experiences of black women in the United States, a group often silenced during the civil rights era during which women's rights translated primarily to white women, and black rights often identified solely with black men. Her focus on black women dovetail's with what **Alice Walker**, a contemporary of Morrison, calls Womanism. While not declaring herself for or against any singular movement, Morrison has, on several occasions, written upon her complicated relationship with both of the aforementioned movements. *Sula* garnered Morrison several accolades, including a nomination for the 1975 National Book Award in fiction, as well as the distinction of becoming an alternate selection for the Book-of-the-Month-Club, a feat rare for a young, black, female writer.

Morrison's star would only rise from that point on. While working as a visiting lecturer at Yale University, Morrison published *Song of Solomon* in 1977. Markedly different from her previous efforts, her third book tells the story of Milkman Dead, and does so from a distinctly male perspective. The book differs significantly in style, as the perspective does not shift as dramatically, and the novel itself is far more plot-oriented than any of her previous or subsequent work. All of this combined to produce Morrison's first bestseller. Although *Song of Solomon* represented a departure of sorts, Morrison further solidified her commitment to writing both to and about the black community —an aesthetic not meant to limit readership, but rather one that simply speaks to her implied audience. Speaking to this issue, Morrison once noted that although Emily Dickinson did not have her in mind as the reader, she had no problem reading and understanding her; in the same way, while her own community defines and shapes what she writes, it does not define or limit who may read it. The success of *Song of Solomon* makes this evident.

After the success of her third book, Morrison increasingly entered the national spotlight. Her success as an author, an editor at Random House, and as a professor, led President Jimmy Carter to appoint Morrison to the National Council on the Arts. She also received popular notoriety; during the publication of her fourth novel, *Tar Baby*, Morrison appeared on the cover of the March 30, 1981 issue of *Newsweek* magazine. *Tar Baby* took place on a small Caribbean Island and marked her most contemporary storyline to date, as well as the first to focus on the interaction of both white and black characters. While not as successful as her previous efforts, it was increasingly becoming evident that any new Morrison novel would garner attention, and that the standards set for her were high, a reality that would only increase in intensity.

Two years later, in 1983, Morrison left Random House after nearly 20 years; a year later she was named Albert Schweitzer Professor of the Humanities at the State University of New York in Albany. While there, she wrote the play, *Dreaming Emmett*, about Emmett Till, a young black man from the North who, after unknowingly breaking the "rules" of the Jim Crow South, was lynched for purportedly whistling at a white woman. The play was performed but never published. In the same year Morrison published her only short story, titled "Recitatif." The title references a musical term referring to a type of speech that blends heightened and ordinary language. The story itself concerns two women and details several meetings they have over a long period of time wherein the race of the characters is never made clear, although one is black and the other white.

Both ventures outside the realm of the novel highlight two of Morrison's decision to not shy away from exploring the complicated racial division. Moreover, her decision to write for the stage illuminates Morrison's decision to merge the written and spoken voice. Morrison's elaborates on the merging in "Rootedness: The Ancestor as Foundation," wherein she describes her vision of having the African American novel playing the role that music once did. In her attempt to inculcate the characteristics of black art into her work, Morrison notes that her writing ought have "the ability to be both print and oral literature: to combine those 2 aspects so that the stories can be read in silence, of course, but one should be able to hear them as well" (Morrison, 59). Morrison takes this vision of writing within and for a black culture even further, proclaiming that she does not feel the need to "translate" as if she is writing to an "other," a criticism she notes in other established writers.

Nowhere does her aesthetic become more evident than in her fifth novel, *Beloved*, published in 1987, which would prove to be her masterpiece. For this book she received the Pulitzer Prize in Fiction. The novel builds upon the true story of Margaret Garner, a slave who, when confronted with the possibility of her and her family being returned into slavery, attempted to kill her children. Garner succeeded in killing one, and this act became the inspiration for the character of Beloved, the name on the tomb where the murdered child rests. The ghost/reincarnation of Beloved, first in spirit form, then in physical form, haunts Sethe and Denver. The spirit is ousted from the house, only to return in physical form. *Beloved* would later (1998) be made into a movie starring **Oprah Winfrey** and Danny Glover.

Beloved is often included in lists of best American novels, and has even been recognized as one of the greatest novels of all time. The novel is also regarded, in some circles, as difficult and elusive, both in structure and theme. Moreover, some have criticized Morrison of unfairly treating male characters, a sentiment carried over from the more male-centered Black Arts Movement, and echoed in contemporary conservative movements. For the most part, however, Morrison does not dignify such claims with counter remarks. Rather, she continued to focus upon her work as a professor and was named the Robert F. Goheen Professor in the Council of Humanities at Princeton University; her appointment made her the first black woman to hold a named chair at an Ivy League University.

In 1992, five years after the publication of *Beloved*, Morrison publishes her sixth novel, *Jazz*, as well as a book of literary criticism, *Playing in the Dark: Whiteness and the Literary Imagination. Jazz* represents possibly her most experimental work—and one that like *Beloved*, had as its inspiration, *The Black Book*. Included in the collection was a photo of a young girl in Harlem, who when asked to identify her attacker, refused to implicate her lover. Morrison plays on this theme, summarizes the basic plot from the outset of her novel, and then, like a jazz performance, riffs on the original tale, improvises with various timeframes and perspectives, adding layer and layer to a performance that attempts to capture, in print, the essence of jazz.

Playing in the Dark, Morrison's only full length work of academic criticism, offers an exploration of the evolution of literary criticism in the United States within the context of race; more specifically, Morrison details what she calls the "Africanist Presence" in American literature, and how the avoidance of race informs and shapes both the discourse surrounding texts as well as how the literature itself is written. The book draws from three lectures Morrison delivered; the most recognized stems from "Unspeakable Things Unspoken: The Afro-American Presence in American Literature," wherein she offers an examination of the work of Herman Melville within the context of the "Africanist Presence."

Morrison received her greatest honor in 1993 as she became the first black woman to win the Nobel Prize in Literature. In her much anthologized acceptance speech, Morrison tells the story of an old woman and several children; however, as is the case with a good deal of her work, simple dualism does not suffice. The old woman does not teach the children a lesson, nor does the woman simply learn from youth; together, through mutual respect and hard work, they challenge one another; in this speech, as Carolyn C. Denard notes in her introduction to *What Moves at the Margins*, both the children and the old woman "have been on a quest to figure out what is authentic about the other" (Morrison, xii). The focus on authenticity harkens back to Morrison's desire to capture the essence of black art, the oral quality, onto the written page—it is an authenticity that disallows "either/or" patterns of thought.

Over a decade after *Beloved*, which continued to be taught, discussed, and lauded with accolades, and five years after receiving the Nobel Prize, anticipation for Morrison's seventh novel was immense. Making the hype even more intense, Oprah Winfrey chose her new book, sight unseen, for her televised book club. Unprecedented amounts of hardcovers were sent out to bookstores. The book, what Morrison had intended to title *War* (until dissuaded by her editor) would be titled *Paradise*. It begins: "They shot the white girl first." From that opening line, readers are introduced to The Convent, a refuge of sorts for women who have lost their way. The book itself is divided into sections titled and told from the perspective of these women. It is a challenging, heavy, beautiful, and complicated narrative, and the readers on the Oprah Winfrey show resisted—many claiming it was too difficult. Overall, the reception of *Paradise* proved mixed, and sales did not match anticipated numbers.

Around this time, Morrison began to work within yet another genre and partnered with her son, Slade. Together, they published several children's books. The first collaboration, *The Big Box* (1999), and their later collaboration, *The Book of Mean People* (2002), both extend the discussion Morrison begins in her Nobel Prize acceptance speech: how do generations perceive one another and what are the implications of their actions. Both books offer a pointed critique of "standard" interpretations of childhood, and like her novels, refuse to cast things as either/or. However, such nuances can be difficult for her intended audience, and as many reviewers note, these books are still directed at more of an adult audience. Morrison and her son also published a *Who's Got Game?* series of three books based upon the Aesop fable, the ant and the grasshopper.

Morrison's eighth novel, *Love*, about a dead hotel owner, Bill Cosey, and the two surviving women from his life, his widow and granddaughter, was published in 2003. The novel was seen by many as a return to form, with its short but dense narrative and ability to pack in a great deal in such a short amount of time. Morrison followed this novel with a non-fiction effort titled, *Remember: The Journey to School Integration* (2004). In Morrison's most recent novel, *A Mercy*, she writes of the United States in the end of the seventeenth century, prior to independence. In this book, she once again employs challenging narrative structure while following the lives of several characters, black, white, and Native American. She also meditates on a question raised in *Beloved*: how far would a parent go to prevent a child from enduring enslavement.

Presently, while Morrison's work as a novelist has catapulted her into the upper echelons of the American Literary establishment, her work as a teacher, an editor, and an essayist has allowed her to keep in touch with a range of U.S. culture. She continues to hold a professorship at Princeton. She also sits on the editorial board of *The Nation* magazine. She received an honorary Doctor of Letters from Oxford University in 2005. Indeed, the sheer breadth of her professional accomplishments is impressive, and certainly makes the 5–8 years between novels understandable.

Moreover, Morrison's work as an essayist is ongoing, and she was recently offered a fine treatment in *What Moves at the Margin: Selected Nonfiction*, published in 2008. Edited by Carolyn C. Denard, the collection spans the length of Morrison's career, covering both personal and professional writing. Included are stand-alone essays discussing her grandparents, literary essays that help explain her aesthetic, often within the context of her predecessors and contemporaries, essays that stand as forwards to edited collections, and topical essays that offer commentary on current events, including a reaction to the events of September 11, 2001. The book ends with her acceptance speech for the Nobel Prize in Literature.

In addition to her fiction and her essays, Morrison has granted countless interviews throughout the years, both in video and print. Danielle Taylor-Guthrie's *Conversations with Toni Morrison*, published in 1994, offers an excellent compilation of interviews. In fact, at times, Morrison's commentary has found its way into public discourse, including her near infamous observation that Bill Clinton was our first black president. Taken out of context, then President Clinton was able to use that label to his political advantage. During the 2008 presidential campaign, Morrison clarified her statement to *Time* magazine as follows:

> People misunderstood that phrase. I was deploring the way in which President Clinton was being treated, vis-à-vis the sex scandal that was surrounding him. I said he was being treated like a black on the street, already guilty, already a perp. I have no idea what his real instincts are, in terms of race.

Morrison then publicly endorsed **Barack Obama** for president of the United States, while declaring her respect for Hillary Clinton.

Morrison once wrote unapologetically that art must be political. It is the refusal to accept boundaries, to fit into prescribed roles, that has informed her career. Not only do her characters challenge perceptions and limited definitions ascribed to them, Morrison herself, by continuing to work professionally and successfully in so many fields, by explicitly noting that she writes for her people and to her people, and by striving to reach a place where race does not matter, continues the work she mentioned in her speech at Princeton—indeed, she is able to teach values not by telling her readership, or her students, what values to have; rather, Morrison is able to teach values simply through her living example, through her words, her actions, her choices, and most evidently, within the printed words she leaves for us on the page.

Michael Perry
Rockford University

FURTHER READING

Beaulieu, Elizabeth Ann, ed. *The Toni Morrison Encyclopedia*. Westport, CT: Greenwood Press, 2003.

Jimoh, A. Yemisi. "Toni Morrison." *The Literary Encyclopedia*. October 25, 2002. http://www.litencyc.com/php/speople.php?rec=true&UID=3214.

Mori, Aoi. *Toni Morrison and Womanist Discourse*. New York: Peter Lang, 1999.

Morrison, Toni. *What Moves at the Margin: Selected Nonfiction*. Edited by Carolyn C. Denard. Jackson: University Press of Mississippi, 2008.

Stein, Karen F. *Reading, Learning, Teaching Toni Morrison (Confronting the Text, Confronting the World)*. New York: Peter Lang, 2009.

Taylor-Guthrie, Danille, ed. *Conversations with Toni Morrison*. Jackson: University Press of Mississippi, 1994.

Redferns/Getty Images

Motown Records

Motown Records was founded by Berry Gordy on January 12, 1959, in Detroit, Michigan. Motown is easily the most iconic record label in the history of popular music. The word "Motown," a nickname for Detroit, the Motor City, came to describe not only the record label, but also the sound developed by the label's musicians. Motown is a soulful form of popular music built around well-crafted tunes and gorgeous vocal harmonies. In the 1960s, Motown became "the sound of Young America," as Gordy liked to describe it. The label's stable of artists produced hundreds of smash hit singles, many of which are considered classics of American popular music. "Hitsville U.S.A." read a sign on the front of Motown's headquarters on West Grand Boulevard in Detroit. This was no overstatement. The label produced more than 100 top-10 pop singles between 1963 and 1969. For many years, Motown Records was America's largest black-owned business. Motown moved out of its Detroit offices in 1972. Sixteen years later, Gordy sold the company to MCA Records. Currently, Motown is a subsidiary of the massive Universal Music Group. In spite of its frequent ownership changes in recent years, the Motown brand retains its legendary position on the American cultural landscape. A list of the label's most iconic performers itself serves as a brief history of American music in the last 50 years: **Stevie Wonder**, The Temptations, Diana Ross and the Supremes, Smokey Robinson and the Miracles, The Four Tops, **Marvin Gaye**, Martha and the Vandellas, the Spinners, the Isley Brothers, The Jackson 5, Rick James, Lionel Richie, **Michael Jackson**, Boyz II Men, and Erykah Badu.

Berry Gordy is the father and mastermind of Motown Records. He was born into a middle-class family in Detroit in 1929. A high school dropout, Gordy fought in the U.S. Army during the Korean War. Gordy bounced from job to job for a few years before using his family connections to get involved in the local nightclub business. While managing a club in Detroit's "Black Bottom," Gordy came into contact with a soulful young R&B vocalist named Jackie Wilson. Wilson and Gordy began writing and recording together with the help of Gordy's producer friend Billy Davis. Davis helped Wilson score a record deal with Brunswick, a subsidiary of Decca Records which produced primarily R&B singles. Wilson scored a hit on the R&B charts in 1957 with "Reet Petite." Gordy invested his share of the royalties in a venture he initially called Tamla Records, a new Detroit-based label which began signing local R&B talent to recording contracts. Making connections with talented young artists was easy for Gordy. He knew many of the city's finest groups through his work as a nightclub entrepreneur.

The name Tamla disappeared in April 1960 when Gordy rechristened the label Motown Records. (Later, the name "Tamla" was used as a subsidiary brand of Motown Records.) Gordy quickly signed a strong stable of artists including The Miracles, Mary Wells, and Barrett Strong. For the first decade of the label's history, Motown focused primarily on releasing singles, which reflected the era's common sense within the music industry. Albums sold far more slowly than more affordable, radio-friendly singles. Gordy played a hands-on role both on the production and distribution side of the music. Paternalism characterized Gordy's relationship with the label's musicians and employees, whom he referred to as the Motown "Family." (In fact, many members of the extended Gordy family played prominent executive roles at the label.)

Berry Gordy selected soulful yet broadly accessible material for his artists. From the beginning, he intended for Motown's music to have crossover appeal on the pop charts. To ensure that Motown had a continuous stream of high-quality material, Gordy aimed to create his own Tin Pan Alley at Motown's "Hitsville U.S.A." building on the West Side of Detroit. Gordy quickly found his primary songwriting team in Brian Holland, his brother Edward Holland Jr., and Lamont Dozier. The Holland-Dozier-Holland trio served as songwriters and producers on many of Motown's biggest hits. Their first major hit came in 1961 with The Marvelettes' "Please Mr. Postman," which reached number one on the pop charts. Holland-Dozier-Holland combined to write 30 number-one hit singles.

Motown signed primarily vocal groups and individual singers. The label relied on their superb house band for its recording sessions. "The Funk Brothers," as the group of Motown session players came to be known, combined a smooth rhythm section with an exuberant set of string, horn, and keyboard players. Gordy and his artists & repertoire (A&R) man William "Mickey" Stevenson hired musicians with backgrounds as jazz session players. They shared the sense that jazz session players had a unique ability to create atmosphere in a song. Music historians have noted that The Funk Brothers played on more number-one hit singles than the Beatles. To this day, the members of The Funk Brothers (James Jamerson, Benny Benjamin, Dennis Coffey, Joe Messina, Earl Van Dyke, and Joe Hunter, among others) remain in obscurity.

Berry Gordy cultivated a wholesome, clean-cut image for Motown artists. The performers acted like ladies and gentlemen in their public appearances. They dressed sharply and avoided controversial subject matter in their songs. Motown strove for perfection in its image, its sound, and its performance. Several of the label's vocal groups incorporated dancing into their performances, including The Temptations, The Miracles, The Four Tops, The Supremes, and The Jackson 5. The group's dance moves were as crisp as their suits. Motown acts displayed great showmanship without being specifically showy. Motown's qualities translated incredibly well to television, making acts such as The Temptations and The Supremes mainstays of the era's variety shows. The total performance package displayed by Motown artists remains unmatched.

The year 1961 marked the explosion of the Motown sound. The Miracles' "Shop Around" climbed to number two on the pop charts in February. The angelically voiced Smokey Robinson fronted the superb Detroit vocal group. The Miracles' soulful harmonies distinguished the group from its doo-wop ancestors. Moreover, The Miracles' delivery demonstrated a stronger pop sensibility than their grittier peers on the R&B charts. The polyrhythmic percussion and exuberant horn playing on "Shop Around" showed the producer's familiarity with the modern studio techniques being pioneered by the likes of Phil Spector. Toward the end of the calendar year, The Marvelettes' "Please Mr. Postman" became the label's first number-one hit single. The yearning, Gordy-penned tale of puppy love transformed The Marvelettes into the label's first female superstars.

Major hits by Mary Wells ("Two Lovers" and "You Beat Me to the Punch") and The Contours ("Do You Love Me") provided Motown with sufficient capital to begin developing a larger stable of artists. Gordy signed his former session drummer Marvin Gaye, Martha and the Vandellas, The Temptations (originally known as The Elgins), The Supremes (originally known as The Primettes), and a blind 12-year-old named Steven Morris, who producer Stevenson rechristened "Stevie Wonder." Many of these artists didn't deliver hits initially, but their tenures in the Motown "Family" transformed them all into major stars by the mid-1960s.

Mary Wells and The Miracles were the major early stars on the label. Wells's girlish demeanor had a great deal of crossover appeal, making her the label's most consistent hit producer in its early years. Her career peaked in 1964 with the release of "My Guy," which went to number one on the pop charts and became Wells's signature song. The Miracles' followed up "Shop Around" with 1962's "You've Really Got a Hold on Me." The first of The Miracles' great tearjerkers, "You've Really Got a Hold on Me" made it into top 10.

To promote the Motown brand, Gordy took his stable out on the road for a national tour. Various Motown Revues began touring the country in 1962, playing to large, racially mixed audiences in the urban North and typically segregated audiences in the South. The tours helped promote the label's hit singles while providing junior performers the opportunity to hone their skills on stage. The Motown Revues began by playing the established "Chitlin Circuit" of predominately black venues, but the explosion of Motown's popularity transformed the economic model of touring for black artists, just as it transformed the economics of the recording industry for black artists. Motown became mass culture. The demand for Motown singles helped increase the overall amount of music recorded by black artists exponentially. Public demand to see The Supremes or The Temptations in concert persuaded promoters to book Motown groups in much larger venues.

A 1963 live recording of one Motown Revue concert became the first hit single by "Little Stevie Wonder." "Fingertips Pt. 2" featured Wonder on harmonica. It reached number one on the pop charts, making Wonder the youngest singer in history to achieve that chart position. Later that year, two of Motown's most prominent acts, The Supremes and The Temptations, began their reigns as the label's top hit makers.

Following a string of unsuccessful early singles, The Supremes emerged in 1964 as the world's most popular female vocal group. The trio of Diana Ross, Mary Wilson, and Florence Ballard sang with elegance, soulfulness, and charisma. Their version of the dreamy "Where Did Our Love Go" reached number one in the summer of 1964, the first of five consecutive Supremes' singles to top the charts: "Come See About Me," "Stop! In the Name of Love," "Baby Love," and "Back in My Arms Again." In the mid-1960s, the group scored other major hits with "You Keep Me Hanging On," "I Hear a Symphony," and "You Can't Hurry Love." Based on chart figures, The Supremes were the most successful American musical group of the 1960s.

The Temptations were the most successful male vocal group of the 1960s. Founded in 1960 as The Elgins, The Temptations were a five-piece singing machine: tenor David Ruffin, bass Melvin Franklin, baritone Paul Williams, baritone Otis Williams, and high tenor Eddie Kendricks. Their combination of scintillating pop melodies, tender vocal harmonies, and flawless footwork transformed the group into radio royalty and television favorites. The Temptations' greatest hits ("My Girl," "Ain't Too Proud to Beg," "Get Ready") have long been etched on the collective conscience.

The mid-1960s were certainly Motown's Golden Age. The label produced a number of other major stars, adding further prestige to The Supremes and The Temptations' launching pad to superstardom. The Four Tops, another Detroit-based male vocal group, built soaring harmonies around lead singer Levi Stubbs' tender vocals. Their best-known singles, "Baby I Need Your Lovin'," "I Can't Help Myself," and "Reach Out, I'll Be There," all merit recognition as American standards. Martha and the Vandellas were Motown's number-two female vocal group in the mid-1960s. Their massive hits "Nowhere to Run," "Heat Wave," and "Dancing in the Streets," evoke the spirit of the times as well as any singles. Martha and the Vandellas' music has been a staple of movie soundtracks for decades. The Miracles, soon to be renamed Smokey Robinson and the Miracles, continued recording classic single after classic single in the mid-1960s. From the seductive "Ooh Baby Baby" to the heart-breaking "Tracks of My Tears," The Miracles could second every emotion running through an adolescent's heart. Marvin Gaye and Tammi Terrell paired on a number of excellent duets including "Ain't Nothing Like the Real Thing," "Ain't No Mountain High Enough," and "You're All I Need to Get By." "The Prince of Motown," as Gaye was nicknamed, scored a number of other smooth, soulful hits including "I Heard It Through the Grapevine," "How Sweet It Is to Be Loved by You," and "Ain't That Peculiar."

The explosion of Motown's popularity in the mid-1960s made Berry Gordy one of the most well-known figures in the music industry. Events conspired to make Motown's undisputed reign on the top of American popular music short-lived. The late 1960s proved an extremely tumultuous time at Motown Records, mirroring the rest of the country. The July 1967 Detroit Riots, which led to the deaths of 43 people and the Michigan National Guard laying siege to the West Side, cast a pall over the city. Soon after the riots, Gordy initiated an initially secret plan to move the company out of Detroit. The multi-year process relocated the vast majority of company operations to Southern California. The loss of Motown Records was a devastating blow for a city already facing the perils of racial conflict, deindustrialization, and an exponentially rising crime rate.

The 1967 departure of the Holland-Dozier-Holland songwriting team from the Motown "Family" removed a key aspect of the label's success: the superb material with which Motown provided its performers. Holland-Dozier-Holland quit Motown after a dispute with Gordy over the songwriting team's share of the royalties. Litigation between Motown and Holland-Dozier-Holland dragged on for more than a decade. Gordy replaced Holland-Dozier-Holland with the rising husband and wife songwriting team of Nickolas Ashford and Valerie Simpson. Ashford-Simpson penned such classics as Marvin Gaye's "I Heard It Through the Grapevine" and Gaye and Terrell's "Ain't No Mountain High Enough."

Conflict at the label extended beyond their songwriting team. Barry Gordy, the sometimes-lover of Diana Ross, intervened in a conflict between Ross and bandmate Florence Ballard. Gordy rechristened the group "Diana Ross and the Supremes" to indicate Ross' executively endorsed leadership in the group. He soon fired Ballard and replaced her with the first in a series of new Supremes. Ross' role in the Supremes waned in the early 1970s as she pursued a solo career. A power struggle emerged among The Temptations as well. David Ruffin wanted to be acknowledged as the group's front man just like Diana Ross was with The Supremes. The Temptations worked through their troubles and continued recording for many more successful years.

The intense political climate of the late 1960s caused a great deal of conflict at Motown. Whether it was the Civil Rights Movement or the Vietnam War, Gordy wanted Motown Records to stay out of the controversy. He wanted the label to remain accessible to people of all political persuasions. Events conspired to make this an untenable position. The assassination of **Martin Luther King, Jr.** and the escalation of the war in Vietnam pushed a number of Motown artists to become more politically active in action and song, particularly Marvin Gaye.

Gaye had been pushing the label to stay culturally "relevant" for years. By the late 1960s, he wasn't the only Motown artist pushing for the label to embrace more political material. Edwin Starr's iconic "War" (1970) was one of the label's earliest forays into explicitly political content. To deal with a complex array of social issues, Gaye moved outside of the label's single-based recording style. He self-financed the 1970–1971 sessions which became Gaye's masterpiece, *What's Going On* (1971). Gaye wrote the title track, "What's Going On," after talking with his younger brother Frankie about his experiences in Vietnam. The pleading, soulful song became a major hit and an important anti-war anthem. Other songs on the album dealt with urban poverty, racism, and environmental issues. *What's Going On* is considered one of the most important albums of all time. Politically, it inspired many black artists to delve more explicitly into social issues in their music. Aesthetically, it encouraged Motown artists to embrace the album as a musical format.

Stevie Wonder took the lead in embracing the album format. Now in his twenties, Wonder moved away from the pop music of his youth in favor of a more sophisticated, thematically based sound. Like Gaye, Wonder incorporated contemporary politics into his songwriting. The new direction in Wonder's recording career began with *Music of My Mind* (1972), the first in a series of critically acclaimed and wildly popular releases. Baroque yet soulful, political yet sensual, the new Stevie Wonder recorded five consecutive masterful albums in the early to mid-1970s. *Innervisions* (1973), *Fulfillingness' First Finale* (1974), and *Songs in the Key of Life* (1976) garnered Wonder a trio of Grammys for Album of the Year, making him the first artist in history to achieve this feat.

The label's top new stars of the early 1970s were The Jackson 5. Marlon, Jackie, Jermaine, Tito, and Michael Jackson of Gary, Indiana, helped the label stay true to the moniker the "Sound of Young America" during the new decade. Combining the dancing prowess of The Temptations and the youthful exuberance of Stevie Wonder, The Jackson 5 began their recording career with Motown by accomplishing something no other artists had in the history of popular music. Their first four singles, beginning with 1970's "I Want You Back," all reached number one on the pop charts. Eventually, the Jackson family, with the exception of Gordy's new son-in-law Jermaine, jumped to CBS Records, but, in their seven years at Motown, The Jackson 5 became the label's best-selling artist of the 1970s.

During the 1970s, Gordy used his new proximity to the film industry to expand Motown's operations into screen productions. Gordy's on-again, off-again girlfriend Diana Ross starred in the company's first stab at film production, *Lady Sings the Blues* (1972), a biopic of **Billie Holiday** based on the singer's memoir. The film was one of the top box office hits of 1972. It earned five Oscar nominations as well, including a nomination for Ross for Best Actress. The film's soundtrack topped the charts in February 1973. In 1975, Ross starred in the rags-to-riches melodrama, *Mahogany*. The film's soundtrack fared better on the charts than the film did at the box office. Perhaps Motown Productions' best-known film was 1978's *The Wiz*, an urban retelling of *The Wizard of Oz*. The film starred Diana Ross as Dorothy, Michael Jackson as the Scarecrow, **Lena Horne** as the Good Witch of the South, and **Richard Pryor** as the Wiz. The film flopped at the box office, posting a $10 million loss for Motown. *The Wiz*'s box office failure pushed Motown out of the movie business.

News for Motown wasn't all bad in the late 1970s. Several new artists became platinum sellers for the label. Much of the label's new success came as a result of their move toward funkier soul artists. The Commodores, fronted by the charismatic Lionel Richie, scored major hits in the late 1970s with "Still," "Three Times a Lady," "Easy," and the ubiquitous funk classic "Brick House." Richie dropped The Commodores in the early 1980s and went on to become one of the top recording artists of the 1980s. Funkmaster Rick James and the Stone City Band rose to prominence on the back of songs such as "You and I," "Mary Jane," and "Super Freak."

The Motown of the 1980s was a rather pared down entity. Although The Commodores and Rick James continued scoring hits for the label, many of Motown's original stars had either quit recording or left the record label. The label's continued profits in the 1980s came largely as a result of nostalgia. The 1960s reunion comedy *The Big Chill* (1983) featured Motown music prominently. The film and the accompanying soundtrack, which included Marvin Gaye, The Temptations, and The Miracles among others, were both major hits. Gordy staged a 1983 for-television Motown reunion. Filmed in March but broadcast in May, *Motown 25* served as a final hurrah for the independently-owned Motown Records. The show featured reunions of The Temptations, The Supremes, The Four Tops, and one of Marvin Gaye's final live performances with his old label mates, a stirring rendition of "What's Going On." Gaye was murdered by his father in a domestic dispute less than a year later.

Michael Jackson stole the show that evening. Riding high on the astronomical success of *Thriller*, Jackson performed his current hit, "Billie Jean." His dazzling dance routine included his first public performance of the "Moonwalk." The audience at the Pasadena Civic Auditorium went from awestruck to exuberant as they watched Jackson perform the seemingly superhuman move. Prior to the King of Pop's performance, The Jackson 5 reunited for a medley of their greatest hits.

In 1988, Barry Gordy sold Motown to MCA Records. Over the past 20 years, a series of mergers had bounced control of Motown Records from one multinational conglomerate to another. Currently, The Universal Music Group owns Motown Records. The Motown moniker continued to be a lucrative brand name as acts including Boyz II Men in the early 1990s and Erykah Badu in the late 1990s and 2000s recorded multi-platinum albums and number-one hit singles with the reformulated label. In recent years, classic Motown recordings have remained in the public eye as well. Motown music has been a staple of Karaoke singing since its inception in the late 1980s in Japan, cementing many songs' status as timeless standards while providing continued revenue streams to the songs' copyright holders. Countless hip-hop deejays have sampled the music of Motown artists, creating continuity between contemporary urban music and its sonic forefathers and mothers. The legacy of Motown Records remains a vibrant force in American popular culture.

Clayton Trutor
Boston College

FURTHER READING

Early, Gerald. *One Nation under a Groove: Motown and American Culture*. Ann Arbor: University of Michigan Press, 2004.

George, Nelson. *Where Did Our Love Go?: The Rise and Fall of the Motown Sound.* Urbana: University of Illinois Press, 2007.

Posner, Gerald. *Motown: Money, Sex, and Power.* New York: Random House, 2002.

Smith, Suzanne. *Dancing in the Street: Motown and the Cultural Politics of Detroit.* Cambridge, MA: Harvard University Press, 1999.

Waller, Don. *The Motown Story.* New York: Scribner, 1985.

Library of Congress

Elijah Muhammad
(1897–1975)

Elijah Muhammad was born Elijah Poole in October 1897 in Sandersville, Georgia. Emerging from this typical small town in the Jim Crow South, Muhammad became one of the most famous and controversial black leaders of the twentieth century. From the mid-1930s until his death in 1975, Muhammad led the Nation of Islam, a religious, black nationalist movement that produced such well-known and diverse adherents as **Malcolm X, Muhammad Ali,** and **Louis Farrakhan.** Elaborating the teachings of his obscure and visionary mentor, W. D. Fard, Muhammad preached a religion that emphasized the dignity of black people by promoting black social and financial self-sufficiency and asserting that blacks, not whites, were a historically superior race. Such an approach, while bringing meaning and dignity to thousands of followers, created enemies across the spectrum. His teachings unnerved the vast majority of white Americans who were not accustomed—as were many of their black fellow-citizens—to having racial vitriol directed against them. Muhammad's program also stood in direct opposition to the nonviolent desegregationist agenda of leaders such as Dr. **Martin Luther King, Jr.**, at times exploding in controversial rhetorical attacks against the famous civil rights leader. In time, Muhammad's controversial philosophy and leadership choices created schisms within the Nation of Islam itself, alienating such figures as Malcolm X and Muhammad's own son, Wallace. Nevertheless, Muhammad's ability to direct a significant but fractious movement for some 40 years and to influence many notable disciples and opponents solidified his legacy in the history of the United States during the twentieth century.

Young Elijah grew up in the small towns of turn-of-the-century Georgia, where he received a dual education that would forever influence his thinking. His father was a Baptist minister, and from an early age Elijah expressed a genuine interest in his father's Christian theology. However, his constant probing of the Bible led to disputes with his father. Although officially converting under perceived pressure from his family, Muhammad's religious inheritance was ambivalent. While he would soon break emphatically with Christianity, he constantly utilized language and themes inherited from his father's religion.

Of even greater significance to Muhammad were the stark exigencies of the Jim Crow South. As was common of many black families attempting to make ends meet, Elijah and his siblings worked hard from an early age, chopping wood and selling it to anyone they could. While Elijah left school perhaps as early as the fourth grade, he received a brutal education when he witnessed the lynching of an 18-year-old acquaintance. Elijah was struck less by the brutality of the act—he had grown up with his grandparents' stories of slave life—but he simply could not understand how such daring violence could occur "in the midst of his own people" with "all our grown men right there" (quoted in Clegg III, 1997, 10).

In 1919, Elijah married Clara Evans, and by April 1923 he and his young family decided to leave Georgia and seek a better life in industrialized Detroit, Michigan. While largely free from the lynching and Jim Crow laws of Georgia,

Detroit was equally challenging to many black families who struggled to find consistent work separated from traditional social networks. The Poole family was no exception. By the early 1930s, Elijah was consistently unemployed and drinking heavily, ashamed of himself, but unable to find the work necessary to support his wife and five children. Although he no longer feared the emasculating effects of Georgian mob violence, the economic emasculation of U.S. industrial capitalism was no less profound.

In 1931, Elijah's brother convinced him to attend a meeting where a mysterious prophet named W. D. Fard (pronounced Far-rod) preached that all black people were descended from a dignified, Asiatic race whose religion was Islam. African Americans, Fard claimed, had been eclipsed in their cultural and economic prosperity by a devious race of "white devils" who had viciously enslaved them and whose long reign on the earth would soon come to an apocalyptic end. To add luster to his image, Fard claimed royal parentage from Saudi Arabia, his remarkably fair complexion notwithstanding. He supported his doctrines with numerous passages from the Bible and the Quran, and his charisma drew scores of black followers to his new sect, the Allah Temple of Islam which he soon renamed the Nation of Islam (NOI). Elijah was so impressed by Fard that he approached him after the meeting. "[You are] that one we read in the Bible that he would come in the last day under the name Jesus," Elijah remembered declaring to Fard (quoted in Curtis IV, 2002, 69). Well-versed in the scriptures, Fard cryptically responded in the Christ-like language of the New Testament gospels: "Yes, I am the one, but who knows that but yourself, and be quiet" (quoted in Clegg III, 1997, 22).

The nearly instantaneous faith and devotion of Elijah impressed Fard, and within one year Fard promoted Elijah to Supreme Minister (second only to Fard himself) and bestowed on him the name Elijah Karriem to replace his "slave" surname Poole. This was a common practice in the NOI, as Fard gave his male followers Muslim surnames or simply the surname 'X' to free them psychologically from names that usually originated with Anglo-Saxon slave masters. For one year, Fard worked closely with Elijah and instructed him in the aberrant doctrines of their sect. "He used to teach me night and day," remembered Elijah, "We used to sit sometimes from the early part of the night until sunrise" (quoted in Evanzz, 1999, 81). Although the new teachings of Fard were undoubtedly bizarre, they provided a powerful explanatory myth to many urban blacks who had experienced the ravages of both poverty and racism.

Fard, and later Karriem taught that a powerful, god-man initially took shape from a spinning atom of life that emerged from the void before time. This god-man was "the Original Man," and possessed black skin, ever-expanding knowledge, and an incredible creative power. He took the name Allah or God, and he created other black, god-men like himself. These divine humans proceeded to fashion the cosmos, taking a particular interest in cultivating Earth for their habitation. Once Earth was completed, these Original People took up residence on Earth as one united Black Nation of Islam. For trillions of years the Original People grew and peopled the earth. Over time, the Tribe of Shabazz emerged as the strongest and most insightful. Taking up residence in East Asia (Africa), Egypt, and later commissioning a settlement in Mecca, they co-existed peacefully but powerfully with rest of their brethren. All of the tribes continued to practice "Islam."

However, this peaceful hegemony was not to last. First, a leader of the Tribe of Shabazz, not content with his lot in East Asia, decided to settle sub-Saharan Africa with a remnant of the Shabazz. Though not particularly pernicious, this remnant became entirely detached from their "Muslim" cultural and religious heritage. These were the ancestors of contemporary sub-Saharan, black Africans. Second, India to the east of the Shabazz began to explode into religious controversy as group and group left the teaching of Allah. It was from these controversies that Hinduism and Buddhism emerged as rival religions, and the ethnic Native Americans broke away from the Original People, forced by Allah to walk to North America "completely guideless . . . because of their disobedience" (*Muhammad Speaks*, October 12, 1973).

While these challenges were bad enough, the Shabazz soon faced their greatest challenge from an extremely skillful but devious god-man, a Meccan named Yacub. Yacub used his gifts to cultivate an evil desire to dominate the Original People. Realizing his designs, the leaders of Mecca banished him and his followers to Greece, where he used his skills to genetically craft a race of "white devils" with which to retake Mecca. The "white devils" were inferior to the Original People in both physical strength and mental power, but what mental power they did possess was all cleverly channeled into "tricknology"—a combination of lies and underhanded science—to deceive and master opponents. Despite continual assaults on the Middle East, the white devils failed to conquer the Shabazz. Frustrated, they turned their tricknology to the Western Hemisphere and sub-Saharan Africa to conquer, corrupt, and enslave the peoples disconnected from Islam. It was therefore Fard and Karriem's mission to call the disconnected black race back to their ancient religious roots and to prepare them for the imminent apocalypse in which Allah would once and for all destroy the white devils.

Although these teachings were clearly offensive to most outside observers, they provided a powerful explanatory myth to the members of the fledgling NOI. The emphasis on the exploitative and deceitful nature of whites made sense to those who had experienced slavery, sharecropping, lynching, and who had suffered the most during the Great Depression. Even the progressive reforms of President Roosevelt and the New Deal were frequently denied black citizens through redlining—the selective application of government funds for civic improvements and home loans—and other forms of economic racism. NOI history accounted for what appeared to adherents to be centuries of pathological white behavior; it made sense that whites would act this way because that was how they were created. As Muhammad rhetorically asked his followers, "Who has been our aggressors and murderers ever since we have been in America? Who, by nature, was made quick to shed blood—even his own?" (Muhammad, *Message to the Blackman in America*, Ch. 4). NOI doctrine also inspired culturally displaced African Americans with tales of a venerable tradition in which they could participate and regain a lost dignity. Finally, the promise of an impending apocalypse provided hope for swift deliverance from current oppression.

Despite Fard's initial success, he did not have long to foster his movement. The police had been tracking his various Muslim sects, and decided to arrest Fard in November 1932 in connection with a mysterious murder in which the perpetrator claimed to hear from the "gods of Islam." Fearing a general uprising of Muslim protest, the police decided to banish Fard from Detroit in May 1933. According to Supreme Minister Karriem, prior to his exodus Fard confirmed that he was Allah come in the flesh and Fard also renamed Karriem, "Muhammad, Messenger of Allah," commissioning him to continue as the leader of the NOI. Though Fard allegedly removed to Chicago for a year, he disappeared for good in June 1934.

The departure of Fard in 1933 marked the advent of a crucial period for the NOI and the increasingly beleaguered Muhammad. When Muhammad declared that Fard was Allah come in the flesh and that Muhammad was his sole prophet, he provoked an outcry from other NOI leaders in Detroit, Chicago, and Milwaukee. Consistently opposing Muhammad, these leaders managed to force him out of Chicago and then Milwaukee, and overall membership of the NOI loyal to Muhammad plummeted from some hundreds to tens in all three cities. Nevertheless, Muhammad managed to leave behind a faithful lieutenant in each city: Timothy Rozier in Detroit, Malik X in Chicago, and Sultan Muhammad in Milwaukee.

Until 1942, Muhammad used Washington, DC, as a base to proselytize numerous eastern cities such as Baltimore, Cleveland, Pittsburgh, and Atlanta. Meanwhile, he took advantage of the Library of Congress and read extensively to better understand his teaching in light of history and current events. During this time his family remained in Chicago, guided by his resilient wife Clara Evans. To preserve his anonymity, he used a number of aliases including Mr. Evans, Muhammad Rassoull, and Gulam Bogans, and it was under the latter name that the FBI arrested him for draft evasion on May 8, 1942.

While Muhammad was in exile, his few followers in the Midwest had managed to recover some of their numbers, and the emerging NOI, while still small, was proving to be disciplined and determined. On several occasions, dozens of NOI men and women appeared in court in support of accused brethren, silently but firmly communicating their determination that authorities not interfere in their religious life. At times, confrontation with authorities erupted in violent but unarmed confrontation where Muslim men asserted themselves in defense of their women.

Despite posting bail and briefly consolidating his position in Chicago, the government convicted Muhammad of draft evasion and he began his prison sentence at FCI Milan Prison on July 23, 1943. While Muhammad was in prison, the NOI suffered another large decline in numbers, but this decline was heavily influenced by the incarceration of numerous men who determinedly followed Muhammad's example and refused to sign up for the draft. When he finally emerged from prison in August 1946, many committed converts—some converted in prison—emerged with him to join those who had remained loyal. Muhammad thus emerged as a martyr and his leadership would never again be in serious doubt.

In the jubilant years of post–World War II economic expansion, Muhammad finally established himself as an enduring icon of black America and the pre-eminent leader of the largest group of black Muslims. Building on previously established NOI doctrines and practices, he managed to build a national religious-economic network that would remain strong until his death in 1975.

NOI practical teachings fell under the general and related ideas of *separatism* and *self-help*. Because whites were inherently oppressive, Muhammad advocated complete separatism from all aspects of American society and even argued that a separate black nation be established within the United States. In addition to avoiding the draft, followers were instructed not to vote, and to sent their children to special parochial schools called Universities of Islam where NOI theology accompanied traditional academic subjects. Maintaining a degree of coherence with traditional Islam, the NOI forbade members to eat pork, smoke, drink alcohol, use drugs, or commit fornication. The organization also forbade dancing and swearing. Gender roles were rigidly defined with men and women sitting separately in religious meetings, and strict rules proscribing most contact between unmarried people of opposite gender.

This separatism and discipline allowed the NOI to develop its second goal of economic *self-help*. Given his theology and experiences, Muhammad insisted, "We must stop relying upon the white man to care for us. We must become an independent people" (Muhammad, *Message to the Blackman in America*, Ch. 76.6). He argued that Muslims should pool their resources, establish and patronize exclusively Muslim businesses, and educate themselves to be successful entrepreneurs. He directly linked the dietary, sexual, and moral disciplines of the NOI to such a vision. Cleanliness and strict gender roles established the self-respect necessary to run a successful business, and abstaining from vice and luxury goods allowed the NOI to gradually build wealth rather than squandering it back to whites.

By the late 1940s, the NOI counted hundreds of followers and had established a collective farm in Michigan, a grocery store, a bakery, and a restaurant all heavily supported by adherents. Furthermore, an increased emphasis on ritual and tradition helped unite the growing national movement. Muhammad now regularly wore his iconic fez with a star and crescent emblazoned on the front, and he instituted the use of a national flag and anthem. In 1950, he inaugurated the annual celebration of Savior's Day to honor the memory of Fard and bring together NOI followers from across America. But while all of these developments would undoubtedly yield important fruit, it was Muhammad's smallest seed that would yield the greatest increase.

In 1949, a letter reached Muhammad from an obscure drug dealer serving time for burglary in Norfolk Prison Colony outside of Boston. Its author was Malcolm Little, who had recently converted to Islam and was now seeking Muhammad's spiritual direction. For three years, the two exchanged letters, and Malcolm emerged from prison with an unyielding devotion to both Muhammad and the NOI. Muhammad, for his part, rightly discerned the immense potential of his new convert and quickly made him a prominent minister. His foresight was rewarded tenfold as the newly christened Malcolm X went on to found thriving temples in Cincinnati, Boston, and Philadelphia, before a grateful Muhammad appointed him head minister of Temple No. 7 in New York in June 1954. In just a few short years, Malcolm used his compelling combination of zeal, charisma, and intellect to become the face and spokesman of the NOI. It is no wonder that Muhammad, his mother, and his wife Clara all affectionately referred to Malcolm as "son" (quoted in Evanzz, 187).

Throughout the 1950s the NOI attracted thousands of converts, thanks to Malcolm's proselytizing and Muhammad's shrewd leadership. To realize his goal of economic independence, Muhammad sought to attract members of the black middle class, while being careful not to alienate them with too much rhetoric denouncing *any* cooperation with whites (which was necessary for initial access to capital). However, it was precisely Muhammad's anti-white stance that made the NOI distinctive and appealing to thousands of marginalized blacks throughout the country. Thankfully for Muhammad, the nascent Civil Rights Movement stirred up a hornet's nest of racial questions that helped attract further converts.

Throughout the 1950s and 1960s, Muhammad and Malcolm distinguished themselves as iconic leaders opposed to the civil rights agenda. "Martin Luther King is a fool for wanting integration," declared Muhammad again and again, and when King helped to lead the famous March on Washington in 1963, Malcolm could only dismiss it as the "Farce on Washington" (quoted in Evanzz, 232, 266). In turn, King and other notable civil rights leaders—**Thurgood Marshall** and NAACP Secretary Roy Wilkins among them—made no secret of their contempt for the NOI's message promoting "hatred among men" (quoted in Clegg, 129). While this ideological divide within the black community was profound, the debate helped both sides. The Civil Rights Movement unearthed the deep, intransigent roots of white racism, and while the brutal backlash against integration swelled the ranks of King and the NAACP, it also ironically justified Muhammad's message that whites would never allow blacks to be their social and economic equals.

While NOI membership multiplied, Muhammad consolidated his control of a growing economic empire. He appointed his son Raymond Sharrieff as Supreme Captain of the Fruit of Islam—a disciplined, uniformed, but unarmed organization composed of all NOI males and used for enforcing NOI discipline. His sons, Elijah Jr., Herbert, and Akbar were likewise given prime leadership roles. While this arrangement was not necessarily problematic, when combined with the access to tithes and business revenues, the NOI leadership—heavily dominated by Muhammad's family—began to acquire a reputation for greed and hypocrisy. By the late 1950s, Muhammad and his family controlled numerous Muslim businesses in Chicago, and owned enough real estate and luxury cars to raise eyebrows. As early as 1956, Hamaas Abdul Khaalis, one of the few major leaders outside of the Muhammad family, began to harbor doubts and then ultimately broke with the NOI over the opulence of its leadership. Khaalis went on to found a more traditional Islamic sect known as Hanafi Islam, and he would later mentor the famous NBA star Kareem Abdul-Jabbar.

Despite accusations of nepotism and corruption, the NOI continued to grow and by 1959 had gained national prominence. On May 31, 1959, Muhammad delivered an address in Washington, DC that drew an audience of 10,000, some of whom were white members of the press. Both from the podium, and in a rare media interview, Muhammad delivered his message of black separatism, self-help, and the imminent destruction of the white race to a national audience.

While this national attention helped to draw even more converts—with attendance peaking at perhaps 40,000 or 50,000 in the mid-1960s—it also intensified public scrutiny. Shortly after the speech, Mike Wallace and Louis Lomax of WNTA-TV produced a harsh documentary entitled "The Hate that Hate Produced." Splicing together Muhammad's vitriolic rhetoric, they raised the specter of a potential race war instigated by hundreds of thousands of angry black Muslims. Likewise, the early 1960s saw a flurry of criticism from other black Muslim groups such as the Muslim Brotherhood and leaders such as Talib Ahmad Dawud eager to distance themselves in the public eye from the controversial Muhammad.

Despite this scrutiny, Muhammad expanded the reach of his message by beginning to publish his own NOI newspaper entitled *Muhammad Speaks* in 1960. In a remarkable display of capitalistic autocracy, Muhammad simply decreed that each Muslim male was required to buy a certain number of papers, and then find a way to sell them. While helping to fill the Chicago coffers, *Muhammad Speaks* also proved extremely effective at spreading the ideology of the NOI and allowing Muhammad complete editorial control of his message.

While this platform extended Muhammad's ideological access to new converts, his personal actions in the early 1960s dealt the NOI a blow from which it would never quite recover. In 1960, his former secretary secretly bore a child out of wedlock, and despite her claims that it was Muhammad's, she was excommunicated from all contact with any NOI members. Were this an isolated incident, Muhammad might have been able to overcome the accompanying firestorm, but by 1963 there was no question that Muhammad had engaged in numerous extramarital affairs as several former secretaries emerged to claim him as the father of their children.

Muhammad's estranged son, Wallace, already questioning the religious legitimacy of his father's message, took it as confirmation of his father's heterodoxy. Likewise, Muhammad's son Akbar, who was studying in Egypt, fell out with his father and left the NOI when he heard the news. Malcolm X, Muhammad's star minister was devastated. How could Allah's prophet commit so many egregious sins? Malcolm frantically sought to first disconfirm the rumors, even going so far as to secretly meet with several of Muhammad's mistresses. When his investigations confirmed his worst fears, he was able for a time to convince himself that Muhammad was perhaps God's messenger but also a man with human temptations. In the interest of both the unknowing Muslim faithful and the reputation of the NOI, Malcolm met with other ministers to discuss the implications of the news. He was flabbergasted by the reactions of many leaders such as Louis X of Boston (later Louis Farrakhan), who seemed not in the least surprised.

If news of the affairs caused Malcolm to doubt his faith, Malcolm's consultations with other NOI ministers raised doubts in Muhammad's mind about Malcolm's loyalty and continued usefulness. On November 22, 1963, President John F. Kennedy was assassinated, and Muhammad, fearing further public scrutiny ordered his ministers to keep silent on the matter. However, when baited by the press Malcolm could not resist. "[B]eing an old farm boy myself, chickens coming home to roost never did make me sad," he declared (quoted in Clegg, 200). While the statement was intentionally cryptic, the press had a field day, and Muhammad was livid at the apparent defiance and decided to test the extent of Malcolm's power and loyalty.

To isolate Malcolm without entirely alienating him, Muhammad, encouraged by many other jealous ministers such as Raymond Sharieff, John Ali, and Louis Farrakhan, removed him from his position as head minister of Mosque No. 7 in New York. Malcolm's already doubt-ridden soul could no longer tolerate such a blow, and on March 8, 1964 he publicly left the NOI and turned the full fury of his mind and charisma against his former mentor. For almost one year, the former spokesman of the NOI publicly articulated the numerous criticisms of greed, philandering, and aberrant doctrine, which carried the full force of his inside perspective. Muhammad and his loyal ministers in turn excoriated and even threatened Malcolm. James Shabazz of Chicago suggested that Malcolm "should be afraid for his future" and in an FBI-taped phone conversation with an unknown Boston member, Muhammad, after mentioning Malcolm's name insisted, "With these hypocrites, when you find them, cut their heads off" (quoted in Clegg, 218–219).

On February 21, 1965, Malcolm X was shot and killed in front of his wife and family while attempting to give a speech at the Audubon Ballroom in New York City. The convicted assassins were Talmadge Hayer, Thomas 15X Johnson, and Norman 3X Butler, all of the NOI Mosque No. 7 in New York. While Elijah Muhammad could not be directly linked to the crime, few doubted his connection to the gruesome murder. At best, Muhammad inspired fanatical followers with a yearlong barrage of violent rhetoric; at worst he ordered the death himself.

The loss of Malcolm was partially mitigated by the conversion of Muhammad Ali in 1964, and throughout the late 1960s Ali's charisma and success continued to attract young converts to the NOI. Likewise, in 1965, Wallace Muhammad reconciled with his father, perhaps equally motivated by financial needs and a long-term vision to reform the NOI from within. NOI businesses continued to grow through the early 1970s, and membership also received an initial boost with the rise of the Black Power movement of the late 1960s. Leaders of Black Power such as **Stokely Carmichael** praised the legacy of the few leaders such as Muhammad who advocated separatism and violent self-defense of black dignity.

In the late 1960s, Muhammad's health, which was always precarious, began to decline and he decided to allocate the vast majority of responsibilities to his lieutenants, though he never relinquished his power over these leaders. The NOI continued to attract thousands of followers across the country, but by the early 1970s, violent, gang-style conflicts both internally and with other groups such as the Young Muslims and Hanafi Islam began to undermine the NOI's appeal. Financially, the NOI took in more money than ever (some tens of millions), but debts were also running high on massive building projects.

On February 25, 1975, Elijah Muhammad died of congestive heart failure, exacerbated by previous conditions of asthma and diabetes. He appointed Wallace Muhammad to succeed him, and Wallace promptly began reforming the NOI along more traditional Sunni lines. Muhammad Ali likewise converted to Sunni Islam. By 1976 Wallace had renamed the organization the World Community of Islam in the West (WCIW) and repudiated his father's claim to being the divinely inspired Messenger of Allah. Instead Wallace began to preach that the Muhammad of orthodox Islam was Allah's final prophet. Wallace also dismissed the NOI's hateful racial ideology. For three years, Louis Farrakhan submitted to Wallace, but by 1978 he resurrected the old Nation of Islam with a few thousand followers who yearned for the controversial old theology. However, this group never approached the wealth or influence of Muhammad's NOI. The fact that Elijah Muhammad's NOI could inspire numerous other iconic black Americans but could not survive his death establishes his legacy as an enduring icon of black America.

Johnathan Koefoed
Boston College

FURTHER READING

Berg, Herbert. *Elijah Muhammad and Islam.* New York: NYU Press, 2009.

Clegg, Claude Andrew. *An Original Man: The Life and Times of Elijah Muhammad.* New York: St. Martin's Press, 1997.

Evanzz, Karl. *The Messenger: The Rise and Fall of Elijah Muhammad*. New York: Pantheon Books, 1999.

Gardell, Matthias. *In the Name of Elijah Muhammad: Louis Farrakhan and the Nation of Islam*. Durham, NC: Duke University Press, 1996.

Lincoln, Eric C. *The Black Muslims in America*. Boston: Beacon Press, 1961.

Lomax, Louis E. *When the Word Is Given; a Report on Elijah Muhammad, Malcolm X, and the Black Muslim World*. Cleveland: World Publishing, 1963.

Muhammad, Elijah. *History of the Nation of Islam*. Phoenix: Secretarius MEMPS Publications, 2008.

Walker, Dennis. *Islam and the Search for African American Nationhood: Elijah Muhammad, Louis Farrakhan, and the Nation of Islam*. Atlanta: Clarity Press, 2005.

Wright, Lewis E. Jr. "Elijah Muhammad's Political Thought on God and Authority: A Quest for Authenticity and Freedom." *Journal of Religious Thought* 51, no. 2 (Winter–Spring, 1994–1995): 47–75.

AP/Wide World Photos

Negro Baseball Leagues (1880s–1950s)

From the early years of the formulation of the American colonies to the late 1960s, the United States was virtually two dual societies: one black and one white. They were separate and totally unequal. Black society was left with inferior products in housing, jobs, and education, though one area in which black society did not believe it was deprived was in its leisure endeavors. Foremost among American culture's outdoor sporting endeavors was the grand old game of baseball. Black society's thirst for the game was answered by the creation of the fast-paced, slick fielding, showboating, entertaining Negro Baseball Leagues. These leagues lasted until the 1950s and games were attended by blacks and whites.

The topic of blacks in American society predates the founding of this nation. Race was also a major issue within black society, as blacks even disagreed over the term they wished to use to describe themselves. This debate has included terms such as Colored, Negro, Black, and African American. Participants of the first black baseball leagues referred to themselves as "Colored," which is consequently the term used to identify these players in this chapter. From around 1911 until the mid-1950s, players in these baseball leagues described themselves as "Negro," so that term is used in this chapter to relate to the leagues during that time period.

The first baseball league for Colored players was developed in the mid-1880s. It should be noted, that Negro League Baseball was always open to white players. In other words, these leagues were technically integrated. Most baseball leagues were integrated until the late 1880s, when the color line was formally drawn, segregating professional mainstream baseball leagues to only whites.

Many teams participated in the leagues during those early years, including the Pittsburgh Keystones, the Cuban Giants of Trenton, New Jersey, Gorhams of New York, Lord Baltimores, Boston Resolutes, and the Norfolk Red Sox. Other areas that had early teams were Boston, Philadelphia, and Louisville. The first black professional baseball team was organized in 1885. The Argyle Hotel of Babylon, a resort hotel built in 1882 in Long Island, New York, actually sponsored the team, which was composed of the black waiters working at the hotel. The team players served as an attraction for the guests of the hotel and played nine games their first season. They played against the best white teams of New York City and Long Island, winning six games, losing two, and tying one during that early season. The members of this successful team were Ben Holmes on third base, A. Randolph on first, Ben Boyd on second, William Eggleston as short stop, Guy Day as catcher, Milton Dabney in left field, Charles Nichols in right, and George Parego, Frank Harris, and R. Martin as pitchers.

Other players found success on the field as well. Sol White, a baseball player and historian of the Colored Base Ball Leagues, held remarkable records himself. Standing five foot nine and weighing 170 lb, he participated in the mainstream white leagues for five seasons before the color line ban around 1888. He never batted below .324 during his years in the mainstream leagues. He was also advertised as the only player with a college education; although

White attended Wilberforce University for a couple of years, there is no evidence that he obtained a degree. The advertisement about his education was about a particular league, because Moses "Fleetwood" Walker played for three years at Oberlin College in Ohio in the late 1860s before playing professionally as White's contemporary.

Other accounts claim that the team sponsored by the Argyle Hotel actually consisted of players from three semi-pro black teams: one from Washington, DC called the Manhattans, and the Keystones and the Orions from Philadelphia. The newly combined team was named the Cuban Giants. According to the other account, any duties performed by these men as waiters, bellhops, or porters, were purely coincidental to their primary responsibilities as baseball players. The early years of the Colored Base Ball Leagues were dotted with short-lived teams, players of questionable skills, poor attendance at times, and poorly financed ownership. Some owners and promoters actually put local town players in uniforms to compete against true professionals who traveled through the area. Ambrose Davis, who owned the Gorhams of New York, was the first African American owner of a salaried black team. He was also one of the owners who jumped at the opportunity to buy up the outstanding talent pool on a team that was folding. On occasion, he gobbled up the best players on a team that consistently beat his squad. After the Cuban Giants badly beat his Gorhams in two consecutive games, Davis signed the better players of the Giants to contracts that were more lucrative on his own team, even though it was the middle of a baseball season. He brought George Stovey, Clarence Williams, Frank Grant, and White from the Cuban Giants to his Gorhams. Each of those black players had experience playing in the white professional leagues. Stovey, along with Moses "Fleetwood" Walker, formed one of the first black batteries in white professional baseball, with Grant pitching and Walker catching. Walker is noted as the first black player in professional baseball.

The Giants remained a popularly used team name through the early years of the Colored Base Ball Leagues. In some cases, a city might have two teams with the name Giants. There were the Cuban Giants (later named the Genuine or Original Cuban Giants), the Cuban X-Giants, the Chicago Columbia Giants, the Chicago American Giants, the Leland Chicago Giants, the Philadelphia Giants, the Brooklyn Royal Giants, and the Page Fence Giants. The name Giants also remained popular with the teams that comprised the Negro Leagues from 1920s to 1950s. The reasons for the name's popularity with the Negro League teams are probably varied. One theory, though, suggests that the name was used in imitation of the National League's extremely successful and popular New York franchise. Regardless of the names used to identify the teams, the Cuban Giants of Argyle Hotel remained a force throughout the era of the Colored Base Ball Leagues, ultimately serving as the progenitor of the Negro Baseball Leagues.

Members of the Colored Base Ball Leagues lived during a notably difficult time in the history of the United States. They performed at a time and era when a black person's life was considered of little value to many in the majority white society. This era, known historically as "The Progressive Era" in the United States, saw African American citizens markedly separated from the rest of society via legal court sanctions. The U.S. Supreme Court ruled that segregation was indeed legal with its decision in a Louisiana railroad car case, known as *Plessy v. Ferguson.* The ruling in this case legally separated blacks from the rest of American society for nearly 60 years. Yet despite these social impediments, black society participated fully in the great American pastime of baseball. Social movements including the Niagara Movement, **Booker T. Washington**'s industrial education movement, and the formation of the National Association for the Advancement of Colored People (NAACP) challenged the limitations black people faced. Although they were separate from mainstream leagues, Colored Base Ball Leagues provided entertainment and diversion for African Americans during this tumultuous time. The early years of Colored Base Ball provided the foundation of what became the glory years and folklore of baseball in black culture, "The Negro Leagues!"

As the twentieth century began, and segregation in the United States became more entrenched, African American society paralleled white America. Black America developed a mass communication system through the Associated Negro Press. This news service linked the sporting and educational worlds of black society. The Associated Negro Press writers were talented and operated within a world that lent little credence to the white world that surrounded them. As one reporter of the time argued,

> There was no white world as far as the black world of that time was concerned . . . We were not even aware of the white world in the sense that it meant anything of consequence to the world in which we lived . . . Our heaven and our glory was in Harlem; not at Harvard, but at Howard and Lincoln, Clark and Morris Brown, Tuskegee and Alabama State, and finally Florida A&M and other schools west of the Mississippi, Wiley and Grambling. All joined in possession of the black world. Nobody cared about Georgia Tech, nobody worried about Auburn. Nobody even worried about Notre Dame. We had our own. We had our Howard Bisons. We had our Golden Tuskegee Tigers, and that was the thing the black press wrote about. These were the things that we celebrated and that marked the Headlines that made the black press important. And of course the Beautiful verses and beautiful lines of men like **Langston Hughes** and Countee Cullen.

The communication system and outlet to African American society and culture was alive and well. The Associated Negro Press helped to provide national exposure for the Negro Baseball Leagues of the twentieth century.

The Negro League baseball teams provided some of the leisure and downtime relief available to the black educated, middle-class, and elite of the era. The Negro Baseball Leagues provided far more than pure entertainment to the community, just as the Associated Negro Press offered more than just communication.

List of Professional Negro League Baseball Teams

Algoma Brownies
All Nations
Argyle Hotel Athletics
Atlanta Black Crackers
Atlantic City Bacharach Giants
Baltimore Black Sox
Baltimore Elite Giants
Birmingham Black Barons
Brooklyn Eagles
Brooklyn Royal Giants
Buffalo (International League)
Chattanooga Black Lookouts
Chicago American Giants
Chicago Columbia Giants
Chicago Giants
Chicago Union Giants
Chicago Unions
Cincinnati Buckeyes
Cincinnati Clowns
Cincinnati Tigers
Cincinnati-Indianapolis Clowns
Cleveland Bears
Cleveland Browns
Cleveland Buckeyes
Cleveland Cubs
Cleveland Elites
Cleveland Giants
Cleveland Hornets
Cleveland Red Sox
Cleveland Stars
Cleveland Tate Stars
Cleveland Tigers
Cole's American Giants
Columbia Giants of Chicago
Columbus Blue Birds
Columbus Buckeyes
Columbus Elite Giants
Cuban Giants
Cuban House of David
Cuban Stars East
Cuban Stars West
Cuban X-Giants

Dayton Marcos
Detroit Stars
Detroit Wolves
Ethiopian Clowns
Harlem Stars
Harrisburg Giants
Harrisburg-St. Louis Stars
Havana Red Sox
Hilldale
Homestead Grays
Houston Eagles
Indianapolis ABCs
Indianapolis Athletics
Indianapolis Clowns
Indianapolis Crawfords
Jacksonville Red Caps
Kansas City Kansas Giants
Kansas City Monarchs
Leland Giants
Long Branch Cubans
Louisville Black Caps
Louisville Black Colonels
Louisville Buckeyes
Louisville White Sox
Memphis Red Sox
Miami Ethiopian Clowns
Milwaukee Bears
Mobile Black Bears
Mohawk Giants
Monroe Monarchs
Montgomery Grey Sox
Nashville Elite Giants
New Orleans Eagles
New Orleans-St. Louis Stars
New York Black Yankees
New York Cubans
New York Gorhams
New York Harlem Stars
New York Lincoln Giants
New York Lincoln Stars
Newark Browns
Newark Dodgers

Newark Eagles   Stars of Cuba
Newark Stars   St. Louis Giants
Page Fence Giants   St. Louis Stars
Pennsylvania Red Caps of New York   St. Paul Gophers
Philadelphia Giants   Toledo Crawfords
Philadelphia Pythians   Toledo Tigers
Philadelphia Stars   Washington Black Senators
Philadelphia Tigers   Washington Elite Giants
Pittsburgh Crawfords   Washington Pilots
Pittsburgh Keystones   Washington Potomacs
Royal Poinciana Team   Wilmington Potomacs
Seattle Steelheads   Zulu Cannibal Giants

In the face of hardening segregationist policies, the leadership of the educational elite within the African American community, led by **W. E. B. Du Bois** and others, launched efforts to reaffirm, reconstruct, and build Black American Culture. This awakening is described as the Harlem Renaissance. This renaissance took place in all aspects of black society, and entrepreneurs and investors of Negro League Baseball redesigned and restructured their product as well. The end result of their efforts was the Negro Leagues.

Negro League Baseball entered a new era of prosperity and change beginning in 1920 until its demise in the 1950s. Rube Foster founded the "Negro National League" of baseball. Foster, acting in a role similar to that of a commissioner, ruled this league until it matured. The league became very successful. A second league, entitled the Eastern Colored League, was organized in 1923. From 1924 to 1927, the two leagues played four Negro World Series. The Eastern Colored League folded in 1928, however, and most of the teams in the league returned to playing on an independent status. Foster himself became ill and died in 1930. The league he founded folded in 1931 due to lack of leadership and difficulties caused by the Depression. Problems with ownership and appropriate funding shifted some teams from one city to another, which also meant that these teams had to change their names. (See the List of Professional Negro League Baseball Teams.) The Great Depression deeply affected the black community, causing additional stress and struggle in a community that already fought racism. Money for leisure activities, such as paying to attend a baseball game, was just not readily available for most blacks. Most Negro League teams survived this era by moving back and forth across the country, playing games in one town or city after another. This system of movement became known as Barnstorming.

Stability returned to Negro League Baseball when, in 1933, Gus Greenlee established the second Negro National League. An East–West All-Star game developed with the advent of this new league. This yearly game surpassed even the Negro League World Series in popularity each year through attendance and fan interest. From the mid-1930s to the late 1940s, legends of the players and some of the teams of these leagues grew and became lore. The pitching of Satchel Paige and the home run-hitting of Josh Gibson were two of the many celebrated tales.

In mainstream major league baseball today, the names of Cy Young, Ty Cobb, and Babe Ruth reign as legendary. In the Negro Leagues, Paige (real name Robert LeRoy Paige), Cool Papa Bell (real name James Thomas Bell), and Gibson (real name Joshua Gibson) served as heroes. In fact, many in the black press referred to Ruth as the white Josh Gibson. The legends of men such as Paige, Bell, and Gibson made the Negro Leagues what they were. Paige, for example, pitched until he was 61 years old. Born on July 7, 1906, in Mobile, Alabama, he pitched his last three innings of professional major league base-ball for the Kansas City A's of the white American League in 1965. He then pitched his last season in 1967 for the Indianapolis Clowns of the Negro Leagues. Yet Paige's glory years lasted from 1926 to 1950 when he played with the Negro Leagues. He pitched over the years in the Negro Leagues for the Chattanooga Black Lookouts, Birmingham Black Barons, Baltimore Black Sox, Cleveland Cubs, Pittsburgh Crawfords, Kansas City Monarchs, Santo Domingo, Santo Domingo All-Stars, Newark Eagles, Mexican League, Satchel Paige's All-Stars, New York Black Yankees, Memphis Red Sox, Philadelphia Stars, Chicago American Giants, and the Indianapolis Clowns.

> Age is a case of mind over matter. If you don't mind, it don't matter.
>
> —Satchel Paige

Paige was an important figure throughout the majority of the Negro Leagues' duration. One tale of his athleticism describes a game he pitched against Gibson's team. Paige, a right-handed pitcher, had never pitched against Gibson in a crucial game-on-the-line type of situation. He intentionally loaded the bases in the last inning to bring Gibson to the plate. Gibson struck out on three pitches.

Paige finally received an opportunity to pitch in the white major leagues in 1948. In 1971, he was inducted into the National Baseball Hall of Fame. He died on June 8, 1982, just before his seventy-sixth birthday. No player epito-mizes the lore and legacy of the Negro Leagues more than Satchel Paige.

Josh Gibson similarly symbolized the lore of the Negro Leagues through his power-hitting. He was born on December 21, 1911, in Buena Vista, Georgia and played in the Negro Leagues from 1929 to 1946 as a catcher. The primary teams for which he played in the Negro Leagues were the Homestead Grays and Pittsburgh Crawfords. He also played two years in the Mexican League and one year in Santo Domingo. Gibson's batting ability riveted crowds who came to see him play. He hit with an individual swing that reliably produced home runs.

Tales of Gibson's power-hitting were second to none in baseball. He was credited with hitting home runs completely out of Yankee Stadium in New York, Griffith Stadium in Washington, DC, and a stadium in Pittsburgh. These feats led reporters to cover the Negro Leagues. Wendell Smith of the *Pittsburgh Courier* and Sam Lacy of the *Baltimore Afro-American Ledger* reminded readers that Gibson may not have had any hitting equals. Not even Babe Ruth hit as well as Gibson! There were always discussions in the black community as to who actually hit more home runs, Ruth or Gibson. One thing is for sure: no player, other than Satchel Paige, received more notoriety in Negro League accounts as Gibson. He died on January 20, 1947, of a stroke. Gibson was inducted in the Baseball Hall of Fame in 1972. At that time, he was only the second player from the Negro Leagues to be so named.

James "Cool Papa" Bell, hailed as the fastest man to ever play baseball, played in the Negro Leagues from 1922 to 1950. He was born on May 17, 1903 in Starkville, Mississippi. He played for the St. Louis Stars, the Detroit Wolves, the Kansas City Monarchs, the Homestead Grays, the Pittsburgh Crawfords, the Memphis Red Sox, the Chicago American Giants, the Detroit Senators, and the Kansas City Stars. He also spent time playing for teams in Mexico and Santo Domingo. His fame came from his speed, which, together with quickness, is one of the most admirable qualities an athlete can possess in the eyes of many African Americans. Even athletes of large stature with extreme strength and power must be swift. Cool Papa Bell had speed to spare. Stories abound of his scoring from first base on a bunt by Satchel Paige while they played against a group of white major leagues. Bell was said to twice have hit the ball to the shortstop in a game and beat the throw to first base; the person playing shortstop against Bell was said to be **Jackie Robinson**, who in 1947 became the first black player to play in the modern white major leagues. This also gives some perspective of the quality of the skill level and play in the Negro Leagues. Though Robinson received an opportunity to play in the white major leagues, many other players from the Negro Leagues who were considered to have better physical skills never got a call or were well past their peak-playing days.

Bell, a centerfielder, was a switch hitter and threw left-handed. The best, albeit exaggerated, description of Bell's speed was that he was able to turn off the light switch and be in the bed before the room got dark. In his 25 years of Negro League participation, Bell was credited with a .341 lifetime batting average. In exhibition games against white major leagues, he is reported to have batted a .391 average. Bell died on March 7, 1991, in St. Louis, Missouri.

The talent of these three men demonstrates why the play of the Negro Leagues was of such high quality. Accounts of their talent also show the thrills and enjoyment that fans would experience and come to expect upon attending games played in these leagues.

Another aspect of Negro League Baseball that is very rarely spoken about is its female ownership. At a time when most of the United States truly thought women did not belong in such arenas, women owned teams in the Negro Baseball Leagues. For example, Effa Manley was the owner of the Brooklyn Eagles, turned Newark Eagles, from 1935 to 1948. At that time, she was the only female owner of a team in baseball. A white female raised in a household with a nonbiological black father, she was very well received in Negro League Baseball circles. She was well ahead of her time for involvement in such business ventures. Players under her contract included Larry Doby, an infielder who was the first black player in the white major American League division, playing with Cleveland the same year that Jackie Robinson played with the Brooklyn Dodgers, pitcher Don Newcombe who later played in the major leagues with the Dodgers and won the National League's Cy Young and MVP awards in 1956, and infielder/outfield Monte Irvin, who also was selected to baseball's Hall of Fame. Manley's reign as owner of the Eagles and her dealings with owners of the major leagues earned her induction in baseball's Hall of Fame in 2006.

> They used to say, "If we find a good black player, we'll sign him." They was lying. —Cool Papa Bell

Though segregation prevailed in American society, African Americans forged ahead with all aspects of their lives. In some areas, such as baseball, they produced a product so outstanding that white society on many occasions spent their leisure funds attending Negro League Baseball games. As social customs began to change, so did changes to racial custom and institutions. Black baseball ended as Major League Baseball integrated. In many ways, the Negro Leagues began to decline when Jackie Robinson joined the Brooklyn Dodgers. Despite this demise, the Negro Baseball Leagues remain a vital part of American baseball. The history and glory of the Negro Baseball Leagues are stored and still collected in The Negro Leagues Baseball Museum in St. Louis, Missouri, primarily through the efforts of John "Buck" O'Neill, a former player and lifelong historian of the leagues. O'Neill, himself, was on the 2006 baseball Hall of Fame ballot, though he was not selected and passed away a few months after the balloting. There, however, is always next year for induction to the Hall. The Negro Leagues' greatest ambassador has passed, but he leaves a lifetime of glorious history for all to cherish.

James R. Coates
University of Wisconsin, Green Bay

FURTHER READING

Brashler, William. *Josh Gibson: A Life in the Negro Leagues*. New York: Harper and Row Publishers, 1978.

Holway, John. *Blackball Stars: Negro League Pioneers*. West Port, CT: Meckler Publishing Company, 1988.

Holway, John. *Black Diamonds: Life in the Negro Leagues from the Men Who Lived It*. West Port, CT: Meckler Publishing Company, 1989.

Holway, John. *Voices from the Great Black Baseball Leagues*. New York: Da Capo Press, 1992.

Peterson, Robert W. *Only the Ball Was White*. New York: McGraw Hill Publishing, 1984.

Riley, James A. *The Biographical Encyclopedia of the Negro Baseball Leagues*. New York: Carroll & Graf Publishers, Inc., 1994.

Robinson, Frazier "Slow," and Paul Bauer. *Catching Dreams: My Life in the Negro Baseball Leagues*. Syracuse, NY: Syracuse University Press, 1999.

Ruck, Rob. *Sandlot Seasons: Sport in Black Pittsburgh*. Urbana: University of Illinois Press, 1987.

Ted Streshinsky/Corbis

Huey P. Newton (1942–1989) and Bobby Seale (1936–)

Huey P. Newton and Bobby Seale emerged as symbols of ultra-militant black radicalism beginning in October 1966 when they founded the Black Panther Party for Self Defense (BPP). Dedicated initially to organizing blacks to protect themselves and their neighborhoods against police brutality in Oakland, California, the BPP developed as a revolutionary, broad-based self-help, political and social action organization. Its signature *"Ten Point Program"* (TPP) demanded major reforms to improve the circumstances and conditions of life for blacks and other oppressed peoples in the United States. "We want land, bread, housing, education, clothing, justice, peace and people's community control of modern technology," the TPP declared in its final summary point. Spreading nationally, particularly to urban centers with significant black populations, and later internationally, the BPP drew attention dramatically with its militancy and deadly clashes with law enforcement. Newton's and Seale's public images grew with the BPP to almost legendary dimensions as friends and foes contrived, exaggerated, and fabricated accounts of their actions and intentions. Their images soared, particularly in the late 1960s-counterculture, especially after Federal Bureau of Investigation (FBI) Director J. Edgar Hoover in September 1968 publicly declared the BPP "the greatest threat to the internal security of the country" and virtually ordered FBI agents and assets to harass and destroy the BPP, its members, and supporters (Cleaver and Katsiaficas, 8).

Newton and Seale were both southern-born: Seale in Dallas, Texas, and Newton in Monroe, Louisiana. They migrated with their families to Oakland in 1945, part of a rising wave of Southern blacks moving to opportunities World War II created. They met for the first time almost 20 years later as students at California's northern Alameda County's Merritt College. Then sitting on Grove Street at the fringe of west Oakland's black ghetto, the public community college preached and practiced a mission of self-development. It reached out to educate the ill-served and underserved, and Seale and Newton stood as prime examples of students Merritt aimed to reach. Seale had left Oakland High School with failing grades his senior year. Six years later and three miles away, Newton had graduated from Oakland Technical High School but could not really read. The Oakland public schools had failed both.

Intellect and desire brought Seale and Newton to Merritt. Seale started taking occasional classes there in 1962. He had done three years in the U.S. Air Force, learning to work as a sheet metal mechanic. On returning to Oakland, he put his skill to work at various aerospace plants and through night classes earned a diploma from Berkeley High School. The younger Newton worked at improving his reading by matching sight with sound as he followed words of poetry, recorded by film actor Vincent Price in his distinctive voice.

Newton then tackled *The Republic*, poring at least a half-dozen times over the ancient Greek philosopher Plato's Socratic dialogues discussing dialectical forms of government and the meaning of justice. Hooked on learning, Newton became especially interested in the operation of political community. He enrolled for a year at San Francisco Law School. Its evening program established in 1909 catered to part-time students such as Newton. Studying to be a lawyer turned out not to be Newton's calling, but he continued eagerly to improve not only his mind but his world. Taking classes at Merritt, he found in Seale a kindred spirit.

Seale and Newton pushed to learn more to better themselves and their community. In the Afro-American Association at Merritt, they joined with others to get the college to offer its first black history course—often reputed the first in the nation outside of historically black institutions. The two joined with others to produce their own political consciousness seminars. They devoured and debated writings of radical giants. The French West Indies-born psychiatrist and philosopher Frantz Fanon's analysis of the effect of colonial subjugation in *Black Skin, White Masks* (1952) and *The Wretched of the Earth* (1961) formed for them a foundational radical critique of blacks' position in the United States and throughout the African Diaspora.

Chinese Communist leader Mao Zedong's direct action philosophy, preaching "all power comes from the barrel of a gun," along with that of the Argentina-born guerrilla revolutionary Ernesto "Che" Guevara, added to Seale and Newton's developing militancy. They also admired Robert F. Williams whom the National Association for the Advancement of Colored People (NAACP) dismissed in 1959 as president of its Monroe, North Carolina, branch for urging a black guerrilla war of self-defense. Exiled in Cuba and later China, Williams subsequently became chairman of the Revolutionary Action Movement and of the Republic of New Africa. Another hero was the black Muslim minister El-Hajj Malik El-Shabazz, who gained fame as the Nation of Islam spokesman **Malcolm X** and was slain in February 1965.

Seale and Newton saw the promise of radical, community-based black self-development. Their vision leaped beyond institutional parameters. They wanted something more mass-based than the NAACP founded in 1909 or the Congress of Racial Equality founded in 1942 or the more recent Student Nonviolent Coordinating Committee (SNCC) founded in 1960 or even the fledgling Organization of Afro-American Unity that Malcolm X formed in June 1964 on returning from his last pilgrimage to Africa. Seale and Newton wanted what they saw as a direct action people's movement.

With a view of moving beyond analysis to action, Seale and Newton put their views into practice on October 15, 1966: They co-founded the BPP. Seale was chairman, and Newton was minister of defense. Protecting the community was the BPP's first order of business. Newton and Seale saw black neighborhoods under siege in Oakland and elsewhere. That accounted for the phrase "self-defense" in the BPP title and for the TPP's Point 7: "all Black and oppressed people should be armed for self defense of our homes and communities."

Violence against blacks routinely occurred as a political tool of colonialist racist oppression in the BPP view, and the immediate, primary perpetrators were police departments and other law enforcement agencies used "to carry out [the official] program of oppression against black people, other people of color and poor people inside the united [sic] States," Point 7 declared.

Enlisting as members a like-minded handful, Newton and Seale formed Panther Police Patrols to watch Oakland Police Department (OPD) operations in black neighborhoods. They put the OPD and other law enforcement agencies on notice that eyes and ears with cameras and tape recorders were vigilant for police brutality and were ready to respond with guns in hand.

The BPP was not looking for a fight. Opposing aggression, it preached defense with an aim to stop violence, not to start it. An example of the violence the BPP opposed occurred on April 1, 1967, when a Contra Costa County sheriff's deputy shot to death black 16-year-old Denzel Dowell for an alleged theft in North Richmond, 15 miles north of Oakland. The sheriff's office hardly took notice of the incident. It rebuffed family and community inquiries into justification, as if police owed no public explanation for the killing. Sheriff Walter Younger refused to investigate the circumstances or even officially question his deputy about the killing.

Seale seized on the shooting. He mounted a BPP rally at Dowell's family home to publicize the tragedy and the BPP's cause. He orchestrated a series of subsequent rallies to galvanize attention on the BPP. At the Dowell home, BPP members openly carried guns, as they did on Panther Patrols. California law let them do so as long as the guns were not loaded or pointed to menace anyone. The sight of blacks with guns in the streets and shadowing police ignited a firestorm. The immediate attention swelled BPP ranks. It also swelled police rancor that made the BPP an official target.

The BPP had begun to excite public imagination and indignation. Oakland's Conservative Republican California General Assemblyman Donald Mulford within days of the rally at Dowell's family home showed the extent of official reaction against the BPP. He introduced an amendment to the state penal code section 602.7 treating public disturbances. With a clear focus on the BPP, he proposed changing California law to prohibit "the carrying of firearms on one's person or in a vehicle, in any public place or on any public street."

The California State Assembly Committee on Criminal Procedure scheduled a hearing on Mulford's bill on May 2, 1967. Feeling the BPP in the law's crosshairs, Newton and Seale seized the opportunity to shift from being mere targets to reveling as the center of attention. They organized a caravan to the state capitol in Sacramento. They wanted a media event, and they created one.

Chairman Seale marched with 29 gun-toting male and female BPP members onto California's capitol steps on May 2, 1967. After posing there for photos and a few quips, the cadre entered the building. They sought the visitors' gallery. They wanted to see the committee hearing on Mulford's bill. Perhaps more, they wanted to be seen at the hearing. The armed BPP presence panicked capital guards, legislative staffers, and others. Governor Ronald W. Reagan, himself, reportedly ducked for cover at the sight of gun-toting blacks. In the melee, BPP members found themselves on the main floor of the California Assembly.

No fracas occurred, but legislative business did halt. The BPP intended no invasion, yet seeing the black cadre created chaos among fearful whites. BPP members stayed cool and followed directions. Returning to the capitol steps, Seale heightened the event's news value by reading soon-to-be famous BPP Executive Mandate Number One.

> "The Black Panther Party for Self-Defense calls upon the American people in general and the black people in particular to take careful note of the racist California Legislature which is now," Seale explainded, "considering legislation aimed at keeping the black people disarmed and powerless at the very same time that racist police agencies throughout the country are intensifying the terror, brutality, murder, and repression of black people." (Newton, 1972/1995, 12)

The BPP manifesto linked racism in the United States at home and American racism abroad. Tapping into protest against the Vietnam War, Seale called U.S. military action in South East Asia "a racist war of genocide" in line with America's "barbaric treatment for non-white people." The war fit historically, he said, with the United States' slaughtering Indians, enslaving blacks, interning Japanese-Americans, and dropping atomic bombs on Hiroshima and Nagasaki. "All testify to the fact that toward people of color the racist power structure of America has but one policy: repression, genocide, terror, and the big stick," the manifesto continued (Newton, 1972/1995, 12).

Seale invoked the dawning of a new era of resistance. He declared an end to the days of blacks simply begging, demonstrating, petitioning, or praying. Such methods resulted in more repression, not less, he said. "The Black Panther Party for Self-Defense believes that the time has come for black people to arm themselves against this terror before it is too late," he insisted. "A people who have suffered so much for so long at the hands of a racist society, must draw the line somewhere. We believe that the black communities of America must rise up as one man to halt the progression of a trend that leads inevitably to their total destruction," the BPP chairman concluded (Newton, 1972/1995, 12).

The startling publicity coup over, the BPP cadre left for the 80 miles back to Oakland. Sacramento city police interrupted the ride. Blocks from the capitol, they arrested 26 Panthers and confiscated 15 guns. Perhaps officials had not wanted to chance a shootout at the capitol or add to the media circus there, but apparently they wanted the BPP not to go unpunished for brazen behavior.

News headlines blared the BPP's feat at the capitol. The BPP had indelibly established itself with an image of challenging governmental power. That idealized vision leapt ironically from most of the news coverage seeking to discredit the BPP as a fringe group of dangerous extremists. The largest circulation newspaper in California's capital led the parade. "Capitol Invaded," the evening *Sacramento Bee* front-page headline virtually screamed that May 2. The flagship of the nationwide McClatchy chain added two stark photos of rifle-toting BPP members in their black berets and black sunglasses outside the capitol. It proved an image to love and hate.

Seething official hostility to the BPP spilled over on October 28, 1967, when OPD Officer John F. Frey's early-morning traffic stop of Newton turned deadly. Frey reportedly ordered Newton out of the car he was driving, after reviewing his license and registration. Frey's probable cause for the stop never clearly emerged. Nor were subsequent events ever completely clarified. What did emerge clearly was a scuffle between Frey and Newton. During the struggle, Frey drew his service revolver and shot Newton in the stomach. Several gunshots then felled the 23-year-old Frey. He died at the scene. Shots also hit Frey's partner, patrolman Herbert C. Heanes, in the chest, knee, and arm. Police arrested Newton at nearby Kaiser Hospital and charged him with murdering Frey.

Prior to the Frey shooting, San Francisco Bay Area newspapers carried occasional notes of Newton's confrontations with police. His arrest for killing Frey put Newton on front pages far and wide in a developing international news story. Reporters from around the world flocked to focus on Newton's prosecution. He became a New Left *cause célébre*. His image became the face of the BPP. In fact, he rose as a cult figure, a symbol of black militancy, and an instant legend. Popular discussion imbued him with characteristics of heroic outlaws in folktales and lore decrying inequities and subordination.

"Free Huey" rang as a BPP rally cry. Hundreds converged on the Alameda County Courthouse on January 28, 1968, for a preliminary hearing in Newton's murder trial in California Superior Court. Still recovering from his wounds, Newton energized supporters with his upraised clenched fist saluting their solidarity with him. About 400 supporters crowded the 10-story courthouse, and 80 or so managed entry into the courtroom itself. On February 17, 1968, Newton's 26th birthday, more than 5,000 supporters attended a Huey P. Newton Defense Fund celebration at the Oakland Auditorium Arena.

Newton's trial for first-degree murder, kidnapping, and assault with a deadly weapon upon a police officer began in earnest in July 1968. It dragged on more than eight weeks, into September. Throughout, hundreds thronged the Alameda County Courthouse to keep "Vigil for Huey Newton. Peace and Freedom," placards declared. The scene was a spectacle. America's criminal justice system appeared on trial with Newton. Supporters portrayed him as the black Everyman whom the official United States systematically stripped and scapegoated. Young black males like the 26-year-old Newton perennially served as grist for America's prison machines, which in the BPP and many other perspectives operated as primary institutions of oppression, separating the hard black male core from society. Newton's trial again illustrated for many, the United States' refusal to allow assertive, self-assured black men liberty to live. It either killed them, shipped them to be killed in places like Vietnam, or put them in prison, as it sought to do with Newton.

Jaundiced eyes worldwide were fixed on the United States' treatment of blacks at the time of Newton's trial. Promises of improved conditions touted with milestones such as the Civil Rights Act of 1964 and the Voting Rights Act of 1965, gained in the momentous civil rights push since the 1950s, appeared less hopeful in the spring and summer of 1968. The assassination of Rev. **Martin Luther King, Jr.** in April and the rioting it sparked across the nation scorched bright predictions of continuing civil rights successes. The August rioting at the Democratic National Convention in Chicago, Illinois, further demonstrated the depth of discontent. The United States faced hard looks from without and from within.

The outcome of Newton's trial appeared a flashpoint. Panther and police spokespersons talked of the prospect of violence when the jury returned its verdict. None occurred on September 9, 1968, when the seven women and five men announced their transparent compromise verdict. With the lone black serving as foreman, the jury found Newton guilty of voluntary manslaughter. It rejected the prosecution's first-degree murder charge, with the possibility of execution in the gas chamber, and also acquitted Newton of assault with a deadly weapon upon a police officer.

Trial Judge Monroe Friedman sentenced Newton to 2–15 years in prison. Newton's sister Doris collapsed at the courthouse, but all was relatively calm. A bomb blast on October 4, blew out more than 100 windows at the courthouse and surrounding buildings, but nothing directly connected the bombing to Newton or the Panthers.

The verdict confirmed BPP friends and foes. Newton supporters took his conviction as further proof of the racial injustice and oppression of America's ruling system. FBI Director Hoover and other reactionaries took Newton's conviction as part of redoubled efforts to restore their repressive vision of law and order. And as Hoover announced the day before the Newton verdict, the BPP headed the official list of internal security threats. As the most visible BPP figure, Newton had stood as something of the United States' public enemy number one in Hoover's eyes.

The FBI director loathed Newton as he had loathed the Rev. Martin Luther King Jr. Hoover detested even the inkling of a Black Messiah or any kind of leader who might electrify and unify blacks. With Newton in prison, King dead, and Malcolm X before him, Hoover had worries about BPP chairman Seale. He had plans, too. Seale had long been under attack as the BPP voice and most visible Panther next to Newton. An Alameda County jury convicted Seale on April 11, 1968, on a felony charge for carrying a loaded shotgun while demonstrating outside the city prison at the Oakland Hall of Justice where Newton sat awaiting trial. Seale would be hounded for years. Yet he proved an irrepressible survivor. Other BPP members were not so lucky.

The FBI and other police agencies appeared intent on sending as many BPP members as possible to join Newton in prison or beyond. The FBI's secret—and later disgraced—domestic surveillance counterintelligence program run since 1956 under the codename COINTELPRO targeted the Panthers. So did local law enforcement. Destroying the BPP became an official priority, and repeated bloody attacks occurred. The pattern appeared before Newton's trial. In an hour-long shoot-out on April 6, 1968, for instance, Oakland police wounded BPP Minister of Information Eldridge Cleaver and killed 17-year-old BPP member Bobby Hutton. Another shootout occurred in San Francisco in November 1968. An SFPD stop of a Black Panther Black Community News Service panel truck with Eldridge-Cleaver-for-President banners ended with three police officers shot and eight blacks arrested.

Official hostility fell not merely on BPP members with guns. The backlash hit BPP community service programs also. It disrupted free breakfast programs that fed schoolchildren hot meals and free clinics providing legal aid, medical care, or senior assistance. Officials villified such programs as BPP propaganda devices to win hearts and minds in black communities by bribery. They took no account of the actual social services the BPP delivered as "survival programs" and which police purposely destroyed.

The official crackdown on the BPP provoked its own backlash. Many understood the repression for what it was. Rather than backing away from the BPP, they embraced it. That response was clear from the first attacks on the BPP. The "Free Huey" campaign made the response chic. That showed again in Bobby Hutton's funeral at the Ephesians Church of God in Christ in Oakland on April 12, 1968. Protesting police tactics drew a throng, including such celebrities as author **James Baldwin** and actor Marlon Brando. Seale charged police with murdering Hutton when he was unarmed and was surrendering to custody. The crackdown seemed to be scaring away few. Rather, it appeared to be creating BPP heroes and martyrs. And the pattern continued, as shown in Chicago in December 1969 when a joint task force of FBI agents and state and local police shot and killed Fred Hampton, the BPP Illinois deputy chairman.

BPP support spiked in the face of official harassment. The BPP newspaper, *Black Panther*, of November 1, 1969, touted the party's growth to more than 2,000 members in 32 chapters across 15 states. Chapters flourished particularly in major urban areas on the East and West Coasts. Baltimore, Boston, Los Angeles, Newark, New York, Philadelphia, San Diego, Seattle, and Washington, DC, all had thriving chapters. So did Midwestern cities such as Chicago, Denver, and Pittsburgh.

As an astute publicist, Seale understood how to turn official actions and allegations to the BPP's favor. He understood and capitalized on Newton's becoming a chic radical idol. He continued to spread the faith, embellishing Newton's image. The publicity promoted his own image, too. He became much sought-after as a proxy for Newton and also in his own right. Radicals and reformers invited his presence, and he used such invitations to promote the BPP.

Violence at the Democratic National Party Convention in Chicago, Illinois, in August 1968 further propelled Seale to national attention. In the wake of various melees and what was dubbed a "police riot," Mayor Richard J. Daley directed to rout a protest rally with upwards of 10,000 demonstrators, Seale found himself under federal grand jury indictment with others who became known as the Chicago Eight. The central charge was conspiracy to violate what perversely was part of the Civil Rights Act of 1968. Called the Anti-Riot Act, it criminalized crossing state lines with the intent to incite a riot. After his trial opened in September 1969, Seale's courtroom shouting against the injustice and racism of the proceedings led U.S. District Court Judge Julius Hoffman to order him bound and gagged and eventually to sever Seale's trial from what then became the Chicago Seven.

Seale faced serious problems in Chicago, but not there alone. In August 1969, officials in New Haven, Connecticut, filed charges connecting Seale to the kidnapping and murder of Alex Rackley, a New York BPP member and suspected FBI informer whose mutilated body turned up in the Cogninchaug River near Middlefield, Connecticut, two days after Seale spoke nearby at Yale University in New Haven. Police charged Seale with being present at Rackley's torture and with ordering his murder.

The FBI had heavy hands in prosecuting Seale in Chicago and in Connecticut. Four carloads of heavily armed FBI agents and local police had arrested Seale in Berkeley, California, in August 1969. The agents then took him for arraignment before a U.S. commissioner and charged Seale with flight from Connecticut to avoid prosecution. When Seale posted bond on his $25,000 federal bail, San Francisco police re-arrested him on the Connecticut kidnap and murder warrant. The orchestrated events, including the Connecticut charges, smacked of a setup to railroad Seale, defense attorney Francis J. McTernan told reporters. The lawyer pointedly asked how Seale could be guilty of fleeing to avoid prosecution when he knew nothing of the Connecticut charges until the FBI pounced on him in Berkeley.

U.S. marshals extradited Seale from California even while his attorneys were in court arguing the invalidity of federal custody. The feds took Seale first to Chicago. In March 1970, they delivered him to Connecticut Superior Court in New Haven. California attorney Charles R. Garry, who had defended Newton in the Frey shooting, defended Seale with associated counsel from Connecticut lawyer David N. Rosen.

Seale's trials in Chicago and in New Haven made him a *cause célébre*. Not only an FBI bull's-eye but a public spotlight seemed fixed on him. His book *Seize the Time: The Story of the Black Panther Party and Huey P. Newton*, published in January 1970, fed attention. The prosecutions stirred a frenzy. A 1970 May Day celebration brought 12,000 demonstrators to New Haven streets to support Seale and his fellow 8 Black Panthers then awaiting trial. Leslie M. Seale, Bobby's wife, became a frequent speaker at protest rallies.

Seale and Newton appeared to swap places in mid-1970. Just as Seale led "Free Huey" rallies while Newton was on trial, Newton now led "Free Bobby" rallies while Seale was on trial. Newton had gained release from his prison sentence in the California Men's Colony at San Luis Obispo in

May 1970 when the California Court of Appeals for the First District overturned his manslaughter conviction because the trial judge failed to instruct the jury properly on Newton's defense. (California subsequently dropped its case after two mistrials.)

Seale's trial in Connecticut eventually paired him with Ericka Huggins, the 23-year-old BPP Connecticut organizer. The proceedings produced extenuated theater that further raised Seale's and Newton's celebrity amid rallies that combined anti-racist and antiwar protests with Viet Cong flags flying next to "Free Bobby" banners. Legal maneuverings dragged the case from 1970 into 1971. Jury selection itself took four months. Points large and small became heated issues for court debate. Whether prison officials could force Seale to shave his inch-long goatee while awaiting trial became a point of extended court hearings, for example. Seale sat in administrative segregation for more than three months at Connecticut's State Correctional Center in Montville because he refused to shave as prison regulations demanded.

In May 1971, after 22 days of testimony the New Haven jury of seven whites and five blacks finally began deliberations. When the eight women and four men appeared deadlocked, Connecticut Superior Court trial Judge Harold M. Mulvey in a startling and controversial decision not only declared a mistrial but dismissed all charges against both Huggins and Seale. Public outcry clashed in declaring the outcome both a travesty and a triumph of justice. It sickened BPP opponents and thrilled BPP supporters.

The dismissed charges in New Haven did not set Seale free. He remained jailed, facing a four-year criminal contempt of court conviction Judge Hoffman had imposed in Chicago, exercising summary powers under Rule 42(a) of the Federal Rules of Procedure. In 1972 the U.S. Court of Appeals for the Seventh Circuit reversed the contempt convictions. By then Seale had spent parts of almost three years imprisoned. Like Newton, who was imprisoned from late October 1967 to May 1970 on charges that failed to hold up under legal scrutiny, Seale had been snatched away from developing the BPP at a crucial time.

Focused on staying alive and getting out of jail at least distracted Newton and Seale. Others in the BPP took over parts of its operation and significant expansion. Members became used to directions from other than Chairman Seale or Minister of Defense Newton. Minister of Information Eldridge Cleaver had especially garnered a following. His 1968 best-selling book *Soul on Ice* and his being the presidential candidate on the Peace and Freedom Party's 1968 slate focused considerable attention on him. Yet, on the run from U.S. law enforcement, he had exiled himself to Cuba and then Algeria to avoid prosecution stemming from an April 1968 shoot-out that left two Oakland policemen dead. A rift in the BPP became undisguisable in developments surrounding 21 pro-Cleaver Black Panthers indicted in New York City in April 1969 for conspiracy to commit murder and arson. Newton expelled the 21 in February 1971. When Elaine Brown became BPP chairman later that year, sexist resistance to her leadership further split Panthers.

Dissention in BPP ranks resulted in large part from the continuing FBI assault. Also the FBI fomented friction between the BPP and other black radical organizations, especially with Ron Maulana Karenga's Organization Us. Something of a rivalry already existed among Seale, Newton, and Karenga. All had been students at Merritt College. Their organizations clashed violently in January 1969 as the BPP and Us competed for dominance at the University of California at Los Angeles campus.

Sharp public focus on Seale and Newton made each a celebrity apart from the BPP, which appeared sadly sinking in social significance in the 1970s. The BPP's expanded agenda continued to embrace highly relevant issues in black communities. Its anti-drug campaign, illustrated by the BPP's 1970 pamphlet "Capitalism Plus Dope Equals Genocide," showed its currency. Yet shifting from its hard-core black nationalism to more Third World reach with Marxist-Leninist emphasis on class struggle rather than racism thinned BPP support. Waning radicalism and growing political conservatism further cooled public ardor for the BPP even while it remained warm to Newton and Seale as celebrities.

The two rode publicity waves on the lecture circuit and in publishing. Seale's 1970 *Seize the Time* continued to be hot. Newton's 1972 book *To Die for the People: The Writings of Huey P. Newton*, which future Nobel Prize-winner **Toni Morrison** edited, neatly summarized the BPP's origins and objectives. Newton's 1973 *Revolutionary Suicide* provided provocative autobiographical context for the BPP movement. In 1978 came *A Lonely Rage: The Autobiography of Bobby Seale.*

The BPP's founding pair appeared fixed as cult figures by the mid-1970s. They would continue as public figures even as the national mood changed with the Watergate scandal that resulted in President Richard M. Nixon resigning in August 1974, the official end of the U.S. Vietnam War in 1975, and the economic slump that closed the 1970s. Newton persisted in the 1970s with his formal education. He earned a bachelor's degree from the University of California, Santa Cruz, in 1974 and a PhD there in 1980. His doctoral dissertation, "War Against the Panthers: A Study of Repression in America," resounded with his analysis of U.S. social control devices. He remained harassed in and out of prison until August 22, 1989, when a 24-year-old black reputed drug dealer gunned him down in Oakland a few blocks from the 1967 Frey shooting. In 1993 Newton's widow, Fredrika, established the Huey P. Newton Foundation, a nonprofit educational organization.

Seale continued with community public service. Using his talents as a publicist he revived his image with his 1987 cookbook *Barbeque'n with Bobby* and became a corporate spokesman for Ben & Jerry's Ice Cream. In 2002 Bobby Seale's REACH Inc. began to pursue community education. It emphasized human rights and promoted projects to combat juvenile delinquency. It continued in its own way creative cooperative community development.

The end was perhaps not what the BPP cofounders envisioned in the 1960s. Yet the radical image Bobby Seale and Huey P. Newton burned into history with the flash of the Black Panther Party they created forever emblazoned them as radical black icons.

Thomas J. Davis
Arizona State University

Donald F. Tibbs
Drexel University

FURTHER READING

Cleaver, Kathleen, and George Katsiaficas, eds. *Liberation, Imagination, and the Black Panther Party: A New Look at the Panthers and Their Legacy.* New York: Routledge, 2001.

Jones, Charles E., ed. *The Black Panther Party Reconsidered.* Baltimore: Black Classic Press, 1998.

Newton, Huey P. *Revolutionary Suicide.* New York: Harcourt Brace Jovanovich, 1973; reprint, New York: Writers and Readers, 1995.

Newton, Huey P. *To Die for the People: The Writings of Huey P. Newton.* New York: Random House, 1972; reprint, New York: Writers and Readers, 1995.

Newton, Huey P. *War against the Panthers: A Study of Repression in America.* New York: Harlem River Press, 1996.

Newton, Huey P., and Erik Erikson. *In Search of Common Ground: Conversations with Erik H. Erikson and Huey P. Newton.* New York: Norton, 1973.

Seale, Bobby. *A Lonely Rage: The Autobiography of Bobby Seale.* New York: Times Books, 1978.

Seale, Bobby. *Seize the Time: The Story of the Black Panther Party and Huey P. Newton.* New York: Vintage, 1970.

U.S. Department of Defense

Barack Obama (1961–)

Barack Hussein Obama was born August 4, 1961, in Honolulu, Hawaii to Barack Obama, Sr. and Ann Dunham. His father was born of Luo ethnicity in Nyanza Province, Kenya. Obama, Sr. grew up herding goats with his father, a domestic servant to the British. Although reared among Muslims, Obama, Sr., eventually became an atheist. Obama's mother grew up in Wichita, Kansas. During the Depression, her father worked on oil rigs, and after the Japanese attack on Pearl Harbor he signed up for service in the U.S. Army. During World War II, Dunham marched across Europe as a member of General Patton's army. With her husband away at war, Dunham's mother found a job on a bomber assembly line. After the war, the Dunhams benefited from the free education provided by the G. I. Bill, bought a house through the Federal Housing Program, and moved to Hawaii.

During the same time period, Obama's father earned a scholarship to pursue his educational ambitions in Hawaii. Obama's parents met as students at the East–West Center of the University of Hawaii at Manoa. After having their first child, Barack Hussein Obama, they separated when he was two years old and later divorced. Obama's father went to Harvard to earn a PhD in economics, and eventually returned to Kenya. His mother married another East-West Center student that she met in school, Lolo Soetoro, from Indonesia. In 1967, the family moved to Jakarta, where Obama's half-sister Maya Soetoro Ng was born. As a young child, Obama attended schools in Jakarta, where he learned the Indonesian language, the language spoken in class.

Four years later when Barack Obama (commonly known throughout his early years as "Barry") was 10, he returned to Hawaii to live with his maternal grandparents, Madelyn and Stanley Dunham, and later his mother, who also returned to Hawaii (she died of ovarian cancer in 1995). As a fifth grader, Obama gained entry to the esteemed Punahou Academy, graduating with honors in 1979. As one of only three black students at the school, Obama experienced his first exposure to racism, and became conscious of his black identity. In his memoir, Obama described how he struggled to reconcile social perceptions of his bi-racial heritage. He had met his African biological father only once, when he was 10 years old, after his parents divorced and before Obama, Sr. died in a car accident in 1982. Obama admitted using alcohol, marijuana, and cocaine during his turbulent teenage years. The love and support of his white maternal grandparents helped him through these years of coming to understand his racial identity.

After high school, Obama matriculated to Occidental College in Los Angeles, studying there for two years. He performed well in college and transferred to Columbia University in New York, where he graduated in 1983 with a degree in political science. After graduation, he worked at Business International Corporation, a company that provided international business information to corporate clients, and NYPIRG. Two years later, Obama moved to Chicago and began work as a community organizer. Obama worked with low-income residents in Chicago's Roseland community and the Altgeld

Gardens public housing development on the city's South Side. During his early years in Chicago, Obama, who said he "was not raised in a religious household," joined the Trinity United Church of Christ. He also traveled to Kenya for the first time to visit relatives and to pay his respects to the graves of his father and paternal grandfather.

After a few years of community organizing in Chicago, Obama decided to attend law school and entered Harvard Law School in 1988. He served as the first African American editor of the *Harvard Law Review*, an elected and prestigious position, and graduated magna cum laude in 1991. Obama returned to Chicago to practice as a civil rights lawyer, joining the firm of Miner, Barnhill & Galland. In addition to practicing law, he also taught at the University of Chicago Law School and helped to organize voter registration drives during Bill Clinton's 1992 presidential campaign. During this time, he wrote an autobiography that was published in 1995 entitled *Dreams from My Father: A Story of Race and Inheritance*. The book was critically acclaimed, and won a Grammy for the audio version of the book. Obama's hard work and public exposure encouraged him to run for the Illinois State Senate as a Democrat. He won election in 1996 to the Illinois General Assembly from Chicago's South Side neighborhood of Hyde Park.

During his years in the State Senate, Obama worked with both Democrats and Republicans in drafting bi-partisan legislation on ethics, expanded health care services, and early childhood education programs for the poor. He also created an earned-income tax credit for the working poor in Illinois. Obama also worked with law enforcement officials, after a number of inmates on death row were found to be innocent, to require the videotaping of interrogations and confessions in all capital punishment cases. In 2000, Obama made an unsuccessful Democratic primary run for the U.S. House of Representatives seat held by four-term incumbent candidate Bobby Rush.

Following the September 11, 2001 attacks in New York, Obama was an early opponent of President George W. Bush's desire to go to war with Iraq. Still an Illinois state senator, Obama spoke out against a resolution authorizing the use of force against Iraq. At a rally at Chicago's Federal Plaza in October 2002, he stated, "I am not opposed to all wars. I'm opposed to dumb wars." He continued, "What I am opposed to is the cynical attempt by Richard Perle and Paul Wolfowitz and other arm-chair, weekend warriors in this Administration to shove their own ideological agendas down our throats, irrespective of the costs in lives lost and in hardships borne." Obama agreed that Iraq dictator Saddam Hussein was a bad person, and that the world would be a better place without him. He disagreed, however, with the position of the executive branch that he posed a threat to the United States or neighboring countries in the Middle East. He argued instead that "the Iraqi economy is in shambles, that the Iraqi military a fraction of its former strength, and that in concert with the international community he can be contained until, in the way of all petty dictators, he falls away into the dustbin of history." Obama predicted that should the United States go to war against Iraq, in the aftermath it would require an occupation "of undetermined length, at undetermined cost, with undetermined consequences."

He predicted that invading Iraq without international support or transparent reason for war would only increase anti-American sentiment through the Middle East and the Arab world, and would "strengthen the recruitment arm of al-Qaeda." The war with Iraq began in 2003, inspiring Obama to run for the U.S. Senate seat vacated by Illinois Republican Peter Fitzgerald. In the 2004 Democratic primary, he earned 52 percent of the vote, defeating multimillionaire businessman Blair Hull and Illinois Comptroller Daniel Hynes.

That summer, Obama gained the invitation to deliver the keynote speech in support of John Kerry at the 2004 Democratic National Convention in Boston. The speech would propel the Senate-hopeful into the national liberal mainstream and would mark the beginning of his immense popularity within the Democratic Party. Obama emphasized the importance of unity, and made veiled jabs at the Bush administration and the diversionary use of wedge issues. "We worship an awesome God in the blue states, and we don't like federal agents poking around our libraries in the red states," he said. "We coach Little League in the blue states, and yes, we've got some gay friends in the red states. There are patriots who opposed the war in Iraq, and there are patriots who supported the war in Iraq. We are one people, all of us pledging allegiance to the Stars and Stripes, all of us defending the United States of America."

After the convention, Obama returned to campaign for his U.S. Senate bid in Illinois, and national media attention followed. His original opponent in the general election, Republican primary winner Jack Ryan, a wealthy former investment banker, withdrew from the race in June 2004, following public disclosure of unsubstantiated sexual allegations by his ex-wife, actress Jeri Ryan. Two months later, diplomat and former presidential candidate Alan Keyes, also an African American, accepted a strategically selected Republican nomination to replace Ryan. In three televised debates, Obama and Keyes expressed opposing views on stem cell research, abortion, gun control, school vouchers, and tax cuts.

In the November 2004 general election, Obama received 70 percent of the vote to Keyes's 27 percent, the largest margin of victory in Illinois history. Obama became only the third African American elected to the U.S. Senate since Reconstruction. After the ceremony swearing him into office on January 4, 2005, Obama embarked on his first effort, partnering with Republican Senator Richard Lugar of Indiana on a bill that expanded efforts to destroy weapons of mass destruction in Eastern Europe and Russia. He also joined forces with Republican Senator Tom Corburn of Oklahoma to create a Web site that tracks all federal spending. He also worked with Democrat Russ Feingold of Wisconsin to eliminate gifts of travel on corporate jets by lobbyists to members of Congress. In addition to working well with others, Obama also voiced important positions individually. He became the first person to raise the threat of avian flu on the Senate floor, to speak out for victims of Hurricane Katrina, to push for alternative energy development, and to champion improved veterans' benefits. During his dedicated work in the U.S. Senate, he also managed to write and publish his second book, *The Audacity of Hope: Thoughts on Reclaiming the American Dream*, in October 2006.

Obama continued to aspire to higher offices of public service. On February 10, 2007, in Springfield, Illinois from the steps of the State Capitol Building, Obama announced his candidacy for President of the United States. The site of Senator Obama's announcement held symbolic meaning because it was also where Abraham Lincoln, in 1858, delivered his historic "House Divided" speech. The location, therefore, was also symbolic not only because it historicized and gave meaning to Obama's message of unity and hope, but because it also signaled just how far the United States and African Americans had come since the era of slavery and Emancipation. Obama's campaign promised progressive change and a fundamental shift in America's political culture. He promised to bring Americans of all persuasions together in the common cause for freedom and democracy, end the war in Iraq, increase energy independence, and provide universal health care. As the U.S. economy plunged into recession and financial crisis between February 2007 and November 2008, moreover, Obama assured a reeling American public that his policies would reverse the nation's economic downturn, and put it back on a stable and prosperous track.

Obama's campaign stunned pundits and political experts during the primary season with his broad-based appeal and fund-raising acumen. He raised a record $58 million during the first half of 2007, and set another fund-raising record with $36.8 million in January 2008, the most ever raised in one month by a presidential candidate in the Democratic primaries. Obama's primary foe during the primaries was the formidable New York Senator, and former First Lady, Hilary Rodham Clinton. Together, Obama and Clinton waged an epic battle for the Democratic nomination, as Obama and Clinton fought to be the first African American and the first woman nominated for president by a major political party.

Obama proved himself to be a serious contender early in the primary season by tying Clinton for delegates in key primaries, including New Hampshire, and securing more delegates than Clinton in the Iowa, Nevada, and South Carolina elections and caucuses. On "Super Tuesday" in February, a day on which the largest number of states hold primary elections, Obama won 20 more delegates than Clinton. After Super Tuesday, Obama won the 11 remaining February primaries and caucuses. He and Clinton split delegates and states equally in the March 4 contests of Vermont, Texas, Ohio, and Rhode Island; Obama closed the month with victories in Wyoming and Mississippi.

As Obama ascended and revealed himself to be the leading contender for the Democratic nomination, his blackness and U.S. race relations became explicit issues on the campaign trail. Despite his early attempts to present himself as new age candidate who transcended race, he and his staff were forced to address respond to his racial identity and its meaning for a campaign and a society in which race taxed the mind and ensnared the heart. Indeed, even though people of color and progressive whites had made tremendous gains since the era of Jim Crow, race and racism still mattered. Race, as Pauli Murray argued, is "the atmosphere one breathes from day to day, the pervasive irritant, the chronic allergy, the vague apprehension which makes one uncomfortable and jumpy. We know that the race problem is like a deadly snake coiled and ready to strike, and one avoids its dangers only by never-ending watchfulness." Even though Obama did not want to allow his race to define his bid, Americans' racist fixation on his heritage and associations, forced him to address the relevance of race in the 2008 election.

Early in the primary, black people were divided in their support for Obama. Most blacks had long support the Clintons because of their symbolic and strategic support of black Americans, whereas others scrutinized Obama's racial status, questioned his "authenticity," and withheld their support as a result. Black-oriented radio shows, National Public Radio (NPR), scholarly forums, Sunday morning news shows, and religious leaders weighed in on his racial legitimacy. Obama's bi-racial heritage, and his immigrant, Kenyan father, give many so-called native blacks pause. His history did not parallel that of most people of African descent born in the United States. Some African Americans argued, therefore, that only a black candidate whose ancestors were enslaved in the United States, or who experienced the pain associated with our nation's racial past, could genuinely grasp what it means to be black in the United States and represent the political interests of African Americans.

Many blacks believed that this notion was narrow-minded and divisive, and they argued that at time when black Americans, whether by birth or by choice, were moving to channel their collective political capital into a formidable voting block, they could ill-afford to squander time arguing about who was "really" black. A bevy of black scholars, religious leaders, and critics dissected Obama's every move. Harvard law professor, Charles Ogletree, and Arizona State University political science professor, Michael Mitchell, came to Obama's defense, noting that his record, particularly as it related to civil rights, was consistent with the voting patterns of the majority of African Americans. Obama, however, did two critically important things that helped convince the majority of black Americans to support his campaign. He proved himself to be a legitimate candidate, and he delivered a direct and rhetorically remarkable speech on race relations in the United States, entitled "A More Perfect Union," on March 18, 2008.

In the address, Obama spoke directly and candidly about who he was and where he came from:

> I am the son of a black man from Kenya and a white woman from Kansas. I was raised with the help of a white grandfather who survived a Depression to serve in Patton's Army during World War II and a white grandmother who worked on a bomber assembly line at Fort Leavenworth while he was overseas. I've gone to

some of the best schools in America and lived in one of the world's poorest nations. I am married to a black American who carries within her the blood of slaves and slaveowners—an inheritance we pass on to our two precious daughters. I have brothers, sisters, nieces, nephews, uncles and cousins, of every race and every hue, scattered across three continents, and for as long as I live, I will never forget that in no other country on Earth is my story even possible.

Many black Americans decided to endorse Obama candidacy, however, after Bill and Hilary Clinton made public statements that angered blacks and exacerbated white racial fears. Following Obama's victory in the South Carolina Democratic primary, Bill Clinton reminded observes that "Jesse Jackson won South Carolina in '84 and '88," and ultimately failed to secure the Democratic nomination. Many blacks believed that Clinton's implicit message was that the African American vote was insufficient to propel Jackson, Obama, or any other black presidential candidate to the Democratic nomination. Large numbers of blacks also believed that Clinton's message was meant to scare white voters into believing that their ballots would be wasted on Obama, who did not, conventional wisdom held, have a realistic chance of winning. On the eve of the 2008 West Virginia primary, Hillary Clinton angered many black people when she, like Bill Clinton, appealed to working-class white voters by labeling Barack Obama an "elitist." Most African Americans viewed this as a duplicitous way of saying Obama was "uppity": a black person who does not know his or her "place."

As it became increasingly clear that Obama was in position to clinch the nomination, the United States played host to a flurry of racist comments, editorials, and actions directed at Obama, his family, and all African American. On September 4, Republican Representative, Lynn Westmoreland of Georgia, dispensed with subterfuge stating clearly and unapologetically that Michelle and Barack Obama were "uppity." T-shirts that depicted Barak Obama as the monkey, Curious George, were printed and sold in the South, conservative talk-show host, Bill O'Reilly, referenced "a lynching party," when commenting on **Michelle Obama**, conservative pundit, Ed Hill described the fist bump that Michelle Obama shared with Barack Obama after a campaign speech as a "terrorist first jab," Fox News Network ran captions under televised video footage of Michelle Obama that read "Obama's Baby Mama," an "art" exhibit in New York City displayed a giant photograph of the Obamas daughters, Sasha and Malia, under a caption that read "Nappy Headed Hos," and some of his campaign offices were vandalized and defaced with racist epitaphs.

Obama revealed little if any anger or bitterness over these acts, as he continued to vie for the nomination. In April, May, and June, he won North Carolina, Oregon, and Montana, seized the lead in the number of pledged delegates and Superdelegate endorsements, on June 3, passed the threshold to become the presumptive Democratic nominee. On that day, he delivered a passionate victory speech amidst thunderous applause in St. Paul, Minnesota. Clinton, reluctantly, suspended her campaign and endorsed him on June 7, calling upon Democrats to "declare together with one voice right here, right now, that Barack Obama is our candidate and he will be our president."

On Thursday, August 28, 2008, the 45th anniversary of **Martin Luther King, Jr.**'s "I Have a Dream" speech, Barack Obama took the stage on Invesco Field at Mile High Stadium in Denver, Colorado, alongside his running mate Senator Joe Biden of Delaware, and accepted the Democratic Party's nomination for president. In doing so, he became the first African American to lead a major party ticket. On one of the most historic and electric nights in U.S. history, Obama addressed an estimated 84,000 people, many of whom cheered, embraced, and cried as they affirmed Obama's nomination and celebrated the transcended moment. His speech was viewed on television and the Internet by over 38 million people. Even Republican observers hailed the achievement. Former president Bill Clinton described Obama's accomplishment as "a 21st-century incarnation of the old-fashioned American dream. His achievements are proof of our continuing progress toward the more perfect union of our founders' dreams . . . Barack Obama will lead us away from the division and fear of the last eight years back to unity and hope."

> We worship an awesome God in the blue states, and we don't like federal agents poking around our libraries in the red states. We coach Little League in the blue states, and yes, we've got some gay friends in the red states. . . . We are one people, all of us pledging allegiance to the Stars and Stripes.   —Barack Obama

Obama clinched the Democratic presidential nomination and immediately turned his attention to Senator John McCain of Arizona, the Republican nominee for president of the United States, and his running mate, Governor Sarah Palin of Alaska. The contrasts between McCain, an extremely wealthy, surly, 71-year-old, white, former Navy pilot and Vietnam prisoner of war, and Obama, a charismatic, seemingly unflappable black man from a broken home and humble beginnings, who rose from poverty and dislocation to graduate from Harvard Law School and become professor and community organizer in Chicago, went beyond the political to the personal. Obama and McCain waged a large close battle between August and November of 2008, with Obama attacking McCain as out-of-touch and in league with Bush's failed economic and foreign policy, and McCain casting Obama as inexperienced, too liberal, and dangerous by virtue of his extremely limited associations with William "Bill" Ayers, a 1960s radical turned university professor, who engaged in despicable acts of domestic terrorism when Obama was eight years old.

In the end, McCain could not withstand Obama's momentum, message of redemption, and ability to tap into the American people's disappointment and yearning for a new direction. On November 4, 2008, Barack Obama won the election by a wide margin in the popular vote, and slim edge in the

Electoral College, and became the 44th President of the United States. In the process, Obama also became the first African American to serve in the nation's highest office. Several factors led to Obama's victory. The election transpired amidst a severe economic crisis, the United States' involvement in wars in Iraq and Afghanistan, the United States' eroding prestige in international affairs, and a nation that had become increasing polarized, narrow, and cynical about its prospects for a brighter future. Try as he might, McCain did not separate himself from the failed economic and foreign policies of his fellow Republican, the former president George W. Bush, who, by the time he left office, registered the lowest approval ratings in the history of the U.S. presidency. In addition, nearly all African Americans who voted cast their ballots for Obama, and the former Senator from Illinois garnered the majority of young voters, labor, teachers, urbanites, women, and other people of color. His message of changes resonated, and the diversity he embodied gave faith to many that his election would reaffirm the American dreams in ways that the election of McCain never could have.

Most importantly, McCain's Republican base was divided and in some cases in disarray. McCain had long been perceived as a firebrand Republican spoiler, who undermined party unity in the pursuit of his own, often-unpredictable, and centrist brand of conservatism, and his selection of the largely unknown, inexperienced, and highly ideological Sarah Palin merely alienated more of his Republican peers, particularly "intellectual Republicans," who bristled at Palin's unimpressive pedigree, naïveté, and lack of "ideas." The consequence of these perceptions and actions was the defection of moderate and intellectual Republicans, and right-leaning Independents, for the Democratic ticket. Unlike McCain, Obama was able to unite his party behind his candidacy. Despite its testy 2008 primary and internal divisions, virtually all wings of the Democratic Party threw their support behind Obama, even if they had reservations. To garner the support of moderate Republicans and conservative Democrats, Obama touted personal responsibility, called attention to the problems associated with of single parent households and "deadbeat dads" in black America. Furthermore, he handled each potential problem in his campaign proactively and with unsurpassed grace.

The implications for Obama's victory are yet to be determined, what is certain, however, is that the United States is a different country than it was in 1865, 1900, or 2000. Chattel slavery was abolished in 1865, de jure segregation was outlawed in 1954, black American's citizenship and voting rights were affirmed in 1965, and white supremacy, though still alive and malignant, is usually denounced publically and looked upon as antiquated and utterly reprehensible. The ability and eagerness of Americans of all backgrounds to embrace each other as fellow human beings and citizens exists in the twenty-first century in ways that were unimaginable only one generation ago. The election of Barack Obama as President of the United States is a substantive measure of this seismic shift in American life, and his very person is the embodiment of the

United States' promise. Indeed, during the fall of 2009, Obama was awarded the Nobel Peace Prize for galvanizing millions in the interest of peace and prosperity for the nation and the world's diverse populations. His rise to power, however, was not the final chapter in African American history, nor did it eradicate the many problems that confronted modern black America. African American history endures, and the struggle to fulfill and maintain America's promise for freedom and justice for *all* continues.

Matthew C. Whitaker
Arizona State University

FURTHER READING

Editors of Time-Life Magazine. *The American Journey of Barack Obama*. New York: Little, Brown and Company, 2008.

Ignatius, Idi. *Time President Obama: The Path to the White House*. New York: Time, 2008.

Obama, Barack. *The Audacity of Hope: Thoughts on Reclaiming the American Dream*. New York: Crown Publishers, 2006.

Obama, Barack. *Change We Can Believe in: Barack Obama's Plan to Renew America's Promise*. New York: Three Rivers Press, 2008.

Obama, Barack. *Dreams from My Father: A Story of Race and Inheritance*. New York: Times Books, 1995.

Department of Defense

Michelle Obama (1964–)

Michelle Robinson Obama became the First Lady when her husband, **Barack Obama,** swore the oath of office on January 20, 2009. They are the first black couple ever to reside in the White House. She is the mother of Malia and Sasha, the sister of Craig Robinson, and the daughter of Fraser and Marian Robinson. She has attracted considerable admiration among some, and considerable vitriol and disgust from others. She grew up on the South Side of Chicago in a working-class home before attending Princeton and Harvard and earning her law degree. Her primary message as First Lady is to working women and mothers, because she had many years balancing work and family life as a lawyer and hospital administer before the presidential campaign. She keeps her husband grounded with her sharp wit and intelligent mind, and is a stable force for her girls.

The Robinson roots go back to South Carolina. The first Fraser Robinson was born there in 1884 in Georgetown County. The county was filled primarily with African Americans, freed people and their descendants, many of whom were relatives and children of Robinson. His eldest son, Fraser Robinson II, left the family stomping grounds and moved to Chicago sometime before 1934. His sister soon joined him in the Windy City. They moved north during the Great Migration, when many African Americans travelled north in search of greater freedoms and industrial jobs. Five hundred thousand moved to Chicago alone. He gave the family name to his first son, Fraser Robinson III, who was born in Chicago. When he grew up, Fraser III took a government job at the water treatment plant; he worked his way up from janitor to operating engineer. In his early thirties, Fraser was diagnosed with multiple sclerosis, an autoimmune disease that attacks the brain and spinal cord. On the campaign trail, Michelle frequently spoke about how much of a role model Fraser was for his family. As he slowly lost control of his body, he nevertheless kept going to work every day, using canes and then crutches to support himself.

Fraser, full of jokes, and his wife Marian Robinson brought a lot of laughter and joy into their home. Marian, one of seven children, was a native of Chicago. She talked to her children constantly, making them feel as if they were intelligent enough to talk to an adult and ask any questions they wanted. She treated them seriously, but also with humor. Sometimes, in the middle of a spanking, she would just start laughing and laughing.

The Robinsons settled in a small apartment on the South Side of Chicago, a vibrant area of black families, small commercial businesses, the University of Chicago, and Mayor Richard Daley's home neighborhood. Daley controlled Chicago through the Democratic Political Machine from 1955 to 1976. The Machine handed out government jobs in return for political activities. Fraser Robinson worked as a volunteer precinct captain, urging people from his area to vote according to the machine. Chicago politics were nasty while Michelle was growing up, which left a sour taste in her mouth for the whole enterprise. Not only did it seem like the purview of the cold and power-hungry, but she did not believe that politics could really change anything.

In 1962, the Robinsons welcomed Craig and then a year and a half later, on January 17, 1964, Michelle LeVaughn. She received her middle name from her father's mother. The two children formed a tight bond, punctuated with frequent bouts of competition. Michelle raced along, trying to keep up with her brother in all things—sports, academics, and music. She was always known as Craig's sister until the presidential campaign when he became Michelle's brother. During the campaign, she described him as her mentor, friend, and protector. Craig and Michelle had aunts, uncles, and cousins scattered throughout the city, giving them a strong sense of security.

Michelle learned early about her family's dedication to education. Her parents were willing to forgo many luxuries and even necessities so that she would get a superior education. For high school, Michelle attended a magnet school many miles from her house. She rode the elevated train, or "el," and then walked through an industrial area of town to get to campus. The magnet school was self-consciously devoted to integrated education. It tried to enforce a quota that divided the school among black, white, Hispanic, and Asian students. The racial composition of Chicago made achieving the percentages difficult and the administration had to actually lower standards for white students to bring more into the school. Students got along quite well in the school, fostered cross-racial friendships, and excelled academically.

In Michelle's memories, she struggled through high school, without very much support from the school. None of her high school teachers remembered her as a student when journalists sought them out. In contrast to her brother, who could ace tests without studying, Michelle had to work very hard for her every success. Craig remembered that when he went out to play basketball after school, Michelle would stay at her desk studying. After he came home and plopped in front of the TV, she would still be studying. Though Michelle was not encouraged to pursue an Ivy League education by her high school counselor, she was determined to follow her brother to Princeton. He had heard about the school at a summer basketball camp and was recruited to attend in part because of his skills on the court. In 1981, Michelle joined her brother, the basketball star, on the New Jersey campus.

Princeton cultural life shocked Michelle. She was not shy exactly, but kept her own counsel. The school had only been accepting black students for a few years when she arrived. Women had not been welcomed for much longer. Of all the Ivies, Princeton had the reputation as the most Southern, the longest to resist admitting black students, and the least likely to accommodate their needs. The campus had an informal dormitory system where students all chose individual "eating houses" in which to sleep, eat, and socialize. Because the administration did not oversee these houses, they could not force them to accept black students, yet a major part of university life took place within their halls. When Michelle arrived, black students were given a special orientation. The students were not quite sure what message to take from this session. Were they only supposed to socialize with each other?

Faced with persistent unfriendliness by white classmates, and questions about their qualifications, Robinson and the other black students did tend to stick together. Students questioned them about their SAT scores, because many white students were convinced by rumors about Affirmative Action that the black students were not actually qualified to be on campus. Newspapers were slipped under black students doors with op-eds arguing that their presence was bringing down the intellectual atmosphere of the university. To shelter themselves from these barbed comments, black students spent a lot of time at the Third World Center, a building designed to give students of color a gathering space on campus. On one episode of "The View," Michelle and Whoopi Goldberg discussed how difficult it was to be among the first black students on campus, expected to be a diversity-teaching tool for all the white students. This was a common experience for the first generation entering educational institutions after the Civil Rights Movement opened many of them to black students.

Taking all her thoughts and confusions about the previous three years into consideration, Robinson buried herself into her senior thesis for her sociology degree (she minored in African American Studies). As one of the few documents she wrote which is now on public record, this piece has been dissected repeatedly in the media. It was a nuanced bit of research examining how black Princeton alumni related to their communities, particularly the working-class and poor, after they had left for college. Robinson structured her questionnaire around her own troubled musings on how she would reintegrate into the South Side after all her experiences over the previous three years. Would she be able to relate to those who stayed in Chicago? Michelle felt as though she had to choose between the culture of the South Side and the culture of the Ivy League. By her graduation, she decided she would try to unite both.

Those sentences where Robinson favorably described Black Nationalism have drawn the greatest scrutiny. She had been able to succeed at Princeton because of the strong support network of black students. It is not surprising that she would speak positively about blacks supporting each other, but later conservatives, in particular, questioned whether she and her husband would govern all of the United States, or just African Americans. A major Google search for Michelle Obama is still, nine months after the inauguration, "Michelle Obama racist." Criticisms such as these tended to patently ignore the whole of Robinson's life, during which she has consistently urged people to unite across racial lines, and focus only on those pieces that most easily fit the feared persona.

After graduating cum laude in 1985, Robinson headed to Harvard Law School. Again, those around her were skeptical that she could make it into such a prestigious school. She not only was accepted, but excelled. She joined several clubs and worked for the legal aid bureau, a student-run law firm helping poor people with legal cases. During one summer, Robinson returned to Chicago to intern at the Sidley Austin law firm. She had been directed there by a white Princeton professor. After graduation, she joined the law firm as a junior associate.

Robinson had a mixed experience during her years in corporate law. Her boundless energy demanded a job that was more rigorous than those usually accepted by new lawyers. She wanted to be working on the law, not just gathering data for older lawyers. She also desired a position in a part of law that would keep her interest. Her assignment to the marketing department, intellectual property group satisfied for a time; that group was more congenial and relaxed than the rest of the firm. The older lawyers in the department recognized her abilities and gave her more challenging work. Even so, she did not like the corporate way of life and felt unfulfilled. Even though other lawyers enjoyed her company, she did not make any lasting friendships.

One relationship started at the law firm did survive. Barack Obama arrived in 1989 as a summer associate after his first year at Harvard Law. His reputation long preceded him. Robinson began to hear rumors about the black man who had been on the editorial board of the *Harvard Law Review*, a major accomplishment. She heard, too, about his unusual upbringing by a white mother and grandparents in Hawaii. Dismissing the rumors, she figured he would be weird and would fail to live up to her high standards. In interviews, Craig has frequently commented on his sister's incredibly high expectations of the men she dated. While she would go out and have fun, she rarely found anyone worthy to bring home to meet the parents. She expected someone with ambition, an intellect to match her own, and someone who reminded her of her beloved father.

Obama did not immediately win her over upon his arrival. The law firm assigned her as his mentor, and she thought it would be inappropriate to date him. Plus, she wondered how it would look if two of the very few black members of the firm started dating. He, however, took one look and decided she was worth pursuing. He asked her out several times without acceptance, but she did not long resist the full force of his charisma directed her way. Her colleagues noticed that the two would sit in her office, focused entirely on each other and the conversation at hand, their whole bodies subtly conveying their total interest in the other. Obama chose his early date spots with care, very conscious of what he wanted to convey to this intelligent, beautiful South Sider. The first movie he took her to was **Spike Lee**'s "Do the Right Thing," letting her know that even though he grew up far from the center of black America, he understood the issues and emotions that spoke to black Americans. On another date, he took her to a church basement, where a group talked about how to help their community. She sat still, captivated by the passion for the poor pouring out of this Harvard-educated man.

Robinson and Obama soon realized how much they complemented each other. Where she was funny and vivacious, he was quiet and thoughtful. Where she saw the details, he saw the big pictures; he dreamed immense dreams and she figured out how to make them reality. Robinson was rooted in the South Side black community (a community Obama had purposefully chosen to become part of), with a stable emotional upbringing, and large extended family. Obama had an exotic background with many fascinating international trips, yet shared the moral character of her father. At the same time, their intellects, their senses of humor, and their driving passions meshed. They realized they could endlessly challenge each other to work harder to make the world a better place, becoming and achieving more together than they could individually.

To be sure about her own opinions of the young lawyer, Robinson took him home to meet her parents and her brother. At one point, she asked if Craig would take him out back and challenge him on the basketball court. The Robinsons as a family had long believed that a man's character was revealed in how he took the court. Returning sweaty and happy, Craig assured his sister that this was a good man.

Obama returned to Harvard to finish his law degree and they carried on a long-distance courtship. In the interim, Robinson began to rethink her position in the law firm. When two people very close to her passed away, she began to ponder the purpose of her life. In 1990, her Princeton classmate Suzanne Alele died of cancer. Throughout her young life, Alele followed her passions and never acted in a certain way just because it was expected of her. Then in 1991, Fraser Robinson III finally succumbed to MS, dying in the car on the way to work. Barack wrote in his first book that Fraser was "as good and decent a man as I've ever known" (B. Obama, *Dreams from My Father*, 439). In her DNC speech, Michelle said she "felt his presence in every grace filled moment of my life" (M. Obama, DNC speech). Thinking about the lives of these two dear ones, Robinson decided she wanted a career motivated by passion instead of by money. She wanted to devote her life to helping her community in Chicago, not protecting the intellectual property of corporations. Some of her concern arose out of a persistent feeling of guilt about making so much money when many of her cousins and childhood friends could barely get by.

Robinson contacted several different individuals throughout Chicago, looking for work that she would find more meaningful. In 1991, Valerie Jarrett responded to her letter and invited Robinson to interview for a position in Mayor Richard M. Daley's administration (this was the son of the machine politician Richard J. Daley who controlled Chicago during Robinson's childhood). She was ready to give Robinson the job by the end of the interview, but Robinson said she wanted to talk to her fiancé about it. She suggested that the three of them get dinner and discuss the position. Obama wanted to ensure that his future wife found a position that she would thrive in, and that would also not conflict with their values. By the end of the dinner, Obama assured Jarrett that she had passed his test.

Before they were married, Obama took Robinson to Hawaii and Kenya to meet his family. His grandparents in Honolulu expressed admiration for the Chicagoan in their own ways—his grandfather said she was quite a looker and his grandmother noted with approval how practical she was. Obama realized how many traits that his grandmother and future wife shared, especially their Midwestern practicality. His grandmother and half-siblings in Kenya also took to Michelle almost immediately. She picked up many Luo words right away and did her best to learn the culture. Family and friends came from all over the world to attend the union of Michelle Robinson and Barack Obama on October 3, 1992, in Chicago. They were wed at Reverend Jeremiah Wright's Trinity United Church of Christ, which had been the church that brought Obama into the faith and which the couple attended regularly. Members of the wedding party wore Kente cloth and tuxes.

Married life surprised Michelle at first. On some level, she had been expecting the life her father and mother had. Fraser Robinson got up every morning, went to work, then came home and had dinner with the family. Marian stayed with the children, volunteered in the community, and made the family meal each evening. Michelle and Barack were constantly busy, too busy for a regular meal time each evening. Barack practiced law, taught at the University of Chicago, and continued to cultivate relationships with Chicagoans from all walks of life. When money troubles threatened, he began the book which became *Dreams from My Father*. Each evening he would sequester himself in his cubbyhole and write. Michelle served as assistant commission of planning and development in the mayor's office before founding the Chicago branch of Public Allies, an AmeriCorps program that trained young people for public service. The people she worked with remembered her intense desire to deliver concrete outcomes, and also her willingness to pitch in. If anything was needed, even licking envelopes, she was ready to do it, with a smile and a joke. She exhorted the allies to break down the walls between races and ethnicities, a theme she would return to again and again on the campaign trail.

In 1996, Barack Obama suggested that he run for an Illinois Senate seat. Michelle was very concerned at first. She did not want her husband to have the good sucked out of him by politics, but Barack brought up all the changes he could bring to the community she grew up in. Whenever she objected to one of his plans, he brought up her responsibility to her community. She supported him during his run for the Illinois State Senate, even while pregnant with their first child. Malia was born in 1998. She traveled and gave speeches on his behalf, and when he won, she had to adjust to seeing her husband even less often because he commuted to Springfield several days a week. In 2000, he lost the race for a seat in the U.S. House of Representatives; Michelle hoped that would be the last race, but Barack suggested he run for the U.S. Senate four years later. When he won the U.S. Senate seat in 2004, they bought a condo in Washington, DC, for Barack for the weekdays. He commuted home on the weekends; Malia and Sasha (born 2001) got used to their father being only a weekend father, though he made an effort to attend their recitals and games. Marian Robinson stepped into some of the gap, helping Michelle with the girls while the younger woman continued to pursue her career. Robinson teased her daughter about the strict rules they kept, including only an hour of television, organic foods, and bedtime at 8:30 p.m.

Michelle successfully balanced a working life and a vibrant family, in part because she had such an extended network of support. She rejoiced at the birth of each daughter and at her role as a mother, indeed often citing motherhood as her primary identity, but also did not give up her administration jobs outside of the home. Knowing how hard it is for many modern American women to find this balance, she has taken up the work/life balance as a part of her goals for her time as First Lady.

In the interim, Robinson Obama had moved from Public Allies to the University of Chicago Hospital, where she was hired as a community liaison. It was her job to convince the uninsured to use community clinics rather than the emergency room as their primary care facilities. She set up several health fairs offering free care to school children and administered a wide network of people working in the same efforts. Some newspapers in Chicago criticized the way she expanded the program, saying that it was salaries and budgets like hers that made hospital costs so large. When she joined a couple of corporate boards in the wake of Barack's election to the U.S. Senate, she received more criticism for using Barack's position to her own advantage.

Not particularly mushy or romantic, the Obamas keep each other their toes. After Michelle had been bugging Barack to propose for a few months, he finally took her to a nice dinner and had the servant deliver an engagement ring with the dessert. At her look of shock, he said, "That kind of shuts you up, doesn't it?" (Mundy, 114). Just before Barack went on stage to give the speech at the 2004 Democratic National Committee that brought him into national spotlight, Michelle whispered in his ear, "Just don't screw it up, buddy!" (Mundy, 171). She had spent the day calming him down and giving him support as opinions were thrown at him from all sides. Michelle frequently told interviewers about Barack's failure to pick up his socks, and about asking him to pick up ant traps on the way home from a major political fundraiser. Their children began grounding them even more as they have aged. After Michelle woke up the girls to tell them that their dad had secured the Democratic nomination, 10-year-old Malia said that yes, her dad as the first black president would be a major milestone, but so would Hillary's presidency have been for women. Malia, the moment after Michelle went backstage after delivering the DNC's keynote address in 2008, told her mom that they needed to have a slumber party that night. Though they are funny and straightforward, they also represent romance to many in the nation. After the inauguration, many women started to talk about how they wished their husbands would look at them the way Barack still looks at Michelle, or hold them during a dance the way Barack held Michelle during the inauguration balls—as if she was entirely precious and the center of his whole world (even though he was, in concrete fact, the center of the entire world's attention at that moment).

When Barack first broached the subject of running for president, Michelle was again concerned about the way it would affect their family. There were few things that could take Barack away from his wife and daughters more than a seat in the U.S. Senate, but a campaign for president was certainly one of them. She also knew it would be a strain on their finances, even though their income had been raised substantially by the sales of *Dreams of My Father* following the 2004 DNC speech. She also worried about Barack's safety. Powerful black men have often been targeted for assassination in the United States' history. Indeed, Alma Powell asked that her husband, **Colin Powell**, not run for president precisely because she feared he would be killed. Michelle finally decided, though, that the future of her children's world was more important than her concerns about her family, legitimate though they were. She did ask that the secret service be assigned to Barack early in the campaign, which it was.

Robinson Obama kept her hospital position at first, but as the campaign heated up, she resigned from her position at the hospital and started on the campaign trail full time. Her mother looked after the girls during the week, giving her the freedom to travel and give speeches. Some of Michelle's statements brought fierce criticism, though she accepted it as one part of the campaign. Most of the criticism arose when she compared the world she lived in with the experience of African Americans in the past.

The Obamas slogged through a very long primary campaign against Hillary Clinton, which was only finally decided a few months before the Democratic National Convention. They then faced down John McCain, pulling ahead when the economy took a dramatic downturn in September 2008. Obama won the election in November and was sworn in January 2009. Michelle, Malia, Sasha, and Marian Robinson moved into the White House. It was the first time that his family had joined Barack in Washington, DC. They rejoiced that they would finally be able to be together in the mornings and the evenings, even though the presidential schedule is highly demanding.

Michelle is listed as a member of the Administration on the whitehouse.gov Web site, along with President Barack Obama, Vice President Joe Biden, Dr. Jill Biden, and the Cabinet. She devotes her energies as First Lady to supporting military families, women's work/life balance, and promoting national service. Michelle Robinson Obama is trying to decide what kind of a First Lady she wants to be. She has retreated somewhat from the limelight since the inauguration, paying attention to her girls' education and normalcy, while giving speeches in support of her husband's programs. One has to wonder just how vast Fraser Robinson's enthusiasm would be if he could see his daughter now.

Lauren L. Kientz
Michigan State University

FURTHER READING

"The Ellen Degeneres Show," September 8, 2008. http://www.youtube.com/watch
   ?v=ngqUSlVQfbY.
Mundy, Liza. *Michelle: A Biography.* New York: Simon & Schuster, 2008.
Obama, Barack. *The Audacity of Hope: Thoughts on Reclaiming the American
   Dream.* New York: Crown Publishers, 2006.
Obama, Barack. *Dreams from my Father: A Story of Race and Inheritance.* New York:
   Three Rivers Press, 2004.
Obama, Michelle. Democratic National Committee Speech, August 25, 2008. http://
   www.youtube.com/watch?v=790hG6qBPx0.
"The View," June 18, 2008. http://www.youtube.com/watch?v=59twO1fJwtQ.

The Illustrated London News Picture Library

Jesse Owens
(1913–1980)

Born in abject poverty in the American South, James Cleveland Owens, better known as Jesse, rose to become one of the true icons in the world. Owens became known not just in the world of sports, but renown for his humanitarian and friendship endeavors in many parts of the world. At the height of his fame and glory, Owens won four gold medals in the 1936 Berlin Olympic Games, setting or tying the Olympic and/or world record in all four events. Owens's athletic success during the games' uncertain and tense international political climate was amazing, especially when compared to the historic statistics of the Olympics at that time.

On September 12, 1913, Oakville, Alabama sharecropper Henry Cleveland Owens and his family awaited the arrival of their then twelfth member. Emma Fitzgerald Owens delivered that new family member, who was named James Cleveland Owens. James, called J. C. by his family members, was the 10th of the eventual 11 children in the family. While Henry worked as a sharecropper, Emma took in other people's clothing for sewing and ironing to help with extra money in the household. Jesse, like most of the other children in the house, picked cotton to help with the household income. Still the family of four girls, seven boys, and mother and father lived in extreme poverty.

Illiteracy was the normal ingredient for sharecroppers of Henry Owens's generation throughout Alabama, and most other regions of the South, and he was no exception. Due to their illiteracy, most sharecroppers, including Henry, never used money for food, even when shopping at the grocery store in Oakville. The sharecroppers' inability to read, write, or do math did not help them. Henry and Emma Owens made sure that their children would not meet with the same fate of illiteracy that captured Henry's existence. With the laws of the nation changing, openly allowing for all children—including African Americans who were previously excluded from formal education in some states—to be formally educated, the Owens couple stressed the importance of reading and a formal education to their children.

Jesse admitted that he was the only one of the boys who did not help with much of the hard work during those sharecropping days. It was not because he was too young or small that he did not help; it was because of his illness. Each winter he became ill with pneumonia, and at least twice believed he was close to death. His family consequently kept him away from the hardest tasks. Emma was the person given credit by Jesse for pulling him through those terrible periods of illness for him in Oakville.

Henry Owens decided that his life would have to change, if not for himself, at least for his wife and children. He summoned his family and told them of his intent to move the family to the North. The new environment of the North was indeed a very strange one for Jesse. He and his family moved from an environment where the races were isolated from one another to one that was open and free by comparison. Jesse now attended a school with white children. While living in Oakville, he could barely go to school, and attending school with white children was simply out of the question. Many of the white students that

Jesse went to school with may have been new to this city and country themselves, but they nevertheless were white and in the same schools as him—a totally new experience for Jesse. Integrated schooling was not a possibility open to him in Oakville. He also wore clothing that covered his body. This was new to Jesse, as he always wore either second-hand clothing that were his older brothers, or clothing that was so worn they were more rags than clothing. With the Northern climate of Cleveland being much colder than that of the Southern climate of Oakville, clothing that covered more of the body was appropriate. So, together with his shyness, Jesse's desire to please his teachers and other adults led him to allow himself to be called Jesse rather than J. C., because he didn't want to cause a problem.

Jesse's participation in athletics was to change the world in which he lived. He was able to obtain a high school education, and then received a scholarship to one of the largest colleges in the country. This opportunity came at a time when segregation was still the law of the land. While attending Fairmont Junior High School in Cleveland, Jesse met the man who would become his coach, mentor, and longtime friend, Charles Riley. Owens learned a great deal about life as well as track and field from Riley, including good manners.

During his senior year, Owens ran a time of 9.4 seconds for the 100-yard sprint, and ran the 220-yard sprint in 20.7 seconds. His 100-yard dash time tied the national record and placed Owens on the national scene. Owens's times gave him national acclaim and recognition. After graduating from high school, he accepted an offer to attend The Ohio State University in the fall of 1933. According to Jesse,

> There were no athletic scholarships at Ohio State University then, not even if your marks had been good, nor even if you'd learned how to use your legs to become the world's fastest human the year before.

Jesse also worked part-time to make ends meet and asked that his father be given some type of employment by the university.

Owens's popularity was very evident from the beginning of his career at Ohio State. By 1935 he had really come into national prominence. The National Intercollegiate Championships of 1935 left no doubt that Owens was no longer just a national figure, but was well on his way to world acclaim. The fans attending the Championships, held at the University of Michigan, saw Owens break five world records and tie another in about an hour's time period. All of this was done while he was injured; he had wrestled with one of his fraternity brothers, and strained a back muscle and sustained other bruises and injuries. On May 25, the day of the 1935 Championships, he was hurting so badly that he couldn't properly warm-up for his sprints or field events. Only moments before the 100-yard race did Owens's back pain subside enough to allow him to participate.

His performance was truly amazing. His times and distances were: 9.4 seconds in the 100-yard sprint and 26′ 8 1/4″ in the long jump, which set a world record that remained unbroken for 25 years. This was also Jesse's only attempt in the long jump for the day. In the 220-yard straight-away sprint, his time was 20.3 seconds, which was also a world record. Jesse won the 220-yard low hurdles in 22.6 seconds—another world record. This day in track and field was truly amazing for the fans, the sport of track and field, and Owens himself.

On July 5, 1935 Jesse Owens married Minnie Ruth Solomon. The wedding took place in the living room of Minnie's parents' home in Cleveland, Ohio. The newlyweds also were to spend their wedding night at Minnie's parent's home. From this partnership three children were conceived, all girls. Gloria Shirley Owens (Hemphill), the firstborn of Owens's daughters, was born on August 8, 1935. Beverly Owens (Prather) is the middle daughter, being five years younger than Gloria. The youngest of the Owens daughters is Marlene Owens (Rankin). These girls were raised to be strong and independent individuals.

> I always loved running—it was something you could do by yourself, and under your own power.   —Jessie Owens

The year 1936 saw a few amazing activities that appeared to be sporting events, but turned out to be far more political and social in nature than they were athletic. Owens's accomplishments were among these activities. **Joe Louis** (boxing), Max Schmeling (boxing), and Marty Glickman (track) were participants in other activities that year that made sports become more political than in earlier years.

Jesse, along with all of the U.S. athletes competing in the Olympics, had to deal with Avery Brundage. Brundage would soon become the president of the U.S. Olympic Committee and one of the most powerful men in track and field worldwide. Brundage was also, reportedly, a Nazi sympathizer during the time that Hitler's Aryan Supremacy Doctrine was propagandized by the Nazi Party.

Owens faced a number of competitors at the 1936 Games. Eulace Peacock, the only person to regularly have beaten Owens in the 100, was unable to pose a threat to Owens because of injuries. Neither Peacock nor Ralph Metcalfe, Jesse's main competitor in the 100-meter run, were threats to Owens in the long jump. Peacock was injured and did not make the Olympic team at all. Metcalfe placed second to Owens in the 100-meter trials final, but still was a part to the team traveling to Berlin. Owens, having set four world records and tied at least one other, was talked about and sought out by the press more than any of the other U.S. Track and Field athletes. Ralph Metcalfe and Eddie Tolan were also known because of their participation in previous Olympic competitions. In fact, before Owens broke the world record in the 100-meter sprint, the record was held by Metcalfe and Tolan. The Olympic Games of Berlin, however, represented the first time the world press could personally meet this new reigning record holder of five world marks.

At this time, Der Fuhrer, Adolph Hitler, and his Nazi Party ruled Germany with a propaganda machine seldom seen anywhere. The major premise of this propaganda was that of Aryan Supremacy and the notion that Germans were "the master race." This was a political ideology that encompassed all aspects of life, including athletic superiority. In fact, various reports remarked that Hitler claimed that the U.S. team had to bring "black auxiliaries" to compete against the superior Nazi Aryan Team. Further, the official Nazi newspaper slandered the African American team members. The newspaper account also suggested that an assistant to Foreign Minister Joachim von Ribbentrop complained to Martha Dodd, daughter of the U.S. Ambassador to Germany William E. Dodd that "the United States had taken unfair advantage by letting non-humans, like Owens and other Negro athletes, compete in the Olympic Games."

The early part of the 1936 Olympic Games began just as Hitler and others knowledgeable about worldwide track and field competition expected they would. The Germans dominated their competitors before home crowds which placed 110,000 people in attendance at the stadium. Although blacks had participated in the Modern Olympic Games almost from its inception, support for their inclusion came mainly from European nations. As far as African Americans were concerned, the 1932 Los Angeles Games were the first to have any significant number of African Americans participate. While most everyone knew of the black athletes the Americans brought, and that some of those athletes (Owens, Metcalfe and Johnson) held or were performing at world or Olympic record times and distances, they would be considered no threat, by reporters, track and field knowledgeable officials and many athletes, to the Aryan athletes assembled by Hitler and his propaganda machine.

During the first day of competition, Hitler observed the early success of the German athletes. He summoned these early German victors, reported to be Tilly Fleischer and Hans Woellke, to his personal box at the stadium and congratulated each of them publicly. This public congratulatory greeting, in his personal box, was done for a Finnish athlete who was victorious also. Next to win a gold medal at those Games was Cornelius Johnson, an African American high jumper. Though Hitler was known to arrive and depart from the competitions at approximately the same time each day, he decided to depart the rest of that day's competition before any congratulatory offers could be extended to Johnson. Explanations and rumors about Hitler's early departure were plentiful. One explanation stated that Hitler arrived and departed on a set schedule each day, and on the day that Johnson won his gold medal it was time for the Fuhrer's departure when the medal presentation ceremony was to take place. It was also rumored that he left because he would not publicly congratulate a black man due to his dislike of Jews and blacks. The rumors soon twisted to the notion that it was Jesse Owens who was snubbed by Hitler. The rumors persisted so long, and were published by so many news organizations, that many believed it to be true. Owens's comments also left readers believing that he indeed was the person slighted by Hitler. In truth, if anyone was snubbed, it was Cornelius Johnson. However, make no mistake about it, Jesse Owens's performance at the 1936 Olympic Games was a major blow to Hitler's Aryan supremacy doctrine as well as to the racial arrogance of the United States.

Jesse Owens, being the most noted of the African American Track and Field participants, was clearly the favorite of the people in attendance. Jesse performed from August 2 to 9 and did extremely well. At the Berlin Games Jesse Owens won the 100-meter sprint, tying the Olympic record of 10.3 seconds. In one heat, he actually broke the world record with a time of 10.2, but this time was disallowed because of the wind speed at his back. He also won the 200-meter sprint, setting a new Olympic record of 21.1 seconds; won the long jump, setting a new world and Olympic record with a leap of 26′ 5 1/4″; and was a member of the world and Olympic record-setting 400-meter relay team with a time of 39.8 seconds.

The U.S. 400-meter relay team was quite controversial, despite its success. According to reports, the coaches pulled the sprinters of the team together on the day of the relay and told them that there would be changes to the team participating in the Olympics. The original members of the team were Glickman, Stoller, Foy Draper and Frank Wykoff. Head coach Lawson Robertson of the University of Pennsylvania told the sprinters that he had heard rumors that the Germans were holding their best sprinter back for the 400-meter relay, so he and the other coaches decided to make changes so that the best possible team was on the track. Of course this was not an accurate statement—in head-to-head competition Glickman and Stoller beat Draper and Wykoff—but Robertson used this excuse just the same to justify the changes. Robertson removed Glickman and Stoller, both Jews, from the team and replaced them with Owens and Metcalfe, both African Americans. Remember that in the eyes of Hitler, the black man was only slightly less offensive to himself and the Nazi party than was the Jewish man. With Robertson's changes, the U.S. team had given Hitler exactly what he had been looking for: a way to prevent Jewish athletes' participation in the Berlin Games.

This particular coaching maneuver meant that Jesse Owens was able to win his fourth gold medal at those Games. Of course the two removed runners were not happy about the move. Neither were Metcalfe and Wykoff truly happy about the move when they reminisced about the incident many years later. One fact remained, however, that Brundage, Robertson, Cromwell, and Hitler could not hide: Jesse Owens.

Fatigued from all the post-Olympic competitions the athletes were asked to participate in throughout Europe, along with receiving very little rest, having no money, and being homesick for his wife and kid, Owens decided not to take part in any further post-Olympic competitions on the advice of his coach and mentor Larry Snyder. Owens instead made plans to return to the United States to take advantage of several reported financial opportunities presented to him.

Avery Brundage, now president of the Amateur Athletic Union (AAU) and American Olympic Committee (AOC), had his assistant Daniel Ferris announce that the AAU was suspending Jesse Owens from all further amateur competition in the United States. Snyder and Owens insisted that the AAU had no right to force participation from Owens and other athletes who did not sign agreements to participate in such competitions. According to AAU guidelines, participation could only be demanded from athletes who had already signed agreements to participate. The AAU for its part said that Owens was insubordinate and did not fulfill his obligations, because he did not participate in the post-Olympic meets as required by the contract agreement with the AAU.

When Owens returned to the United States, he had to face the press and its questions about his suspension and the reported snubbing they believed he received from Hitler. As uncomfortable as it might have been, Owens answered the questions to the best of his ability. His major new dilemma was in what direction he now should take his life. He was reportedly offered significant sums of money to appear with different entertainers, white and African American. Owens's decisions included whether to turn professional, go back to college, take one of the entertainment offers, or try to be reinstated with the AAU. Surprisingly, Owens received a great deal of verbal support from the press in the form of articles and radio commentary, but nothing tangible. Many of these reporters, along with members of the National Collegiate Athletic Association (NCAA) felt that the AAU was indeed manipulating the Olympic athletes, especially Owens and the other athletes who went to Germany. The AAU received all the financial rewards while the athletes received nothing for themselves. Notice should be made, however, that the NCAA and the AAU were at major odds with one another by this point in their existence. So, any support Owens received from the NCAA must be looked upon with a very critical eye. The support Owens received from Ohio State was also very suspect. With the exception of Larry Snyder, the main interest of the university's personnel was in the windfall that would be reaped by them if Owens were to return to school to participate in the track and field program.

Owens in the meantime lived life to its fullest. Since he had just returned to the United States, Owens was participating in one parade after another, most of them in his honor. He and his wife received gifts and accolades from city officials, friends, and well-wishers. Shortly after returning to New York to be in a parade honoring all of the returning U.S. Olympians, Owens signed a contract with professional agent Marty Forkins. Owens soon found out that almost all of the offers for financial reward that he received while in England from various sources were either bogus or reneged. Two that remained open to him were from members of the African American community: one from a vaudeville entertainer, and the other from Wilberforce University, a Historically black College and University (HBCU) located in Ohio.

The IRS placed a lien on Owens's income for back taxes in 1938. By that time Owens had also ventured into a number of other endeavors, including managing a barnstorming basketball team, managing a regional softball team, racing against professional baseball players, taking part in vaudeville acts, opening a dry cleaning business, and of course having a foot race with heavy-weight boxing champion Joe Louis. Owens's athletic endeavors brought fame and fortune, to some degree, to his life. They also brought swindlers and problems with the government over taxes. As anyone who has had any tax encounters with the IRS will attest, few win such high-profile disputes with the government. In other words, Jesse did not prevail against the IRS.

Jesse's introduction to the black athletic revolution, occurring in the United States and elsewhere during the 1960s, took place on the international stage of the Olympics. His reaction to the tactics utilized and the platform chosen (Olympics) to bring attention to black athletes' plight was not unusual. In fact, many segments of the African American community, including the athletes themselves, disagreed on the appropriateness of the tactics used by each arm of the Civil Rights Movement. The major difference was that the athletes' rejection of Owens came on the world stage of the Olympics, and from a chief organizer of the movement, Professor Harry Edwards. Most others from the African American community who disagreed with the revolution did so in anonymity. No one from the African American community would have accepted the insults from Edwards. To be blunt, Edwards was not the only American, black or white, to direct insults at Owens. Several others took the time and effort to put their beliefs of Owens's behavior in writing, addressing him as "boy," "slave," and an Uncle Tom. Owens weathered those indignations with his usual class and dignity, and later even came to understand some of the rationale being used by the "Blackthinkers" for their revolutionary actions.

> The battles that count aren't the ones for gold medals. The struggles within yourself—the invisible, inevitable battles inside all of us—that's where it's at.
> —Jessie Owens

Many individuals, African Americans and whites, did not give credit to Owens for his community involvement, which included working with youth and building what might be deemed positive relationships between the races at home here in the United States. Owens worked with underprivileged youth on a regular basis as a board member of the Chicago Boys' Club. At times this organization served as many as 1,500 youth. Owens also worked for more than five years as the Sports Specialist of the State of Illinois Youth Commission. He was the United States' Ambassador of Sports, which was a position that he was appointed to by officials from the U.S. State Department. Owens even served as special representative of President Dwight Eisenhower to the 1956 Olympic Games hosted by Australia.

After returning home from the 1936 Olympic Games and dealing with various personal difficulties, Owens traveled extensively on behalf of both public and private entities. He made motivational speeches to professional organizations, business meetings, church functions, parent-teacher organizations, and youth groups. In addition to working as an ambassador and consultant,

Owens also had a track and field athletic competition, named by others, in his honor. In 1976, President Gerald Ford presented Owens with the highest civilian honor, the Medal of Freedom. President Jimmy Carter also presented Owens with the Living Legend Award in 1979.

After his death, Owens' family and friends created the Jesse Owens Foundation (J.O.F.). The organization's goal is "to promote the development of youth to their fullest potential." The organization was also established to "perpetuate the ideals and life's work of this Olympic champion and humanitarian." The establishment of the J.O.F. has served as a great resource for research on and about Owens. In addition to serving as a wonderful research source, the J.O.F. has provided funding to assist more than 350 students as they attend college. The scholarships for educational funding are allotted through the Ruth and Jesse Owens Scholars Program at The Ohio State University, which helps with funding for students who accept admission to that institution. Jesse Owens is one of the true icons of sports no matter what era or which athletes he is measured against.

James R. Coates
University of Wisconsin, Green Bay

FURTHER READING

Baker, William J. *Jesse Owens: An American Life*. New York: The Free Press, 1986.

MacAloon, John J. *This Great Symbol: Pierre de Coubertin and the Origins of the Modern Olympic Games*. Chicago: The University of Chicago Press, 1981.

Mandell, Richard D. *The Nazi Olympics*. Urbana: University of Illinois Press, 1987.

Owens, Jesse, and Paul G. Neimark. *Blackthink: My Life as Black Man and White Man*. New York: William Morrow and Company, 1970.

Owens, Jesse, and Paul G. Neimark. *I Have Changed*. New York: William Morrow and Company, 1972.

Rurup, Reinhard. *1936 The Olympic Games and National Socialism*, 2nd ed. USZ, Wien: Institute F. Sportwissenschaften, 1996.

Sears, Edward S. *Running Through the Ages*. Jefferson, North Carolina and London: McFarland & Company, 2001.

Library of Congress

Rosa Parks (1913–2005)

Rosa Parks was born Rosa Louise McCauley on February 4, 1913, in Tuskegee, Alabama. Recognized as the "mother of the modern-day civil rights movement," Parks refused to relinquish her seat on a Montgomery, Alabama, bus on December 1, 1955—the action that led to the famous Montgomery Bus Boycott. Many believe that Parks refused to surrender her seat because she was tired from a hard day's work. For Parks, this was far from the truth. Parks was tired of the racist and discriminatory treatment African Americans endured in a Jim Crow society. Rosa Parks' action on that historic day in December led to a successful boycott, the eventual integration of Montgomery's public transit system, and the hiring of African Americans as public transit operators. The significance of Rosa Parks' action cannot be underestimated. Her decision that day signaled the beginning of a new era in the African American Freedom Struggle—the era of nonviolent direct action activism.

Although born in Tuskegee, Alabama, Parks grew up with her grandparents in Pine Level, Alabama. Prior to Parks' birth, her mother, Leona, was a school teacher and her father, James, was a skilled brick and stonemason. Having married in 1912, James and Leona McCauley moved to Tuskegee to take advantage of employment opportunities and because this city, at the time, was known to have amicable race relations. It was also the location of **Booker T. Washington**'s Tuskegee Institute. Although Parks was too young to remember anything about living in Tuskegee—she was only two years old by the time they left—her life was still influenced by the importance of education and its role in African American uplift.

Affected by the boll weevil's destruction of many Alabama farms in the early 1900s, the McCauley's moved to Abbeville, Alabama where they were supported by James McCauley's family. The extremely crowded quarters and her inability to get along with the McCauleys caused Rosa McCauley's mother's to move, pregnant with her second child, back to her home town of Pine Level. Additionally, Leona McCauley desired to return to her parents and to the career she had pursued prior to Rosa's birth, teaching. Rosa McCauley's father desired to take his chances expanding his building business. These desires led to their separation.

After the move back to Pine Level, Leona McCauley became an itinerant teacher of sorts, travelling long distances to teach at African American schools. Because of this, Rosa McCauley and her younger brother were mostly raised by their grandparents because Rosa's father had disappeared from their young lives by then. Life for young Rosa McCauley was not carefree. From a very early age, she felt the grip of white supremacy and understood the violence that permeated life for African Americans in the United States. In the 1920s after World War I, the Ku Klux Klan, a white supremacist organization that terrorized African Americans, made a vicious comeback. As a result, Rosa McCauley remembered her grandfather going to sleep in a rocking chair with a shotgun in his lap. She also remembered that she and the other grandchildren used to sleep in their clothes just in case a confrontation would force them to have to run from the house (Brinkley, 2000, 23–24).

Growing up in that atmosphere, Rosa McCauley understood early on that U.S. society, at that time, dictated a certain place for African Americans. This place was most certainly separate and unequal from whites. Separate drinking fountains, bathrooms, seating facilities, schools, and neighborhoods. McCauley, however, would not internalize this and demonstrated this when she was a young girl. No more than 11 years old, one day Rosa McCauley was walking down the street in an all-white neighborhood. A young white boy was riding his bicycle and upon seeing McCauley tried to force her off the sidewalk. Unafraid of the white boy and the white woman standing by watching the boy assault her, McCauley retaliated by pushing the boy. She soon learned the white woman was the boy's mother. In fact, the woman told Rosa McCauley that she " 'could put [McCauley] so far in jail that [McCauley] would never get out again for pushing her child.' " McCauley told the woman " 'he had pushed [her] and that [she] didn't want to pushed, seeing that [she] wasn't bothering him at all' " (as quoted in Brinkley, 2000, 28). Southern society dictated that McCauley accept this treatment without any recognition of the wrongdoing of the little white boy. However, McCauley stood up for herself. She attributed her outspoken nature to growing up with her grandfather who was certainly unafraid of racist whites.

At the age of 11, Rosa McCauley began attending Montgomery Industrial School for Girls. This school was one of the few places African American girls could receive quality education as there were no high schools for African Americans in the state of Alabama until 1946. Modeled after Booker T. Washington's Tuskegee Institute, the white founders of the industrial school, Alice White and Margaret Beard, focused on useful skills for African American girls—cooking, sewing, and housekeeping. Although this curriculum was limited, McCauley would later go on to say that she learned much more than domestic science—" 'what I learned best . . .,' " she said, " 'was that I was a person with dignity and self-respect and that I should not set my sights lower than anyone just because I was black . . . We were taught to be ambitious and to believe that we could do what we wanted in life' " (as quoted in Brinkley, 2000, 35).

Armed with this knowledge, McCauley decided she would become a teacher. After finishing the 8th grade at the Industrial School for Girls, she attended Booker T. Washington High School where she completed 9th grade and then to Alabama State Teachers College where she finished the 10th and 11th grades. Rosa McCauley's studies would be stopped short because her of grandmother's illness and the need to return to Pine Level to take care of her. After the death of her grandmother, Rosa McCauley returned to Montgomery, enrolled back in school, and got her first job, but soon she would have to quit again—this time to take of her ailing mother. She " 'was not happy about dropping out of school either time . . . but it was [her] responsibility to help with [her] grandmother and later to take care of [her] mother. [McCauley] did not complain; it was just something that had to be done' " (as quoted in Brinkley, 2000, 37).

Not able to finish school because she needed money to support herself, McCauley began doing domestic work for white families as well as doing sewing jobs for people in her spare time. In her leisure time, McCauley also was an active member of Saint Paul African Methodist Episcopal Church because Christianity was a central part of her life. Pretty soon, political activism would become central as well—but not before she met and fell in love with her husband, Raymond Parks. Raymond Parks was born on February 12, 1903 in Wedowee, Alabama. Ten years her senior, Rosa McCauley would, at first, ignore Raymond Parks's requests to court her. Eventually she acquiesced and they went out. On the second date Raymond Parks asked McCauley to marry him and they were married in December of 1932.

Raymond Parks, a member of the National Association for the Advancement of Colored People (NAACP), was heavily involved in an important instance of activism at the time: protesting against the false imprisonment of the Scottsboro boys—a group of African American male youth accused of raping two white women aboard a cargo train car. Raymond Parks organized a legal defense fund on behalf of the Scottsboro Boys and also served on the National Committee to Defend the Scottsboro Boys. Although Raymond Parks was very involved in the national effort to help the Scottsboro Boys, he feared his wife's involvement because of the danger of violence that threatened those who lent their support to civil rights efforts. As such, Rosa Parks did not attend any of the meetings—even when they were eventually held in her own house for lack of meeting space. Instead, she stayed on the back porch "with her face buried in her lap" (Brinkley, 2000, 41). Rosa Parks would sit still during the meetings because she " 'was very depressed about the fact that black men could not hold a meeting without fear of bodily injury or death' " (as quoted in Brinkley, 2000, 41).

Radicalized by her husband and his involvement in the Scottsboro case and her belief that change only occurred when one exercised his/her right to vote, Rosa Parks attempted to register to vote three times in 1943 and 1944 before finally being certified in 1945. During the time of Rosa Parks's attempted voter registration, white supremacists used several tactics to prevent African Americans from successfully registering to vote simply because of the color of their skin. Many localities implemented voting requirements that made it near impossible for African Americans to register such as poll taxes, literacy tests, grandfather clauses, and the famous "white primary." Using the "white primary" as a restrictive device, many southerners argued that political parties were voluntary organizations that could restrict their membership, thus denying African Americans the right to vote in primary elections. Despite all of these odds, Rosa Parks kept trying and eventually succeeded in registering to vote.

During the same time in which Rosa Parks repeatedly tried to register to vote, she was also involved in the Montgomery chapter of the NAACP. As the chapter's secretary, she worked with chapter president E. D. Nixon on voter registration drives and staffing the chapter's headquarters. Rosa Parks believed that " 'from the start the NAACP...was about empowerment through the ballot box.... With the vote would come economic improvements. We would have a voice' " (as quoted in Brinkley, 2000, 48). In addition to voting rights, Rosa Parks also worked on another issue of great concern to black Montgomery residents: segregation on the city's busses.

Rosa Parks's undying passion for rights and equality for African Americans was only stoked in 1943—her first encounter with the rude and racist bus driver who would have her arrested 12 years later. James F. Blake was a particularly mean-spirited bus driver in Montgomery, Alabama. He was known for his poor treatment of African American passengers. While city law declared certain sections of the bus reserved for whites—the first ten seats—and for blacks—the rear ten seats—it was left up to bus drivers to decide to whom to allot the remaining middle seats. In November of 1943, Rosa Parks boarded James F. Blake's bus, deposited her money, and proceeded to move to the back of the bus. Parks' first mistake was that she entered the bus from the front and not the back. Parks's reason for entering through the front was that the back section of the bus was already so full with African American passengers that it was near impossible for any additional passengers to enter the bus through the rear stairwell.

Therefore, Parks's decided to do what any reasonable person would, enter from the front. Blake, however, was not very happy with Parks's behavior and "sure enough, the driver glared at her, hand near the holster on his hip, and demanded that she exit the bus and reboard it through the back door" (Brinkley, 2000, 58). Parks's decided that she would not exit the bus only to reboard from the back, especially when bus drivers were known to drive off before African American passengers had a chance to reboard. She told the driver this—her second mistake—and he replied that if she did not comply, she would have to get off his bus. With her refusal, Blake began to force Parks's off the bus by pulling her by her coat sleeve. Without struggling at all, Parks was removed from the bus, but not before dropping her purse and purposely sitting in one of the reserved white seats to pick it up. This further incensed James F. Blake, but he could respond no further after she had exited the bus. After this incident, Parks' decided she would never ride on any bus Blake was driving.

Parks continued her activism after this incident and became even more involved with the NAACP by agreeing to advise the Montgomery NAACP Youth Council in 1949. As advisor to the Youth Council, Parks supported Montgomery youth as they challenged segregation in Montgomery, Alabama. For example, libraries were just one public institution that operated under the "separate but equal" status quo. Underfunded and lacking resources, the

African American library branch had very few books. As a result, African Americans who wanted books requested them from the main library and had them delivered to the African American branch. African Americans, however, were not allowed to simply go the main library and check out books directly. The NAACP Youth Council decided to challenge this practice by going to the main library and requesting service directly. Over and over youth went to the main library, but to no avail—the library never changed its policy. Still, Parks encouraged the youth activists to continue their work because it was important that they made their voices heard. Over the next few years, civil rights activists learned the importance of raising their voices for change.

In 1953, Montgomery African Americans caught wind of a bus boycott in Baton Rouge, Louisiana. The previous summer, the Baton Rouge City Council passed an ordinance that declared that all busses have an open-seating policy. By 1953, policy had not become practice and white bus drivers still enforced segregation on the busses. African Americans in Baton Rouge, under the leadership of the pastor of an African American Baptist church, conducted a week-long bus boycott that gave African Americans a platform to demand change. Baton Rouge activists proved that a boycott could be a very successful form of activism. The moment economic activity was threatened, city officials were quick to listen to the demands of African American activists.

The year 1954 would also be an important year in the civil rights struggle. In May of this year, the Supreme Court declared separate public schools for African American and white children inherently unequal and therefore unconstitutional in the *Brown v. Board of Education of Topeka* case. A huge victory for civil rights activists and especially the NAACP, this case paved the way for the activism that would later occur in the 1950s and 1960s. During the summer of 1955, Rosa Parks attended a Desegregation Workshop at Highlander Folk School, a well-known training institute for civil rights activists. At Highlander Folk School, 42-year-old Parks learned, worked, and shared with other civil rights activists, both black and white.

One of the very few places of integrated training for activists, Highlander was founded in 1932 by Myles Horton in Monteagle, Tennessee. In its early period, the School supported the labor movement and was crucial in educating Tennesseans about labor rights. However, in 1953, Highlander began focusing on issues of civil rights and hired educator and activist, Septima Clark, to direct its Citizenship Schools which not only taught African American literacy skills to pass voter registration tests but also about their political rights.

Parks attended a 10-day workshop at Highlander Folk School. Her time at Highlander was unlike anything she had experienced before. She said, "We forgot about what color anybody was. I was forty-two years old, and it was one of the few times in my life up to that point when I did not feel any hostility from white people. I experienced people of different races and backgrounds meeting together in workshops and living together with peace and harmony" (Parks, 1992, 106). After leaving Highlander, Parks would go back to

Montgomery—leaving the ideal world of Highlander behind. Armed with the knowledge, experience, and belief that integration could work, Parks returned to Montgomery and back to her life of work and activism.

While Parks continued her work with the NAACP, there was also another organization that sought to rid Montgomery of segregation as well. The Women's Political Council, founded by Mary Fair Burks in 1946, was a group of African American female activists whose primary focus became integration of the city busses after one of its members experienced poor treatment on the city busses. After presenting petitions to the Montgomery City Council requesting better treatment on the busses and having these petitions ignored, the WPC began planning a boycott. Before a boycott could begin, there needed to be a test case—or a person who could be a plaintiff in a court case. Before Parks's sat down on December 1 and refused to get up, two other young women did so. Both Claudette Colvin and Mary Louise Smith were rejected as test cases because of their so-called questionable backgrounds. While both of these young ladies sat down and refused to get up, inciting a response by angry white bus drivers, neither of these women's cases were backed by the NAACP. Claudette Colvin was rejected because at the time she was pregnant out of wedlock. Mary Louise Smith was rejected because NAACP and WPC leaders thought her father was an alcoholic. Any woman who would be accepted as the test case "would have to be above reproach, have a good reputation, and have done nothing wrong but refuse to give up her seat" (Parks, 1992, 111).

Although Parks's knew the type of woman desired as a test case, that was not reason for action that day. In fact Parks asserted, "I was in on the discussions about the possible court cases. But that was not why I refused to give up my bus seat to a white man on Thursday, December 1, 1955. I did not intend to get arrested. If I had been paying attention, I wouldn't even have gotten on that bus" (Parks, 1992, 113). But she did get on the bus and her action on that day sparked one of the most important events in the history of the Civil Rights Movement.

In 1955, Parks worked as a tailor at Montgomery Fair Department Store. On the evening of December 1, 1955 she had just gotten off or work. Preoccupied with the planning of an upcoming NAACP workshop, when the bus pulled up the stop, she just got on, not noticing that the bus driver was James F. Blake. She boarded the bus, paid her fare, and proceeded to an open seat in the front section of the area reserved for African Americans. The bus continued on its journey, with Parks seated. However, a few stops later, the bus stopped and more passengers boarded. As white passengers filled the remaining seats in the section reserved for whites, Blake turned to the African Americans in the row Parks was sitting and demanded the seats. At first all four of the African American passengers refused to move. Demanding they move a second time, the other three African American passengers moved, but not Parks. She felt if she got up, nothing would ever change for African Americans in Montgomery. In fact, Parks felt "The more we gave in and complied, the worse they treated us"

(Parks, 1992, 115). Tired of this treatment, Parks did not budge. Those who have told Parks's story have falsely attributed the reason for her refusal to get up that day. Parks corrected this misattribution in her memoir. She asserted, "People always say that I didn't give up my seat because I was tired, but that wasn't true. I was not tired physically, or no more tired than I usually was as the end of a working day. I was not old, although some people have an image of me as being old then. I was forty-two. No, the only tired I was, was tired of giving in" (Parks, 1992, 116). And so when Blake finally saw that Parks would not give up her seat he told her she would be arrested. Her response was, " 'You may do that' " (Parks, 1992, 116).

The police came and Parks was arrested. The arresting officers did not mistreat Parks, but picked up her belongings and escorted her to the waiting squad car. They first stopped at City Hall to fill out paperwork, and then proceeded to take Parks to the City Jail. Parks was put in a cell with two other African American women. After requesting her legally required phone call several times, Parks was finally able to call home and ask her husband to pick her up from jail. Before Raymond Parks arrived at the jail, E. D. Nixon and Attorney Clifford Durr, along with her longtime friend, Virginia Durr arrived to bail her out. As soon as Raymond Parks arrived, everyone left to return to the Parks's home. While there, Nixon asked if Rosa Parks would be the plaintiff in the case against the bus company. Before agreeing, Parks discussed the issue with her husband and her mother. At first Raymond Parks was against the issue but he soon agreed and thus Rosa Parks became the test case the NAACP was looking for.

Nixon was ecstatic to have Parks as the test subject because she was just what was needed. Nixon said Parks was " 'honest, she was clean, she had integrity. The press couldn't go out and dig up something she did last year, last month, or five years ago. They couldn't hang nothing like that on Rosa Parks' " (Parks, 1992, 125). Parks agreed. She said, "I had no police record, I'd worked all my life, I wasn't pregnant with an illegitimate child. The white people couldn't point to me and say that there was anything I had done to deserve such treatment except to be born black" (Parks, 1992, 125). While the NAACP was planning its case for Parks upcoming court appearance on December 5, 1955, the Women's Political Council was also busy.

Under the leadership and activism of JoAnn Robinson, the president of the organization, the WPC put into action what it had been planning all of those years—a bus boycott. Overnight, Robinson photocopied 35,000 fliers to publicize the boycott of the city's busses—an act that would coincide with Parks's trial date. Robinson's fliers asked every African American "to stay off the busses Monday in protest of the arrest and trial" of Rosa Parks. In addition to the boycott that was planned for Monday, African American ministers in the city also planned a mass meeting for that evening.

On December 5, as African Americans boycotted the busses, Rosa Parks went to her trial. Represented by Charles Langford and Fred Gray, Parks pled not guilty of violating segregation laws. James F. Blake testified against her as well as a white women who claimed there was a seat further back that Parks could have taken. Not called to speak on her own behalf, Parks was convicted of violating segregation laws and was fined $10 plus court costs. Intending to appeal the verdict, Parks, her husband, and her lawyers left the trial and went to the mass meeting at Holt Street Baptist Church.

The main item on the mass meeting's agenda was whether or not to continue the bus boycott. Some felt that African Americans could not sustain the boycott, especially given that so many of them depended on the city's busses to get to work, school, and across town. Also, many felt that continuing the boycott was dangerous to all involved. However, after Dr. **Martin Luther King, Jr.**'s speech, there was no question that the boycott would be continued. Dr. King, the newly appointed president of the new Montgomery Improvement Association (MIA) addressed the church: " 'There comes a time when people get tired. We are here this evening to say to those who have mistreated us so long that we are tired—tired of being segregated and humiliated; tired of being kicked about by the brutal feet of oppression' "(as quoted in Parks, 1992, 138). After King's remarks, another minister, Reverend Ralph Abernathy, presented the list of demands the MIA would submit: "1) Courteous treatment on the busses; 2) First-come, first-served seating, with whites in front and blacks in back; 3) Hiring of black drivers for the black bus routes" (Parks, 1992, 140). The crowd signified their agreement by standing and cheering.

On December 8, the ministers of the MIA presented their demands to the city commissioners and they were rejected. The boycott continued as the MIA continued to negotiate with city officials. African Americans in the city of Montgomery sustained the bus boycott by walking and by creating an intricate private cab system. Middle-class African Americans who owned cars donated their cars to the cab pool that transported mostly working-class African American women to their destinations across town. Many African Americans suffered economically from their participation in the boycott. Employers fired workers who participated. Raymond Parks eventually quit his job and Rosa Parks was fired for no "apparent" reason. In February 1956, Fred Gray filed a civil action lawsuit with the U.S. District Court against the mayor of the city of Montgomery, W. A. Gayle. After nine months tied up in the courts, the Supreme Court ruled in *Gayle v. Browder, et al* that segregation on busses was unconstitutional. The Supreme Court ruled that the integration would begin on December 21, 1956. The MIA agreed that the boycott would continue until this date.

After the Bus Boycott, Rosa Parks moved, with her husband to Detroit, Michigan where they lived the rest of their lives. While in Detroit, she worked as a staff person for U.S. Representative John Conyers. She also continued her activism by attending the 1963 March on Washington and the 1965 Selma to Montgomery March, both historic events in the history of civil rights activism. The late 1970s were particularly hard for Parks as both her mother (1977) and husband died (1979). She was honored, however, by the NAACP in 1979 when they presented her with the Spingarn Medal for outstanding achievement. In the 1980s she received many awards including the Martin Luther King Jr. Award (1980); the Martin Luther King Jr. Nonviolent Peace Prize (1980); the Service Award from *Ebony* Magazine (1980); and the Eleanor Roosevelt Women of Courage Award (1984). In 1996, she received the Presidential Medal of Freedom. Three years later she received the Congressional Gold Medal.

Rosa Parks passed away on October 24, 2005. The entire nation mourned the loss of Parks and she was lain in state at the U.S. Capitol Rotunda, the first woman and second African American to receive this honor. Rosa Parks is a symbol of freedom in U.S. society. When asked to name those who have stood for justice in the midst of injustice, Rosa Parks is always mentioned. However, many only know very little about the life of the woman who refused to relinquish her seat that day. Influenced by her grandfather and never one to sit idly by in the face of injustice, Parks did something that was always in her nature: stood up—by sitting down—for a cause she thought was right. And, as a result, her action sparked one of the most influential social movements in the history of the United States.

Crystal Marie Moten
University of Wisconsin-Madison

FURTHER READING

Brinkley, Douglas. *Rosa Parks*. New York: Penguin Lives, 2000.

Morris, Aldon D. *The Origins of the Civil Rights Movement: Black Communities Organizing for Change*. New York: The Free Press, 1984.

Olson, Lynne. *Freedom's Daughters: The Unsung Heroines of the Civil Rights Movement from 1830 to 1970*. New York: Touchstone Books, 2002.

Parks, Rosa, with Jim Haskins. *Rosa Parks: My Story*. New York: Scholastic, 1992.

Robinson, Jo Ann Gibson. *The Montgomery Bus Boycott and the Women Who Started It: The Memoir of Jo Ann Gibson Robinson*. Edited by David J. Garrow. Knoxville: The University of Tennessee Press, 1987.

Shipp, E. R. "Rosa Parks, 92, Founding Symbol of Civil Rights Movement, Dies." *The New York Times*, October 25, 2005.

AP/Wide World Photos

Sidney Poitier (1927–)

Sidney Poitier was born in Miami, Florida, on February 20, 1927. Rising from a childhood of poverty and obscurity, Poitier became one of the best-known actors of the twentieth century. During the 1950s and 1960s, Poitier was the only African American actor to achieve lead roles in major motion pictures. He was the first African American actor to win acclaim solely for his acting abilities. The characters Poitier portrayed were a move away from the stereotypical and often racist depictions of African Americans in earlier films such as *Birth of a Nation* and *Gone With the Wind*. Poitier's work was recognized in 1963 when he became the first African American to win an Academy Award for Best Actor in a Leading Role. In 1967 and 1968, with three back-to-back major motion picture releases, Poitier was the top actor at the box office. Poitier's roles helped gain momentum for the burgeoning Civil Rights Movement, as well as establish a place for African Americans as serious actors within Hollywood.

The road to Hollywood did not begin easy for Poitier. Poitier's parents, Reginald and Evelyn, were small-time tomato farmers from Cat Island in the Bahamas. Poitier was born premature while his parents were in Miami selling their produce. Convinced that his newborn son would soon die, Reginald set about making funeral arrangements and bought a tiny casket. Evelyn, however, went to a fortune-teller where she was told not to worry about her new son, as he would live and grow up to be an important man. After making Reginald dispose of the casket, the family settled into temporary residence in Miami until their son was well enough to travel home to Cat Island. The luck of Poitier's premature birth in Miami granted him automatic citizenship to the United States, which would be beneficial later in his life.

Poitier grew up in Arthur's Town, Cat Island, Bahamas, and was the youngest of Reginald and Evelyn's seven surviving children. The family lived in a small house built by Reginald, and everyone participated in farming. While the family grew tomatoes for sale in Florida, they also maintained a small subsistence garden which provided much of their food. Poitier grew up amidst poverty, and he often wore flour sacks that his mother bleached and sewed into clothing. The family had no electricity.

While life on Cat Island was relatively primitive compared to the United States, Poitier found his childhood there to be ideal. When not helping on the farm, Poitier was fishing, exploring the island, or daydreaming. His island explorations helped foster his athletic physique, while his constant daydreams facilitated his imagination and his capacity for creating characters and acting. Poitier also found Cat Island ideal due to its lack of racism. While a few whites had residences in Arthur's Town, the color of one's skin was not tied to power as it was in the United States or other regions of the Caribbean. Many prominent members of the community were black. Poitier thus grew up without the surroundings of discrimination.

The Great Depression hit Cat Island hard and in 1938 the Poitiers moved to Nassau to try and make a better life. Instead they found continued poverty, as the soil proved infertile for tomatoes. Evelyn spent her time crushing boulders into gravel to sell. Poitier's older brother spent time in jail for attempted extortion, and Poitier himself began to turn to a life of petty theft, even spending a night in jail for stealing corn. In Nassau, Poitier had his first experience at a movie theater and also his first exposure to racism and discrimination. In January 1943, due in part to Poitier's constant petty crimes, his father sent him to live with his older brother in Miami, Florida. Poitier, now 15 years old, arrived in Miami with a new set of clothes and three dollars cash.

Poitier arrived as an American citizen but immediately found himself out of place in U.S. society. His skin color, his Bahamian accent, and his lack of education made life difficult from the start. In Miami, Poitier learned painful lessons about racism, including an incident while working as a delivery boy. Poitier attempted to deliver a package to the front door of a house, only to have an irate white woman tell him that he must use the service entrance. Not understanding, Poitier simply left the package on the porch. That night, the Ku Klux Klan marched through his neighborhood searching for him.

Poitier worked a series of menial jobs in Miami but was unhappy with his life. He attempted to run away to Tampa twice, but both times his brother brought him back to Miami. Eventually, Poitier found work in a resort outside Atlanta and, after six weeks of work, had enough money to leave. In the spring of 1943, Poitier boarded a bus bound for the farthest place he could find: New York City.

In New York, Poitier's prospects continued to look grim. Although he delighted in the subways of the city, he found himself unable to afford room and board. After spending some time sleeping on rooftops, Poitier found work as a dishwasher and rented a tiny room. In August of 1943, during the riots in Harlem, Poitier was shot in the leg by police as he ran out of a department store that was being looted. As winter approached, Poitier found himself cold and alone in the city with no winter clothes.

Attempting to escape the freezing streets, Poitier decided to join the Army. He lied about his age and joined a medical company stationed at a veterans' hospital on Long Island. Poitier learned that the army was no respite from discrimination, and he loathed the strict discipline of army life. Rather than admit he was only sixteen, Poitier chose instead to pretend to be insane to gain a Section 8 and release from service. After throwing a chair at a superior officer, Poitier landed in a military hospital where he spent time with a psychiatrist in regular weekly sessions. Narrowly avoiding a court martial, Poitier was released from duty in 1944.

Although he was desperate to return home to Nassau, Poitier did not have the money he needed to travel. A letter to President Franklin Roosevelt asking for a hundred dollars went unanswered. Poitier returned to his work as a dishwasher until an ad for actors caught his eye. Poitier assumed acting would be a job like the many he already had, and went to his first audition at the American Negro Theater (ANT) in 1945. With no formal theater experience or training,

Poitier's first audition was a complete catastrophe. He was asked to leave in the middle of the audition, with the helpful suggestion that he find work as a dishwasher. Crushed by the implication that he would never achieve anything above washing dishes, Poitier was determined to prove everyone wrong. Rather than accept the idea that he was worthless, he would become an actor.

Poitier needed to develop an American accent, and he spent countless hours listening to the radio and mimicking the voices of the announcers. He worked hard to improve his literacy and read as often as possible between his work as a dishwasher. Six months after his initial rejection, Poitier returned to the American Negro Theater for a second audition, this time for a place in their School of Drama. Despite another lackluster audition, the school accepted him, primarily due to the dearth of male students. After a three-month trial period, his talents had not improved enough and Poitier was asked to leave. Instead, he worked out a deal to work as the janitor for the school in return for one more semester.

Poitier's first role was as an understudy for **Harry Belafonte** in the play *Days of Our Youth*. When Belafonte missed a private production for a Broadway producer, Poitier got his chance. He was offered the role of Polydorus in the all-black cast production of *Lysistrata* on Broadway. He also gained a role in an ANT production of *You Can't Take It With You*. In 1948–1949 he joined a touring production of *Anna Lucasta*, before taking the stage in the play *Freight*. Poitier was on his way to a career in acting.

At the end of 1949, Poitier auditioned for a role and made a screen test for Twentieth Century Fox. He was given the lead role in his first film, *No Way Out*, and headed to Hollywood. *No Way Out* cast Poitier as Dr. Luther Brooks, an African American professional in a racist world. On the set, Poitier learned Method acting from the director, Joseph Mankiewicz. *No Way Out*, which came out in theaters in 1950, was one of the first movies to cast an African American as an educated professional. *No Way Out* created a nonthreatening image of African Americans that challenged the way white Americans viewed race, and moved beyond the stereotypes of sex-crazed men and bumbling fools portrayed in earlier films.

In early 1950, Poitier gained a screen test with director Zoltan Korda, who was preparing to direct the film version of Alan Paton's novel, *Cry, the Beloved Country*. Poitier was cast as a South African priest, Reverend Msimangu, and shooting commenced in South Africa at the end of 1950. Due to South Africa's stringent apartheid policies, Poitier and the other black actors were legally listed as indentured servants of Korda. *Cry, the Beloved Country* focused on the themes of social injustice and colonialism which gave rise to the system of apartheid and racial discrimination in South Africa. While not a box-office success in the United States, *Cry, the Beloved Country* did create black characters with more depth and challenged some racial assumptions.

In April 1951, Poitier married Juanita Hardy, who worked as a model and a dancer. Steady acting jobs continued to elude Poitier, and he and friend John

Newton opened a barbecue restaurant in Harlem called Ribs in the Ruff. His work on the World War II drama *Red Ball Express*, released in 1952, provided little income to support his family. A small role in 1953's *Go, Man, Go*, about the Harlem Globetrotters, also did not ease his financial woes. Poitier attended acting classes when he could, but remained heavily involved in the restaurant to help make ends meet.

Poitier's break would not come until 1954, when Metro-Goldwyn Mayer (MGM) Studios began planning a film version of *Blackboard Jungle*. Although the studio sought out teenagers with limited acting experience to help give the movie a realistic feel, Poitier was contacted for a role. Despite being 27 years old, Poitier was cast as high school delinquent Gregory Miller. On his arrival in Hollywood, Poitier met with the studio's lawyer, who requested that Poitier sign a loyalty oath. Throughout the early 1950s, the House Un-American Activities Committee (HUAC) scoured Hollywood searching for those with communist ties. Poitier's friendship with **Paul Robeson**, a known communist sympathizer, placed Poitier in danger of being blacklisted and denied work. Poitier told the lawyer he needed time to think over the loyalty oath, but never returned. The director, Richard Brooks, told Poitier to ignore it, and shooting commenced on the film.

Blackboard Jungle focused on the exploits of juvenile delinquents in the U.S. school system, with Poitier portraying one of the ring leaders. Poitier's performance won critical acclaim, and the film was featured at the Cannes Film Festival and played throughout Europe. In the United States, the film faced censorship due to its controversial topic; it only made the film more popular and helped make Sidney Poitier a more recognized actor. Poitier found an agent, Martin Baum, and shut down Ribs in the Ruff. In 1955, Poitier was signed on for the film *Edge of the City* with John Cassavetes, which explored an interracial friendship among dockworkers. Again, Poitier won the critics over. Also in 1955, Poitier worked on *Something of Value* alongside Rock Hudson, about the Mau Mau revolt in Kenya. Poitier again received praise for his work. This was followed with 1956's *Mark of the Hawk*, which examined missionaries in Africa, but was received poorly at the box office, and 1957's *Band of Angels* starring Clark Gable.

In early 1958, Poitier made *The Defiant Ones* with Tony Curtis, playing escaped convicts bound to each other by handcuffs. Again, this film explored topics of racism and interracial relationships. The film was shot in one month to release Poitier for a commitment to Samuel Goldwyn for the film version of *Porgy and Bess*. *The Defiant Ones* catapulted Poitier into stardom. Curtis shared top billing with Poitier, and Poitier achieved his first Academy Award nomination; it was the first time an African-American was nominated for Best Actor. Meanwhile, Poitier worked on *Porgy and Bess* where he began a nine-year romantic relationship with actress Diahann Carroll. The film was released to mixed reviews, primarily due to the stereotypes invoked in the story.

Poitier next returned to Broadway, performing in Lorraine Hansberry's *A Raisin in the Sun*. The drama revolved around the Younger family and their very human problems of survival. Hansberry created characters with depth that would appeal on a personal level to audiences of all colors. Poitier was cast as Walter Lee, and used Method acting to bring some of his personal pain to the stage, helping to shape the character. When the play opened in 1959, it was the first play where virtually all involved, from playwright to director, were African American. It met rave reviews from the critics, and in 1960 Poitier began work on a film version. Like the play, the movie had universal appeal to audiences although it won no nominations from the Academy.

Throughout the early 1960s Poitier's presence increased in the growing Civil Rights Movement within the United States. Poitier sent personal funds to Dr. **Martin Luther King, Jr.**, and in August of 1963, Poitier participated in the March on Washington. Poitier's choice in roles continued to reflect his belief in equality and racial integration in all aspects of American life, and Poitier chose his roles carefully. In 1962, he again portrayed a professional, as a psychiatrist in the film *Pressure Point* alongside Bobby Darin. Poitier's roles continually demonstrated to a multi-ethnic audience that race should be inconsequential; what mattered was a man's character. Poitier thus continued to use his art to aid civil rights in the United States.

In 1963 Poitier assumed one of the most important roles of his career in the low budget film *Lilies of the Field*. Director Ralph Nelson was unable to find financial backing for the film, and cut costs wherever possible. Poitier took a pay cut and was the only big name in the picture. The black and white film was shot over 12 days in Arizona. Poitier played Homer Smith, an itinerant handyman who finds himself helping a group of nuns make repairs to their convent. The sisters convince Smith to stay and build a chapel, even though he knows he will not be paid monetarily for his work. Instead, Smith leaves his newly built chapel with a sense of honor, self-respect, and accomplishment. The critics loved Poitier's portrayal of Smith and the film became an international success and won several awards. In February, Poitier was nominated by the Academy for Best Actor. At the awards ceremony in April 1964, Poitier became the first African-American to win the Academy Award for Best Actor. His acceptance speech was filled with nervous enthusiasm as he fought back tears. He was 37 years old.

The years following his Oscar win were intense for Poitier. In late 1964, he filed for divorce from his wife Juanita, with whom he had four children, and continued his sometimes-romance with Diahann Carroll. He filmed *The Long Ships*, a story of Moors and Vikings, which was unsuccessful in the box office, and he followed with an appearance in *The Greatest Story Ever Told*, a Biblical epic. At the end of 1965, Poitier starred in three movies released within a two-month period, but he was still the only mainstream African American star in Hollywood.

Poitier next starred in 1965's *The Bedford Incident*, which explored themes of the Cold War and nuclear annihilation. Also in 1965 Poitier filmed *The Slender Thread* in which he played a man volunteering at a suicide hotline;

Anne Bancroft played the suicidal caller. His final film of 1965 was *A Patch of Blue*, which tackled interracial relationships and the theme of colorblindness. In the film, Poitier plays Gordon Ralfe, a man who helps a poor and abused white teenager who happens to be blind. Predictably, she falls in love with her savior, but Ralfe restrains the relationship by sending her to a school for the blind. The film contained a passionate interracial kiss, but it was cut for theaters in the South. *A Patch of Blue* won several awards, and became Poitier's most popular film to date, earning him upwards of $700,000.

In 1966 Poitier worked on a western, *Duel at Diablo*, and spent time as a political activist for civil rights. In August of 1966, Poitier flew to London to begin filming on *To Sir, With Love*, the first of three consecutive major motion pictures. *To Sir, With Love* found Poitier back in a troubled classroom, much like *Blackboard Jungle*; this time, however, Poitier was teacher Mark Thackeray. In the film, Poitier teaches his delinquent students self-respect and gives them hope for the future, while suffering racial discrimination at the hands of students and peers. While the film does explore some issues of race, *To Sir, With Love* also reflected anxiety over social problems in big cities across the globe. The film spoke both to older and younger generations of moviegoers, and was a box office hit, becoming the highest grossing film of Poitier's career thus far.

The following month, September 1966, Poitier returned to the United States to work on a police drama, *In the Heat of the Night*. At Poitier's insistence, the filming was moved from Mississippi to a small town in Illinois to avoid racial confrontation. In the film, Poitier played Virgil Tibbs, a Philadelphia detective mistakenly arrested for murder in a small Southern town. After his release, Tibbs is given orders to help the local sheriff, Gillespie, portrayed by Rod Steiger, find the true killer. The film is imbued with the theme of racial discrimination, as Tibbs is constantly forced to prove himself as both a detective and a man. Gillespie makes fun of Tibbs' first name and his racial background, asking what they call him in Philadelphia; Tibbs erupts with anger, proclaiming, "They call me Mr. Tibbs!" The climax of the film occurs when Tibbs questions a wealthy white man about the murder, who then slaps Tibbs across the face; without hesitation Tibbs slaps the man back. Unlike other films, *In the Heat of the Night* avoids an overly saccharine ending; Gillespie and Tibbs solve the murder, but never overcome their hatred for each other. The film was an instant success.

By mid-1967, while his romance with Diahann Carroll crumbled and a race riot gripped Detroit, Poitier enjoyed the immense success of his two films. He gained the honor of becoming the first African American actor to place his handprints in the cement outside Grauman's Chinese Theater in Hollywood, California. In November, he started his own production company, another milestone. Poitier continued his work for civil rights, giving a speech for the Southern Christian Leadership Conference (SCLC), and aiding Martin Luther King, Jr., in fund-raising events.

Poitier's final film released in 1967 was *Guess Who's Coming to Dinner*, with stars Katharine Hepburn and Spencer Tracy. Hepburn and Tracy play Christina and Matt Drayton, a liberal-minded couple who have their politics tested when their daughter Joanna (Joey) brings home her fiancé, played by Poitier. While Dr. John Prentice has impeccable manners and is a successful and well-known doctor, the Draytons, especially Matt, cannot help but judge Prentice by his skin color. Prentice's parents are equally upset by the match. The perfection of Prentice serves to emphasize the ridiculous way in which he is judged. The film was almost scrapped due to its controversial interracial engagement, but the persistence of director Stanley Kramer and the power of the film's three stars helped filming commence.

Like *To Sir, With Love* and *In the Heat of the Night*, *Guess Who's Coming to Dinner* was a success at the box office. Poitier had three top box office hits in a six-month period; he was at the height of his career. *Guess Who's Coming to Dinner* received warm praises but also harsh criticism. Poitier was targeted by critics for his over-the-top caricature of Dr. Prentice, suggesting that the character was simply what white audiences wanted to see in an African American suitor. African American audiences ridiculed the qualifications of the doctor which did not resemble the average African American male's experiences or opportunities in the United States. Audiences balked at Prentice's overly deferential attitude to the white family. Kramer received hate mail regarding the film. Poitier was not nominated for any Oscars that year, although his films and his costars were.

While 1967 was the pinnacle of Poitier's acting career, the following years saw a slow but steady decline in his work. Poitier continued to release films on a regular basis, but his role as the advance guard of African American actors was fading. In April 1968 Poitier attended the funeral of Dr. Martin Luther King, Jr., and in June he served as an honor guard at the grave of slain presidential hopeful Robert F. Kennedy. At the end of 1968, while working on the film *The Lost Man*, Poitier met his second wife, model and actress Joanna Shimkus. In 1969 Poitier released a sequel to *In the Heat of the Night*, titled *They Call Me Mister Tibbs!*, and reprised the role of Virgil Tibbs for 1971's *The Organization*. During the 1970s, more African Americans achieved fame in Hollywood and their roles diversified. Hollywood began to embrace African American culture and Sidney Poitier was considered a relic from a previous era.

During the 1970s, Poitier began to experiment producing and directing films, as well as continuing his acting career. While the majority of the films found limited success, the comedy *Uptown Saturday Night* was popular with mixed race audiences and made more than $10 million. Poitier returned to Nassau during the early 1970s before settling down with Shimkus and their two daughters in Beverly Hills, California. In 1980 Poitier directed Gene Wilder and **Richard Pryor** in *Stir Crazy*, the first film he directed without acting in; in 1987 he directed **Bill Cosby** in *Ghost Dad*. Poitier continued to work into the 1990s, playing Nelson Mandela in the television movie *Mandela* *and de Klerk*, and starring opposite Robert Redford in *Sneakers*. His last project was a 2001 television movie titled *The Last Brickmaker in America*.

While Poitier's acting career waned after the high point of 1967, his success in Hollywood is still prominent. The films he acted in questioned the rationality of racism in the United States, and presented white America with heartfelt and deep stories of individual African Americans struggling for equality and justice. Poitier's work opened the doors for future generations of actors. Thirty-eight years after winning the Academy Award for Best Actor in *Lilies of the Field*, **Denzel Washington** became the second African American actor to win the award for his film *Training Day*; **Halle Berry** and **Will Smith** also received nominations as Best Actress and Best Actor. The same evening, Poitier accepted an honorary Academy Award for his lifetime of work in film. The prevalence of African Americans in the field, as actors, directors, producers, and writers, is a lasting consequence of Poitier's work.

Rebecca Baird
Arizona State University

FURTHER READING

Goudsouzian, Aram. *Sidney Poitier: Man, Actor, Icon.* Chapel Hill: The University of North Carolina Press, 2004.

Poitier, Sidney. *Life beyond Measure: Letters to My Great-Granddaughter.* New York: HarperOne, 2008.

Poitier, Sidney. *The Measure of a Man: A Spiritual Autobiography.* New York: HarperSanFrancisco, 2000.

AP/Wide World Photos

Colin Powell (1937–)

Colin Luther Powell was born on April 5, 1937, to Jamaican immigrants who lived in the Harlem neighborhood of New York City on Manhattan Island, New York. Powell's career of service ranged from joining the Reserve Officers Training Corps (ROTC) while at the College of the City of New York (CCNY) to serving as the first African American Secretary of State under President George W. Bush. Throughout his working career Powell has exemplified steadfast leadership and the highest code of personal conduct. Powell first garnered national attention while serving as chairman of the Joint Chiefs during the first Gulf War. With a clear and concise manner, Powell explained to the American people the military goals behind the complex situation of repelling Saddam Hussein's invasion of Kuwait in 1990. During Powell's news briefings from the Pentagon the American public was introduced to his style of analytical reasoning and explanation that would remain center stage throughout his career as Chairmen of the Joint Chief of Staff, a potential Presidential candidate, and the Secretary of State.

Powell's outlook on life was shaped by his family's commitment to the power of education and the value of hard work. The neighborhood of the South Bronx, where his family moved when he turned four, also affected his childhood. In this neighborhood Powell grew up with children of West Indian descent as well as other ethnic groups including Jewish and Irish. While he experienced racism in the South Bronx, it paled in comparison to the racism he would experience firsthand in portions of the South later in life.

In 1954, at the age of 16, Powell enrolled at CCNY. An average student in high school and in college, CCNY introduced him to something he excelled at, military service. In his second year in college Powell joined ROTC, which stressed the notions of loyalty, hard work, and love of country. Powell enjoyed his experiences in the program including comradeship and working within a team. During the summer of 1957 Powell attended summer training at Fort Bragg, North Carolina. While the U.S. military had been desegregated under President Harry Truman 10 years previously, the experiences outside the base demonstrated the true face of racism for many African Americans from which Powell for the most part had been sheltered growing up.

In June 1958, Powell graduated from CCNY and became a second lieutenant in the U.S. Army. After further training at Fort Benning, Georgia, Powell was stationed with the Third Armored Division in West Germany. After two years in this position Powell returned to the United States. While back in the States he met his future wife Alma on a blind date arranged by a friend. During their courtship Powell received orders requiring him to spend a year in Vietnam. Not willing to continue their relationship only through letters, Alma wanted to be married. The couple married in her hometown of Birmingham, Alabama, on August 25, 1962.

Once in Vietnam, Powell was briefly stationed in Saigon before being assigned to the A Shau Valley. Serving in an advisory role, Powell worked with a South Vietnamese officer and his unit in constructing a new base camp. Conditions in the field for advisors contrasted sharply with the offices in Saigon due to the heat, poor conditions, and near-total immersion in the Vietnamese culture. At the same time Powell received the news that Alma was expecting the couple's first child.

While serving as an advisor in 1963 danger was ever present for Powell. His unit was attacked by mortar fire from Viet Cong forces. While the danger remained, good news continued to reach Powell in the field. First he learned of his selection into an Infantry Officers Advanced Course held at Fort Benning at the end of his tour. This course promised the potential of later holding some of the highest positions in the U.S. Army. Then on March 23, 1963, Colin and Alma's first child Michael was born and both mother and child were in good health. Both pieces of news reinforced Powell's desire to get home in one piece after the tour in Vietnam.

Powell experienced a brush with danger in July 1963 while assigned with a unit in the field. Traversing a jungle trail, Powell unknowingly came upon an unconventional trap laid by the Viet Cong. While walking, Powell's right leg sank and he felt an immediate pain from a sharpened stick piercing his combat boot and entering the bottom of his foot. This simple weapon called a "punji stick" could prove deadly as the stick was covered in animal dung which could cause a massive infection if left untreated. Powell was able to finish the march on his swollen foot and was flown to a hospital for treatment.

After a full recovery in a short time, Powell's remaining time in Vietnam was spent in the headquarters of the First Army of the Republic of Vietnam. This role differed greatly from his position in the field where he witnessed the war firsthand. From headquarters Powell was granted a better sense of the overall strategy of the conflict. What he saw on some levels concerned him, especially in the use of statistics in explanations of the progress made by the South Vietnamese forces. As he wrote of this notion in his autobiography, "Experts often possess more data than judgment" (Powell with Persico, 99).

Powell returned to the United States and began his training in the Advanced Infantry School in August 1964. This time allowed for him to be back with his family and spend time with his new son. During this period Alma became pregnant again, and Colin's yearlong course allowed him to take an active role in welcoming his new child. The couple's first daughter, Linda Powell, was on April 16, 1965. Within a matter of weeks of her birth Powell completed the course and graduated third out of the 200-member class. The following year Powell remained at the school, this time as an instructor.

Powell's career in the Army continued to rise in 1967 by his selection into the Command and General Staff College at Fort Leavenworth, Kansas. This institution represents an important milestone for any young officer headed for the top positions in the Army and former alumni include Generals Dwight Eisenhower and George Patton. This program is aimed at helping students see beyond the infantry platoon and see the larger strategic military position. Here Powell did not only meet and learn about all parts of the Army, but also the other branches of the service. This 38-week experience of understanding the nuances of a large military operation would pay off later in his military career.

With the Vietnam War escalating in the middle portion of the 1960s a second tour loomed ahead for Powell and his family starting in July 1968. The conflict contrasted sharply from the one Powell left in 1963 when only 16,000 advisors resided in Vietnam. By 1968 half a million servicemen were stationed in Vietnam, and for the American people the conflict and the growing anti-war movement at home could be witnessed on the family television screen every night. As the war had changed, so too would Powell's position during his second tour.

Powell was assigned to the division of Major General Charles M Gettys as a G-3, which was involved in planning the operations for the 18,000-man force. From this position Powell's earlier feeling about an over-reliance on statistical evidence was reinforced. He witnessed politicians who, in his opinion, were detached from the realities of the conflict and demonstrated no clear objective for the U.S. military in the conflict. He also witnessed aspects practiced by the United States that clearly took away from their strength in the field. Chief among these reasons was the draft system that allowed large numbers of the American male population to avoid the service by attending college or by other means. All these failures later greatly affected Powell's belief in the proper use of U.S. military forces. As he wrote in his biography,

> War should be the politics of last resort. And when we go to war, we should have a purpose that our people understand and support; we should mobilize the country's resources to fulfill that mission and then go in to win. In Vietnam, we had entered into a half-hearted half-war, with much of the nation opposed or indifferent, while a small fraction carried the burden. (Powell with Persico, 143)

In July 1969, Powell returned to his family in the United States and they moved to Washington, DC. Here Powell would once again move forward with pursuing his education, this time in a civilian school. He studied for his Masters in Business Administration from George Washington University. While living in Washington, DC, the family welcomed their third child on May 20, 1970, when their daughter Annemarie arrived. Powell earned his MBA in 1971 and returned to the Army.

At age 33, Powell returned to the Army holding the rank of lieutenant colonel, just one rank away from making a one-star general. Armed with his MBA, the Army once again found an interesting opportunity for Powell, as a White House Fellow. This program allowed young leaders in a range of positions from the military and business to spend a year in Washington, DC learning the inner workings of government. Powell's time in this program allowed him to address a problem for the military and also expand his experiences that would serve him well later.

The credibility of the U.S. military after the Vietnam conflict was not high. On many campuses ROTC, the program that ushered in Powell into the military, was banned and students in the ROTC program were insulted. Powell's time in the White House Fellowship allowed him to work with a number of high-ranking government officials in addressing this issue. The Fellowship also introduced him to members of the Nixon administration and allowed Powell to travel with the President to the Soviet Union in 1973 during the warming of relations with the communist nation that occurred with the ending of the Vietnam War.

After completing the White House Fellowship, Powell wanted to return to the Army for the command position of a battalion. The most prestigious commands were in Europe and the United States. However, due to Powell's non-traditional career path his assignment called for him to be stationed with the 1st Battalion, 32nd Infantry, 2nd Division in South Korea. The position was not sought after for it did not allow for Powell's family to live in the country and it included bitterly cold winters.

After the Korean War from 1950 to 1953 resulted in the division of Korea between the Communist North Korea and democratic South Korea, tens of thousands of U.S. troops had been stationed in the South since the war ended. Powell addressed a number of problems in the 2nd Division. One of these problems centered on race. While the U.S. military was desegregated under President Harry Truman, the issue of race still remained a huge dividing factor in daily life in the military. Deteriorating morale conditions resulted in disputes over music preferences and culminated in fistfights between enlisted soldiers. This continued to the point that local restaurant owners in neighboring towns segregated their establishments to cater to one group and avoid potential fights taking place in their businesses. While this system may have stemmed altercations taking place off base, this practice only decreased morale.

Powell addressed this problem by implementing two steps. First, the Army informed local businesses that the segregated system must end. Second, the soldiers were encouraged to come forward with issues instead of letting those issues fester into larger problems. Over time, these steps helped ease racial tensions and also improve morale among the troops.

Powell also addressed improvement of morale of the men in other ways. One problem stemmed from the Army not moving forward in daily operations after ending the drafting of men into the service. At the close of the Vietnam War the system of selecting young men into military service was eliminated. However, in Korea, Powell found soldiers in the all-volunteer force performing duties such as kitchen patrol. A volunteer into the U.S. Army being forced to wash dishes for hours on end hurt morale, and under Powell's recommendation the practice was ended and morale improved. After his battle command tour in Korea Powell once again returned to the United States for more education.

The National War College represents the top level of military learning aimed at educating the top-level officials of tomorrow. Entering the college in 1974, Powell's classmates came from all branches of the service and also from the State Department and the Central Intelligence Agency. Top lecturers educated these students for top-level positions, which for Powell would come quickly. In 1979, he earned the rank of brigadier general. While not the first African American to earn this rank, at age 42 he was the youngest general in the U.S. Army at the time.

The year 1979 proved a crisis year for the U.S. military and the nation. In Tehran, Iran, the U.S. embassy was stormed and more than 50 military servicemen and American civilian workers were taken hostage. This action was in retaliation for the U.S. government's past support of the previous Iranian leader Shah Reza Pahlavi. On the nightly news, Americans would see images of the hostages on television, which only further weakened the perception of U.S. leadership under President Jimmy Carter. In April 1980 Carter decided to act.

A risky operation aimed at capturing the hostages was launched involving an assortment of helicopters and C-130 transport aircraft. In the first stages of the mission, a crash between two aircraft caused the deaths of eight servicemen and the termination of the mission. This failed mission only reinforced the feelings of weakness of the American people about the situation. For Powell assigned to the Pentagon, this failure also reinforced his notions of the use of limited military power, and when utilized to use overwhelming force with a clear mission.

A major shift in the U.S. military and for Powell's career took place with the election of Ronald Reagan to the Presidency in 1980. Reagan selected Casper Weinberger for his Secretary of Defense. Military spending increased 11 percent in the first Reagan budget. Much of this directly affected military services with increased wages and improved housing conditions on military bases. Powell would serve as an aid to Weinberger and the first term of Reagan's presidency presented a number of crisis during which Powell learned lessons that again added to his experiences in handling difficult situations.

> War should be the politics of last resort. And when we go to war, we should have a purpose that our people understand and support; we should mobilize the country's resources to fulfill that mission and then go in to win.   —Colin Powell

The first foreign policy crisis occurred on September 1, 1983 when the Soviet Union shot down civilian Korean Airlines Flight 007 that had unknowingly drifted into Soviet airspace. The meetings addressing the U.S. response to the incident that killed all 269 passengers taught Powell about mistakes that can occur when judgments are rendered with only a portion of the information gathered. Seven weeks later U.S. forces were directly attacked in Beirut, Lebanon. The Reagan administration had placed U.S. Marines in Beirut to serve as a buffer force between the Lebanese and Israeli armies. A total of 241 U.S. military personnel were killed in a truck bomb attack near their barracks. This incident again reinforced Powell's view of the disadvantages of placing military personnel in a combat zone with no clear mission.

After serving as an aid to Weinberger, Powell was promoted to lieutenant general in 1986. This promotion required stationing with the V Corp in

Germany. As a three-star general, he returned to his first overseas assignment some 30 years previously. This time he commanded over 70,000 military service members. However, his time in Germany would be only for a short five months. His ability to handle a crisis called him back to Washington, DC.

In Reagan's second term, the National Security Council (NSC) was reeling from a scandal of secret arms sales to overseas governments against the orders of Congress. Powell took over the position of deputy national security advisor to the President. One of the first actions taken was that the NSC would officially end any actions of secret arms deals. Later Powell would head the NSC and be intimately involved in the arms treaty negotiation with the Soviet Union. Accompanying Reagan to the Soviet Union, Powell aided in the successful arms treaty negotiations toward the end of Reagan's administration.

With the election of George H. W. Bush in 1988, Powell took the position as head of all U.S. Army personnel in the United States and became a full general at age 52. The year 1989 witnessed historic changes in the Cold War with the Soviet Union forces pulling out of Afghanistan after a 10-year war and the Soviet Army cutting the size of its army by over half a million soldiers. These actions Powell saw required a re-evaluation of American military thinking. Central to Powell's thinking was the Army's need for more flexibility in responses in the future other than the massive retaliation model practiced during the Cold War.

Powell continued to promote this change of thinking and tactics after his next promotion, this time to Chairman of the Joint Chiefs of Staff in October of 1989. In this position Powell pushed forward his post-Cold War vision not just to the U.S. Army, but also as Chairman to all branches of the service. These challenges of the post-Cold War period arrived sooner than most imagined with the nation of Iraq invading Kuwait on August 1, 1990.

Iraq, ruled by the dictatorship of Saddam Hussein, had just concluded a brutal war costing millions of causalities with its neighbor, Iran, from 1980 to 1988. At the time Iraq was supported by the U.S. government's response to past issues with Iran. However, the invasion of Kuwait represented a direct challenge to the stability of the Middle East. Thus, the flow of oil and the world economic systems were also challenged. To protect the nation of Saudi Arabia, which bordered both Iraq and Kuwait to the south, President George H. W. Bush supported the sending of U.S. troops. However, placing U.S. military forces in Saudi Arabia presented a number of problems that Powell would have to address.

The clash of cultures between a nation ruled by Islamic law and U.S. forces sent to defend it was multiple. One problem was Jewish religious services were illegal inside the nation. Under Powell's direction Jewish services were held on U.S. warships offshore, thus out of the jurisdiction of Islamic law, and personnel wishing to attend were flown out to the vessel. Another issue was that alcohol is illegal. Powell enforced this law and this aided in the elimination of disturbances between intoxicated service members and the local population.

Powell became a nationally recognized figure during the time leading up to the conflict and during the short war. Technology brought the air campaign against Iraqi forces, which started after the UN mandate to withdraw from Kuwait ended in January of 1991, directly into the living rooms of the American people. Powell also addressed the press and explained in briefings the air campaign and the three-day-long ground offensive.

While Powell is most well-known for his service as Chairman of the JCS for the successful removal of Iraqi forces from Kuwait by a multi-national force, his remaining time in the office presented a number of challenges. These included a successful coup in the Caribbean nation of Haiti, the civil war igniting in the former nation of Yugoslavia, and hunger and genocide in the East African nation of Somalia. These post-Cold War challenges surfaced for the remaining term of President Bush and the beginning portion of the administration of President Bill Clinton starting in 1993. However, after 35 years of service to his nation, Powell retired at a ceremony on September 30, 1993, in which President Clinton awarded Powell the Presidential Medal of Freedom.

With his distinguished military career and his leadership abilities receiving national attention, Powell's move to the world as a civilian hosted a range of grand possibilities including a much-talked-about possible run for the Presidency. However, at a press conference on November 8, 1995 with his family alongside him, Powell stated he was not running for the office. In his remarks he stated,

> To offer myself as a candidate for president requires a commitment and a passion to run the race and to succeed in the quest—the kind of passion and the kind of commitment that I felt every day of my thirty-five years as a soldier, a passion and commitment that, despite my very effort, I do net yet have for political life, because such a life requires a calling that I do not yet hear. (Powell with Persico, 601)

Powell's time in civilian life was multifaceted. In 1995, he wrote his autobiography entitled *My American Journey*, which included a public speaking tour. In 1996, he spoke at the Republican National Convention which was nominating Senator Bob Dole to run for president. Powell spoke of his vision of the Republican Party stating, "The Republican Party must always be the party of inclusion . . . It is our diversity that has made us strong" (Powell, "General Colin Powell Speaks"). In the speech he also spoke of his belief in a women's right to choose in regard to the issue of abortion and his support of affirmative action.

While making his case for not wishing to aspire to the Presidency, Powell did not remain out of the political realm. With the election of President George W. Bush in 2000, Powell was selected as Secretary of State. This choice granted credibility to Bush's cabinet selection due to Powell's impeccable military record and more moderate political views. Powell, serving as the first

African American Secretary of State, not only made history, but also took on a role that few realized at the time would be the most challenging of any Secretary of State in a generation.

With the attacks on the United States on September 11, 2001, the world situation transformed overnight. Confronting the enemy of al-Qaeda not only meant military attacks on their bases in Afghanistan, but to their financial systems and other means of support in nations across the world as well. This latter tactic did not require military interventions, but diplomatic maneuverings directed from the State Department.

Central to Powell's role immediately following the attacks on the United States was Afghanistan's neighboring country of Pakistan. Powell walked a diplomatic tightrope of gathering support in Pakistan from a nation made up predominantly of Muslims unhappy with U.S. efforts in the region in the past. Powell traveled the world not just in gathering support for the war in Afghanistan, but in the United Nations drafting Resolution 1441 which included the line that will be debated for generations to come: "the council has repeatedly warned Iraq that it will face serious consequences as a result of its continued violations of its obligations" (United Nations). Lastly, once the U.S. invasion moved forward into Iraq in March of 2003 Powell focused his attention on the Israeli-Palestinian conflict that included the removal of Israeli forces from the occupied lands left from the 1967 war and the formation of a Palestinian state.

With the re-election of President Bush in 2004, Powell resigned at the start of the second term of the administration in 2005. At age 66, Powell had traveled an amazing road of duty and leadership that started with joining ROTC in the 1950s when the Cold War loomed for the American people. Powell witnessed firsthand the importance of a clear mission and goals for U.S. military personnel in the jungles of Vietnam. In the 1970s, Powell advanced into the upper echelon of military thinking still aimed at confronting communism. During the later portion of the 1980s and early 1990s, Powell aided in ushering the U.S. military into the post-Cold War realm where trouble spots can erupt in places all over the world. Finally, Powell took all this knowledge and turned this into driven leadership in holding the cabinet position of Secretary of State in a time of some of the most diplomatic turmoil since the conclusion of World War II.

Benjamin Hruska
Arizona State University

FURTHER READING

DeYoung, Karen. *Soldier: The Life of Colin Powell*. New York: Alfred A. Knoff, 2006.
Harari, Oren. *The Leadership Secrets of Colin Powell*. New York: McGraw-Hill Companies, 2003.
Landan, Eline. *Colin Powell: Four Star General*. London: Franklin Watts, 1991.

Means, Howard. *Colin Powell: Soldier/Statesman Statesman/Soldier*. New York: Donald I. Fine, 1992.

O'Sullivan, Christopher. *Colin Powell: American Power and Intervention from Vietnam to Iraq*. Lanham, MD: Rowman & Littlefield, 2009.

Powell, Colin. "General Colin Powell speaks at the GOP National Convention." August 12, 1996. *Floor Speeches*. PBS. http://www.pbs.org/newshour/convention96/floor_speeches/powell.html.

Powell, Colin, with Joseph Persico. *My American Journey*. New York: Random House, 1995.

Steins, Richard. *Colin Powell: A Biography*. Westport, CT: Greenwood Press, 2003.

United Nations. Resolution 1441. "Security Council Holds Iraq in 'Material Breach' of Disarmament Obligations, Offers Final Chance to Comply, Unanimously Adopting Resolution 1441." August 11, 2002. http://www.un.org/News/Press/docs/2002/SC7564.doc.htm.

AP/Wide World Photos

Richard Pryor
(1940–2005)

Richard Franklin Lennox Thomas Pryor, III, one of the most influential comedians in U.S. history, was an iconoclastic figure who attacked racial conventions and white supremacy, transcended racial barriers, and challenged the United States' consciousness with biting, derisive, irreverent humor. Pryor's brilliant comic imagination and dynamic use of the straight-talking tones of street language shocked and captivated many Americans, both black and white. He did not simply tell stories; he gave them life, revealing the entire range of black America's humor, from its folksy rural origins to its bawdy urban vernacular. At the height of his career in the late 1970s, Pryor stalked the stage like an antsy puppy and an edgy jungle cat, pursuing the audience and observing them as much as they observed him. He did so while delivering what critics regarded as the most heartrending and piercing comedic view of black life in white America ever witnessed in U.S. history and life. He was explosive yet exposed, ridiculous but keenly aware, streetwise and swaggering but somehow still shy and uneasy. His routines call to mind the anger, short-comings, fortitude, and strengths of all segments of black America, including churchgoing people, the working-class, prostitutes, pimps, and hustlers.

Pryor was raised as the only child of Leroy Pryor and Gertrude Thomas Pryor in Peoria, Illinois. Often described as a small, wide-eyed kid, Pryor learned early on that making people laugh was a powerful antidote to the harsh realities of everyday life. His living arrangements were anything but pedestrian. "I lived among an assortment of relatives, neighbors, whores and winos," he recalled, "the people who inspired a lifetime of comedic material." His parents and grandmother, Marie Carter, were bar and bordello owners. Pryor was raped at the age of six by a teenaged neighbor, molested by a Catholic priest during catechism, and witnessed his mother performing sexual acts with Peoria's mayor. "Sometimes pain is funny later on," Pryor was later to say, an assertion he would support in his comedy for most of his life.

Aside from laughter, he coped with these traumatic experiences by attending the movies as often as he could. Always confined to the segregated "Negro" section of the cinema, Pryor watched a bevy of films and became consumed with the on-screen exploits of John Ford and Howard Hawks. Their works inspired him to seek stardom and wealth.

Pryor, to survive, used his quick wit and belligerent humor to gain respect from the street gangs and bullies in his neighborhood. Although he was highly intelligent, his manic behavior led to his expulsion from school in the eighth grade. He went on to work as a janitor at a local strip club, a shoe-shine "boy," a meat packer, billiard hall attendant, truck driver, and field hand. These experiences, in addition to several brushes with the nation's criminal justice sys-tem and a stint in the army, from which he was discharged for stabbing a fellow soldier during a fight, gave Pryor a unique and ground-level perspective on the black masses in the United States that he translated into honest and hilarious comedic endeavors.

Pryor's first introduction to performance came at age 12, when Juliette Whittaker, a supervisor at a public recreational facility in Peoria, cast him in a local production of *Rumplestiltskin*. Whittaker was so impressed by Pryor's comic ability that she arranged talent shows to showcase his skills. While serving in the army between 1958 and 1960, Pryor performed in many amateur productions. After being discharged, Pryor returned to Peoria, married, fathered a son named Richard Jr., and, motivated by the work of comedians Redd Foxx and Dick Gregory, started performing in local nightclubs.

Not finding it easy to schedule comedic appearances without having a built following, Pryor sought to perform in the public arena in other areas. His first cabaret gig was in his hometown's Harold's Club, where he played piano and sang, quite badly according to Pryor. Quickly realizing that audiences preferred his jokes to his singing, Pryor began working as a professional comic in clubs throughout the Midwest. Indeed, between 1962 and 1964, Pryor became an itinerant comedian on the "chitlin circuit" of small black nightclubs in cities such as Chicago, Cleveland, and St. Louis. He also ventured outside the Midwest and performed in clubs in Greenwich Village, including Cafe Wha?, The Living Room, Papa Hud's, and the Bitter End.

Inspired by **Bill Cosby**, Pryor went to New York in 1963 and gained recognition for his club work as a stand-up comedian, performing on the same bill as celebrities such as Bob Dylan and Richie Havens. While in New York, Pryor also garnered some mentorship from actor, director, and producer, Woody Allen. He eventually performed at the **Apollo Theater**, and he made his television debuts on widely viewed shows such as "The Ed Sullivan Show," the "Merv Griffin Show," and "The Tonight Show with Johnny Carson," in 1964. His first foray into the world of Las Vegas entertainment was as the opening act for Bobby Darin at the prestigious Flamingo Hotel. More hip and controversial than Cosby and the other Vegas acts, Pryor grew tired of performing what he considered to be uninspired, irrelevant, "lilly-white" material, and stormed off the stage of the Aladdin Hotel in Las Vegas in 1967. Pryor maintained, "There was a world of junkies and winos, pool hustlers and prostitutes, women and family screaming inside my head, trying to be heard. The longer I kept them bottled up, the harder they tried to escape. The pressure built till I went nuts."

Though club owners, agents, and advisers urged him to eschew more critical, racialized material, he ignored their requests and drew upon the black experiences he knew well. Seeking authenticity, he began using the term "Nigga" in his material. Using the term "Nigga" or "Nigger" to Pryor was not profane. Rather, it was a term born out of the realities of racial relations in the United States. Pryor saw his role in the use of these terms as one of projection, allowing blacks a conduit through which to speak freely. To Pryor, the lives that most "Niggas" were forced to live is where the profanity resided, not within the word itself.

His first comedy album, labeled *Richard Pryor* (1967), demonstrated his new focus with irreverent sketches and coarse yet sidesplitting routines that addressed various aspects of race and racism in the United States. *That Nigger's Crazy* (1974), Pryor's next album, shocked the record industry by appealing to both white and black audiences. Despite its X-rating, explicit language, and sexual content, the album sold over 500,000 copies and won the Grammy Award for best comedy album of the year. He produced another album the next year, *Is It Something I Said* (1975), which also went gold and won a Grammy award. He wrote for Redd Foxx's popular television series "Sanford and Son," "The Flip Wilson Show," and the Lily Tomlin specials of 1974, for which he won an Emmy Award for best comedy writing.

Pryor became the most popular guest host on "Saturday Night Live" in 1975, and in 1977 he produced, directed, and starred in a series of television specials for NBC. Starring himself, *The Richard Pryor Show* was Pryor's foray into television in the form of a comedy variety series that proved to be both short-lived and controversial. The idea for the show was born from an NBC special that Pryor performed in May 1977, and went into production under the guidance of producer Rocco Urbisci of Burt Sugarman Productions. Even before production started, however, Pryor's show was subject to much scrutiny about its content, and controversy over its time slot. Originally and contractually, the show was slated to run during the 9 p.m. period, not during the middle of what many considered "family hour" on a Tuesday night. Premiering on NBC's 8 p.m. slot on Tuesday, September 13, 1977, it ran opposite of *Laverne & Shirley* and *Happy Days*, two popular show from ABC's network lineup. Not only did this adjustment in time limit Pryor's potential and target audience, but it also limited viewers because of other shows running in parallel slots on other networks. Running in an already dense time slot, and proving to be drastically different from the "bad comedy skits with songs" variety shows that viewers had grown accustomed to, *The Richard Pryor Show* only lasted four episodes.

Many believe that because of all of the controversy behind launching and running the show, and the apparent indifference and incompetence demonstrated by the network during its development stage, that *The Richard Pryor Show* had a predisposition for failure. Pryor's program featured an unpredictable mix of satire, social commentary, conceptual comedy, improvisation, slapstick, and the occasional dramatic bit; it was a true variety show, in many ways ahead of its time. Despite having an original contract to produce 10 shows, Pryor only produced four episodes that ran in consecutive weeks. Throughout the process, interference from the network proved to be a persistent obstacle, even up until the last moment before the first episode aired, when the introductory bit was cut.

Beginning with a close up of Pryor's face explaining that he was not going to give anything up in order to bring his brand of comedy to network television, the introductory bit started off on a very frank, but harmless note. But then, the camera zoomed out to show an apparently nude Pryor with his genitals removed, although in reality he was clad in a full-length body stocking. While the depiction of "giving up" part of himself to bring comedy to the masses was ironic, equally so was the fact that more people saw or heard about the cut clip through different news broadcasts and outlets was greater than the number who would have actually seen the bit if it had been permitted to air. It is no surprise, then, that after Pryor's contractual obligations were filled, he did not pursue any further projects with NBC, nor did the network court him.

Less-than-satisfied with his experience with network television, Pryor's political savvy and desire to learn led him to develop his consciousness off-stage. In 1979, he traveled to Africa, acquiring a newfound sense of the independence, freedom, and pride of African peoples. As a result of this trip, he stopped using the word "Nigga" in his performances and materials, to reflect his more conscious, positive view of black people, as when he was in Africa, Pryor stopped seeing "Niggas" and rather saw everyone as equals to everyone else. During this trip Pryor gained a new respect for those of African descent, citing their both dynamic and sophisticated nature.

In the 1970s, Pryor also began to make his mark on the big screen, appearing in 40 films throughout his career. His first film, *Greased Lightning* (1972), was a biopic about the first African American to make a mark in the auto-racing industry, Wendell Scott. Although the movie was billed as a comedy, no doubt because of its inclusion of Pryor, was actually more serious in nature, conveying Scott's long-suffering humor and determination to succeed, despite racial boundaries and prejudice, in a sport that he loves.

> I woke up in the ambulance, right? And there was nothin' but white people starin' at me. I say ... I done died and wound up in the wrong heaven.
> —Richard Pryor

Later that year, Pryor starred in *Silver Streak* (1972) with Gene Wilder, a film that would later be named by The American Film Institute (AFI) as one of the top 100 comedies. Unlike the other movies that Wilder and Pryor would film together, this was the first and arguably their best, as it showed numerous sides to both actors in this romantic comedy, borderline thriller, script. In 1979, Pryor debuted in his first concert film, *Richard Pryor, Live in Concert*, recorded during a live performance in Long Beach, California, during what many say was the height of Pryor's comedic and creative genius. *Richard Pryor, Live in Concert* set such a precedent for comedic performances and films, that it remains a standard by which work in this genre is judged.

Pryor did not shy away from dealing with controversial issues, nor did he shy away from sharing examples from his own life to make a point or to get a laugh. His material reflected on many aspects of his chaotic life and, often, particular actions. In one performance, he recalled a marital dispute which, in the middle of the argument, he shot his then wife's car. He provided commentary on the death of his pet monkeys, joked about his upbringing and the atrocities he experiences, and offered a description of his near-fatal heart attack: "I woke up in the ambulance, right? And there was nothin' but white people starin' at me. I say … I done died and wound up in the wrong heaven." This quote, among others, reminds us how comedians like Pryor and other entertainers of the day gave voice to disaffected, direct, and forceful blacks.

Pryor's comedy created far more than laughter in his audiences; it often yielded a significant amount of thought and reflection. His far-reaching, in more ways than one, performances warranted numerous marks when Pryor placed his hands in his star on the Hollywood Walk of Fame. Academy Award-winner Louis Gossett, Jr. recognized Pryor as, "the single most reason for us making it in this business. He made it possible for us [black people] to be in this business on equal terms." Composer **Quincy Jones** coined him "a pioneer … who made us understand the truth about us." Indeed, Pryor's material is socially astute and passionate to the point that he expanded our notions of what may be perceived, and even accepted, as funny.

Like many entertainers of the day, and throughout history, Pryor had his own demons to contend with. He was addicted to both alcohol and a variety of drugs, and ended up entering a rehab clinic in 1993. Even after "recovery" Pryor still said, in interviews, that he enjoyed nothing more than some cocaine. "Giving up drugs was like saying adios to the greatest, funniest character I'd ever created," he said. Drug possession, assault, tax offenses, and other charges put him in jail a number of times, adding to his image as a wild man of comedy. Even throughout these circumstances, he retained his sense of humor and critique. Indeed all the dramatic incidents in his life, good or bad, controversial or benign, became part of his stand-up routine, and later, part of his autobiography. *Pryor Convictions* (1994), was both confessional and derivative, drawing materials from his 20 albums, numerous appearances, and turbulent life. Now, Pryor's comedic genius was brought to a different venue: the page. The book was a testament to how Pryor worked, translating reflections of his life into comedic language, even when his life events were anything but laughable.

In the early 1980s, aided by an onslaught of personal problems, Pryor experienced third-degree burns over a third of his body, as the results of a narrowly survived burning incident. Some speculate that this event occurred while Pryor was freebasing cocaine, but Pryor was also noted as saying that he was actually trying to kill himself by pouring rum over his body and setting fire to it. Barely recovered from the previous accident, Pryor was diagnosed with multiple sclerosis (MS) in 1986.

Multiple sclerosis strikes the protective sheath surrounding nerves, affecting, among other things, motor ability, and balance. The first sign that he was sick came on location in Los Angeles about three months earlier, while he was filming the ironically titled *Critical Condition* with director Michael Apted. Pryor recalled the incident:

MS is a very strange disease. I didn't know anything was wrong at first; [it] just crept up on me. Then one very strange day Apted said, "Richard, come here." And I did. Well, I thought I did. My brain told my body, "Go see what the fella wants." But my body said, "I'm gonna f—- with you a bit, Rich." Apted thought I was joking around. He said, "Come on, Richard, stop goofing around." I told him, "Well, I'm not! trying real . . . hard to get there!" They sent me to this wonderful place called the Mayo Clinic for a checkup. They did all these tests on me . . . After a week, I was told I had MS. (*Ebony*, September 1993)

His last film, *Another You*, was eventually made at the end of 1990 and released in July 1991. Playing a con man to Gene Wilder's chronic liar, Pryor gave a performance marked by debilitating physical decline. The disease, however, did not stop him from performing. In 1992, he could still be seen live at the renowned Comedy Store in West Hollywood, cracking jokes about his afflictions and his wheelchair, and still telling probing and entertaining stories that ensnared the hearts and stimulated the imagination of diverse audiences from around the world.

Pryor may have been sidelined by MS, but his presence and message did not subside. He was so adamantly opposed to the use of animals in researching, even his disease, that he used his Christmas card to discourage donations to charities that still fund such tests. He's been honored by PETA, the People for the Ethical Treatment of Animals, for saving baby elephants in Botswana targeted for circuses. In 2000, as the Ringling Bros. and Barnum & Bailey Circus was preparing to open at Madison Square Garden, Pryor gave the Big Top's first African American ringmaster something to think about. "While I am hardly one to complain about a young African American making an honest living," Pryor wrote in a letter to Jonathan Lee Iverson, "I urge you to ask yourself just how honorable it is to preside over the abuse and suffering of animals."

Pryor, along with fellow actor and activist, Alec Baldwin, also crusaded against Burger King's unethical treatment of animals, primarily cattle. They sent letters asking owners of Burger King franchises to use their clout to get the fast-food corporation to meet or exceed the animal welfare standards set by its chief competitor, McDonald's. Pryor's activism came as a surprise to many, because those who did not follow his career closely, and those who were unaware of his childhood marked by abuse and abandonment, could not properly contextualize him identifying with the helpless, violated, and disposed. As his own professional and personal life declined his work on behalf of the less fortunate and vulnerable intensified.

The beginning of the end for Pryor, however, began with Pryor's physical decline. Although his MS prevented him from performing in the last few years before his death in December 10, 2005, from his home in the Encino, which he shared with his two rescued dogs, Homer and Spirit, Pryor continued to catalog the events of his life and the world around him. Pryor will probably never lose his position as a cultural icon. Throughout his life, Pryor reached out and touched millions with his talent, and his ability to bring others closer to each other through the raw and unfiltered lens of outrageous, profane, and scabrous satire was unsurpassed.

While none of the films in which he appeared has qualified for the most prominent awards of merit, Richard Pryor remains a seminal figure in the history of comedy and American entertainment. His acting was never fully cultivated, but his talent loomed large enough to frequently eclipse substandard material. Mere mention of his name will conjure a smile from even the most staid entertainment media critic, and no discourse on contemporary stand-up comedy can occur without utterance of the names Richard and Pryor. Generations of admirers—African American and otherwise—have a story to tell, whether it is the recollection of clandestine audio review of his recordings, having named the comedian as the inspiration for a show business career, or a remembrance of falling over in hysterical laughter at one of the many hilarious bits Pryor perfected during his decades on the popular culture scene.

When Richard Pryor walked off the stage for the last time on December 10, 2005, he did so quietly, with little of the verve and brashness that defined so many of his groundbreaking moments as a storyteller, comedian, recording artist, and actor. For all the direct links made between the late Pryor and post-civil rights comedic icons such as Eddie Murphy, Chris Rock, and Dave Chappelle, the hip-hop generation has had not connected with Richard Pryor and his art. Pryor was a product of another era, but it was in the midst of that era that he redefined how Americans confronted the issue of race and black masculinity, thereby paving the way for mainstream acceptance of hip-hop's own irreverence and provocative nature.

Pryor had little to offer the hip-hop generation, his peers were more demure, less direct, and far less critical than he. It would be the Chris Rocks, Robin Harrises, and Dave Chappelles of the world who would best capture the painful yet often humorous realities of the hip-hop generation. For his part, however, Pryor was much more complex than the profanity that garnered him an audience and a devoted following.

Matthew C. Whitaker
Arizona State University

FURTHER READING

Pryor, Rain. *Jokes My Father Never Taught Me: Life, Love, and Loss with Richard Pryor*. New York: It Books, 2007.

Pryor, Richard, and Todd Gold. *Pryor Convictions, and Other Life Sentences*. New York: Pantheon Books, 1995.

Pryor, Richard. *The Richard Pryor Show, Vols. 1 & 2 Plus Bonus Disc*. Los Angeles, CA: Image Entertainment, 2004.

RichardPryor.com. "History." www.richardpryor.com/0/4113/0/1240 (accessed February 18, 2010).

Schumacher, David, "Richard Pryor's Biggest Fight: Multiple Sclerosis." *Ebony*, September, 1993. http://findarticles.com/p/articles/mi_m1077/is_n11_v48/ ai _13230349/ (accessed February 20, 2010).

Watkins, Mel. *On the Real Side: Laughing, Lying, and Signifying: The Underground Tradition of African-American Humor That Transformed American Culture, from Slavery to Richard Pryor*. New York: Simon and Schuster, 1994.

Williams, John A., and Dennis A. Williams. *If I Stop, I'll Die: The Comedy and Tragedy of Richard Pryor*. New York: Da Cp.apo Press, 2005.